A Minute of Presence for Women

a minute of Presence

of

Presence

FOR WOMEN

Awaken Your Heart
to the God of Wonder

Leigh McLeroy

TYNDALE
MOMENTUM™

The nonfiction imprint of
Tyndale House Publishers, Inc.

Visit Tyndale online at www.tyndale.com.

Visit Tyndale Momentum online at www.tyndalemomentum.com.

Visit the author's website at www.leighmcleroy.com.

TYNDALE, Tyndale Momentum, and Tyndale's quill logo are registered trademarks of Tyndale House Publishers, Inc. The Tyndale Momentum logo is a trademark of Tyndale House Publishers, Inc. Tyndale Momentum is the nonfiction imprint of Tyndale House Publishers, Inc., Carol Stream, Illinois.

A Minute of Presence for Women: Awaken Your Heart to the God of Wonder

Designed by Kristin Bakken

The author is represented by the literary agency of Alive Literary Agency, 7680 Goddard St., Suite 200, Colorado Springs, CO 80920, www.aliveliterary.com.

For information about special discounts for bulk purchases, please contact Tyndale House Publishers at csresponse@tyndale.com, or call 1-800-323-9400.

ISBN 978-1-4964-2284-2

Printed in China

24	23	22	21	20	19	18
7	6	5	4	3	2	1

Introduction

I am convinced that God is present and ever revealing himself in the midst of ordinary human life. Yes, he is the creator of the universe, the author of salvation, the beginning and end of everything that is. He is great. There is none greater. But he is not far away. Not at all. If you asked me for proof of his presence, I would point first to the fact of the Incarnation: "the Word became human and made his home among us," says the Gospel of John (1:14). With the birth of Christ, God put on skin and, as Eugene Peterson has phrased it in *The Message*, "moved into the neighborhood." His coming changed everything.

If you pressed me for further proof, I would point to my own everyday life—because *this* life is the place he keeps on showing up, time after time after time. Not a day goes by that I don't catch a glimpse of him. In checkout lines and waiting rooms. In bells that chime and sirens that wail. In drive-throughs and drop-ins and even at my own front door. These pages demonstrate the ways God has been present in my own life. The stories they tell are in thematic order rather than chronological order, and my hope is that you will recognize yourself in them and consider God's constant presence in your life too.

"Human life," says Michael Downey, "all of it, is the precinct of epiphany—of God's showing, of God's constant speaking and breathing."* It is a wonder to me that this is so. And every time he shows himself, it takes my breath away. My prayer for *A Minute of Presence for Women* is that it will invite you to linger a while in the presence of God and will awaken your heart to his wonder all around you.

> In Your presence is fullness of joy;
> In Your right hand there are pleasures forever.
> PSALM 16:11, NASB

Leigh McLeroy

---

* Michael Downey, *Altogether Gift: A Trinitarian Spirituality* (Maryknoll, NY: Orbis Books, 2000), 35.

Calendar Girl

I've tried going paperless. I have. I have all sorts of convenient tools and apps that stand ready to keep me on track, on time, and on task. But I love my plain, banded folio and its simple, worn pages. Scratched notes fill the columns of each week, reminding me where I've been and where I need to go. Scribbled names record who I've spoken with and perhaps what we've talked about.

Great and small blocks of time attest to what sort of work I've done and what is yet to do. Stray words and phrases are buried throughout the whole stew that might someday bubble into something more substantial . . . or not. My own handwriting on my planner's not-virtual pages grounds me in a way that ether notes cannot. I am, unapologetically, a calendar girl.

Each January I procure a new planner with crisp, white, empty pages. I have no idea what assignments or stories it will catalog. I hope, of course, that its pages will record good work, thoughtfully done. Old friendships maintained. New ones serendipitously explored. Heart-hammering trials endured. Good books read and pondered. Inviting creative challenges met. I cannot possibly predict what will appear on any one page, but I can attest with certainty who will be present behind, before, and on every page: my heavenly Father.

How do I know? Because he was there in the pages of last year's calendar . . . and in all the ones that came before it. He was there when the pages bore notes like "fire" and "move" and "myeloma" and "Memphis." He was there on a beachside balcony in Orlando and in Marcy's guest room in May. He was there in my mother's hospice room and beside me on a bluff high above the Frio River. He will be for me what he has always been: present and the same yesterday, today, and forever.

The pages may be new. The year may be different. But there is no reason to fear the coming contents of this empty planner. The unseen Author of every line is unchanging, good, and true. He is faithful. He can be nothing less. I am a calendar girl, and he is the God of the ages.

———

God's way is perfect. All the LORD's promises prove true.
2 SAMUEL 22:31

a New Thing

Every day in my city I notice an unending barrage of new things. A new drugstore has sprung up on a street I haven't driven down in weeks. A new restaurant or a splash of flowers or a herd of SUV hybrids catches my eye. New billboards proliferate like viruses along each block, advertising new destinations for not-so-new airlines, or new offers for things I've never before thought I needed.

At the grocery store I frequent, another face-lift is underway, and the greeting cards are now where the coffee was. Just this week a new mail carrier assumed my neighborhood route, meaning I've delivered misplaced mail twice in only a few days' time.

In all this newness, I've discovered something new about myself: the thing I like most about new things is that eventually they become old. The newness wears off, and a sweet familiarity settles in. Then I know what to expect. Then I'm not breaking anything in or trying anything out. God, however, is not constrained by my preference for the predictably tried and true. Just when I think I've got him figured out, he challenges my cozy assumptions that he'll do the same thing in the same way that he did the day before.

I know him, yes: I know that Jesus Christ is, as the writer of Hebrews says, the same yesterday, today, and forever (see Hebrews 13:8).

Oh, yes! That's good! I count on that.

But his ways and the Father's ways and the Spirit's ways are not set in stone. He is forever doing something new. No two sunrises or sunsets paint the same pattern in the sky, and no two days ring with identical echoes of his grace. Just this week a flaming red cardinal flew so close to me that I think I might have touched him if I'd been quick enough—and that's never happened before. Ever.

His mercies are new every morning. So who knows what new thing he will surprise me with today?

I am about to do something new. See, I have already begun! Do you not see it?

ISAIAH 43:19

Bare Branches

I'm not sure when the last leaves fell from the tall trees in the yard; Houston winters aren't harsh enough to pinpoint a single killing frost. The leaves simply seemed to let go. Now I'm seeing birds I never noticed before: ten, twenty, thirty at a time, perched in branches listing in the breeze. They'd been there all along, but because I was focused on something else, they were invisible to me.

I was reminded of those "invisible" birds and bare branches during dinner with a dear friend—the kind of friend whose presence makes you breathe easier. A friend whose voice is a comfort, and whose heart has long been open to mine. She is a widow now. Parts of her world that were once lush and full are now emptier, more bare. She is a teacher of the Word—one of my favorites. One whose love and wisdom I've striven to emulate. (She smiles sometimes and says her student has surpassed her, but I don't believe I ever will.)

"How has what you've been through recently changed your teaching?" she asked me as we nibbled plates of Middle Eastern food and caught up with one another's struggles.

I didn't answer right away. I wanted to find the right words. But I knew the truth almost instantly. "Everything is closer to the surface," I told her. "Everything is more intense and real."

"Anything else?" she wanted to know.

"Yes," I said. "I love the people I teach more. Sometimes so much it hurts." Then I asked her the same question.

"I cry a lot more," she admitted. "And I see their hurts. Even the invisible ones. But I want to tell them the truth, even when it's hard. There's no room for platitudes anymore."

Bare branches show us things we never noticed before. Bare branches bring things into clearer focus—sometimes with an awful heart pang, but always with surprising clarity. And bare branches have a beauty all their own.

Since we have a great high priest who has passed through the heavens, Jesus the Son of God, let us hold fast our confession. . . . Let us draw near with confidence to the throne of grace, so that we may receive mercy and find grace to help in time of need.
HEBREWS 4:14, 16, NASB

More

Do you make New Year's resolutions? I normally don't, but this year I am keenly focused on more. Not more stuff or more money, not more power or control. This year I want to love more, give more, and sit more often at God's feet with no agenda in mind but to experience his presence.

Loving God and loving others are precious things. And imagining ways to grow in them is a challenge. But I aim to try.

Loving more will no doubt mean extending myself beyond my safe, trusted circles of family and friends. That's a scary prospect. *What will happen,* I wonder, *if I make it a point each day to tell or show one other person that I love them—and to at least hint that God loves them more?*

How can a person with finite resources give more and more? I can start by sharing what I have, giving what I no longer use or need, and shifting funds from one budget category to repurpose in another. And I can offer up the most precious commodity of all: my time. I confess I often hoard it. Time is the one thing I struggle to relinquish on any terms but my own. I need it, I convince myself. It's mine. Already in this barely begun year I've been asked to part with more of it for causes that are undoubtedly good. How will I know the best way to respond?

I will know by spending time with God. Understanding is a good side effect of a relationship with him. Through uninterrupted, content-to-sit-in-his-presence time—by listening, praising, dreaming big, and feeling small, I will learn to better love and give. I'm convinced this one thing is the key to my year of more. If I fail at this, I'll succeed at nothing.

More. I want more. It sounds selfish, doesn't it? But it needn't be. Open my heart and my hands, Father, and give me more of you! I promise—out of love for you—to keep the giving going in your name.

How precious is Your lovingkindness, O God! And the children of men take refuge in the shadow of Your wings. They drink their fill of the abundance of Your house; and You give them to drink of the river of Your delights. For with You is the fountain of life; in Your light we see light.
PSALM 36:7-9, NASB

Fridays at Avalon

The clock over the long serving counter at Avalon Diner says it's 7:30 a.m. Booths and tables have already filled just an hour after the diner doors opened. Cups clink and conversation hums. With her smile and hairnet in place, Patsy stands at the grill, scrambling the lightest, fluffiest eggs you've ever eaten in your life. Cassie, Sarah, Brenda, and Ronnie deliver breakfast orders amid the cheerful chaos, their moves as smooth as syrup flowing over a hot short stack.

For twenty-five-plus years, my dad and I have met in this midtown diner on Friday mornings and shared what we've come to think of as *our* table—the fourth booth on the right, nearest the kitchen. The space between us—two feet of scarred and slightly greasy Formica—has been filled with conversation, easy silence, tears, and laughter. The distance between Dad's face and mine is measurable. The height and depth and breadth of our shared connection forged over time is not.

Now if one of us sits down at our table without the other, we're quickly asked, "Where's Mac?" or "Where's Leigh?" My oldest niece began to join us when she attended college nearby, and to our friends at Avalon she is "Baby Girl." When she married and had a baby girl of her own, my grandniece made delightful guest appearances. Once, a gentleman dining alone in the booth opposite ours took off his glasses, folded his paper, smiled at our intergenerational gathering, and said, "I'm just enjoying your breakfast." It never occurred to me before that what we were doing was anything but ordinary.

My connection with my heavenly Father is meant to be just as real and intimate and life giving as any ordinary Friday at Avalon. Every day, God lays a meal before his children, and his winsome hospitality beckons us to come and eat and enjoy his presence and love. I know that I belong at that table. I am expected and wanted there, just as I am each Friday in the fourth booth on the right, the one nearest the kitchen, where my earthly father waits for me.

I stand at the door and knock. If you hear my voice and open the door,
I will come in, and we will share a meal together as friends.
REVELATION 3:20

This Old House

The first house I can remember living in was a low-slung, pinkish-brick ranch with a long, long driveway in Refugio, Texas. I had not seen it for decades until a visit to a nearby coastal town made me curious. Was it still standing? Could I find it? Thanks to the magic of GPS (and a little help from reliable, ever-chirpy Siri), I located it with very little trouble and recognized it with even less.

Maybe I sat a bit too long in the car in front of the house, but I couldn't stop staring . . . and remembering. A woman came out into the yard and began to putter around, checking me out but pretending not to. I opened the car door and walked over to explain, but I got out only a few words before I began to weep. "My parents built this house in 1963 . . ."

The woman put her arm around me as if I were a cousin or an old friend she hadn't seen in years, then invited me inside. She led me up to the porch where I'd practiced dancing in my tap shoes (because my mother insisted indoor tapping would scar the linoleum), where I'd cried when our first dog died, begging to go visit him in heaven.

The house Mother had kept bright and squeaky clean was dark and full of clutter, and the owner was apologetic, but I was seeing what she couldn't: a little girl on the kitchen floor, playing with pots and pans; two footie-pajama-ed sisters watching *Captain Kangaroo* in the living room; the bedroom where we said our God-blesses each night before falling into innocent sleep.

At some point in the tour a paper towel was pressed into my hands—I hadn't realized how hard I was crying. I didn't want to go back *there*, to that time and place, so much as I wanted all that I'd experienced there to be made new. Memory is eschatological, it has been said. And it is. It makes us long not only for all that *was* but for all that *will be*—and for the one who says, "Behold, I am making all things new" (Revelation 21:5, NASB).

Compared to what's coming, living conditions around here seem like a stopover in an unfurnished shack. . . . The Spirit of God whets our appetite by giving us a taste of what's ahead.
2 CORINTHIANS 5:2, 5, MSG

Waiting on a Miracle

I don't often spend time on golf courses. Nevertheless, a certain Monday found me on a local course late in the afternoon, waiting near the green on the seventeenth hole as a witness to a potential hole in one. In other words, waiting for a miracle.

If the miracle should happen, it had to be verified, of course, so I waited to see if someone might actually finish the par-three hole with a single shot. If they did, the payoff was quite nice: a trip to Pebble Beach with lots of extras (including more golf). So a friend and I parked our cart and chatted while we waited for the teams to approach—and then watched balls fly through the air and drop in the general vicinity of the flag.

The golfers made their way toward us slowly, but approaching much faster was a dark, thick cloud. The wind was blowing hard, and I could actually smell the rain in the air. We were waiting for a golfing miracle, but a storm was threatening to shut us down. So my friend faced the cloud and silently prayed while I kept watching for a one-in-a-million hole in one. In a few minutes, the menacing cloud that had been heading straight for us literally broke in half and went around us on either side.

And I kept my eyes fixed on hole seventeen, watching and waiting to witness a miracle.

Sometimes our eyes are so focused on the miracle we have in mind that we don't see the miracle at hand. God held a storm back, but he didn't let us witness a once-in-a-lifetime golf shot. He gave us a miracle all right, but it wasn't anything like the one we were there looking for.

God's nearness and his intervention can be as plain as the nose on my face, and I may still miss it. But the miracle that comes unannounced is no less mine, and no less divine. It just may take me a while to see it for what it is.

———

The LORD said to Moses, "How long will this people spurn Me? And how long will they not believe in Me, despite all the signs which I have performed in their midst?"
NUMBERS 14:11, NASB

From the Inside Out

In a note from a friend whose mother had very recently died, I read these words:

> I wear some of her clothes: her socks, her sweaters, her pants; her scarves, mittens, and coats (she was always cold like me!) and think of her embracing my body with her love from the inside out.

Honest confession: I stumbled over her last two words and edited them in my mind to "outside in," imagining that's what she'd meant to say.

I certainly understood the comfort she found in wrapping herself in those clothes. I once wore—every night for a week—the T-shirt of a boyfriend who was traveling abroad, and I felt soothed somehow by it in his absence. The reality of him wasn't in the piece of clothing any more than the reality of my friend's mother resides in *her* garments. But the putting on of temporal things is a visceral reminder of those eternal, intangible realities that we cannot touch or see. And her words were indeed more accurate than those substituted by my edit. The embrace, the presence of a loved one is experienced first in the heart, and it ends—not begins—on our skin. The "putting on" is the last step of remembering and identifying, not the first.

Henri Nouwen writes,

> Anyone who believes, Jesus reminds us, has eternal life (John 6:40). That is the enormous revolution, that in this fleeting temporary world he comes to plant the seed of eternal life. . . .
>
> Become aware of this mysterious presence and life turns around. You sense joy even as others nurse complaints, you experience peace while the world conspires in war, and you find hope even when headlines broadcast despair. You discover a deep love even while the air around you seems pervaded by hatred.*

In the places I will go today—some comforting and familiar, others daunting and strange—I imagine myself "putting on" Christ, and letting his incarnate clothing of goodness, mercy, and rightness with the Father be the outward expression of this one, unshakable reality: he is ever with me from the inside out.

As many of you as have been baptized into Christ have put on Christ like a garment.
GALATIANS 3:27, HCSB

---

* Henri Nouwen, *Turn My Mourning into Dancing* (Nashville: Thomas Nelson, 2001), 48.

Betrothed

He was twenty-five. She was twenty-one. I held her when she was just hours old; loved her before I ever saw her face. My sister's youngest daughter was engaged.

They sat on my sofa and talked about the future. I almost had to blink to see her in the present, not as I remember: at birth, in kindergarten, with pigtails, or in Christmas pajamas and braces. When she looks to the future, she sees the young man beside her clearly. The rest is fuzzy, and she's fine with that unfinished picture, as long as her groom is in it.

She's sure now who she belongs to, even if she's sure about little else. Three years earlier we sat together on a balcony on a cool July night in Aspen, gazing at the moonlit ridge before us and shivering in the chilly mountain air. She was ready to go to college, to test her independence and her ideas. She was sure then about what she wanted, and I'm grateful she's found it.

She's spoken for. Betrothed. And that changes things.

What if we knew and believed that we are spoken for? How would our days be different? What if we viewed our lives as one long, tender engagement—as a prelude to a promised eternity with a strong and faithful bridegroom?

We focus our modern ideas about engagement chiefly on the bride, and on the wedding itself. But the central figure of betrothal in Jesus' culture was the groom: his actions, his provision, his promise. And his betrothal was a binding agreement. No turning back. No second thoughts. Done deal. So the betrothed bride didn't need to fear the future. She was certain of her groom's good intent and confident of their shared life together.

We have no need to fear the future either. Our groom has secured our destiny and prepared our forever home. He will defend us against any thief or deceiver, for he has betrothed us to himself in righteousness, justice, loving-kindness, and compassion (see Hosea 2:19). There's a wedding in our future. Let us count the days with joy.

Your Maker is your husband—the LORD Almighty is his name—the Holy One of Israel is your Redeemer; he is called the God of all the earth.
ISAIAH 54:5, NIV

What Happens

It rains hard on a Wednesday, and you decide not to go out to lunch after all. You stay home instead and meet the mailman, who rings the bell to hand you a package and takes cover under your porch for a few extra moments to chat.

You had planned a trip to the library to finish some research tomorrow, but a cancelled appointment means you can go today instead. Minutes after you arrive, you hear the hushed voice of someone who lives six states away and whom you haven't seen in a decade. Tomorrow he would have been back home.

So much of life is colored by what happens and what doesn't. These two recent occurrences brought me unexpected joy, but their effect was momentary. Other happenings or nonhappenings carry a much greater impact, and their reverberations are far more lasting.

What happens: A husband's unthinkable choice meets a hidden fault line in his marriage, and the ensuing crack breaks into a canyon that will not be filled.

What doesn't: A friend longs to conceive a child and cannot. Every new turn of the calendar page inflicts an invisible blow to her tender heart, laying siege to her firm belief that God's plan for her is good.

What happens: A colleague's chronic illness turns pain and weakness into constant companions, not occasional pests. She masks her discouragement well, but you know—and your heart longs with hers for the bliss of a "normal" day.

What doesn't: The job a talented coworker has earned and would excel at goes to someone else—someone who seems less gifted and less deserving.

Something happens. Something doesn't. And life is changed, not so much by gain or loss, joy or sorrow, as by our response to it.

Today, for what happens and for what does not, may the God of all grace give you his limitless peace and boundless joy. For "who can say where the mourning ends and the dance begins?"*

———

The LORD will comfort Israel again and have pity on her ruins. Her desert will blossom like Eden, her barren wilderness like the garden of the LORD. Joy and gladness will be found there. Songs of thanksgiving will fill the air.
ISAIAH 51:3

---

* Henri Nouwen, *Turn My Mourning into Dancing* (Nashville: Thomas Nelson, 2001), 15.

A Rescue Too

The small gray sedan idling just ahead of me in traffic sported a bumper sticker shaped like a dog's paw. It read, "I'm a rescue. What are you?" My mind immediately went to Burley, my goofy mixed-breed pup whose mother was reportedly a black Labrador, but whose father was anyone's guess. One of a litter of nine, Burley became mine at nine weeks. When people ask, "What is he?" I almost always answer, "He's a rescue."

"He's a rescue" isn't a breed name. It's a story. He's a rescue because he needed a home, and I had one to share. I took one look at his soulful, kohl-rimmed eyes and imagined what a good dog he might become. When someone asked, "Will you take him?" I said, "Yes, I will." I didn't need a dog. I already had one—a very good one—at the time. But Burley needed me.

I naturally thought of Burley when I saw the bumper sticker. But the decal didn't ask about my dog. It asked about me. And the truth is that *I'm a rescue too*. I needed a place where my spirit could be at home, and God said, "Come and live with me. I have room."

I did not earn my oh-so-fortunate adoption. I was chosen not because of any virtues of my own, but because of the love of the one who did the choosing. Had he not plucked me out of my "litter of lostness," I would have certainly been homeless forever. But when I needed him most, he took me in. I'm thinking of getting that sticker for myself. It fits me like a glove. *I'm a rescue. What are you?*

By entering through faith into what God has always wanted to do for us—set us right with him, make us fit for him—we have it all together with God because of our Master Jesus. And that's not all: We throw open our doors to God and discover at the same moment that he has already thrown open his door to us. We find ourselves standing where we always hoped we might stand—out in the wide open spaces of God's grace and glory, standing tall and shouting our praise.

ROMANS 5:1-2, MSG

Twelve Miles of Memory

Ballinger, Texas, is just one of dozens of tiny West Texas towns that are fading fast from the landscape but clinging to the map.

I loved going there as a child to visit my mother's family. Their small-town life was magical to me. In Ballinger I watched Little League games and slurped pickle juice sno-cones. I swam and fished and stayed out too long in the sun, and I loved every minute I spent there.

Last week I returned but not with the same sense of expectation. My uncle's frail health required him to be moved into a nursing facility; my aunt was now alone in the house they had long shared. My sister and I made the six-and-a-half-hour drive to check on them and found the town the same. It always is. But they were not.

"It just happened so fast," she kept saying. "One day we were fine, and the next day we weren't." After a visit with him and lunch with her at the local senior center (we offered to cook; she insisted on going out), I asked if she'd like to go for a drive in the car. Her face brightened. So we did. We drove twelve more miles up the road to the place they had once farmed together. We looked, and she remembered.

Of all the sights I saw that day, here's the one *I'll* remember the most: in the nursing home, sitting in a chair with an oxygen cannula stretched across his face, my uncle reached out for my aunt's hand, and she caught his in midair. They patted each other, then their hands settled together on the arm of his chair, still comforted that the other one was near enough to touch.

One day our God will restore what's lost, mend what's broken, refresh what is weary and old and worn. We'll be at home again. And that will be a day for hallelujahs, oh yes, it will.

"God himself will be with them. He will wipe every tear from their eyes, and there will be no more death or sorrow or crying or pain. All these things are gone forever." And the one sitting on the throne said, "Look, I am making everything new!"
REVELATION 21:3-5

As Good as It Gets

Recently, I saw this sobering bit of graffiti: "This is as good as it gets."

The corresponding spray-painted artwork depicted a somber-looking male face. The image was hard to decipher, but the message wasn't. Even though I know better, the words made me sad. Not that they might be true, but that someone might think so.

Because it's going to get a *lot* better than this.

I'm not sure what your circumstances might be. Maybe sickness or death or unemployment or bankruptcy or a broken marriage or a wayward child or something I can't imagine consumes your every waking thought. And maybe it's tempting to believe that nothing will ever change. Maybe the voice of the enemy is whispering despair in your ear and telling you that tomorrow will bring more of the same.

But that voice is lying.

Nearly two thousand years ago a band of followers of a Nazarene teacher came to see him for who he was: God in flesh. He lived and died before their eyes, and then—for forty days more—he kept showing up, raised and somehow blazingly new, even with his scars. "Wait in Jerusalem," he told them, "for the gift that was promised to you" (see Acts 1:4). Some of them were probably so confused and frightened that they just wanted to go home to business as usual. Others were itching for a political coup, and still others, for a prominent place in a new movement. No doubt some believed, "This is as good as it gets."

It wasn't.

The one who died for them intended to keep on living for and through them. But first, he needed to fill their tiny waiting room with a hurricane of power and gift them with his permanent presence. But even *that* was nowhere near as good as it will get.

One day, he will defeat his archenemy once and for all, administer justice, and reign forever. He will undo the curse, reward his servants, and usher in a new heaven and a new earth. His rightful Kingdom will have no end.

That, my graffiti-splashing doomsayer, will *truly* be as good as it gets. Forever.

No one's ever seen or heard anything like this, never so much as imagined anything quite like it—what God has arranged for those who love him.
I CORINTHIANS 2:9, MSG

Sowing Life

Each Sunday morning at my small, inner-city church, twenty-five or so women gather in Modular D, Room B. The sign on the door says I'm their teacher, but quite often they teach me. Sometimes we have coffee, but not always. Sometimes, when the teacher is feeling a little flush or a client has just paid their bill, we have donuts. But those things aren't why we come. We come because we want to open the Word of God together and be taught by his Spirit. We've pored over Romans and Genesis, been wowed by the miracles and proclamations of John's Gospel, wondered at the beauty of the Psalms, and parked ourselves in the thick of prophecy in Daniel and Isaiah.

In the process, we've been bound up together in the boundlessness of God. Our lives are not alike. Some of us have laugh lines, and some don't yet need to moisturize. Some live in the suburbs and commute in. Others walk from their homes nearby. Some are married; others are not. Some have children; some don't. Some have advanced degrees, and others have GEDs. We are black and white, Hispanic and Asian. We're sisters in God's Kingdom.

I'm honored to be among these saints. I'm thrilled to see them come in, open their Bibles, and say, "We've got to get Joseph out of prison! Are we going to get him out this week?" I'm humbled, too, by their faith. Together we have prayed for jobs, finances, family members, illnesses, test results, travel mercies, and more. We have celebrated together the births of children and grandchildren, engagements and weddings, graduations and new jobs.

Together we are learning to lean on our Father and to love one another. We are finding our way in the world with his help, and seeing the fruits of his everlasting love in one another's lives. We're in this together—and on any given week we'll find a reason to celebrate. He's just that good, and his Word is just that true. We're expectant, and why shouldn't we be? Dream-telling Joseph *was* finally released from prison and put in charge of all of Egypt. So who knows what tomorrow will bring?

The Kingdom of Heaven is like a mustard seed planted in a field. It is the smallest of all seeds, but it becomes the largest of garden plants.
MATTHEW 13:31-32

15

There all along

I sat alone for almost an hour in the place I thought I was meeting friends. I expected to be waiting for at least a few minutes, so I ordered a latte. People-watched. Read the stray, rumpled sections of someone else's paper. And got more and more frustrated by the minute. Had I misunderstood the time? The meeting place? Had plans changed?

After forty-five minutes I ended my own misery and left the restaurant. I'd really looked forward to company—to blending into the laughter and love and conversation that usually characterize our time together . . . but I drove home frustrated instead.

Then my phone rang. "Where were you?" my friend asked. "We were there. Didn't you see us?" I hadn't. I'd watched the door the whole time, and even walked into the other room once to look around. I didn't see them, and apparently, they didn't see me, either. But they were there all along.

Although God always knows my whereabouts, sometimes it feels like we've gotten our wires crossed too. He doesn't show up when (or where) I expect him. I look around anxiously and don't trust his promises enough to wait past my own comfort. I keep moving to mask my confusion and disappointment. And almost always, after the fact, I come to see that he was there all along.

I was sure I was alone once as I cried sloppy tears on the balcony of a remote mountain cabin. I wasn't. He was there. I thought I was alone in the vet's office as I cradled a precious, dying pup and watched his last breaths, but I wasn't. He was there. I believed I was the only person in the hospital waiting room on a Saturday morning, waiting for my father's surgeon to come out and tell me how things had gone, but even though all the other chairs were empty, I wasn't alone. God had been there all along. I may not always be aware of him or recognize his nearness . . . but my Father never leaves me undefended. Ever. He goes before and behind. He's been there all along.

Do not fear, for I am with you; do not anxiously look about you, for I am your God. I will strengthen you, surely I will help you, surely I will uphold you with My righteous right hand.
ISAIAH 41:10, NASB

For Want of a Shepherd

When our pastor of a dozen years left for a new assignment, my church began searching for God's leader for us. For the first time in my life, I sat on something called a "pastoral search committee" and was struck with the enormity of our task. Each of us believed that God already had our new shepherd in sight, in mind. We just had to listen, follow, and find him.

The second time Israel went in search of a king, God led them to a shepherd. Their first king, Saul, was a placeholder in God's providence, but he *looked* the part— even if he failed to fill the role as hoped. Though Saul was the king from central casting, he was deeply flawed. His human flaws alone needn't have sunk him, but his fatal flaw was his failure to follow God. He knew how to lead the parade. He just didn't know how to love the flock and listen to their God.

Our committee proceeded through the necessary denominational steps, talked with one another, engaged our church family, prayed, and began to move forward. At one of our first meetings, we shared with one another what had led us to our church—and without fail, each of us told a story of connection that began with our former shepherd. We told stories of guidance, wisdom, nurture, and presence. The gifts of the shepherd.

Israel's second king tended sheep. God whispered David's name in old Samuel's ear, just like he had whispered Saul's. One could argue that David was a more flawed man than his predecessor—but shepherd-boy-made-king David knew how to follow. And when he failed to do so, his heart broke over his mistakes. Like every good shepherd, he knew the way home, and even when he wandered, he never lost sight of true north. His heart was fixed on it.

Kings and pastors come and go. Their legacies are fleeting for the most part and seldom self-determined. But good shepherds—well, their sheep remember them and know their voice, and follow them in love and gratitude.

I am the Good Shepherd. I know my own sheep and my own sheep know me. In the same way, the Father knows me and I know the Father.
JOHN 10:14-15, MSG

The Quiet Ones

I'd never heard of Euthydemus or Charmantides or Cleitophon. Maybe their names don't exactly ring a bell for you, either. They each appear in Plato's *The Republic*, albeit very briefly. They're not main characters, but they're in the crowd, listening to the dialectic. They just don't add much in the way of words.

So why bother, Plato? Why write them in? Those were the questions my philosophy professor asked as eight of us sat around a table having a conversation about what is, and how we can *know* what is. "If a character has just one line, why not give it to someone else?" he asked. "Or if he has no lines, why have him there at all?"

I listened as my classmates offered their answers, but as I did a huge lump formed in my throat and tears began to run down my cheeks. I remembered a precious widowed and childless aunt, dying in a dreary nursing home in a small West Texas town. I thought of a younger friend with cerebral palsy who probably finds himself on the outside of more than a few circles of his peers. And of another friend who rarely holds the floor but whose heart is a deep, deep river. And I wept. In a graduate class. In front of everyone.

"Have we hurt you in any way?" my professor asked. I shook my head no. Then he asked if there was something I'd like to say, and for one of the few times in my adult life I simply answered no. And I meant it.

Here's what I understood that evening from "the quiet ones"—from the guys who hardly uttered a line in *The Republic*, but whose names are included along with Socrates in the dramatis personae: everyone matters. Even the ones who may not speak a word. Simply by being with us, they change everything. That night I saw their faces, heard their voices, felt their weight. When I came home, I said what I might have said earlier, but did not. I said their names, voicing the gratitude I felt for them. They are the quiet ones, the wordless ones we'd be bereft without. How good of God to let *us* be with *them*.

You are no longer strangers and aliens, but you are fellow citizens with the saints and members of the household of God.
EPHESIANS 2:19, ESV

Inches and Degrees

Just three or four inches can make all the difference in the world. During a drive home from San Antonio to Houston in the season's coldest snap, my back car window refused to stay up. I started the trip warm and toasty, but as the window slid lower and lower, the night air crept in and the temperature drifted down. Still 150 miles from home and driving in the dark, I turned the heat up higher and aimed it at the center of my chest, then alternated its direction between chest, face, and shins every few miles in an inefficient attempt to warm myself.

It didn't seem possible that a scant few inches of space could mean the difference between cozy and uncomfortable. But it did. Already cold when I placed the key in my front door, I felt no less chilled when I stepped inside. I'd turned the heat off when I left home, and my hallway thermostat now read a disheartening forty-nine degrees! All the way home I was just three inches from fine. Finally *at* home, I was a good twenty degrees from the same.

I parked my suitcase, turned on the heat, and as planned, hopped back in the car to sit at the bedside of a dear and dying friend. He barely fluttered open one eye, and although our faces were hardly a foot apart, I wasn't sure he recognized mine. Just the slightest bit of pressure from his weak fingers made me hope that maybe, just maybe, he did. Every labored breath he took made me sharply aware of how close we are to eternity. We're only inches . . . small degrees . . . from glory in every ordinary moment, and we hardly even realize it.

Inches and degrees. Such tiny measures span so much vast real estate. Back home I bundled up in layers, climbed into bed, and waited for the temperature to rise. I breathed in deep, curled up tight, and fell into the arms of the one whose comfort is closer than my skin, believing in nothing more than morning, and a God whose lovely Kingdom comes by inches and degrees.

Bethlehem of Ephratah, though thou be little among the thousands of Judah, yet out of thee shall he come forth unto me that is to be ruler in Israel.

MICAH 5:2, KJV

Borrowers, all

A friend reminded me after a lovely catch-up dinner that I still had a borrowed book of his . . . three years after I'd first asked to read it. (Oh dear. Nailed.) When he told me the book's title, I pictured the cover and remembered its contents, but I couldn't say for sure whether it was still in my possession. I didn't *tell* him this, but I panicked briefly, wondering if I might have sold his missing title along with a stack of my own books, quite by mistake!

A few days later (to my great relief) I located his book and let him know it was coming home soon. Then I began thinking of all the *other* borrowed things I possessed. Borrowed hats, umbrellas, and gloves; borrowed bowls and coffee mugs and spoons; and even a borrowed painting. After that quick inventory, I realized a few items of my own were outstanding as well. But honestly, I don't mind.

Maybe that's because I know that I am a borrower at my very core and always will be.

I borrowed righteousness when I had absolutely none to my name. I borrow grace every day. (More truthfully, every minute of every day.) I borrow strength when mine is waning, and I borrow hope when I can't seem to muster much of it on my own. I borrow power when I am weak, wisdom when I am confused, and courage when I am fearful. I even borrow rest when I cannot seem to stop and peace when I am troubled. The gracious Loaner of all these things never hesitates to give, never grumbles, and never calls in his markers. None of this stuff is mine, and yet he makes it available as if it were. I say shyly, "May I please . . . ?" and "Could I have . . . ?" and "God, I need . . ." and he whispers, "As you wish. For as long as you need." And he never makes me feel ashamed for having asked.

So if you see me in possession of any of these things, you must understand that they are not mine and never were. They're his. He is the gracious giver of all that is good, true, and beautiful—and we are borrowers, all.

"My son," the father said, "you are always with me, and everything I have is yours."
LUKE 15:31, NIV

Falling Together

My family and friends can testify that I am *spectacularly* clumsy. A while ago I was ambling (solo and, I hope, unobserved) along a downtown sidewalk, and I tripped and fell so hard I ripped the knee out of my jeans. (The resulting scab and bruise healed nicely, thanks.) This happens more often than I would like to admit.

Maybe I'm so caught up in what I'm seeing or doing that I'm not attentive to where my feet are going, or maybe I'm just not terribly graceful. In any case, while it's less embarrassing to fall when you are by yourself, it's infinitely better to fall . . . together.

Three times in one weekend I lost my footing. But thankfully not for long, and with no ugly scars to show for it. The first time I fell was down an old rabbit hole of hurt when a few sharp and ill-timed words left me wounded and wanting to hide. But I didn't fall alone. One friend saw and prayed with me. One reminded me that the father of lies was, well, lying to me about myself. A third fed me the dinner I had skipped to nurse my wound in private, three hours *after* dinner at a beautifully set table for one in the kitchen. Thanks to these friends' kindnesses to me, I didn't have to fall far.

The other two tumbles were the literal kind—both on a trail I'd hiked dozens of times before, and in another's easy company. Once going up and again coming down, I lost my balance and slipped to the ground. Both times I let strong hands lift me back up to my feet. It just works better that way, even if it's humbling and not particularly pretty.

I'd like to go through life decidedly upright and steady, but I don't always. I get off kilter and lose my balance *and* perspective from time to time. Maybe you do too. When I fall, it helps to have good company nearby. It helps to have their prayers, wise words, kind acts, and steady hands. While I'd like to hide my stumbles, sometimes falling together is the very thing that keeps me from falling apart.

Two people are better off than one, for they can help each other succeed.
If one person falls, the other can reach out and help.
ECCLESIASTES 4:9-10

Worry Disabled, Fear Disarmed

The very busy executive in the television commercial appears concerned. With a few clicks of his computer keyboard, he pulls up a screen shot—presumably of his distant, suburban home—and watches as his front door opens. Two young teens let themselves in and trudge upstairs, backpacks in tow. Knowing (through video surveillance) that his children are home from school, he returns to the tasks at hand.

Then these words close out the spot: "Worry disabled. Fear disarmed." If only it were that easy.

My worrier often works overtime . . . and fear is close behind it. What if my health plan premiums go up 65 percent this year, and not the "mere" 25 or 40 percent from years just past? What if I or my loved ones are threatened by illness or disability? What if the violence I'm witnessing in other cities visits my own city one lurking night? What if my ability to earn a modest living decreases and the demands for that living increase? Honestly, I laugh now as I remember that in my thirties my most pressing question for the future was, what if I never marry? (The answer: under God, you live, love, and even thrive.)

I'm surprised I even saw the cable company commercial—I hardly turn on the television anymore. I just don't have the stomach to watch.

The truth is, there is nothing new under the sun. Every age—and every day—has plenty of troubles of its own. The antidote to trouble is not denial or avoidance, and the end result does not have to be fear and worry. It can be faith. But only because I am loved by a good and faithful God, and he is working all things for his glory and my good. Worry and fear are disarmed and disabled only when I think of God and his great love for me. He proved it irrefutably once for all in time and history, and he keeps on proving it, day in and day out, through troubles of every kind.

Which of you by worrying can add a single hour to his life's span?
If then you cannot do even a very little thing, why do you worry
about other matters?
LUKE 12:25-26, NASB

Ear to the Ground

In most of the westerns I grew up watching, a good cowboy or Indian could tell when help (or danger) was coming by listening for the sound of approaching hooves. Sometimes a wrangler or warrior would actually get down off his horse and put his ear to the ground to try to sense the faint vibration that might hint at coming reinforcements.

Well, these days my ear is tuned for hoofbeats. I am attentive and straining hard to hear. I know my Father's voice, and I long to take the time to zero in on it through the noise of daily living . . . but for this season at least, the silence has been quite deafening. I don't hear a sound.

"Faith," the writer of Hebrews asserts, "shows the reality of what we hope for; it is evidence of things we cannot see" (11:1). Could it also be the certainty of what we do not *hear*? Trying to explain this mysterious new silent treatment to a trusted friend, I found myself at a loss for words. But yesterday, these few words came, like a silent movie clicking out staccato code on a steady, spinning reel:

> *If it weren't for all the*
> *years and miles and tears—*
> *If it weren't for all the*
> *sudden joys and solid saves*
> *and lavish good—*
> *I'd say that you've gone missing,*
> *or you're sleeping on the job.*
> *But silent isn't absent—*
> *it is simply proof on mute.*
> *I'm calling this a coda*
> *in a lifelong song of presence,*
> *and my ear is to the ground*
> *to hear the thunder of*
> *your cavalry of one.*
> *Come.*

If you hear his voice today, praise him! If you hear only silence, praise him! Keep an ear tuned for the shout that says help's finally on the way.

In that day the people will proclaim, "This is our God! We trusted in him, and he saved us!"
ISAIAH 25:9

Come As You Are

Four word flash cards—the kind some of us used to learn to read—are tucked one after another into a rusted strip of trellis that hangs on my dining room wall. The cards say *come, as, you,* and *are.* They form a simple invitation to gather around the table with no pretense or fuss. I like the thought that friends can come as they are to my home and be fed and blessed.

A few weeks ago at my small inner-city church, we kicked off summer with a church-wide breakfast, organized on the fly by e-mail. Food items were suggested: breakfast casseroles, fruit, baked goods, and juice. But no individual assignments were made. Members just began showing up with their dishes, and the long table in the center of the room got fuller and fuller. It was an unorchestrated embarrassment of riches.

As I watched kids crowd the spread the adults had arranged and displayed, I thought that the body of Christ is not so different from our ad hoc breakfast buffet. Anyone might turn up. Everyone has a place. The table is simple, and the meal is sweet. In God's house, you can come as you are and bring what you've got. The Spirit takes the mix and makes of it something better than the sum of its parts. And no one need go away from the Father's table hungry.

Come as you are. Rich, poor, weak, strong, wise, simple . . . come. Bring what you've got: love, money, time, and talent—or emptiness, worry, and want. Just come.

There's something about a table that begs to be filled. There's something in each of us that longs to be fed. We have what others need. He has something perfect for us all. And really, what could be better than that? Just come as you are, and bring what you've got. He'll do the rest.

The next time you put on a dinner, don't just invite your friends and family and rich neighbors, the kind of people who will return the favor. Invite some people who never get invited out, the misfits from the wrong side of the tracks. You'll be—and experience—a blessing. They won't be able to return the favor, but the favor will be returned—oh, how it will be returned!—at the resurrection of God's people.
LUKE 14:12-14, MSG

Frozen

I should have covered them. Why didn't I imagine that a twenty-three-degree night would turn a half-dozen tropical(!) variegated ginger plants into something resembling well-cultivated straw? Two years before I'd struggled to drape these same plants when a hard freeze was predicted, and in spite of my clumsy efforts, they survived the frost. Not so this time. I left them naked—and was surprised to see how quickly they surrendered, flash frozen, to the bitter cold.

We are not impervious to the elements either. A harsh word, neglect, illness, loss, rejection—all of these can "flash freeze" our souls and deaden our hearts.

Naked to these elements, we wither. But willingly exposed to the sovereign hand of God, we thrive. "In this state of self-abandonment," writes Jean-Pierre de Caussade, "in this path of simple faith, everything that happens to our soul and body, all that occurs in all the affairs of life, has the aspect of death. This should not surprise us. What do we expect? It is natural to this condition. God has his plans for souls and he carries them out very successfully, though they are well-disguised." What sorts of disguises? De Caussade continues, "Under the name of 'disguise' are such things as misfortune, illness and spiritual weakness." The very things that leave us frozen! "But," says de Caussade, "in the hands of God everything flourishes and turns to good. He arranges the accomplishment of his highest designs *by means which deeply wound our natural feelings*."[*]

And this he does (I must often remind myself!) for his own glory and my highest good.

My ginger will come back. I consulted a local gardening source and learned that I should cut away the dead leaves and leave the stalk intact. My front flowerbed won't be attractive. Not for a while. But come spring I'll be looking for the tiny green shoots that whisper life and resurrection to a formerly frozen landscape.

The love of the LORD remains forever with those who fear him.
PSALM 103:17

---

[*] Jean-Pierre de Caussade, *Abandonment to Divine Providence* (New York: Crown Publishing Group, 2012), 95; emphasis added.

The Dessert Table

We were driving along a familiar country road, a dear friend and I, talking about our lives. About struggles and disappointments, about our own doubts and failings, and about how God keeps on showing up in the midst of everything. About how *relentless* his grace is and how much of it we might be missing as we catalog our every hurt and wish for what we don't yet have.

We spoke of small comforts, of new insights, of character and how slowly (and sometimes painfully) it grows. Then there was silence in the car for a mile or two before my friend said, "Don't get me wrong—I'm pleased that he's present and doing a work—but sometimes you just want to go straight to the dessert table."

Amen.

Enough with the vitamins and necessary nutrients of faith. I want the sugar high of blessing, spread out like a banquet for my choosing and my pleasure.

But life is not an endless dessert table set up to satisfy my sweet tooth for ease and comfort. And underneath my friend's words sat this hard and lovely truth: life serves what it serves, and a loving God is sovereign over every bite.

The hard swallows help us to fully savor the loveliest morsels—and to give thanks for them when they arrive. "The human spirit," wrote C. S. Lewis, "will not even begin to surrender self-will as long as all seems to be well with it." * Lewis also says,

> What would really satisfy us would be a God who said of anything we happened to like doing, 'What does it matter so long as they are contented?' . . .
>
> I should very much like to live in a universe which was governed on such lines. But since it is abundantly clear that I don't, and since I have reason to believe, nevertheless, that God is Love, I conclude that my conception of love needs correction. †

Our bitterest struggles are the very things that drive us hungry into his presence. His is the *only* dessert table where there *is* truly fullness of joy and where pleasures last not for a moment, but forever.

In your presence there is fullness of joy; at your right hand are pleasures forevermore.
PSALM 16:11, ESV

---

* C. S. Lewis, *The Problem of Pain* (New York: HarperCollins, 1996), 90.
† Ibid., 31–32.

The Mailman and the Resurrection

I'd never been without a mother, and her loss came so quickly that I'd hardly begun to feel it. The days since her passing were filled with a crazy jumble of emotions, and with a strange emptiness I can't quite describe. The kindness of friends was wide and deep; the levy of family held strong. But if you asked me for one memory that might just remain with me forever, it would be this.

On a Tuesday, Lee the mailman rang the bell. I met Lee on the first day I moved into my house and often saw him through the window as he delivered mail to the box on my front porch. If I happened to be outside sweeping or raking leaves or stuffing the feeder with birdseed, Lee and I would chat—but unless he had a package to deliver, he seldom rang the bell.

For some reason, on that day he did. I opened the door, and there stood my mailman, holding a handful of grocery-store flyers and one random credit solicitation. "Just wanted to say hi and see your face," he said, handing me stuff we both knew I'd throw away. "How's your year going so far?" he asked. "How have you been?" I dumbly shook my head and said, because I couldn't think what else to say, "My mom died on Sunday."

Lee rocked back on his feet and cocked his head. He said he was very sorry. I said, "Me, too." Then he held my gaze with his and said, "But you'll see her again, right?"

"I will," I said. "I will."

He nodded, and we just stood there for a moment—two speechless people who hardly knew anything about each other, except that we agreed on the Resurrection. That's a big thing to have in common with anyone, including a kind mailman who shares your name.

Did God know I needed a reminder of my mother's permanence? Maybe. Did the Holy Spirit whisper to the mailman on his daily rounds, "Ring her bell today"? I think he might have. It surely seems so. That day, the rock-solid fact of the Resurrection made the unbearable, bearable. One day, it will make everything new. Even us.

The last enemy to be destroyed is death.
I CORINTHIANS 15:26

Still Here

I'm a pack rat, although not in the traditional I've-got-stuff-stashed-everywhere sense. I save up memories. The kind that make my nose sting and my eyes fill up with tears. Moments when God seems so close that my heart breaks a little at the awareness of him.

This morning I stretched to set a just-washed plate on the top shelf in my kitchen cabinet, placing my hand on the countertop for balance. When I did, I remembered the evening, two years ago, when an army of women who love God and love me, too, brought salads and themselves and unpacked my belongings with me until the wee hours. Several of those women have moved away, but in the moment of remembering, they were all still here, very near and dear.

Then a snippet of song took me back to a weekend of word and song and food and art and God-ward thought with a ragtag group of believer-artists. And as I write these words, I can see their faces, hear their music, remember their laughter. And they're still here.

Once, on a bright, cold afternoon, I hiked a trail with a new, strong-shouldered friend. At the top we sat on a flat rock overlooking a river. We told our stories, or parts of them, for an hour or more. As the wind blew and the words swirled around us, I wished I could make the sun stand still. Those moments sped by too quickly, but the memories continue to linger with me.

"The physical presence of other Christians is a source of incomparable joy and strength to the believer," wrote Dietrich Bonhoeffer. "Whether it be a brief, single encounter or the daily fellowship of years, Christian community is only this. We belong to one another only through and in Jesus Christ."*

Because of Jesus' life, death, and resurrection, if I've loved you in a moment, I love you still. If my heart has broken at the beauty of a fleeting afternoon, that beauty's with me still. His beautiful breaking puts us together, forever, still.

Father, I desire that they also, whom You have given Me, be with Me where I am, so that they may see My glory which You have given Me, for You loved Me before the foundation of the world.
JOHN 17:24, NASB

---

* Dietrich Bonhoeffer, *Dietrich Bonhoeffer: Witness to Jesus Christ* (Minneapolis: Augsburg Fortress, 1991), 178.

Face Time

There is no substitute for face time. Instant messaging, texting, e-mailing, and tweeting may fool us into thinking we are solidly connected—but these tools are illusory. If our relationships don't have a real-life component, we can become a mile wide and an inch deep.

While speaking by phone to a friend in another state, I realized I didn't have his e-mail address. When I asked for it, he said, "Sure—but if this were an e-mail, I couldn't hear you laugh, or pick up the tone in your voice, or know how many seconds went by before I asked and you answered."

Fair enough.

Technology can fool me into thinking I've connected with dozens of people during the course of a day, when I haven't sat for more than a moment with a single living being. It may make me efficient, but it doesn't help me to know deeply or be deeply known.

Is it any wonder, given our manic reliance on disembodied communication, that we imagine we can somehow know God apart from spending time in his presence? Reading theology is a useful pursuit, but that knowledge will only take me so far if it's not matched by time spent in adoration or praise or confession or pleading before the one I've been reading *about*.

I'm becoming more and more convinced that my commitment to God is evidenced by my willingness to "waste" time—long stretches of it—before his face. The old hymn "Beneath the Cross of Jesus" says, "I ask no other sunshine than the sunshine of his face." That's a holy hunger, one that's not easily satisfied with distant, fleeting sparks. That's a longing for face time, and a confession that nothing less will do.

So if these words have resonated with you, don't just be glad that you and I "connected." Talk about them with someone over coffee. Call a friend you've drifted from and listen for as long as it takes to hear what you've been missing. But if you only do one thing, do this: sit still and expectant before the face of the one who never drifts and whose love never wanes. And when you think you've been there long enough, linger just a little while longer. You won't regret it.

When you said, "Seek my face," my heart said to You, "Your face, O LORD, I shall seek."
PSALM 27:8, NASB

Reading the acknowledgments

Have you ever considered why you buy a book? (You do buy books, right?) Some of the best reads I've found came by way of recommendations—from friends and from strangers. I've bought books a few times for their covers, at least twice for their inscriptions, and often for their authors. I've purchased more than a handful because they were the current buzz, but those have frequently fallen short of the hype.

Lately, I've abandoned these book-shopping techniques for one that is almost always reliable. I've started reading the acknowledgments page. Here authors sometimes list other writers whose thoughts and words have inspired them—or colleagues who have sharpened their thinking—or agents whose suggestions gave their work needed clarity and focus. Editors whose unseen hands made a good work even better are cited, along with friends and family members whose encouragement bolstered the author's faltering will to finish.

Producing a book worth reading is a lot like growing a life worth living. Things worth doing are seldom done easily and rarely alone. And the real story is more often found in the acknowledgments than it is in slick cover copy or reviews.

Names like William and Liz, Howard and Annie, or Lee and Noel may not make the marquee. But they (and hundreds of thousands more) are part of the nurturing community surrounding names that do. Their influence is enormous. Without them, and others like them, what happens on the page simply wouldn't.

It doesn't matter whether or not you've written a book. You're writing a life—and you're not doing it alone. So whose name would be on *your* acknowledgments page, and on whose acknowledgments page would your name appear? Most of our names won't make the headlines or the book jacket. Our impact may not be broad, but it can and should be loving, intentional, and deep. Because there are no small contributors to any glorious endeavor. Not ever.

Greet Mary. . . . Greet Andronicus and Junias. . . . Greet Ampliatus, my beloved in the Lord. Greet Urbanus, our fellow worker in Christ, and Stachys my beloved. Greet Apelles . . . Herodion . . . Tryphaena and Tryphosa . . . Persis . . . Rufus . . . Asyncritus, Phlegon, Hermes, Patrobas, Hermas.

ROMANS 16:6-14, NASB

JANUARY 30
Tell It again!

I love a good story. I always have.

One chilly Sunday evening, tucked into a booth at a noisy taqueria, I heard one I liked a lot.

It was told in tandem and had no doubt been repeated several times already, although it was scarcely twenty-four hours old. The tellers of this particular story were young and in love. One of them is my oldest niece. On Saturday, he had asked her to marry him, and on Sunday we grabbed dinner together so I could hear all about the night before. I'd been anticipating the story for a while, so while we enjoyed generous plates of shrimp tacos and quesadillas, the tale unfolded one more time for my benefit.

She started it. He filled in a few colorful details. Both of them are actors, so the story's execution was as enjoyable as the content. I felt like I had seen the whole thing: the ring in the tiny blue box, the shaking hands, the question, the answer, the pictures and phone calls and oddly timed tears. They told it to me, and they'll tell it again. To their friends. To their extended families. To their children one day, and maybe to *their* children too. I pray that it grows sweeter to them every time they do.

The best stories never get old. No matter how many times you hear them told, you're never sad to hear them again. Martin Luther is reported to have replied, when asked by his parishioners when he planned to stop preaching the same old gospel story to them, "I will stop preaching it when you no longer need to hear it." Clearly, he did not anticipate that that day would ever arrive.

Have you told your story lately? The one about how God found you? About how he rescued you, or comforted you, or healed you? How he held you, tested you, or gave you the desires of your heart? No one else can tell it like you can. You were there. You know the details. Your story bears telling again.

On her left hand, my niece wears the first few lines of a story. I can't wait to see it grow richer and deeper with time and with every telling.

Your name, God, evokes a train of Hallelujahs wherever it is spoken, near and far; your arms are heaped with goodness-in-action.
PSALM 48:10, MSG

Permanent Ink

I sat down to dinner next to a lovely young woman I'd just met, and we began trading bits of our stories over steaming plates of chicken enchiladas.

We talked about food, faith, community, and music. We even discovered a handful of acquaintances we held in common. She told me how she and her musician husband met and how much they loved traveling together at this stage of their lives. I could have listened to her beautiful voice all evening and not grown weary of it.

I knew a bit of her story already, though, and I wondered if she hoped I'd avoid it or acknowledge it. When the conversation veered toward children, I took a risk and asked about the two babies she'd lost just months before. "Did you have boys, or girls, or one of each?" I asked.

"A boy and a girl," she answered without hesitating. "Jack and Lucy."

I asked if those were family names, and she said they weren't. "We thought we were having two boys until they came," she explained. "We had decided on Jack and another boy's name—but we liked the sound of Lucy."

I couldn't (and still cannot) imagine the grief that must have swallowed them. She acknowledged it, saying, "People asked what got us through it, as if they were expecting us to share a good book or a few verses of Scripture we'd clung to." Then she said, "I realized the answer was simply 'Jesus.' He held us."

As she spoke and gestured with her hands, her sleeve slipped away from her wrist, and I saw the tattooed words *Jack and Lucy*.

"My husband has one too," she offered. "We wanted to do something that would last."

I might one day forget these children's names. But their parents will not. They cannot. The names written on their hearts will last longer than the faint wisps of permanent ink etched on their skin. And they'll need no reminder of what to whisper between kisses when they hold their precious children once again. Hearts broken by love always remember. They can do no less.

Can a mother forget her nursing child? Can she feel no love for the child she has borne? But even if that were possible, I would not forget you!
ISAIAH 49:15

February

Ode to a Big Chief (Why I Write)

From my first Big Chief tablet with its pale-blue, alternating solid and dotted lines, I've long been smitten with empty pages. I started writing young—a word nerd from the get-go—and I never stopped. I was writing poetry at eight. Penning short stories to entertain myself at ten. I wrote out my prayers and filled up journal after journal through high school and college, where I was . . . wait for it . . . a journalism major who took literature classes for fun (and easy As).

I'm often asked now, as someone who writes for a living, "How do you become a writer?" I've learned over time that the question is not about me—it's about the questioner. It's less "How did *you* become a writer?" than it is "How can *I* become a writer?" Understanding this, my answer is always the same: *writers write*. They don't simply dream of writing or plan to write someday or talk of writing or read books about how to get published or "build a platform." They sit down before an empty page or screen and paint with words whatever insistent image beats its wings against their mind and heart, fighting to get free.

They write because they have to. They write because the weight behind the words demands the service of a voice.

If I never sold another piece or landed another book contract or received another assignment, I am certain the sight of a Big Chief tablet (or its grown-up cousin, the Moleskine) and the smell of a few sharpened pencils would still make my heart beat faster. And why wouldn't it? I follow a God whose story never gets old. The sky-wide narrative arc of creation, fall, redemption, and restoration lies at the heart of every true and beautiful story, because it's the echo of *his* story. He makes all things new, and in him, all things hold together.

And let's face it: all the Big Chief tablets in the world set end to end cannot contain all the ways to say, "He loves you," to a world that needs to hear it. So I write.

There are so many other things Jesus did. If they were all written down, each of them, one by one, I can't imagine a world big enough to hold such a library of books.
JOHN 21:25, MSG

FEBRUARY 2
Groundhog Day

Remember the movie *Groundhog Day*? Narcissistic meteorologist Phil Connors travels to Punxsutawney, Pennsylvania, to cover the February 2 appearance of Phil the groundhog, and gets stuck. Each morning at 6:00 a.m. his alarm goes off to Sonny and Cher's "I Got You Babe," and no amount of clock smashing will make it stop. Phil is in a time warp. Every day is the same day, all over again. No matter what he tries.

Do you ever feel like it's Groundhog Day? Maybe your job is numbingly monotonous, or the same worry wakes you, day in and day out. Maybe there's a memory you can't shake or a toxic relationship that never seems to heal. Or perhaps an illness has taken up residence in your body and has become your unwanted, constant companion.

Groundhog Day. Nothing changes.

With nothing to break up the landscape, we languish. As C. S. Lewis asserts in his poem "Love's As Warm As Tears," we see only

Deluge, weeks of rain,
Haystacks afloat,
Featureless seas between
Hedges, where once was green.

Once, all of history was just more of the same. Nothing could break the hopeless cycle of sin and death begun with Adam.

But the Resurrection changed everything—changes everything.

What appears to be final, isn't. What feels fatal, won't be. In Christ, loss will be gain, darkness will be light, fear will surrender to hope, and hope will never die. The Groundhog Day warp of futile human monotony was shattered when Christ arose. In him, anything is possible. Will your situation change? It will. How? I can't say. But do you doubt that the God who defeated death can step into your same old, same old and shake things up for your good and for his glory?

I don't. Not for one Groundhog Day minute. It's 5:59 a.m. The alarm's about to ring. God's got me, and I'm hoping to see springtime yet. Who knows? Perhaps today will break the cycle and set me free.

Listen! My beloved! Behold, he is coming, climbing on the mountains, leaping on the hills! . . . [He] said to me, "Arise, my darling, my beautiful one, and come along. For behold, the winter is past, the rain is over and gone. The flowers have already appeared in the land."
SONG OF SOLOMON 2:8, 10-12, NASB

Smelling Smoke

I didn't hear the alarm, but I didn't need to. My dog woke me at 3:25 a.m., crying and barking, and as soon as he did, I smelled smoke. A look outside the bedroom window caused my concern to quickly escalate. Fire trucks were beginning to line the street. When I opened the door to the hallway and confirmed what I had only smelled before, I was wide awake for good.

You always wonder what you would grab if your house was on fire. Now I know. Dog and leash, cell phone and purse. I threw a robe over my nightgown and skipped the shoes. I couldn't find them quickly enough. As I dashed out of the lobby of my building, firemen were on their way in. I met a neighbor in the parking lot who said he'd been walking his dog when he saw smoke rising from the building. As we spoke, the firemen were making their way down the halls, knocking on doors and breaking them down when there was no answer. Neighbors were beginning to congregate in the street and compare notes about what might have happened.

Within minutes the street was filled with fire trucks. Smoke poured from the roofline above my three east-facing windows: bedroom, study, and living room. The news media wasn't far behind: two cameramen prowled the street, panning the curb-sitting residents of my building. They stopped in front of my dog and me. (He is extremely photogenic; my bathrobe, not so much. Even so, I think I might have made the morning news.)

Here's what I learned that day: I could live without my stuff. The apartment suffered only smoke damage and a broken doorjamb, but it could have been much worse. I would have missed my books and photographs, yes—but they didn't matter enough to grab, even when I knew there was a fire. I just wanted out. Also, the threat of danger makes neighbors of us all. Watching your building burn is a surefire barrier breaker. (Maybe we should all talk more when nothing's on fire.) And finally, by the time you smell smoke, the fire is out of control. Don't dawdle. Run.

I'm grateful for my little four-legged sentry. I'm grateful to have smelled the smoke in time. And I'm grateful to see another sunrise.

I lie awake thinking of you, meditating on you through the night. Because you are my helper, I sing for joy in the shadow of your wings.
PSALM 63:6-7

Say the Words

Every Sunday at my home church, we stand and recite the words of the Nicene Creed, which Christ followers have said for centuries:

I believe in one God, the Father Almighty, Maker of heaven and earth, and of all things visible and invisible.

And in one Lord Jesus Christ, the only-begotten Son of God, begotten of the Father before all worlds; God of God, Light of Light, very God of very God; begotten, not made, being of one substance with the Father, by whom all things were made. Who, for us men and for our salvation, came down from heaven, and was incarnate by the Holy Spirit of the virgin Mary, and was made man; and was crucified also for us under Pontius Pilate; He suffered and was buried; and the third day He rose again, according to the Scriptures; and ascended into heaven, and sits on the right hand of the Father; and He shall come again, with glory, to judge the quick and the dead; whose kingdom shall have no end.

And I believe in the Holy Ghost, the Lord and Giver of Life; who proceeds from the Father and the Son; who with the Father and the Son together is worshipped and glorified; who spoke by the prophets.

And I believe in one holy catholic and apostolic Church. I acknowledge one baptism for the remission of sins; and I look for the resurrection of the dead, and the life of the world to come.

Amen.

Each time I say these words together with my brothers and sisters in Christ, I am struck by something particular, because they are particular words. Saying them doesn't make them any *truer*—it just keeps me tethered a little more tightly to the truth I already believe. I can believe in God the Father, God the Son, and God the Holy Spirit, but when I say the words, my heart is stirred all over again. And if I'm fortunate, I'll be saying the words—and rejoicing in every syllable—as I bid good-bye to this world and embrace the life of the world to come.

Even when it may go without saying, it's good to say the words.

Now we live in fellowship with the true God because we live in fellowship with his Son, Jesus Christ. He is the only true God, and he is eternal life.
I JOHN 5:20

No Other Name

All was calm in the airport shuttle van until *she* boarded. "Maria" was slow to get in, giving an earful to the young port authority employee (not) helping her (enough) to arrange transportation to Manhattan. Then she promptly got on her cell phone and began doing business.

"Debbie? No? Then who is this? Where is Debbie? We were supposed to do an interview."

Debbie was actress-choreographer Debbie Allen. I know this because Maria dropped her name multiple times. Clearly, there would be no interview for the "seventeen media outlets" apparently salivating for Maria's story. The unfortunate person on the other end of the line got the same treatment as the port authority kid. The message was simple: they were stupid. She was important. In fact, she said so: "I'm like Barbara Walters or Anderson Cooper. I'm the busiest person in the world." Oh yes, *she did*.

Did the person explaining Debbie's absence not realize what an egregious error had been committed? "I took the red-eye in from LA and had one hour to spare, and I used it to prepare for this interview." Oh, well then. And, "I have Kate Upton all week this week—I'm on my way to the Waldorf Astoria to meet with her, so this was the only time I could do the interview with Debbie." Perhaps next week, her victim must have asked? Uh, *no*. Because "next week I'm in London all week with Tom Cruise."

One name she dropped held my attention, though: *Jesus Christ*. She invoked it after she'd chewed out the kid on the curb, after Debbie's assistant hung up on her, and when a laundry van nearly sideswiped us on the Queensboro Bridge. I held my tongue. I probably shouldn't have. I wanted to say, "Oh—I know *him*! Do you?" Her final reference to Jesus was followed by this: "Do I have to do *everything* myself? [Bleeping] incompetents!"

I have good news for Maria. There is *nothing* we can do for ourselves. We are unable to change the trajectory of our soul's destination. But Jesus can. He knows we are frail and sick and deeply flawed, and he loves us as if we were name-droppable A-listers. Because to him, we are.

This Jesus is the stone that was rejected by you, the builders, which has become the cornerstone. And there is salvation in no one else.
ACTS 4:11-12, ESV

What I Wish I'd Said

Words seldom fail me, but sometimes I fail them. Sometimes I fall short of offering exactly what a moment asks of me. The right words may come later, and leave me feeling like a kid who's managed to untangle herself at the starting line only after the race is done.

A pregnant girl in a dirty pink T-shirt approached me as I spoke with a colleague in a hotel lobby. "Are you from here?" she asked. When we both said no, she paused, then came closer to tell her story. It involved a need for money, as I was sure it would. Should I believe she needed twelve dollars to spend the night in a nearby shelter? If I helped her out, would she use what I gave her wisely? Feeling no strong conviction either way, I gave her what little cash I was carrying. My friend did too.

Later I realized the moment could have been different if I had spoken instead what I *knew* to be true: "What I have is yours whether you've told the truth or not, because grace gives—and grace has given to me. And at this very moment, whatever our motives, God could not love either of us more."

To the shuttle driver who deftly delivered me to the airport in a traffic jam *and* a thunderstorm, then confessed she was likely to be late for a court-mandated anger management class, I only said, "We'll make it . . . both of us." I wish I'd complimented her on how calmly she'd managed the kind of frustrating ride that usually kicks my own blood pressure up a notch. But I didn't. I let the moment pass.

We have the power to bless, encourage, and offer hope with our words. Moment by moment, new opportunities will arise. When the next one does, I pray I'll say what I'll wish I'd said when the moment is gone.

———

A man has joy by the answer of his mouth, and a word spoken in due season, how good it is!
PROVERBS 15:23, NKJV

Marvelous, Wondrous Things

The world is full of marvelous, wondrous things—things I could never figure out on my own. I've encountered these marvels since childhood, and I imagine I'll go right on encountering them until I die. Bread rising. Words of poetry or praise forming in my brain among the formulas and passwords that I store there for everyday, ordinary use. One writer calls such wonders "quotidian mysteries," and they are. Some of these commonplace happenings may be discovered by chance, but many—maybe most—are taught.

I was taught that in water too deep to wade through, I can float or swim. Taught that long shoelaces can be tugged and arranged in a way that holds my shoes firmly on my feet. Taught that the alphabet can morph into words, and words into sentences, and sentences into stories that can take your breath away. Through teachers I have come face-to-face with marvelous things I was once quite ignorant of.

Some of my teachers knew what they were up to. Others had no idea they were teaching me at all. Mrs. Johnson (my kindergarten teacher) knew that "Run, Spot, run" would eventually make a reader out of me. Mrs. Youens knew how to coax a writer out of that shy reader. Mrs. Shumate knew she was teaching her third-grade Sunday school charges to love Jesus and live right—but she couldn't have known which of us would. A boy named Michael taught me how to share my heart, and a man named John taught me broken hearts do mend. I am absolutely certain I would have learned none of those things on my own. For these (and a thousand other wonders) I needed an instructor.

Some of these instructors remain. Many are gone. But I have one teacher who never leaves me. God the Holy Spirit teaches me every day. Which way to go. What words to say. Where to look so I won't miss a single thing he means for me to see. Through him, the school bell rings each precious day and mysteries abound.

This is God's Message, the God who made earth, made it livable and lasting, known everywhere as *God*: "Call to me and I will answer you. I'll tell you marvelous and wondrous things that you could never figure out on your own."
JEREMIAH 33:2-3, MSG

FEBRUARY 8
Learning to Let Go

"It's congestive heart failure," the veterinary cardiologist said. Before that week, I hadn't known such specialists existed. A leaky mitral valve had finally reached its tipping point, and my sweet little companion of eight years was very sick. He still barked at the UPS drivers and at the twin Boston terriers who paraded their sleepy owner past our window each morning. He ate well and let me know when it was time to go outside.

But in spite of regular doses of very expensive medicine, he was not getting measurably better. His rattling cough caught us both off guard several times a day and into the wee hours of the morning, and I felt helpless to soothe it. As he lay curled in my lap, I could feel his heart thumping in his thin, heaving chest.

So I began learning to let go.

I tried to imagine my house without the sound of feet on the hardwood floor, and I pictured the sofa minus his silky self stretched across the back. I considered the strangeness of not being followed from room to room, or of having no need to shoo him away from licking my wet feet when I stepped from the shower. I wondered what it would be like to wake up on cold mornings and not feel his weight plastered warmly along my spine.

I didn't want to give him up, but I knew the choice would not be mine.

Isn't that just like life? So much we can't command and don't expect. Lots of uncertainty. Countless opportunities to practice releasing our tightening grip and to trust the hand that grips us. But even with determined practice, we never seem to get much better. Sometime toward the end of Owen's life, I wrote these words:

> God, help me to let go of what you would have me release, and cling only to that to which you would have me cling. Clarify for me the difference between the two. May the way I spend this day be a pleasing aroma to you. Let its altars be placed closer together, not farther apart. Teach me to order and savor this day so that at its end I will have loved you—and others—well.

Though he brings grief, he will show compassion, so great is his unfailing love.
LAMENTATIONS 3:32, NIV

Weighty Matters

A book I was reading slapped me silly with these few words: "As a species we travel better light than heavy-laden."* I had just schlepped through security and across the terminal with a large purse, a laptop, a jacket, and a bulging folder of editing to complete in flight. I was weighted down—but convinced I needed every extra ounce I toted.

Each day I hear stories of people who are traveling lighter—and most of them not by choice. Their portfolios aren't as fat as they once were. Their list of must-have devices and services is growing leaner too. They're deciding that vacations can be trimmed, or vehicles can be driven less than fully loaded. We're told that this is a very bad thing. Cause for fear, even.

I think it might not be. I think the grudging divestiture of some of these "weighty matters" might yield a positive outcome in the end.

The things I carried into the airport made my shoulders ache. They kept me slightly off balance as I tried to shift their weight to an easier-on-the-body position. Seated, I had to watch them carefully. I was only away for three days. I could have traveled lighter.

When did our stuff get so heavy? When did kindergartners start lugging ten-pound packs? When did a "medium" soft drink begin to tip the scales at thirty-two ounces? When did television screens expand in all their high-def glory to dwarf regular living room furniture? When did we start demanding so much of everything but not making time for the one thing we need most of all?

I could have done without the folder of papers. The flight was only two hours. I could have done without the laptop. I could have done without twenty-five pounds of clothing, shoes, and toiletries for a there-and-back working trip. I once spent ten days in Europe with far less and never felt unequipped or underdressed.

Sometimes carrying more means having less: less freedom, less spontaneity, less curiosity, less contentment. In these weighty matters, I am a very slow learner.

Look at the birds, free and unfettered, not tied down to a job description, careless in the care of God.
MATTHEW 6:26, MSG

---

* Gerard W. Hughes, *God in All Things* (London: Hodder & Stoughton, 2003), 141.

In Distressing Disguise

Mother Teresa is said to have called the lepers and outcasts and dying ones that she and her order served "Jesus in distressing disguise." The man whose body was covered in running sores and flies: Jesus in distressing disguise. The bloated child dying for want of simple nourishment: Jesus in distressing disguise. The infant left in a trash heap: Jesus in distressing disguise. Mother Teresa saw her job as simply loving each and every "Jesus in distressing disguise" that she met.

I'm no Sister of Charity. I don't rescue men, women, and children from the ravages of disease or poverty. I live an ordinary life, but each day I encounter Jesus in distressing disguise. I can love him, or I can turn away.

There's the high-handed, haughty colleague who disdains every opinion but her own: Do I love her as Jesus in distressing disguise, or do I silently judge and then dismiss her? What about the crude critic-in-chief who shames others into submission with his biting words? The self-proclaimed friend who deceives you then disappears like vapor when you need her most? The mean-spirited social critic who blisters openly and with malice those who dare to disagree with him? Jesus again in distressing disguise.

I'm not saying Mother Teresa had it easy loving strangers. I am saying that the most distressing Jesus-in-disguise challenges we face may not be strangers at all. They may be those nearest and dearest to us. (And we to them!) Regardless of the unseemly condition of the man, woman, or child before her, Mother Teresa saw the beauty of Jesus Christ . . . and an opportunity to love him through ministering to one of the least, the last, the lost, or the left behind. Today I'm asking God to help me do the same. My Jesus comes in distressing disguises of every sort, challenging me to love the unlovely or even the enemy in his name. And I want to. Because once upon a time, that's just the way he loved me.

"Lord, when did we ever see you hungry and feed you? Or thirsty and give you something to drink?" . . . The King will say, "I tell you the truth, when you did it to one of the least of these my brothers and sisters, you were doing it to me!"
MATTHEW 25:37, 40

Good Bones

When it comes to real estate, I'm the kind of shopper I hate. I have a good idea of what I'd like, but I waffle. A house could have most of the things on my list and still not feel right. Or it could meet my admittedly quirky criteria but be on the wrong end of the right block. Or need a little too much "fixer-upping."

The cute-outside cottage on the ideal block was already under contract and riddled with goofy mural painting in almost every room. It was as if the owner had picked up a do-it-yourself trompe l'oeil manual and tried every trick in the book. (Let's just say the eye was *not* fooled.)

The neat little house on the historic register had great possibilities but literally no reasonable place for a bed. (Maybe *historic* means "twin bed only" or "roll-up mat"?)

I've heard people say they chose their house because it had good bones, and I'm wondering if there isn't some wisdom there. *Good bones* says, "I see what this could be. The foundation is strong and solid. I could build on this and make something beautiful of it." Readiness says, "I'm willing to begin today."

Once, in a conversation with a friend of mine, I floated a theory I called "first available." (This was when smoking was an option in most restaurants.) It went something like this: when you're really, really hungry and ready to eat and the hostess asks, "Smoking, nonsmoking, or first available?" you say, "First available." Right?

Maybe the house that's supposed to be my home will be the first house I see that makes my heart flutter at least a little, has room for a grown-up bed (and a gas stove, please!), and good bones—and I will see it when I'm really, truly ready to make it my own.

Here's the surest lesson that house hunting has taught me so far: I'm very, very thankful Jesus observed my flaws and decided he could work with nothing more than good bones (or rather not-so-good ones). It is sweet to be his, even though there's no end to the improvements needed to make me wholly inhabitable. Somehow, miraculously, he committed to me, and is making himself more at home every day.

Your love has always been our lives' foundation, your fidelity has been the roof over our world.
PSALM 89:2, MSG

Under Construction

I'm a work in progress. What comes out of me under pressure is not always what I would wish. If you asked a certain group of city employees working on my street, they might swear there's no way the lady in the little gray house is a Christ follower. Their doubt could be traced to the witness of my midafternoon meltdown when I returned home to a front yard and driveway that looked like a bomb crater. With no warning at all, the city had decided to replace the sidewalks on my block and had dug them all up in the middle of the day, leaving a three-foot-wide gap nearly a foot deep across my driveway—when my car was parked in it!

A call to the city's 311 line yielded a six-digit report number and nothing more. So I braved the 107-degree heat and walked a block and a half down the street to where I flagged down a city employee on a bulldozer digging up another driveway. I threatened, begged, and threw a small fit, demanding that he do something to fix the mess he'd created. "Do you care at all that you've made it impossible for me to get out of my own driveway?" I asked.

"Lady," he said, "my boss just said, 'Dig the hole.'" By then I had calmed down enough to realize the stupidity of angering the only person in sight who might solve my problem. So I took a deep breath and asked, "Then do you think I could ask you to fill it?" And he did. He took his bulldozer, filled the hole in my driveway with dirt from down the street, tamped it down, then garnered two more workers with shovels to smooth it out. When they were done, I just said, "Thank you," and went inside.

My front yard is still a mess, and the sidewalk isn't poured. The job is not done. Jesus isn't done with my heart, either. I'm under construction, as surely as the sidewalk in front of my house. What comes out of me is what's inside—and what's inside isn't always pretty. All the digging going on here just proves to me how much work remains.

Let the words of my mouth, and the meditation of my heart,
be acceptable in thy sight, O Lord, my strength and my redeemer.
PSALM 19:14, KJV

They Signed Their Work

The signs on the north and west boundaries of these meandering streets say this neighborhood was established in the early 1900s, so I was quite late to discover its charms. As with most places, I found that I came to know it best when I traveled it by foot. There are discoveries to be made at a walking pace that come no other way.

Even while I'm looking down for errant roots or sidewalk cracks, there is still much to see. One time while crossing a driveway, I noticed an imprint near its curb that read, "Fred Brown, Contractor." Then a few yards up the street, I saw another driveway poured by Fred. As I walked further, I noticed that F. O. Schuller had poured his share of driveways too. After I started looking for names, I began to see them everywhere—even on the steps leading up to my own front porch. Once upon a time, it seems, ordinary workers signed their ordinary work. I'm fairly certain they did not do so until the job was done and up to standard. And I wonder why they don't do it anymore.

Fred and F. O. and the others once had companies bearing their own names. Their work product was, in effect, their signature. If it stood, their reputations stood too. Their names attested to that fact. I even imagine that if, years ago, you wanted concrete poured in this neighborhood, you could dial your rotary landline and even speak to Fred or F. O. personally about the work you needed done!

I sign some of my work but by no means all of it. Much of it is done anonymously for others. But these fellows who in days past signed the work that was their bread and butter have challenged me to do each bit of my own ordinary work as if *my* name were set in stone upon it. Then, long after I am gone, each word I have written will testify that once I worked for a living wage and was never ashamed for the work I did to bear my name. Would you sign your work today?

Whatever you do, work at it with all your heart, as working for the Lord, not for human masters.
COLOSSIANS 3:23, NIV

Why Not Love?

I'm so weary of ugliness in the public square. I'm saddened (and my soul is a little more deadened every day) by the name-calling, the nonstop accusations, and the mean-spirited words hurled, leaked, broadcast, and tweeted. And it's not just politicians who are the problem. The meanness is trickling down to everyday discourse between ordinary folks. I witnessed the following unlovely exchange in a clothing store:

Two women were shopping with two small children in tow—one a three-year-old boy and the other a baby girl. The little boy was standing stock-still, staring at a broken bottle of perfume on the floor. As an employee was moving in to clean things up, she noticed the children's mom had placed the baby girl on one of the store's rolling stock carts.

The employee said, "Oh, please don't do that—she might fall."

The other woman said: "She is not going to let her fall."

The employee said: "Yes, but that's dangerous—she can't be there."

The other woman said more loudly (as the mom held on to the baby on the cart with one hand and the little boy wandered off on his own): "She isn't going to fall. Her mom's *watching* her."

The employee tried again: "Yes, ma'am, but we can't have her up there for liability reasons."

Then, this angry retort: "You don't care about the baby. You just don't want to get sued. You think she can't watch her own baby."

When the young employee tried again to politely explain herself, the older woman cut her short: "I know what you care about . . . and I don't want to hear anything else from you. This conversation is *over*."

I can't change the world, the toxic climate in halls of power, or the attitude of a hostile shopper. But in a world where meanness has become room temperature, I can choose love instead. Gracious responses. Acts of kindness. A caring word. Eye contact. A smile. A listening ear. These I can do. And so can you. Let's just love.

When we take up permanent residence in a life of love, we live in God and God lives in us.

I JOHN 4:17, MSG

The Easy Road

The amusement parks of my childhood featured dozens of colorful rides. I stood in meandering lines for what seemed like hours to enjoy them for no more than a minute or two. Some lifted you off the ground and spun you silly; others dropped you in a speeding, clattering cart off the highest point in the park. But a few rides were slow and meandering and offered not even a hint of danger.

I liked those best when I was small.

No roller coaster for me. No going upside down or backwards at breakneck speed with my arms high above my head. I favored the carousel and the sputtering cars I couldn't help but drive in a straight line. Even then I liked control. The one-way car track had a raised metal rail in the center—no way I could have gone off road on that. And the carousel never reversed, ever. Every horse had the same view.

Only now do I see that what seemed like freedom wasn't. I could have gone to the park every day for a year and nothing would have changed one iota except the color of the tiny car I rode in. The park was not real life. It only mimicked real life. The sense that nothing bad could ever happen was imaginary, and the threats were predictable and tame.

A few decades later, the center rail is gone. Movement in any direction is possible. Nothing is certain . . . or safe. I *can* go off road, whether I mean to or not. Much is different, but one thing is the same: I never went to the park alone. Not ever. And I am not alone today. Nothing, no one, no surprise or sameness can snatch me out of the Father's hands. That is fixed. That is certain. That will never change. Ticket, please? Let's ride.

In all these things we overwhelmingly conquer through Him who loved us. For I am convinced that neither death, nor life, nor angels, nor principalities, nor things present, nor things to come, nor powers, nor height, nor depth, nor any other created thing, will be able to separate us from the love of God, which is in Christ Jesus our Lord.
ROMANS 8:37-39, NASB

A Trick of the Eye

Someone has said that one of the most crucial aspects of writing is noticing. I don't disagree. Oh sure, there are tricks of the trade, but if a writer's eyes and heart are not alert and awake to all that is around her, if she is not keen to notice the smallest sights and moments and unspoken words, well—you and I won't likely read her work for long.

As readers, we're looking for recognition: for the moment when we say, "Yes, of course, I've seen that too." Or, "Oh—that's like the conversation I had with my spouse last night." Or, "That makes me think of that little deli in SoHo."

If a writer really notices, her readers see what she sees, even if the image they perceive is not exactly the same as the one she describes. The words on the page create something more substantial than simply ink on paper. They take shape in the reader's mind, connecting with a thousand tiny synapses of memory and resonating as real.

Last Friday I watched a hummingbird hover near the blooms off my front porch. I decided that I would stay and watch as long as she enjoyed my hedge. I've never seen something so small work so hard to stay in motion. On Sunday morning as a storm was brewing, I opened the screen door to smell the rain and feel the pregnant breeze stir. I swear I sensed the thunder before I heard its rumble: just the tiniest contraction in advance of the big event.

As real as these moments were to me, I suspect they were only quick renderings by God in one reality that strongly hint at another. Someday I will climb through the frame of this world and enter another. Someday a hummingbird might rest easily in my hand, and I may surf the wind that blows before a storm. Someday I will know that what I thought was the real world was only a taste of what would come, and even so, be grateful for the preview that was mine.

Now we see through a glass, darkly; but then face to face: now I know
in part; but then shall I know even as also I am known.
I CORINTHIANS 13:12, KJV

Assisted Suffering

Brittany Maynard's stage 4 glioblastoma was steadily overtaking her body, and no viable treatment could stop it. *Salon* magazine touted Brittany's choice to kill herself before her cancer could as "brave," claiming that all "religious arguments against physician-assisted suicide fall flat."*

A steady stream of magazine covers and news stories demonstrated that Brittany was indeed beautiful. She became the face of assisted suicide. But does assisted suicide demand a face? And if she were *not* so young and beautiful, would Brittany's face have been chosen? Disagreeing with her decision to wrestle her life from God's hands is not a popular stance. Dissent to her decision—for any reason—is seen as cold, uncharitable, and judgmental. Her story makes one thing very clear: it is no longer popular to trust God.

I am not in the situation Brittany faced: I cannot with any certainty estimate the amount of sand left in the hourglass of days God has ordained for me. Yet her story has made me long for the world to see a different face—the face of *assisted suffering*. Where are the magazine covers touting the bravery of those who have received news of their dying and chosen to live—daily placing themselves in God's good hands and trusting in his mighty providence? Where is the applause for those who have embraced suffering and the loss of strength and beauty and bodily function with a peace that passes understanding?

Perhaps today you are a caregiver in need of grace. May God grant you all that you need to love well, for as long as God ordains. If you are sick, or struggling, or dying—or loving someone who is—please know that you are deeply respected, and loved. Your bravery is not unseen. Your reward is sure. Your sacrifice is beautiful. And you, and only you, will know the precious, blessed beauty of loving to the end. May you struggle well and dwell in the house of God forever.

You saw me before I was born. Every day of my life was recorded in your book. Every moment was laid out before a single day had passed.
PSALM 139:16

---

* Joanna Rothkopf, "Brittany Maynard's Brave Choice: Why Religious Arguments Against Physician-Assisted Suicide Fall Flat," *Salon*, October 19, 2014, http://www.salon.com/2014/10/19/brittany_maynards_brave _choice_why_religious_arguments_against_physician_assisted_suicide_fall_flat/.

Unspoken Alleluias

This phrase from the Benedictine breviary that I sometimes use for morning and evening prayer has pricked at me like a tiny burr in the heart: "From Ash Wednesday until the Easter Vigil, Alleluia is not said at any point in the entire Office." In my little prayer book normally brimming with praise, the *alleluia*s have gone missing for the forty days of Lent. None *at any point* from Ash Wednesday until Easter.

So when my small group leader asked us what we were observing (either giving up or giving attention to) during Lent, for a fleeting moment I thought of saying, "I'm fasting from alleluias." But the truth is, I cannot. No matter what the prayer book might omit, praise springs up from my heart unbidden and unchecked. Whether or not my mouth forms the words, they are ever present, even in this season of somber introspection and repentance:

Alleluia for the smell of rain and the wildflowers that carpet the banks of the bayou! Alleluia for hot coffee and a good book in the still-dark hours of the day! Alleluia for the prayers of friends, and the Spirit who shapes and forms them! Alleluia for spring tomatoes and cucumbers and their fresh, earthy sweetness! Alleluia for the gift of walking and for the places my feet might take me! Alleluia for music and poetry that pierces the heart, for singers who sing and writers who write! Alleluia for words to praise him with, and the breath to form them this day!

No alleluias? No. Most definitely *not*. I'd more easily give up sleeping, or eating, or breathing air in and out. Without thanksgiving—and without knowing who to thank for every ounce of goodness I can see—my heart would shrivel and my soul would shrink. Some seasons are meant for solemnity. I get that. But I know too much, have seen too much, have been given too much in the last hour alone to leave out praise. It simply wouldn't do, no matter what the book might say.

When he reached the place where the road started down the Mount of Olives, all of his followers began to shout and sing as they walked along, praising God for all the wonderful miracles they had seen.
LUKE 19:37

Still Standing

I don't typically put furniture together. I'm in no way a spatial thinker. But when one of the bookshelves in my house toppled under its word-filled weight, I bought a new one . . . in a box. It included a daunting number of long and short screws, dowels, cam bolts, cam locks, shelf supports, and various pieces of "wood product"—113 in all. Oh, and a lengthy instruction booklet with these words on page 11: "Feel confident that this will be a fun and rewarding project. The final product will be a quality piece that will go together smoothly and give years of enjoyment."

I dutifully counted my pieces and parts. I readied the required equipment—a Phillips screwdriver and a hammer. (The hammer I was never instructed to use but assumed later it was to hit myself over the head with in a severe mercy, or to break the entire assembly into splinters in frustration.) I arranged all of this into separate piles on my living room floor, then dove in.

I had to retrace my steps twice, taking apart pieces I had wrongly connected. I cried once. I took a five-minute break, lying in a fetal position on the rug. Three hours later I finished, with no pieces left over (always a good sign). The next morning the bookcase was full of reshelved books, and it is still standing: at least as good as its parts, and better than my skill.

The bookshelf-assembling process reminded me that I, too, am a work in progress: at least as good as my God-designed parts, and even better than the skill of this do-it-yourself assembler. Sometimes the process is anything but "fun and rewarding." Sometimes I read the instructions and mean well, but I still get things wrong. Sometimes I look at the picture of the end product I'm aiming for (let's call him Jesus) and find it hard to believe I will ever resemble him. I'm not there yet. There are errant pieces to be secured, tightened down, and locked into place. But today, by the sheer, brilliant, and benevolent work of a good and wise God—I am still standing. And if that isn't proof of grace, nothing is.

No one can lay any foundation other than the one we already have—Jesus Christ.
I CORINTHIANS 3:11

Bring It

I don't typically watch pro basketball on TV. But when I recently clicked past a Lakers-Celtics game, I stopped long enough to notice a little ritual I liked a lot. In the hard-charging, body-banging game, I noticed a touch. That's all. Just a touch.

It was the player at the free-throw line who received the touch. After each shot, whether he made it or missed, his teammates on the floor stepped in for a brief touch that seemed to say, "We're here. Up or down we've got your back." Sometimes what we need most is to know that someone is out on the floor with us, regardless of whether our next shot clangs or swooshes.

I assume most NBA players make millions of dollars playing the game—and that they know they're good at it. But still, the touch is reassuring. I'm pretty competent at what I do too, although sharing words isn't a quick way to riches. But lately, I've needed encouragement. And one touch at a time, I've gotten it. Others in the game with me have stepped in at just the right time to say, "Bring it. We're with you." And I'm grateful.

Grateful for the housewarming wind chime on the back porch that rings when the breeze picks up. For the two hanging plants that appeared on the front porch the week before last—an unexpected burst of lavender joy. For the farmers' market granola left on my porch swing and for the envelope in the mailbox from my agent—the one with twenty dollars tucked inside and a note to let me know he and his wife were thinking of me. I doubt jocks get teary eyed at the free-throw line, but I did then. It's not the gifts themselves; it's the goodness they represent.

I am not alone. And neither are you. And these "free-throw touches," these serendipities of encouragement, are straight from heaven—no matter what package they arrive in. Are you struggling? Weary? Wondering if help will come? Here's a touch from one teammate to another to remind you someone's got your back. So step up to the line and keep bringing your best game, whatever challenge lies ahead.

We take our lead from Christ, who is the source of everything we do.
He keeps us in step with each other.
EPHESIANS 4:15-16, MSG

Heaven or the Hampton?

From Henderson, Texas, to Paris, France, I've stayed in very few hotels that actually delighted me. For me, a hotel is a place to sleep. Don't bother me with extras. That's why the Hampton Inn in Brownwood, Texas, caught me off guard. The week my youngest niece turned nineteen, my sister and I drove west to her college in Brownwood to visit. I anticipated a long drive, a fun visit, and a mostly miserable night away from my own bed. But that's not what I got.

The drive was long, and the visit was fun. But the Hampton was a total surprise. If you're ever in Brownwood, you really should give it a try. The desk clerk was friendly and helpful. The lobby was spacious and clean and full of comfortable seating. A large, neat stack of newspapers sat waiting for any news-seeking guests like me. The business center had a serviceable computer with faster-than-dial-up speed *and* a printer . . . and both worked. The fitness center was well appointed too.

Our room was spotless and larger than in some four-star hotels. And the bed—well, I liked it better than my own! Even the aesthetics were thoughtful, down to the tiny black-and-white photos next to each room number.

Why am I going on about the Hampton? Because I never expected so much from tiny Brownwood. Because I've been disappointed in far more recognizable places. And because I believe part of the pleasure of these accommodations was how unexpectedly nice they were. Do you ever assume you know exactly where God will turn up and how? And do you sit at those spots and await the big "Ta-da!" only to be let down? I sometimes do.

If I do this for long, I miss whatever delight God has orchestrated elsewhere—because he is the God who parts water that's never before split and who causes old women to bear children and small armies to route legions. He's the God who helps young shepherds slay giants and arrives late to funerals to raise the dead. (It's all in the book. I highly recommend it.)

As I sat on my four-pillowed, duvet-covered Hampton Inn bed, God reminded me of this. And today, I am eager to discover when—and how—he will surprise me again.

All humanity finds shelter in the shadow of your wings.
PSALM 36:7

School Days

The sun hadn't come up yet when I pulled into the parking lot. Two bright-yellow school buses stood side by side near the building's entrance, and the campus was quieter than it would be for the next fifteen hours or so. Despite the predawn darkness, classroom windows were already aglow with light as early arriving staff, teachers, and students began another school day.

More than three hundred pre-K through eighth-grade students come here each day to learn. But it's more than a school. God's love permeates every nook and cranny. I could give you numbers: 100 percent of the students live in poverty or extreme poverty; 93 percent come from single-parent homes; median household incomes are just over $8,000 a year . . . but somehow this place coaxes hope out of these grim realities.

I come to this school once a month with a small group of friends. In the wee hours, we move quietly from room to room, upstairs and down, and pray. We pray for the students whose lockers line the walls, whispering their names one by one. And we pray for the teachers who bear Herculean struggles with kids whose environments rarely support academic achievement. (It's not unusual for students under the age of ten to get their younger siblings dressed for school and to the bus and to arrive breathless at having *just* made it one more day.)

One morning I lingered in the language/writing lab and in the upstairs hallway overlooking a city basketball court notorious for drug trafficking and violence. I prayed for C—— and his teacher, who are having a rough time. Tucking a small note inside her locker, I prayed for R——. I sat in the teacher's lounge and whispered thanks for these heroes who could make more money (and face fewer struggles) elsewhere but who choose to teach at this school instead. My friends and I huddled before we left to share what God had shown us and to pray again together.

Does it make a difference? I believe it does. Because it doesn't take a village. It takes an *army* on its knees. Draw these children to you, Father, with cords of love. Never let them go.

Show me your unfailing love in wonderful ways. By your mighty power you rescue those who seek refuge from their enemies.
PSALM 17:7

Ready to Be Filled

Days ago, I stood in a newly completed, not-yet-opened theater with the actors, designers, and technicians whose work will be soon offered there. It is to become the permanent home of one of my city's oldest resident theater companies, and the only one committed to doing its work to the glory of God. The move will come after a wait of more than twelve years (longer if you count the dreaming).

The space is beautiful. It is the culmination of a founder's vision, many donors' generosity, an architect's plans, builders' craftsmanship, and the prayers of who-knows-how-many believers in the dream. It is a promise fulfilled, ready to be filled.

Many months ago when the theater's foundation was poured, treasured Bibles were buried in its slab. Yesterday, artists inscribed Scriptures on its freshly painted walls. New carpet will soon be laid in the aisles. On a chilly evening now only weeks away, its seats will be filled, actors will take the stage, and the building will become what it was made to be: a place where stories are told and hearts are encouraged, emboldened, and inspired.

The long-awaited and temporarily empty theater is ready to become what it was created to be.

What dreams, visions, gifts, and desires has God poured into you? What collaborations are at the core of you, waiting to be expressed? What promises have been sealed into the foundation of your life, waiting for time and faithfulness to bring them to fruition?

The building I stood in was complete . . . but not yet brought to life. But when the curtain goes up for the first time, when the audience and performers are assembled, bringing their own longings, gifts, and aspirations to the moment, then it will become a theater. And God willing, that window of creative promise will open again, and again, and again.

The curtain is going up on a new day. What will you do with its powerful concoction of potential and promise? By the providence of the Father, the presence of the Son, and the power of the Holy Spirit, may you be found ready and fill it well.

You belong to God, my dear children. You have already won a victory over those people, because the Spirit who lives in you is greater than the spirit who lives in the world.

1 JOHN 4:4

Pin This

I could be infected by the Pinterest virus in a nanosecond—and I know it. The first time I saw the embarrassment of visual riches there, I felt my heart beat a little faster. That kitchen! Those bookcases! Floral designs! Gorgeous fabrics! One visit felt like inhabiting a Pottery Barn on steroids. While some might be able to pin in moderation, I fear I couldn't stop with just a few curated collections. This kind of eye candy would quickly get out of hand with me. (As in, "Excuse me, officer—I was just assembling the components of my ideal, imaginary living room while commuting.") While *your* pinning might represent a benign hobby, mine would more clearly resemble a demanding addiction.

Too much of a good thing isn't good for anyone, right? And who *really* hangs a chandelier in their closet, or has a rustic, rolling ladder installed in their pantry to reach the top shelf? Real life is not so exquisitely pinnable. Most of us live in semi-organized chaos, not in stunning vignettes. Real life is messy. It just is. And even if we *could* manage to make our lives resemble the pictures on Pinterest, we couldn't keep them that way for long.

I fight the longing for perfection every day. God, in his goodness, keeps me humble by not allowing me to come even close to it. My life contains messes I'd rather not display. Fears and anxieties I'd like to stack out on the curb for heavy trash day. Confusion and sadness that I'd just as soon throw a tarp over and ignore. Pin this? I don't *think* so.

God sees my heart. It's rarely stunning, and it's seldom neat. But it's all his. And every messy, unwanted bit I'd like to hide he gently uncovers and begins to expose, set right, reorder, and rearrange. One day it will be lovely. He's promised:

What marvelous love the Father has extended to us! Just look at it—we're called children of God! That's who we really are. . . . And that's only the beginning. Who knows how we'll end up! What we know is that when Christ is openly revealed, we'll see him—and in seeing him, become like him. All of us who look forward to his Coming stay ready, with the glistening purity of Jesus' life as a model for our own."
I JOHN 3:1-3, MSG

FEBRUARY 25
You Will See Me

On the first Sunday of each month, my little church observes Communion. Our elders stand at the table, ready to serve those who make their way to the front. Some come alone, like me. Others come in family groups or as couples. Some stand with bowed heads and clasped hands. Some kneel, even though we have no kneeling benches.

To each person who comes, an elder says, "This is the body of Christ, broken for you," and "This is the blood of the new covenant, poured out for you." Then the elder prays for him or her by name. I look forward to these few moments and savor them—wanting them to linger like the bread on my tongue and the sweet taste on my lips.

Not long ago a saint of the Lord—upwards of eighty, with the kindest twinkling eyes—met me at the table with these words: "Leigh. What a privilege this is for me." I felt tears spring to my eyes and begin their slow slide down my cheeks. I didn't bother to wipe them away; I knew more would follow. After I swallowed the bread and set down my empty thimble cup, he placed his hand on my shoulder and prayed over me.

"You will see Me," Jesus told his disciples at that last meal with them. "Because I live, you will live also" (John 14:19, NASB). And I *do* see him. As I pause to take in the wonder of such ordinary moments, I see him in that dear elder's eyes. I see him in the family with their arms intertwined, encircling faithful generations. In the friend whose baby will arrive soon, and in the newlyweds struggling to make ends meet. I see him in the musicians who take the elements in even rhythm with each other, barely missing a beat between them. In the face of the woman who I know longs for a husband and in the quiet dignity of the wounded veteran who cannot kneel at all.

These are his people, joined in his remembering feast. And this is my family, with Christ's reflected glory so bright on them that they seem to shine too. My heart almost breaks for loving them—and for the joy of seeing him afresh in them.

I will not abandon you as orphans—I will come to you.
JOHN 14:18

One Bright Red Bird (Redux)

I wrote *The Beautiful Ache* in 2007. It's a personal book, but its topic—longing—is universal. "If I find in myself a desire which no experience in this world can satisfy," said C. S. Lewis, "the most probable explanation is that I was made for another world."*

Things can change a lot over the years, but the longing expressed in at least one chapter of *The Beautiful Ache* remains. "One Bright Red Bird" expresses the desire to hope against all hope . . . to believe the unbelievable, to have confidence in the unseen.

Back then, I wrote of the desire for a husband and children—a family of my own. That longing, for a never-married, childless woman, can be intense. Mine certainly was. Honestly, I'm a little embarrassed when I read those pages now. A part of me wishes I hadn't said so much. But what I wrote was true.

You might think, many years hence, that because I am still unmarried and childless, I believe less in hope. But you'd be wrong. The power of hope is stronger in me than it's ever been, regardless of what is hoped *for*. Hope is powerful stuff indeed. And while I can only see in part, God sees the whole of my story—from beginning to end.

Last weekend in the little hamlet of Round Top, Texas, I wandered into a tiny shop called Blue Door Decor and spied . . . *one bright red bird*. When I saw this cardinal, I thought immediately of the book's chapter and decided that this tiny icon of hope was going home with me. The bird is perched on the top of the armoire in my living room as a reminder that more exists than I can see, and that my God is still a God of hope. A cardinal is not ashamed of his color. This red bird reminds me to not be ashamed of my hope. My God knows. He sees. He is good.

In *The Beautiful Ache* I write, "'Don't make me hope,' I've said to God more than once. 'It hurts too much.' But hoping is fertile ground, and having hope is much more reasonable than not having it. Especially with a God like ours whose specialty is nothing less than the impossible."†

I stand by those words. Still.

I wait confidently for God to save me, and my God will certainly hear me.
MICAH 7:7

---

* C. S. Lewis, *Mere Christianity* (New York: HarperCollins, 1980), 137–38.
† Leigh McLeroy, *The Beautiful Ache* (Brenham, TX: Lucid Books, 2010), 100.

Not a Day Goes By

Not a day goes by that I don't hear a story that makes me shake my head in disbelief at the gone-wrongness of the world around me.

Like the story of the United States Air Force Academy cadet who posted a Bible verse on the whiteboard of his dorm room door and started a firestorm.

He wrote, "I have been crucified with Christ. It is no longer I who live, but Christ who lives in me. And the life I now live in the flesh I live by faith in the Son of God, who loved me and gave himself up for me" (Galatians 2:20, ESV).

The verse was not up for long before the cadet was asked to remove it. Apparently, it deeply offended some students and faculty, who then reported it to a human rights organization, which filed a complaint. An academy official ordered the student to remove the "offensive" message; he did so. But the representative of the organization that complained insisted that *removing* it was not enough; the cadet must be punished.

Not a day goes by that I don't see increasing hostility to persons of faith—particularly the Christian faith, which is often described (as it was in this case) as fundamentalist extremism. I'm not sure I know what a *fundamentalist* is, although I suspect these same objectors would be quite willing to describe me as one. And extremist? Well, perhaps. But not in the way the critics intend. It *is* extreme to say, as Paul did, that the man he once had been was no more and that in his place Christ dwelt. To say that his old passions had died and been replaced by new ones. Especially in a world bent on denying or perverting the truth of the gospel and insisting every other idea be protected while only one is abused.

Not a day goes by that I don't breathe thanks to God for his promises or praise him for his provision. Not a day goes by that I don't believe in his glorious return to judge the living and the dead and to rule and reign in righteousness. A lot is wrong with us, but still he loves us. And not a day goes by that his mercy is not made clear somehow, somewhere. Look for it today.

Let your unfailing love and faithfulness always protect me.
PSALM 40:11

Maurice in Transit

Maurice got on the Portland commuter train and walked slowly past me and the other passengers in the car. As he did, he glanced down at my feet and said, "Nice pedicure." The two guys next to me laughed. After a few minutes Maurice addressed me from several seats away: "I hope you didn't take offense," he said. "I just noticed your feet right off. They look good. I mean, I like the color and everything."

"No worries," I told him. "No offense taken." We rode a few more minutes in silence, then he stood, ambled forward, and sat down across from the two men on my side of the car. "My name's Maurice," he said, extending his hand to me. I shook it politely, but I didn't really look at him.

"You going to work?" he asked.

"Sort of," I said. "More like a meeting."

"Is your company big?" he wanted to know.

"My company's just me," I told him.

"Oh," he replied. "I don't mean to be forward or anything, but you're different. You're not from around here, are you?"

"No," I said. "Texas."

"Texas! Well, my pastor's from Kill-in, Texas."

Kill-in didn't register at first. Then I took a wild guess. "Kil*leen*, maybe?"

"Yeah, that's it! Killeen! I'm livin' out in California, see—I just came here to hook up with some friends."

I nodded, but honestly, I was trying hard to end our chat. I couldn't quite figure out his angle and assumed that Maurice was flirting, looking for money, or a little of both. Either way, he was undaunted by my lack of enthusiasm.

No matter how uninterested I appeared, he kept on pitching lines to me. My stop was finally called, and I stood. "Have a nice day, Maurice," I said. I smiled. He did too.

Now I'm wondering if I don't sometimes look like Maurice to people I meet: angling for any conversational advantage and the chance to sell them on something, like me or my faith, perhaps. I decided that being sized up and targeted for a hard sell isn't particularly flattering. Even if the hustler is polite. Thank you for the lesson, Maurice.

Sanctify Christ as Lord in your hearts, always being ready to make a defense to everyone who asks you to give an account for the hope that is in you.
I PETER 3:15, NASB

March

Cruisin'

My first big-girl bike was a shamrock-green Schwinn with reverse brakes, no gears, and a basket. My sister's was identical. I rode this simple two-wheeler a few blocks down the street to elementary school each day of my first- and second-grade years. I wasn't "going green"; I was simply going where the state of Texas required me to go, in the manner in which my parents instructed me.

When we moved to a bigger city, I began to take the school bus to school. My bikes were more complex, including the bright-gold, curve-handled ten-speed I took to college and used to zip from one corner of the sprawling campus to the other.

Lately I've been wishing for that green Schwinn again. Maybe it's the way spring has blossomed in my sleepy neighborhood, but I itch to go cruising again on two wheels. And not bent over, clicking through gears to get there, but the way I did all those years ago: slowly, with my head up, noticing things around me.

There is a cost to moving through life too quickly. Speeding along may be a time-saver, but it's not a lifesaver. Focusing on small things rather than the broader view may seem shortsighted or even irresponsible, but limits do not necessarily mean loss. In fact, whole worlds can open up in the smallest, most obscure vistas. They might appear on my own block—and I could perhaps catch a glimpse of one today. But only if I choose to cruise instead of dart and dash.

Calvin Miller writes, "The believer who wants an in-depth affair with Christ must not allow time clocks and ledger sheets to destroy that wonderful holy leisure by which we make friends with God."*

Perhaps I'll find a new, modern cruiser. Maybe I'll find a used one in good condition, or one in a nostalgic, bright-green hue. But I can still cruise without it, allowing myself moments where I may catch the gently blowing wind of another world and focus my heart on the subtle glimpses of it.

No eye has seen, no ear has heard, and no mind has imagined what God has prepared for those who love him.

I CORINTHIANS 2:9

---

* Calvin Miller, *The Disciplined Life* (Bloomington, MN: Bethany House, 2011).

West

He sat on the curb near the westbound interstate on-ramp with a ratty duffle bag at his feet and a sign in his lap. As I pulled closer to make a right-hand turn, I imagined I knew what his message would be. I anticipated "Hungry, Please Help" or "Need Work" or "Homeless Vet." But his hand-lettered SOS had only one word, and it wasn't a word I expected. It simply said "West."

The sign didn't say how far west he wanted to go or the final destination he had in mind. He only revealed a hoped-for trajectory and the patience to wait for someone moving in that direction who was willing to carry him farther along. It struck me that he had something to teach me: in matters of direction, I sometimes use too many qualifying words.

I, too, am dependent on someone to carry me where I need to go. But I wonder if I don't weigh my directional requests down with so many particulars that moving me there is more complicated than it should be. I'd like to get to holiness, but without too much heartache, please. I'd like to live in Christlikeness, but I'd prefer to dawdle on the way, enjoying the worldly scenery and lingering in alluring roadside parks of selfishness until my options narrow.

But what if my hand-lettered directional sign simply said "Jesus," and I was willing to take any route to get to him? What if I could be content with straight shots and meandering back roads as long as they kept me moving toward him? What if speed mattered to me less than abiding and I was willing to keep any company that would carry me closer to his heart? It might not be an efficient journey, but it would almost certainly be an interesting one. How could it not be?

Tonight I'm wondering how far west the man with the sign might be. He wasn't in the same spot when I returned to it later that day. And neither, I pray, am I.

Listen for GOD's voice in everything you do, everywhere you go; he's the one who will keep you on track. Don't assume that you know it all. Run to GOD! Run from evil! Your body will glow with health, your very bones will vibrate with life!

PROVERBS 3:6-7, MSG

Learning to Love My Limits

I don't *want* a supersized Diet Dr Pepper, thank you. A medium, heavy on the ice, will do just fine. And I don't covet any more space than the 1,457 square feet I happily call my own. I don't need a newer car, more clothes in my closet, or more things to fill my rooms. I have enough. More than I need.

It's not that I am unambitious. My head is still turned by beauty of all sorts. I hope to keep being asked to do meaningful work that matters to me. I hope to write more books, teach more lessons, craft more poems. I hope to grow (in depth and not just breadth) my circle of friends. Plenty of longings still tug at my heart—but they don't break it. Not anymore.

Every now and then I wonder what it might be like to have my own place in the country to get away to, although it's perfectly nice to be loaned the keys to someone else's now and then. And when people ask about the children they assume I have, I choose to remember the ample opportunities God gives to practice my own improvised brand of mother love.

Finally, after so many years of wanting, seeking, and striving—I'm learning to love not just my gifts but my limits. There are things I cannot do and may never do. Things I don't currently have and may never have. I could focus on these and become resentful, or I could consider how those limits refine my desires and my heart for the better.

G. K. Chesterton writes, "The thing which keeps life romantic and full of fiery possibilities is the existence of these great plain limitations which force all of us to meet the things we do not like or do not expect."*

There is no shame in admitting that I am kept from some things and lacking others. In all things I have more than enough. *I have him and this life that he has given.* And I am certain I will never come to the end of the fullness of either.

He makes peace in your borders; he fills you with the finest of the wheat.
PSALM 147:14, ESV

---

* G. K. Chesterton, *Heretics* (Simon and Brown, 2010), 87.

In Praise of Our Differences

One of the longest-running sitcoms in recent history featured six singles in their twenties and thirties who, apart from their personality quirks and ways of earning a living, were practically interchangeable in a huge melting pot of a city. They were all one race, all at one socioeconomic level, and all about relationships, all the time. Nothing bigger than themselves ever hit their radar. They were the center of their universe, and the show's longevity proved that America loved to watch.

But television was once the land of aliens. *My Favorite Martian* moved in, and the neighborhood was never the same. *The Beverly Hillbillies* hit Los Angeles in their old jalopy, and delightful cultural confusion ensued. *I Dream of Jeannie*'s buttoned-up Major Nelson lived innocently (but precariously) with a real live magical genie found in a bottle on the beach. And Mr. Ed, the talking horse, lived in Wilbur Post's garage. No same-same there.

In truth, we *don't* all fit in. We shouldn't. It's so much more interesting when we don't. John Piper said, "I am wired by nature to love the same toys that the world loves. I start to fit in. I start to love what others love. I start to call earth 'home.' . . . It is a terrible sickness."

Those of us who follow Christ can take comfort in our alien status. Ours is a citizenship in an invisible Kingdom, and that citizenship binds us together. In Christ, I have family in England and Brazil and Zambia and India. My relatives live around the world, down the street, across tracks, and beyond borders. The more we mix it up here, now, the more at home we'll feel when we finally arrive on our true homeland's shore. Heaven will be delightfully diverse. God said so.

So here's to neighbors of all kinds. And to the wonderful surprises our differences allow us to discover.

Everyone was there—all nations and tribes, all races and languages. And they were *standing*, dressed in white robes and waving palm branches, standing before the Throne and the Lamb and heartily singing: Salvation to our God on his Throne! Salvation to the Lamb!

REVELATION 7:9-10, MSG

Bread Crumbs

In a fairy tale remembered from childhood, Hansel and Gretel leave a trail of bread crumbs behind them to find their way home out of a dark and threatening forest.

Sometimes life's challenges mount in ways that leave us a little lost—or a lot. Aches multiply. Sorrows crowd us. Fears press in. And their cumulative, prolonged effect causes a loss of perspective that is understandable, yes, but frightening nonetheless.

You don't need to hear my list of woes. Each of us has her own. But what you might need to hear is this: the Bread of Life is present, and he himself is the way back home. When the pain of settled darkness seems too much to bear—when we don't know whether to go right or left, to lie down or get up—he leaves us precious pieces of himself to comfort, guide, and encourage. He came, after all, to give himself away.

My trail of bread crumbs from the Father's hand has included a snippet of long-loved music on the car radio. Words on a page found just in time. A leap into my lap, a deep sigh, and a full-body snuggle from forty-seven-pound Burley when I was swimming in lonely tears. A vase of flowers on my doorstep. A kind word from a stranger. A bright-blue, cloudless sky and a few moments to sit underneath it. Found photographs. A saved voice mail of my mother's voice. My father's voice sounding normal again. My sister's laugh. These may seem insignificant, but such crumbs are life to me—and although my own hand has not laid them down, I am picking them up and savoring each one. I know where they lead, and I want to be in that place.

Darkness comes. It always has. It always will. But the Bread of Life has come, and he keeps on coming too. He heaps morning manna. Breaks Communion loaves. Drops grains of wheat at the far corners of a harvested field. He leaves markers of himself through the dimmest of days and weaves a ribbon of remembrance of his goodness over time. We have history, he and I, and he shows me every day that he means to bring me out and guide me safely home.

Jesus replied, "I am the bread of life. Whoever comes to me will never be hungry again."
JOHN 6:35

Not My Home

I knew when I moved into my little rented 1920s bungalow that my stay would not be permanent. But honestly, I didn't expect to go so soon, either. My phone rang while I was visiting a retreat site where I would soon be teaching—and I saw my landlord's number. With very little preamble (he's usually very chatty), he told me he'd listed my home of five years for sale and had an appointment to show it *that afternoon* at two thirty. And that two more buyers would be coming to look the next day.

I felt like sitting down for a good cry, but I couldn't. I had to stuff my emotions and smile my way through another half hour of planning, then make the hour-long drive home. I pulled in to the driveway more tired than weepy. I didn't have the energy tears would require. So I went inside, sat down on the sofa, and told my beloved pup I was sorry, but it looked like we were moving again. Because this place is not my home. Not my home.

God has a new place for me. I can't see it yet. I don't know where or what it will look like, or how long I will stay there. I am longing to sink my roots down deeper than I ever have before and *stay*, but I am moving again—and probably not for the last time. *Because this is not my home.*

My more-nomadic-than-I'd-like lifestyle keeps me from getting too comfortable with a place on a map, but maybe that's a good thing. I know I have serious nesting tendencies and that I could become complacent and unwilling to venture out when God says go. So I'm looking at my things again and asking, do I really need this? And should I give this away before I go? The answers are easy: no, I don't. And yes, I should. Because this is not my home.

One day I'll move for the last time. One day I'll be settled. Until then, I am my heavenly Father's girl, and he's leading me to the place he's prepared for me. I know I'll love it, sight unseen—because any place he is is home.

He will conceal me there when troubles come; he will hide me in his sanctuary.

PSALM 27:5

He Brings Me Word

"Let the morning bring me word of your unfailing love," David writes (Psalm 143:8, NIV). I love that he asks God, "Bring me word." I understand that to mean "I need to hear from you, God, early and often—and to know beyond a doubt it's your voice I am hearing and no other."

I, too, want to hear from God . . . but even so, I question his delivery at times. Still, he's faithful to bring me word of his unfailing love. It's in a favorite Emily Dickinson poem on the walls of a waiting room where I'd rather not have been:

> *Hope is the thing with feathers*
> *That perches in the soul,*
> *And sings the tune without the words,*
> *And never stops—at all.*

It's in a trio of well-timed kisses pressed to my forehead in a single day—each one received as a sweet benediction from God himself.

He brings me word of his love through the prayers of the saints, spoken for me when my own heart is too fearful or frazzled to form them myself. He brings me loving words from the Word alone: passages committed to memory and called to mind when they're most needed, or read to me by friends who could not possibly have known how desperate I was to hear exactly the lines they were speaking. And he brings me tangible words in action spelled into my hands: a warm peach, a soft back pillow, a front-porch fern, and a happily walked dog—living words from the Father that say, "See how I care for you, little one?"

My Father brings me word, over and over again, of his unfailing love. Not because he's afraid I'll stop trusting him . . . but so that I'll become more and more glad that I do! By these reminders and a hundred more, he brings his love for me front and center and proves that it is no mistake to depend on him for everything . . . and that there is no shame—ever—in lifting my soul up to him.

I'm certain of his unfailing love. How could I not be? He brings me word of it every single day.

Let me hear of your unfailing love each morning, for I am trusting you.
Show me where to walk, for I give myself to you.
PSALM 143:8

Considering the Sparrows

My eyes aren't working so well. For months I've struggled to read small print with my contact lenses *in*. I used to laugh with my non-lens-wearing friends who were already awkwardly adjusting to the distance between their eyes and menus or instruction manuals, smugly thinking myself impervious to the little indignities of age. Let the record show I am not immune to Father Time.

Thankfully, my optometrist offered a suggestion that spares me reading glasses or bifocal lenses, and so far it is working well. Using monovision (strengthening one contact lens and weakening the other), I am learning to adjust as my eyes compensate for each other, calling dominance over the visual task at hand the way a second baseman and a center fielder might negotiate a midrange pop fly. ("Got it! Mine!")

Somehow, without my brain engaging, my eyes do their work and focus appropriately. If only my heart would learn to do the same.

Lately, I've been focusing on what isn't. What I don't have that others do. What isn't in my portfolio or my living room or my name. Who isn't in my corner or by my side. My perception is distorted. I am not easily discerning the fine print. I no longer recognize beauty or abundance up close—only at a distance. I'm not sure when this happened, just as I'm not sure exactly when my eyes could no longer manage small fonts well. One day I just knew.

Instead of considering the sparrows or lilies, I started focusing like a laser on my own lack. Instead of looking with gratefulness at the past and learning from it, I was gazing at the future with fear.

"Look at the birds," Jesus said. Really look. Focus, see, and consider. "See how the wildflowers grow," he instructed. They're not so different from you. They're small and transient, but deeply valued and exquisitely made. They haven't manufactured a thing, yet they always seem to have enough. Do you *see* them? I do. My eyes are adjusting to the reality of the season. I'm struggling less and considering the sparrows more. And it's about time.

Look at the birds. They don't plant or harvest or store food in barns, for your heavenly Father feeds them. And aren't you far more valuable to him than they are?

MATTHEW 6:26

Flying Inside

Halfway into a day of jury selection, the judge let our group go for lunch. We'd been escorted by an officer of the county through an underground maze of concrete tunnels before taking an elevator to the courtroom on the twentieth floor. When we were released four hours later, a cafeteria eighteen floors down was suggested. Most of us trudged there, waited some more, ordered, and then sat down with our lunches.

I chose the table nearest to one of the only three windows in sight and had hardly sat down when a small bird flew low across the room, fluttered against the windowpane, then flew off again. Repeatedly for the next thirty minutes, it approached one of the windows, found no opening, and circled the room before trying again. Each time I watched, my heart sank a little more. At the end of the day I would be set free, but apart from some powerful intervention this little lost sparrow would still be flying inside.

I know that sense of futility—of being trapped—and I'll bet you do too.

Maybe you're stuck in a job that doesn't fit, a marriage that is not working, or a role you never asked for or aspired to. Maybe a cycle of addiction or compulsion or regret keeps you coming to the same barricaded place over and over again. Maybe grief smothers you, or maybe anger has you in its grip. Whatever the constraint, you know the feeling of racing the wind and going nowhere. Of flying inside.

At the end of the day, I found the street again and was free. But what of the sparrow's plight? Was she still flying inside? When we are trapped, isn't that our secret? We may be unable to change the circumstances of our particular constraint, but we can, every now and then, still manage to fly. We are always free to hope, to think, to dream. We can pray, trust, and even thank our God for the good we've known and may yet know. In spite of our surroundings, our restrictions, our constraints, we can be flying inside.

You have been my helper; do not leave me or abandon me, God of my salvation. . . . I am certain that I will see the LORD's goodness in the land of the living.
PSALM 27:9, 13, HCSB

Embraceable Inconsistencies

I'm neat. Not compulsively neat, but orderly. I like things to make sense. Like when the conclusion of a good book somehow affirms its beginning. Or when I intuitively reach for something in the place it should be . . . and it's there.

But while there's comfort in finding things as you expected and where you expected, there's also something a little thrilling about noticing the odd placements of life. Like spotting a single azalea blooming in my hedge more than a month after the thousands of others have faded and fallen. Or opening the newspaper and seeing that the predictable-as-rain sports section has been completely redesigned. Or discovering that my favorite neighborhood coffee shop has stopped making pistachio muffins and begun experimenting with cranberries.

Just when the routine becomes sweetly ordinary, God seems to specialize in shaking things up a bit. In a movie review I read recently, one of the actors was asked if the audience was meant to like his character—whether he was meant to be a "good" person or a "bad" one. He replied, "As an actor, I have always felt there is a risk in trying to reconcile everything about a character. *You must embrace the inconsistencies.*"

That last phrase intrigued me enough to tear out the paragraph surrounding it and leave the scrap of newsprint on my bedside table for later pondering. *Embrace the inconsistencies.*

Do you suppose a road closing could be an embraceable inconsistency? What about a harsh word from a normally gentle friend? Or a snowstorm in April or a last minute gate change at the airport?

And if I could learn to embrace the smaller, relatively painless inconsistencies in life, do you suppose I could ever learn to love the larger?

I hope so.

I'd like to embrace weakness so that strength can be showcased. I'd like to embrace emptiness so that fullness might be wildly celebrated. I'd like to do this because I'm the beneficiary of one of the most illogical, unpredictable, unexpected inconsistencies of all.

We have this treasure in jars of clay, to show that the surpassing power belongs to God and not to us.
2 CORINTHIANS 4:7, ESV

Words and Pictures

As a little girl, my favorite hours in school were spent in the library with my nose pressed into the pages of a book. In elementary school I made a beeline for the books with a Caldecott Medal on the cover: they were the ones with the most beautifully illustrated stories. Once I began reading chapter books, the illustrations took a back-seat to the rhythm of words on each page. Pictures were nice but no longer essential.

I'd almost forgotten the importance of words *and* pictures when a new friend reminded me over plates of breakfast tacos and cups of steaming coffee. He had brought along a book that contained a true story of his father, with the pages marked that bore his dad's name. Like the book nerd I still am, I was delighted to read the words—but my friend had also tucked a dozen or so photographs of himself and his father inside the book. Together the words and pictures told his story. That's what words and pictures do.

Near the same time, another friend read a story to me that I've been drawn to more than once—the story of a woman with a chronic illness that medicine had not healed. But she'd heard of a man who might help her, and she was determined to risk getting close enough to him to find out. This woman followed Jesus into a crowd and with one well-timed touch grasped the hem of his cloak. She thought she was unseen, but he felt power spill from his body to her need that miraculously made her well. She was caught—not in shame but in affirming, healing love.

The same friend who read this story asked me to picture it, and I tried. But I couldn't quite imagine how it was. No matter: two days later *another* friend e-mailed a picture of what I'd tried to conjure but couldn't. That faith-filled reach toward powerful goodness . . . I can see it now.

Words are good. I make my living with them, and they are my first love. But pictures tell the story like nothing else I know.

The Word became flesh, and dwelt among us, and we saw His glory, glory as of the only begotten from the Father, full of grace and truth.
JOHN 1:14, NASB

a Contemplative at the Car Wash

Open-air parking and a pair of seventy-year-old oak trees sent me to the car wash. I could have done the job with a hose and a bucket, but I happened to pass a drive-through car wash on my way home. A perky girl chirped her greeting on-screen then told me to select my wash and insert cash or credit card. Two tokens for vacuuming dropped with a clink when I did so. Next I drove toward the rolling belt that captured my tires and pulled me forward.

Then the real fun began.

I was on a track I could not see, moving at a rate of speed I could not control. I couldn't back up. Moving arms and brushes assaulted my car, flinging foamy soap every which way and slapping the windshield and windows with surprising force. Once the brushes descended completely, my vision was obscured. I could have been around the corner from my home or in Ukraine, for all I could tell. I heard threatening thumps just inches away, and my car rocked slightly as it eased forward. I couldn't see where I'd started or how near or far the end might be. I didn't know what spray or gel or finishing agent would come at me next.

The car wash is a lot like life.

I may entertain the illusion of control, at least for a while. But not for long. I'm in a groove that won't let me go and moving under a power not my own. I can't manipulate the mess and motion around me or command the things threatening me to stop. But I'm held. And safely. No matter what threats assail me or for how long, I *will* be released at the appointed time—buffed, blown dry, and clean, and surely better for the worry and wear.

Imagine receiving far more than eight dollars' worth of spiritual tutoring not three minutes from home! If the owners of the car wash knew what they were dispensing along with the foam and film and spray, I bet they'd find a way to charge extra.

Who will separate us from the love of Christ? Will tribulation, or distress, or persecution, or famine, or nakedness, or peril, or sword? . . . In all these things we overwhelmingly conquer through Him who loved us.
ROMANS 8:35, 37, NASB

What Doesn't Belong

Some things just go together. Others don't. Pickles and chocolate don't belong together. Ditto to bacon and chocolate. Not in my book, anyway. But once on a road trip, I found a place selling both of these bizarre food combos. Their sign said so. I wondered when I saw it if anyone actually came looking for a pickle dipped in chocolate or had a secret hankering for a slice of chocolate-covered bacon. Maybe customers simply decided, "That's really weird, but I'll give it a try." Because pickles and bacon don't belong with chocolate.

Sometimes (like in that roadside store) it's easy to spot what doesn't belong. But sometimes it is not. It's harder for me to see that nursing a quiet grudge does not go with being saved by grace, or that habitual gossip shouldn't flow from a redeemed heart and mouth. That gluttony doesn't belong with gratitude or that pride is out of sync with servanthood.

The truth is, because I am a saved-by-grace daughter of the Most High God, sin doesn't belong in my life. It shouldn't sit easy with me. Ever. I should never think it natural to keep on sinning, having once tasted living water. Sin and the Spirit of the resurrected Christ should not comfortably cohabit in me. The idea that I would nurse some secret, repetitive sin should be as absurd to me as the idea that I would pine for a chocolate-covered pickle.

The longer I walk with Jesus, the easier it should be for me to spot what doesn't belong and simply pass on it. I was not tempted even for a second to plunk down a chocolate-covered pickle or piece of bacon to go with my Diet Dr Pepper. They held virtually no appeal. May my favorite petty sins hold even less!

You know that he appeared in order to take away sins, and in him there is no sin. No one who abides in him keeps on sinning; no one who keeps on sinning has either seen him or known him.

I JOHN 3:5-6, ESV

Along the Beam

Once upon a time I trusted my eyes fully and without hesitation. But the older I get, the less I rely on them to tell me all that I need to know.

More and more, I trust not just what I can assess empirically, but also what becomes known to me in the process of experiencing a thing. I used to refuse to budge unless I could see and understand the next steps to be taken. Now I am more willing to suspend entrenched beliefs or secret disbeliefs and simply, as C. S. Lewis says, "look along the beam."

In his essay "Meditation in a Toolshed," Lewis describes the distinction between looking at a thing and looking along it. Looking *at* a beam of light in a dark toolshed, he saw only the light but saw nothing by it. But when he moved into the beam of light, letting it fall on his eyes, he saw, framed by a crack in the door, the leaves on a tree outside and the sun.*

There is much to be said for contemplating the beam, for examining a thing by standing apart from it and gazing at it to learn and observe. But there are things that may be apprehended fully only by gazing along the beam—by stepping into the light and letting it illumine what it will. I can give a hundred good reasons why I believe that Jesus Christ is the Son of God and have placed my faith in him. I can point to eyewitness testimony, the detail of Scripture, the fulfillment of Old Testament prophecy, and more. But those proofs are arrived at by examining the gospel the way a scientist would examine some theory or specimen. They tell a part, but not the whole.

I believe the gospel is true because God has revealed its veracity as I have gazed at the world along the illuminating beam of his love. By the gospel, everything is clearer. By it, I am changed in ways I could never have imagined or dared to hope. "I believe in Christianity as I believe the sun has risen," said Lewis, "not only because I see it, but because by it I see everything else."†

Me, too, Jack. Me, too.

———

[Christ] is the image of the invisible God, the firstborn of all creation.
COLOSSIANS 1:15, NASB

---

* C. S. Lewis, "Meditation in a Toolshed," in *God in the Dock: Essays on Theology and Ethics* (Grand Rapids, MI: Eerdmans, 2014), 230–31.
† C. S. Lewis, "Is Theology Poetry?" in *The Weight of Glory* (New York: HarperCollins, 2001), 140.

Waffle House Goodness

Five-year-old Josiah was having dinner with his mom at a Waffle House in Prattville, Alabama, when he spied a man near the door who looked dirty and disheveled. Curious about the man, he began to pepper his mother with questions. Did anyone know him? Why was he standing there alone? Didn't he have a friend?

Josiah's mother told her son the man was probably homeless, then tried to explain what *homeless* meant. He didn't have a place to live. He was poor and maybe hungry. Josiah took that in . . . then had one more question: would his mother buy dinner for the man without a home?

She agreed. Only, when he sat down at a table, no one waited on him. Undeterred, Josiah brought him a menu. "Because you can't order without one," he reasoned. Josiah's new friend ordered a cheeseburger, and when Josiah's mom assured the man that he could have whatever he wanted, he asked if he could add bacon to it. (Yes.)

When his food came, the homeless man prepared to eat—but Josiah had one more question. Could they pray? Both bowed their heads, and Josiah prayed. The man who ordered the bacon cheeseburger cried. Josiah cried. His mother and the eleven other customers in the Waffle House cried. Then the homeless man ate dinner and went on his way—and Josiah and his mother went home.

"I just wanted to say the blessing with him," Josiah said later when asked about his prayer. And he did. But he didn't just *speak* the blessing. For a few moments he *became* the blessing—and served up a little Waffle House goodness for everyone in the room.

An adult might look at a homeless man and see a systemic social problem. But Josiah saw a *person*. An adult might fear embarrassment or "an incident." But a child saw no cause for fear. An adult might resist praying in public, but a child wanted to say a blessing over someone's meal.

Josiah's act made news—good news. And there can never be enough of that.

———

In a turbulent world where people are either dying or being rescued, we are the sweet smell of the Anointed to God our Father.
2 CORINTHIANS 2:15, THE VOICE

Thrown Away

I don't know Emily—the twenty-five-year-old who gained fifteen minutes of fame by filming her own abortion and posting it online for the world to see. I know nothing about her except what she's chosen to display, but my heart aches for her, for the father of her child, and for the young life she so cavalierly ended.

I don't consider myself a crusader. But I grieve at the alarming rate at which new lives are tossed away in our culture. I watched Emily's video because I wanted to look head-on at the upside-down world in which I live, even when the reality of it hurts like crazy. I saw a heartbreaking, three-minute, laughing, posturing video that said nothing at all about Emily's child, its father, her family, or any of her friends. "I found out I'm pregnant," she says to the camera. Then she laughs. "Hey—I'm pregnant." She purses her lips and shakes her head. "I'm not ready to have children." In the next frame she laughs again, then says, "I'm going to be having an abortion tomorrow morning." She claims midprocedure that she's comfortable with her decision and "feels completely supported by everyone." But you don't hear from "everyone." Only from her.

Reader, know this: I am flawed. I am selfish. I'm a sinner saved by a God whose grace is so over the top it still takes my breath away. I've made mistakes. I have regrets. I'm not throwing stones. I know better. But I'm stunned by how smoothly death can be minimized and by how able I am to edit my own story in ways that hide sin and sorrow and elevate self. I know how it feels to try to justify yourself . . . to put on a smiling face and claim you're just fine, thanks. And I'm ashamed of that. Like Emily, I've thrown goodness away with both hands and praised my own autonomy. I just didn't make a movie of it. *Lord Jesus Christ, have mercy on us. Have mercy on us. Have mercy on us. Amen.*

The LORD is the portion of my inheritance and my cup; You support my lot. The lines have fallen to me in pleasant places. . . . You will not abandon my soul to Sheol; nor will You allow Your Holy One to undergo decay.

PSALM 16:5-6, 10, NASB

Behind and Before

I was late for an appointment, driving down a narrow residential street shaded by a canopy of trees. In front of me was a very tall, very long moving truck. For half a block it crept along, causing a furious shower of foliage each time its top brushed the underside of the canopy.

Then it stopped. Dead still. Right in the middle of the block—banked on one side by a flatbed truck full of lumber and on the other by a curbed, manicured esplanade.

At first I thought this truck's driver might be dropping off a delivery. But he wasn't. He was stuck. And because *he* couldn't move, neither could I. As the driver and several workers from the construction site pondered the dilemma, other cars began to stack up behind me and honk.

No one seemed to know how to clear the jam ahead of me, and I could feel my frustration rising. I was hemmed in behind and before, late, and agitated. I got out of my car and explained to the people honking behind me that they might use their time more fruitfully by organizing the cars behind *them* to back up to the nearest intersection and turn around. But they didn't speak English, and my Spanish wasn't quite good enough to explain the plan. And flinging my arms and stamping my foot just made me look silly.

In the fifteen minutes it took for this urban uh-oh to clear, I had time to think. And what I thought was this: *I am enclosed, behind and before.* God says so. And while my present "enclosure" was most frustrating and unpleasant, being hemmed in by God need not be so. "You go before me and follow me," wrote David the king. "You place your hand of blessing on my head" (Psalm 139:5). How I feel when I am enclosed, trapped, or stuck depends entirely upon *who I am stuck with.* God himself has hemmed me in. I am held fast in his embrace. He knows my past. He controls my future. He holds me firmly in the present *with him.*

It is good for me to be held fast between his hands.

"I am the Alpha and the Omega—the beginning and the end," says the Lord God. "I am the one who is, who always was, and who is still to come—the Almighty One."
REVELATION 1:8

The Trouble with Running away

I ran away often as a child. For reasons it would probably take a solid year of therapy for us to unravel, my sister and I—both under the age of ten—invented a childhood game we called "running away from our boyfriends." We didn't have boyfriends or know anyone who did. Even so, we routinely ran away from ours.

The game began when we called up our boyfriends and told them we were leaving. Then we gathered our dolls, packed their clothes up in our tiny red pasteboard suitcases, and ran away. (Usually just down the hall.) There were several things wrong with this game. First, they were our boyfriends, not our husbands, but we had babies. Second, we always came back home only to leave again in a day or two.

I don't have a red pasteboard suitcase anymore. Or any dolls. But I still feel that urge now and again to run. I just disappear, Houdini-like, from places or situations that find me feeling uncomfortable or out of place. If I can't physically escape, I let silence make a moat around me, keeping risk or vulnerability at bay.

I would like to learn another way. Because the trouble with running away is that you never learn what happens when you stay. It could be something painful . . . or something exquisitely good. There are indeed times when removing yourself from danger is necessary, but running often means never risking the possibility that staying put might just be the greatest adventure of all.

In Jesus' story of the Prodigal Son, the stay-at-home brother resented the runaway one. He couldn't understand why he didn't get more credit for staying put. Or why the runaway was welcomed with a feast. When he told his father how he felt, the old man reminded him: "All I have has been yours this whole time." The young man could have pressed in and enjoyed what was his, but he did not. Even though he stayed, his heart was far away from his father's.

Habits of the heart don't change overnight. But stories can be rewritten, even one line at a time. So I'm resisting the urge to run, and learning to stay and love what has long been mine.

His father said to him, "Look, dear son, you have always stayed by me, and everything I have is yours."
LUKE 15:31

Castles in the air

A tall fence rings a construction site the size of a city block. The fence bears images of the unbuilt coming attraction: a condominium, pedestrian center, and retail village combo with Tuscan influences and a breezy California name. The dirt beyond this barrier once supported a quirky retail strip from the 1940s. (My hometown doesn't get too sentimentally attached to its older buildings.)

With no "steak" to see beyond the fence, the "sizzle" is screened onto it in large, lush photographs with choice verbiage. The models in the photos are expensively dressed and perfectly groomed. Their surroundings are more opulent than their clothing. "Dream lifestyle fulfilled," one section of the fence promises. "No weekdays . . . only weekends," says another. Now I'm a poet at heart, and I don't expect every message offered to be a literal one. But no Monday, Tuesday, Wednesday, Thursday, or Friday, ever? I understand the subtext: every day will seem like the days you most enjoy. But I happen to think some of those middling, ordinary days can be pretty fine too.

More promises are made about this coming castle in the air. "Where romantic tomorrows become reality," reads one message. "Where you get younger every year," boasts another. (What? Is a Botox clinic planned for the retail village somewhere? Or perhaps a tiny fountain of youth in an aisle of the promised "haute couture grocery"?)

The fence, I have decided, is really selling dreams. Desires. But all that it presently hides from peering eyes is a lot of graded dirt. The last message I saw on the canvas of the fence said, "Totally refined living." No variation. No speck of the unexpected. No surprises. Just luxury and ease, utter refinement, all the time.

Even if I could afford a home in this upscale development, I'm actually dreaming of something a little bolder. Something hard won (but not by me) and a lot truer. A very different kind of "Master-planned" community. It's been prepared for me, and I'll recognize it when I see it. I won't even need to read the signs on the fence to know I'm home.

They were looking for a better place, a heavenly homeland. That is why God is not ashamed to be called their God, for he has prepared a city for them.

HEBREWS 11:16

The Pig or the Parlor?

G. K. Chesterton once said that "original sin . . . is the only part of Christian theology which can really be proved."* I like that. Chesterton was a robust lover of life and of God—but he knew all too well what kind of stuff he was made of. Our own hearts may whisper that we are desperate sinners who need grace, but our culture does its very best to convince us that we are perfect. That we don't need forgiveness. We just need a better opportunity or a fatter bonus. But would that really do it for any of us?

When I read the first three chapters of Genesis, I sometimes put myself in Eve's place. I imagine the Garden: its lush vegetation, the sweet smells of flowers in bloom, the curious animals and even more curious Adam. I think of what bliss it would be to have a personal playground with only the slightest limitations. For half a second, I imagine that I might have fared better in paradise. But who am I kidding?

"Tie ribbons around a well-washed piglet," writes Donald Barnhouse, "put him in a parlor and see which will change first—the pig, or the parlor."† It's not an elegant illustration, but it does the trick. Environment didn't affect Adam and Eve, and it won't transform me. I am deeply, hopelessly flawed. I wouldn't thrive in—or even survive—any paradise left to my own devices.

Don't get me wrong. I don't glory in being a "pig," or a walking advertisement for original sin. I glory in being flawed and human and rescued not by better surroundings, but by God's amazing grace. When my ancestors in Eden sinned, he allowed the consequences of those actions to fall on them. They were banished from the Garden—but they left wearing the sin covering he lovingly provided for them.

We're still torn. We still struggle with sin. And he still covers us. No parlor will ever change a pig. No perfect set of circumstances will ever keep me from sin. Only Christ's sacrifice can cover me. Only his grace can return me to paradise and make it feel like home.

Thanks be to God through Jesus Christ our Lord! . . . There is now no condemnation for those who are in Christ Jesus.
ROMANS 7:25–8:1, NASB

---

* G. K. Chesterton, *Orthodoxy* (Chicago: Moody, 2009), 28.
† Donald Grey Barnhouse, *The Invisible War* (Grand Rapids, MI: Zondervan, 1965).

Get a Move On

I hate to move. Doesn't everyone? Thinking only of the books I will have to pack makes me break out in a cold sweat. And knowing that six years of accumulated stuff is waiting to be sorted and boxed up too—well, it's overwhelming.

But it's not just the packing. I hate the thought of moving because over the past six years I've made my home in this place. I love the curve of the sidewalk leading up to the front door, the familiar squeak of the hardwood floors. I love hearing the nearby church bells ring and the neighborhood girls shriek, "Owen!" and come running when I walk my friendly puppy. I am extremely fond of the hedge of azaleas that has just begun to bloom again and of how the towering tree in my front yard bends to kiss the branches of my neighbor's tree, making a perfect canopy between our homes.

But as much as this feels like my home, I cannot stay. I do not own it. I am only its tenant for as long as the owner wishes, and now he wishes to live here himself. So I am working hard to fall out of love with this place and find a new spot for my books, for Owen, and for me. I try to picture myself elsewhere, even though just now, I can't. Still, I know God has a place selected, and I want more than anything to recognize it when he shows it to me. I want to go where he wants me to be. Even if it's a place nothing like this one.

Maybe you're in transition too. Maybe God is calling you closer to himself through uncertainty or trial or tears. Maybe he is simply asking you to follow in the steps of Abraham and go out by faith to a place he's yet to reveal. (Maybe it will be even better than the place you now call home. I hope so.)

God won't let us stay in one place forever. Let's get a move on, you and I, and see what the landlord of everything has in store.

By faith Abraham, when he was called, obeyed by going out to a place which he was to receive for an inheritance; and he went out, not knowing where he was going.
HEBREWS 11:8, NASB

MARCH 22

The Illusion of Control

I live in a city of nearly five million people, on a quiet street with nice neighbors. Lovely shops, cozy restaurants, a bayou hike-and-bike trail, and at least a half dozen coffee shops are minutes away. Our neighborhood association grooms the esplanades with care, and an informal neighborhood alert system keeps us apprised of any suspicious activity nearby.

If you walked down my street, you'd think it was full of people without a care in the world. People in complete control of their neat-as-a-pin lives. But control, I'm learning, is an illusion.

I'm reminded of that every time I see someone on a street corner with a crudely lettered sign and a plastic cup for handouts. Their faces change, but almost always there's a sign that sums up the bearer's plight in a handful of words. I'll bet once they thought life was controllable. I'm sure each one used to live somewhere else. Somewhere better.

Far from my neighborhood, a national talk show host with an audience of twenty million held up a sign that said "Addicted to Prescription Painkillers." He appeared to have an enviable life. He appeared to be in control. Recently I heard a precious woman tell of how, after being abused and evicted, she lived out of her car in a superstore parking lot. She did so for a long time before she went to her boss and spoke the words that would have been printed on *her* sign: "I'm homeless."

So I'm wondering what's behind the illusion of control in me—and in most of the people I see every day whose lives look near perfect. Which of us would have a sign that says "Toxic Marriage" or "Adultery" or "Liar" or "Addict"? Whose sign would say "Lonely" or "Cancer" or "Unresolved Anger" or "Compulsive Shopper"?

The truth is, we're not in control—none of us. No matter how enviable our lives appear. No matter how neat and attractive we seem. That's why I'm relieved that the one whose sign said "Jesus of Nazareth, King of the Jews" tells us to come and find rest in him.

Come to me, all of you who are weary and carry heavy burdens, and I will give you rest.
MATTHEW 11:28

Swimming Naked

I haven't actually swum naked. Not in the literal sense. I'm not opposed in theory to judicious skinny-dipping—but I have never been presented with what I would consider a "just right" opportunity to do so. (I imagine your relief, even as you read . . . and your vague concern about where this might be going.)

Not to worry.

I am thinking about grace. About how revealing it is. About how daunting it feels to shed my warm, comfortably arranged notions about goodness and knowledge and spiritual striving and works of compassion, and to stand shivering on the water's edge, wondering if what I believe and nothing more is really enough.

The only ones who'll know for sure are the ones who dare to dive in naked.

If I *were* to skinny-dip, I'd swim alone or choose my company awfully well. I'd choose my spot well too and time my plunge to the appropriate nanosecond. In other words, everything about the maneuver would be tightly managed and controlled.

Now that I think about it, maybe I *have* swum naked. I'm sure at least once or twice when I was small I must have been freed of my swimsuit or diaper and allowed to splash about in a plastic pool in nothing but my skin. But the older we get, the more we have to hide—right? What may have been charming at two is almost unthinkable today. We have too much grown-up pride to deliberately go uncovered for long.

But where my faith is concerned, pride is a luxury a woman in love cannot afford. Because the one who covers my sin and shame is the same one who calls me out, who bids me to shed my layers of self and striving and brave the waters with him. He is all I need.

The thought of such filled-up freedom makes me tingle down to my toes and yearn to feel—even more than safety—grace's cool, clean water on my skin. Nothing less . . . and nothing more.

Let me put this question to you: How did your new life begin? Was it by working your heads off to please God? Or was it by responding to God's Message to you?
GALATIANS 3:2, MSG

Detour

Those bright orange signs with the bold arrows that say "Detour"? Those arrows are deceptive. The way back or out or across is seldom a simple straight line or even a neat, ninety-degree turn. Detours meander. They can leave you lost before the way is found again.

A recent drive to a downtown courthouse started out uneventful enough, and I knew a back way I believed would avoid any further traffic snarls. But before I was halfway there, the street was abruptly shut down in a knot of cranes and barricades and huge mounds of blasted asphalt. Detour!

For fifteen minutes I meandered east, then north, then west before I could go south again. I went through neighborhoods I didn't know existed on streets whose names I'd never heard. I followed the signs placed periodically that didn't seem accurate, and I finally arrived at my destination, on time.

On another trip, a traffic accident on a major feeder road sent me searching for a new way home. I wanted to go east on the freeway, but police sent me west through a residential neighborhood. Every detour I tried put me on the same clogged feeder again. Three times. For the next hour, I traveled in a half-mile series of circles. Finally, I took a toll road in the wrong direction, paying $1.25 to bypass the accident. When I finally turned onto my street, I saw a *possum* sitting not ten yards from my driveway. I prepared to detour again, but as I slowed down, it turned and slowly lumbered across the street toward a neighbor's house. (Thank goodness.)

I'm sure I'd never before taken either of the routes just described, and I likely won't take them again. Yet twice in less than a week, I've been lost and surprised only a few miles from home.

Is your way crooked? Are the streets unfamiliar? The lights glaring? The company odd? Have faith. Steer around confusion, believing a sovereign hand will guide you. God knows the way because he *is* the way. Trust him all the way home.

It is You who blesses the righteous man, O LORD, You surround him with favor as with a shield.
PSALM 5:12, NASB

I Repent

I grew up in a Southern Protestant tradition whose congregants never burned Palm Sunday's fronds for Lent's ashes, and so the liturgy and pageantry of my first Ash Wednesday experience was oddly unfamiliar. The content of the homily was not, though: it resonated with the images and phrases of thousands of cumulative "sin and Savior" sermons heard since childhood.

The subject was repentance.

It's an uncommon word, really, and not at all a popular one. Repentance simply means to recognize the wrong in something you've done and to be truly sorry about it—so sorry, in fact, that you deliberately change your ways or habits to avoid doing it again.

Saying, "I repent" recognizes that the solution for sin is not my intent to do better, but the ever-fresh supply of forgiveness and grace available to me in Christ Jesus. The ashes, the sorrow, are on me. But the forgiveness and the grace that my cross-shaped Lenten smudge signifies are utterly, completely on him.

Years ago, the pastor of my parents' church sat in our suburban living room and explained to me God's plan for saving repentant sinners. I got it, but I was only eight. When he asked if I had any questions, I had just one. I wanted to know if Jesus' sacrifice on my behalf was good for every sin I'd committed up to now and every one I'd commit in the days to come. (Even then I realized I had far more potential as a sinner than I did history.) He assured me that it was so. I told him I was *in*.

Each time an ash-covered thumb brushes down then across my forehead in two quick strokes, I say in my heart, "I repent." I expect I'll be confessing it until the day that I die, followed by a deep sigh of thankfulness and an unbidden surge of joy.

I could keep trying, of course, to justify my sins to God and to camouflage them from others. But if I succeeded (which I wouldn't), it would mean no gain for me. Because repentance is the very invitation he is waiting for. By the power of the Cross, Wednesday's ashes become Thursday's grace when I say the words "I repent" and mean them.

He has removed our sins as far from us as the east is from the west.
PSALM 103:12

My Last Google

Breakups are hard. Whether you've been together a month or a dozen years, you can expect to grieve the loss of a relationship. (If you don't grieve it, maybe you didn't *have* a relationship.)

Once, on a Resurrection Sunday, Google and I parted ways. And I have grieved. Google was fast. Familiar. Convenient. We got on well.

But when I turned on my computer that afternoon and was greeted by a doodle honoring the eighty-sixth birthday of farm workers' organizer Cesar Chavez, I was done. Chavez has been dead for twenty years or so. But for a couple of thousand years, the holiday celebrated that year on March 31 has been someone else's day— and he is risen and alive. His name is Jesus. He is the Messiah of the Jews, the Savior of all peoples, the once-for-all propitiation for sinners of every stripe, and the one whom more than two billion Christians call Lord.

I may or may not choose to celebrate Cesar Chavez. But I worship Jesus Christ. And while I don't expect the powers that be at Google to agree with me on that, common decency would seem to suggest that placing a Messiah-like drawing of anyone other than the Son of God on Google's home page on Easter Sunday is at best in poor taste and at worst a mean-spirited poke in the eye to every single Christ follower on the planet.

The day may be coming when following Jesus is cause not only for ridicule in the public square but also for persecution at every turn. A day when Christians are not simply deemed intolerant and thus are marginalized but are also caused to suffer injustice and violent opposition to their faith. It will certainly not be the first time. If that day comes for me, I pray I will have the strength to not just stand, but to also love my enemies well. And to remember that Jesus has already been crowned King of kings and Lord of lords.

One day, a light will dawn in the gathering clouds . . . and every knee will bow and every tongue confess that Jesus Christ is Lord, to the glory of God the Father, no matter whom Google exalts.

Awesome is God from his sanctuary; the God of Israel—he is the one who gives power and strength to his people. Blessed be God!
PSALM 68:35, ESV

She Blooms

Grief makes gray of everything, and lately it has leached most of the color from my world. But last week, the same awful week that placed a final mark of punctuation on my sadness, the lone rose bush in my backyard sprang to Technicolor life. And it hasn't stopped blooming yet.

I don't know for sure, but I am guessing that bush was planted by one of the spinster sisters who once inhabited my home. It's *that* old. (And bless them, so were they.) Last spring it yielded very few flowers, and most of those were spotted and misshapen. So in the fall I pruned it back. Way back. And then forgot.

Now it's defied the shears, the mixed-up weather of this past winter, and my own sadness and is effortlessly yielding cutting after cutting for vase upon vase—each flower a bright-pink exclamation mark to interrupt the gray. Something inside the bush said, "Bloom!" And so it has.

I marvel at the God who flips a switch each spring and turns on color as abruptly as if I'd stepped into Oz. At how sleeping things awake and offer beauty in good time. I see him do this in my front yard and in back, along the interstate and down the block. And I want him to do it in me.

I want to awaken to the call to bloom and defy the gray of a heavy season. To burst with color and beauty and life—not in spite of everything, but *in* and *through* everything. To let go of secrets itching to shout themselves out. And to free each loveliness that clamors for an opening. I want to burst with color against all odds, declare my Maker, and so declare it spring. I want someone to say, "She blooms—summer, autumn, winter, spring."

I will be like the dew to Israel; he will blossom like the lily, and he will take root like the cedars of Lebanon. His shoots will sprout, and his beauty will be like the olive tree and his fragrance like the cedars of Lebanon.
HOSEA 14:5-6, NASB

On Sign Language

During Holy Week, two particular signs caught my eye. Both bore changeable letters, and both carried seasonal messages. The first sign was outside a nursery and greenhouse and said simply "He is risen." Its unembellished statement of truth was a bit surprising; after all, there is nothing overtly religious about the nursery business. In fact, in a multicultural city like mine, such words were sure to offend at least a few potential plant buyers.

Within yards of that sign, another outside a jewelry store said "Buy a carat for some bunny you love." It took me a second or two to register the pun, but the proximity of the two signs and their widely divergent messages struck me as a perfect picture of the world we live in.

On the one hand, God's truth still breaks through the clutter in straightforward ways. On the other, we humans exhibit a stunning ability to trivialize the holy and make light of weighty things. (Is Easter really a big time for diamonds?) The two signs were almost the same size and even looked similar. But their sentiments could not have been further apart.

One was selling something. The other meant to give something away.

"He is risen" may be one message among the hundreds of thousands in the marketplace, but it is *the* message that changes everything. "He is risen" means that death is not the last word—and what seems like the end isn't. "He is risen" means that hope is not audacious . . . it's entirely reasonable. "He is risen" is the true arc of the greatest story ever told.

Hope is not a nice, optimistic feeling. "Hope," says N.T. Wright, "is what you get when you suddenly realize that a different worldview is possible, a worldview in which the rich, the powerful, and the unscrupulous do not after all have the last word. The same worldview shift that is demanded by the resurrection of Jesus is the shift that will enable us to transform the world."*

That's a lot of power for three simple words.

Where, O death, is your victory? Where, O death, is your sting?
I CORINTHIANS 15:55, NIV

---

* N. T. Wright, *Surprised by Hope: Rethinking Heaven, the Resurrection, and the Mission of the Church* (New York: HarperCollins, 2008), 75.

As Dark as It Gets

Johann Sebastian Bach's *St. John Passion* was first performed on Good Friday in Leipzig, Germany. I heard it for the first time nearly three hundred years later in a small Lutheran church in Houston, Texas.

The libretto combines the text of John's Gospel, stanzas of old church hymns, and poetic text. As it was sung in German, I followed the English translation in my lap, but I could have closed it and understood. The familiar story unfolded on a current of sheer emotion, carried along by the music's inflection and intensity and the sometimes harsh, sometimes hushed interplay of voices.

Loud, angry cries of "Kreuzige ihn!" needed no footnote. The music itself told me the moment my Lord said, "It is finished!" Then a mournful soprano voice sang, "Dissolve in tears my heart, in floods of weeping in honor of the Most High. Tell the earth and the heavens your anguish: your Jesus is dead!"

That's as dark as it gets.

Have you ever been in utter, total, can't-see-your-hand-in-front-of-your-face darkness? The kind of darkness that makes you wonder if there will ever be light again? Maybe the darkness you remember is not a physical darkness. Maybe it was a moment when you lost something so precious that you thought the sun couldn't possibly bring itself to rise again. Maybe you thought, *This is as dark as it gets.*

It wasn't.

As dark as it gets was when the Father's only Son gave up his final breath and it looked like death had won. *As dark as it gets* was when communication ceased between the Father and the Son—when two who'd never been apart suddenly were. *As dark as it gets* was a sealed tomb, a buried promise, and the empty hours between Friday and Sunday.

As dark as it gets happened once. It will never be that dark again.

"Rest well, sacred limbs," the chorus sang as the music ended. "I no longer weep for you: sleep well, and bring me, too, to rest. The grave which is reserved for you no more dismays me: it opens heaven's gates for me and closes those of hell." It's already been as dark as it will ever be.

Why do you seek the living One among the dead? He is not here, but He has risen.

LUKE 24:5-6, NASB

Deeper Magic

I confess, I've had a long string of king crushes, starting with the made-for-television bachelor-prince who searched with a slipper in his hand for a girl named Cinderella. After him came kings named Simba, Henry V, Aragorn, Aslan, and Arthur. These and other kings have come and gone, charming though they were. But when I was eight, a greater King stole my heart, and I fell hard. I haven't recovered; I don't expect I ever will.

Jesus is my King. It's as simple as that. He's come to inhabit my heart and my life, and he paid the ultimate price to make me his. How could you not love a king who would lay down his life to spare yours?

Circumstances have placed me this Easter season in a land called Narnia—a land I haven't visited in quite some time. It's as beautiful as I remember. Maybe more. And Narnia's king—Aslan—still makes my heart beat faster. Bound, sheared, and strapped to a great stone table, Aslan exchanges his life for that of a snarky boy named Edmund; he surrenders to the White Witch and dies.

Edmund's sisters, Lucy and Susan, run back to the spot of Aslan's execution and find the Stone Table broken, but they see no Aslan. Then a familiar voice speaks, and Aslan is with them, assuring them he is very much alive. Susan asks him, "But what does it all mean?"

And here, I give you Aslan's answer: "'It means,' said Aslan, 'that though the Witch knew the Deep Magic, there is a magic deeper still which she did not know. . . . When a willing victim who had committed no treachery was killed in a traitor's stead, the Table would crack and Death itself would start working backward.'"[*]

I am the traitor. He was the willing victim. Death has come undone and "everything sad is coming untrue,"[†] because Jesus, the only Son of God, has become and is ever my now and future King. There's the deeper magic.

He was pierced for our rebellion, crushed for our sins. He was beaten so we could be whole. He was whipped so we could be healed.
ISAIAH 53:5

---

[*] C. S. Lewis, *The Lion, the Witch and the Wardrobe* (London: HarperCollins, 2000), 163.
[†] This title of an album by Jason Gray (2009) alludes to J. R. R. Tolkien's *The Return of the King* (New York: Houghton Mifflin, 1994) in which Sam Gamgee asks, "Is everything sad going to come untrue?" (page 230).

It Won't always Be like This

In times of challenge or discouragement I sometimes invite hope by reminding myself, "It won't always be like this." I won't always struggle with health issues . . . or finances . . . or strained relationships . . . or lost opportunities. I won't always feel sad or afraid or exhausted or overwhelmed or hurt.

Then I think of friends who I know must be telling themselves the same thing: the new mom with very little margin in her day, operating on minimal sleep; the too-young widow learning to live without her precious husband; the wife whose husband is not the man she thought she'd married; the smart-as-a-whip dynamo whose business is floundering; the parents of a child with a mysterious, debilitating illness; the father who aches for the return of his adrift and angry son . . .

But it won't always be like this.

How do I know? Because Jesus Christ is risen. Because in his story life follows death like a hound on a scent. "For everything there is a season," the writer of Ecclesiastes opined, "a time for every activity under heaven" (3:1). And times change.

The very words that encourage me in challenging times should resonate in the midst of blessing, too, making me deeply grateful for every good gift, because even the best ones are fleeting. A fiery sunset. An unexpected dinner with dear but distant friends. An old hymn sung afresh whose words burst bright and new. A good day of writing. A road trip for no reason. Kind words from a stranger. I drink these in because it won't always be like this—and because remembering these joys deepens them.

If today is full of sorrow or fear or loneliness, take heart and hope: it won't always be like this. And if it is filled with quiet joys, celebration, comfort, or tenderness, then rejoice and give thanks: it won't always be like this. In either case God is good, and the day is his. And so are you.

Whatever was, is. Whatever will be, is. That's how it always is with God.
ECCLESIASTES 3:15, MSG

a Saltwater Girl

Her name was Jane. I had the good fortune to work with her on a church staff for seven sweet years. When I began the job, I was thirty-six and she was eighty-four. She used to joke that she was so mean it took being baptized in salt water to clean her up. But she wasn't mean. She was spunky and opinionated and full of life. And she loved Jesus long and well.

"Getting old is not for sissies," she used to tell me. "You've got to be tough to keep on living!" She also confessed that heaven grew sweeter as it became populated with people she'd known and loved. I can attest to the truth of that now; then I wasn't so sure.

Once we were roommates for three days on a staff retreat. She made me laugh so hard my sides hurt every night. And whether or not my light was out, each night she got in bed, turned over on her side, and was asleep in a matter of seconds. She was the living embodiment of decades of our church's history. She once tapped a photograph of a former pastor and said, "He was smart, but he stayed two years too long." I blinked at her frankness, but Jane called it as she saw it.

She was the most alive, vibrant, winsome woman—yet she never married and had no children. I used to look at her and secretly think, *Oh God—don't let me become like her!* Now I remember her and implore him to do just that: to make me a beautiful, loving woman who's stretched out in pursuit of the life God has planned for me.

Today is her birthday. A few days before she died at ninety-one, I asked a pastor who'd been to see her how she looked. "Like a girl getting ready for her first date," he said. "She looked me straight in the eye and said, 'Don't you dare pray me back. I'm ready to go.'" He didn't disobey. Happy birthday, dear Jane. I'm so glad you're home.

———

The spacious, free life is from GOD, it's also protected and safe. GOD-strengthened, we're delivered from evil—when we run to him, he saves us.
PSALM 37:39-40, MSG

Sometimes a Light Surprises

You think the day is going to be ordinary. You do. You think that if you just put one foot in front of the other—and do it often enough—you'll arrive at the finish line unscathed. You don't expect wonder. You don't expect beauty. You don't anticipate the need to drop everything and offer praise.

But "sometimes a light surprises."

Sometimes a light surprises the Christian while he sings;
It is the Lord, who rises with healing in His wings;
When comforts are declining, He grants the soul again
A season of clear shining, to cheer it after rain.

Many moons ago I had a vinyl album by gospel singer Cynthia Clawson called *The Way I Feel.* I think I wore it out on the turntable, it held so many beautiful songs. One of them was an arrangement of the hymn "Sometimes a Light Surprises" by William Cowper. It began with the slow pull of a bow across the strings of a cello— a mournful sound. Then it built and built into a crescendo of fully orchestrated praise. I loved the music, but it was years before I really understood the words.

Sometimes a light surprises. Once, as I was driving along Interstate 10, the sky seemed to catch fire near a little town called Flatonia, Texas. The late afternoon light collided with something in the lower atmosphere that caused the clouds to combust over the local Dairy Queen . . . and I pulled into the parking lot, drove around back, climbed out of the car, and pulled up the camera on my phone. Because while my heart was turning somersaults, my mind was calmly advising, *You'll want to remember this.*

I pointed the camera skyward . . . but what I really wanted to do that afternoon was fall on my knees. I wanted to kneel on the solid earth there in ordinary Flatonia, because glory doesn't visit the interstate every day. Or maybe it does, but I'm just not positioned to see. On this day, my heart and my eyes were peeled, and I saw.

Sometimes a light surprises. But when it does, will we stop and take it in?

The heavens are telling of the glory of God; and their expanse is declaring the work of His hands. Day to day pours forth speech, and night to night reveals knowledge.

PSALM 19:1-2, NASB

Rounding the Curve

A loved one lies in a nursing home three hundred miles away, her present life dim and faint compared to the bright history behind and the brighter glory ahead. She is rounding the curve. There is no going back.

An e-mail asks for prayers for a dear friend's mother, removed from the ventilator and allowed to take as many breaths without it as she will, until, the note said, "she'll be able to go Home."

There is a curve we round that opens up the final stretch. Sometimes we see it coming. Sometimes we don't. But it is certain and absolute. And for the Christ follower, at its end lies the door we've been fumbling toward our whole lives. It is not cause for dread. Only the gospel, said Martin Luther, can "make death into sugar, and turn all ills, of which there are plenty, into delectable wine."*

We travel toward the curve. Winding or sharp, lingering or brief, we navigate the one-way road between earth and eternity. The race is not timed. The ribbon is not visible. But once begun, we only move forward, never back. There are memories—both sweet and bitter—behind us and unimaginable glory ahead, but the only beauty that exists *now* is somewhere along the curve. We find it here, or nowhere. The joy discovered here is a real-time taste of something deeper. Something that lasts.

When my sister and I were little, we couldn't wait to top the last hill on the highway to the sleepy West Texas town where my maternal grandparents, aunt, and uncle lived. We knew the landmarks and sat up straighter in the backseat when they appeared: a railroad bridge, a water tower, a high hill. We eagerly anticipated what waited there for us. Loved ones. Laughter. Hugs. Food. Gifts. Welcome. We didn't dread the last curve or the crest of the final hill. We strained to see it; longed for it with the pure, sweet longing reserved for only the dearest things.

May God give us the grace to wholeheartedly embrace every last inch of the curve and to live in confident expectation of the longer, lovelier road ahead.

I've got my eye on the goal, where God is beckoning us onward—to Jesus. I'm off and running, and I'm not turning back.

PHILIPPIANS 3:13, MSG

---

* Eugene F. A. Klug, ed., *Sermons of Martin Luther: The House Postils* (Grand Rapids, MI: Baker, 1996), 1:116.

Prepare to Meet Thy God

The Billy Graham Center Museum in Wheaton, Illinois, chronicles not just the life of the world's most famous evangelist, but also the history of evangelistic revivalism in the United States from its earliest days. The usual suspects are there, of course—Jonathan Edwards, George Whitefield, Sojourner Truth, Billy Sunday, and George Beverly Shea—but Johnny Carson was a surprise (Graham appeared on his late-night show), as was Johnny Cash (a personal friend of Graham's).

The image from the museum that I can't quite shake, though, is a small, odd one: an ornate plate (perhaps prepared for some turn-of-the-century church banquet or celebration) inscribed on its face with the message "Prepare to meet thy God."

I chuckled when I saw it. Imagine sitting down to a fine meal and seeing that foreboding message on your dinner plate! (It might make you suddenly wish for a food taster.) The words on the plate were spoken by the prophet Amos to the people of Israel: "Prepare to meet your God in judgment!" (Amos 4:12). Amos was telling the people to turn from their sin, because one day they would answer to God. And so will we.

But beyond a warning, "Prepare to meet your God" could also describe a lifestyle of loving devotion to the one with whom we will spend eternity. When I love my neighbor, I am preparing to meet my God. When I pray or worship or work or create, I am preparing to meet my God, who is the object of my worship, the recipient of my prayers, the impetus for my work, and the source of my creativity. I am coming to know him better and to love him more—and therefore, I am preparing to meet him with joy when we are finally face to face.

"Prepare to meet thy God" may have once been a phrase used to sober up sinners to the prospect of meeting a holy, judging God—and it may well have worked for many. But for those for whom Jesus has borne God's judgment, it's the sweetest of all invitations: in all you do (today!) prepare to meet your God.

Know that you were redeemed from your empty way of life inherited from the fathers, not with perishable things like silver or gold, but with the precious blood of Christ.

I PETER 1:18-19, HCSB

Eyes to See

My four-legged office assistant isn't seeing so well. For several days now his eyes have been irritated, red, and seepy. The vet advised that I try dosing him with Benadryl for a couple of days to see if he might be suffering from allergies. I did. No change. An ensuing office visit revealed both an eye infection and "inadequate tear production." The planned course of treatment involves two messy ointments applied twice daily to his cornea. Meanwhile, Owen squints like an old man who's lost his bifocals.

Our present eye ordeal has made me think of my own vision. I'm wondering about the eyes of my heart. Jesus referenced this spiritual vision often. He said things like "Your eye is like a lamp that provides light for your body" and "When your eye is healthy, your whole body is filled with light" (Matthew 6:22). He told his followers, "Get rid of the log in your own eye" (Matthew 7:5). Years later, the apostle John wrote to the church at Laodicea that Jesus was able to provide "ointment for your eyes so you will be able to see" (Revelation 3:18).

I need my Father's eyes. I need him to help me see beyond the surface to the things that really matter. I need his Holy Spirit to reveal to me my own sin. I need the "heart eyes" of Jesus to see and feel the needs of others around me. I confess that sometimes I am squinting and tentatively moving here and there in feeble response, unsure, unsteady, unseeing.

I'm beginning to more keenly understand the words to one of my favorite hymns:

Be Thou my Vision, O Lord of my heart;
Naught be all else to me, save that Thou art;
Thou my best thought, by day or by night,
Waking or sleeping, Thy presence my light.

It is his presence that brings light. It is his presence that gives sight. It is his presence that chases away the darkness. May his presence do these things for me—and you—this very day, and give us eyes to see.

I pray that your hearts will be flooded with light so that you can understand the confident hope he has given to those he called— his holy people who are his rich and glorious inheritance.
EPHESIANS 1:18

APRIL 6
Finding the Thing

A friend and I set aside one day each year in October and one in April for our pilgrimage to a tiny Texas town, where with thousands of others we comb rural acreage in search of delights. Past years have yielded a stereoscope, an enamel bread box, a Bible bookplate of Luther at Worms, and a dirt cheap pair of pink-and-peach Elsa Schiaparelli costume earrings. Each year we have our eyes peeled for what we call "the thing"—that unique find that fits our particular tastes and interests.

One year, I found it at a shop called Clutter. It was an illustrated sheet titled "Writing" from what might have been a Sunday school curriculum. The birdseed type at the bottom of the page said that "Writing" was lesson number eight in a book called *Manners and Customs of the East* published by the Society for Promoting Christian Knowledge in London.

The text described how children in the Middle East learned to write: first in the sand, then on leaves of trees or on skins or parchment. "This," I read, "made their books very dear, so that each person could not have a book of his own." It ended with "We ought to thank God that printing has made books so cheap that even a poor man may buy a Bible for himself, and read it at home; and that there are kind and rich people who get books printed for the poor; so that every poor child may learn to read the word of God."

For me, it was "the thing." And for ten dollars, I carried home a neat amalgamation of my love of God, books, writing, the Word, and one-of-a-kind items that tell a story. My antique-store find synchronized several loves at once. The best things always do. And every one of them is an echo of the truest, most perfect thing: the moment when all of history and prophecy and obedience and love caused a King to die and a curtain to tear and a Roman soldier to whisper in awe, "This has to be the son of God" (see Matthew 27:54).

Does it get more perfect than that?

Don't be afraid. I know you're looking for Jesus the Nazarene, the One they nailed on the cross. He's been raised up; he's here no longer.
MARK 16:6, MSG

Odd Hours

Once upon a time I had a schedule—certain hours for work, for sleeping, for study, for devotions, and for leisure. I remembered with longing that mostly missing schedule as I washed and dried my hair at three in the morning one day. Then on another day as I finished editing an article at eleven at night, and once more as I eased my car onto the freeway barely six hours later at five fifteen.

My not-so-smart phone had clearly *not* received the message that we were in an extended period of scheduling turbulence.

Alarms kept reminding me of the times things *used to* happen: a favorite Bible study I stopped attending when work deadlines mounted. A beloved small-group meeting that conflicted with an evening graduate school class. A once seldom-missed weekly date with my dad on Friday mornings. Twice-daily reminders to pray the Examen (short prayers of reflection) at midday and evening. Once-every-third-week Sunday school teaching and once-a-month committee meetings. Ah yes. Such were my once well-ordered days!

But in a confounding season of odd hours, the memory of my former schedule grew fainter by the turn of each calendar page. Yes, I *did* fall asleep over my computer at two in the afternoon. And yes, I *did* breathe out a prayer of thanks for the bright, round, golden-orange moon I met at four in the morning. Yes, I baked cookies at eight in the morning and grocery shopped at ten at night. (No lines!) And at each odd hour I was reminded of what hadn't changed . . . and of what has always been true.

God is never constrained by my schedule—erratic or organized. He keeps watch over me as I sleep, at midnight or at midafternoon. He sees my going out and my coming in, even if the neighbors don't. He knows the moment before dawn when the songbirds begin to sound their cries, and the hour I finally sigh and fall asleep. And he is no more or no less present in my ordered days than he is in the odd, uneven hours.

He will not let you stumble. . . . Indeed, he who watches over Israel never slumbers or sleeps.
PSALM 121:3-4

APRIL 8

Hands-On

When my church installed its new pastor, a single moment from that joyful occasion gripped my heart: our leader on his knees before the gathered assembly, wearing like a mantle the hands of the elders of the church as they prayed over him. I knew the moment was rich when I saw it unfold, but later, looking at the photographs, I kept coming back to that shot of the hands-on prayer.

Our former pastor was beloved. There was no drama involved in his departure. He simply accepted God's call to another church. First we grieved. Then we rested in the sovereignty of God, trusted in the process our denomination outlined for us, formed a search committee, and moved ahead. For a year, the seven of us on the committee held our church in our hearts and sought God's leader in his time. In the process we learned what church should teach at every turn—to hear, love, and respect each other—and we learned to seek God *together*. In our backgrounds, our giftings, our personalities and quirks, we were as diverse as the church family we were serving.

The differences that made our work a struggle at times made it a blessing in the end. Isn't that just like God? He was faithful. He brought our pastor to us, and he brought us together in that decision. And as hard as it was to say good-bye to the shepherd we loved, my heart was full when I recognized the shepherd who would lead us forward. That picture is more than a record of an event. It is a snapshot of our family of faith, of the process we've been through, and of God's great faithfulness to us, his beloved bride.

We don't do this Christ-following walk alone. Ever. The prayers of the saints surround us, and we are empowered together on our knees. Church is a hands-on affair. Not just in service projects and Sunday worship, but in support of each other through the power of the Holy Spirit. We're never out of our Father's reach when we're within reach of one another.

I ask you to make full use of the gift that God gave you when I placed my hands on you. Use it well.
2 TIMOTHY 1:6, CEV

Over the Cliff

If only I had a nickel for every time I heard the phrase *going over the fiscal cliff* during the 2012 budget crisis. Would we? Wouldn't we? And whose fault would it be if we did? Once an anemic deal was struck, I thought, *Finally! I'm done with this cliff business!* But I'm not. Not by a long shot. Every test of faith is a cliff: illness, loss of a loved one, financial stress, job uncertainty. The churning waters below these all-too-common cliffs are threatening, indeed. Even the strongest swimmers could go under for good. Many do.

But I am slowly learning this secret: you can't be afraid to fall. Even if you know the landing will be hard. Even if you're terrified the instant your feet leave firm ground. The building of faith is a hundred little cliff dives, one right after another. And then a hundred more. The question is not if but when. And how.

This is how: with Jesus. Ask yourself, *Am I loved?* Then look to Calvary for your answer. God went over the cliff for you and me and never looked back. He took the fall for you. Take the leap with him.

Every time I hear the story of Abraham and Isaac, I ponder how old Abe did it. How did he obey the awful command to take the son he loved and lay him on the altar? How did he raise his arm and grip the knife and prepare to slaughter his God-promised future? How did he lean over that cliff and take the free fall of faith?

One painful step at a time. Moment after moment of assured love and then a cliff-diving leap of faith. Impossible love. Impossible faith. Over the cliff and into his arms again, trusting nothing but the Father's good intent.

Dicker all you want. Deal. Try to strike a bargain. Back away from the edge then approach it again. Cry. Swear. Sweat. Or let go and lean into God himself. There is nothing more glorious than a cliff of his design. But you'll never know until you fall.

Abraham took the wood of the burnt offering and laid it on Isaac his son. And he took in his hand the fire and the knife. So they went both of them together.
GENESIS 22:6, ESV

My Own Backyard

Last spring, I discovered figs on a tree whose distinctive trifoliate leaves I should have easily recognized but did not. In late summer, tiny green and red peppers grew on a bush I had assumed was merely ornamental. And not long ago I discovered another fruitful serendipity: two yellow lemons, ripe and ready to pick, on another small (and previously unremarkable) tree.

I planted none of these trees or shrubs; they simply came with the house. Honestly, I didn't pay much attention to them. But quietly, without my examination or intervention, things in my yard began to grow. They exist because someone else thought of them. They are mine because I have taken up residence in the place where they were planted. My own backyard, it seems, is full of surprises.

Sometimes I discover other things I have not planted or cultivated. Rich, desirable fruits like goodness, kindness, gentleness, joy, patience, and love. That these things exist does not surprise me—anymore than I'm surprised that lemons or figs grow on their appointed trees. The amazing thing is that such things exist *in me*—because I did not put them there. My heart is hospitable soil for this kind of fruit only because it's been turned and tilled by the mighty love of Christ.

I can do nothing either to sow or to nurture this uncharacteristic crop, save to be receptive to its Sower. It is the Spirit's presence that makes these sweet fruits grow, and Christ's love that whets my appetite for them. "We were dead to God. We were unresponsive; we had no true spiritual interest; we had no taste for the beauties of Christ. . . . He made us alive. He sovereignly awakened us to see the glory of Christ (2 Corinthians 4:4). The spiritual senses that were dead miraculously came to life."*

Because he did these things, and only because he did, I can relish transplanted beauty in bloom, right in my own backyard.

We have received not the spirit of the world, but the Spirit who is from God, that we might understand the things freely given us by God.

I CORINTHIANS 2:12, ESV

---

* John Piper, *Future Grace: The Purifying Power of the Promises of God*, rev. ed. (Colorado Springs: Multnomah, 2012), 79.

APRIL 11
On My Knees

I do not come from a faith tradition that regularly kneels. Sometimes I wish I did (although I'm sure my knees do not!). I've most often prayed sitting, sometimes walking or standing, and more rarely lying faceup or facedown. Kneeling, not so much.

But lately my body wants to kneel. I can't explain why, after decades of Christ following and God worshiping, I have the strong inclination to hit the ground when I listen and speak to God, but I do. The urge feels natural, like the tugging awareness of hunger or thirst, so I follow it. Many predawn mornings now, I ease myself out of bed and kneel for a few moments before I begin the duties of the day.

Author Annie Dillard says, "How we spend our days is, of course, how we spend our lives. What we do with this hour, and that one, is what we are doing."* If this is true (and I think it might be), then my kneeling is a good thing. Living low—even for only a minute or two—is a good practice for me, lest I think too highly of myself.

I've heard that men still kneel before kings on ceremonial occasions, and I've known more than a few who took a knee before the woman they wished to marry when they proposed. But those are momentary, public niceties, not well-worn habits done corporately or in private.

I'm new to this posture, so I can't say for certain if it's changing me, but I believe it might be. For this season, at least, I am on my knees. God is as he is and has always been: near, above, beside, and within. May it ever be so.

I bow my knees before the Father, from whom every family in heaven and on earth derives its name, that He would grant you, according to the riches of His glory, to be strengthened with power through His Spirit in the inner man, so that Christ may dwell in your hearts through faith.
EPHESIANS 3:14-17, NASB

---

* Annie Dillard, *The Writing Life* (New York: HarperCollins, 2013), 32.

One-of-a-Kind Mug Number Ten

I love wrapping my fingers around a mug filled with hot, aromatic coffee, morning or night. I like the weight of my numerous mugs, their irregularities, and the random stories behind them.

A few weeks ago, I ordered a handcrafted mug to support one of my favorite virtual gathering places, a community of writers, singers, and other believing artists whose work I enjoy.

When my mug arrived, I immediately liked its heft, its roughness, and its rich ocher color with splashes of scarlet inside. I liked the nicely curved handle, wide enough to slip three fingers through, and the mug's lettered rim. But it took a few days before I noticed something else about my mug: the tiny numeral ten etched just beneath the handle, reminding me that of the dozens of mugs crafted for this fund-raising purpose, mine was tenth in line. And although I've not seen the others, I am certain that while they might appear similar, none is quite like this one. Mug number ten is one of a kind.

You are too. And so am I.

God's creativity is so limitless that he has never, in the creation of bodies and souls, crafted the same one twice. For all of our similarities, we are different down to the very contours of our finger pads. The desires of our hearts, the gifts we bear, the abilities we possess—these are unique. No two alike, anywhere, ever. C. S. Lewis opined that there are no ordinary men or women, that each of us is shot through with something utterly eternal.* And he was right.

We might not have unique numbers etched on our surfaces, but we are fearfully and wonderfully made just the same. Mug number ten's beauty is a testimony to the skill of its potter, and your own particular ins and outs are a great shout of praise to your maker too. Glory be to God for molding and shaping you just as you are. He has done well, indeed.

The thing molded will not say to the molder, "Why did you make me like this," will it? Or does not the potter have a right over the clay, to make from the same lump one vessel for honorable use and another for common use?

ROMANS 9:20-21, NASB

---

* C. S. Lewis, "The Weight of Glory," in *The Weight of Glory* (New York: HarperCollins, 2001), 46.

Finding Mr. Perfect

Who says there's no Mr. Perfect? I beg to differ; I'm looking at him now. My own Mr. Perfect is tacked to the bulletin board above my desk. He is about three inches tall, made of red rubber, and encased in plastic. He's got the biceps and washboard abs of a G.I. Joe doll, and his well-proportioned arms are stretched wide. He's labeled "Mr. Perfect—Grows three to four times his size in water!" I've never immersed him. But if he grew twenty times, he'd still be too short for me, even without heels.

Someone gave me this novelty Mr. Perfect as a joke, but every time I see him, I'm reminded of the absurdity of expecting perfection in any sort of package. (Or of being perfect myself.) Why? Because perfection is an illusion. And because I could wait a lifetime for perfect and not find it or become it. I'm pretty sure that perfect exists only in fairy tales, or for nanoseconds at a time. Give any of us much longer than a wink, and we'll blow our shiny cover for good. In fact, let me come clean right here and now: I am flawed. I've never been perfect. (Airbrushed once; perfect not one single time.)

Perfect may be nice to look at, but it's only a wavy mirage. As soon as you get close enough to touch it, perfect goes fuzzy at the edges and then disappears entirely. But flawed, well, that's another story. Flawed invites honesty and enjoys community. Best of all, flawed is the very condition of mine that God the Father embraced when I pled for his mercy and first tasted grace.

Mr. Perfect has no hope of growing, ever. He'll be three inches tall and encased in plastic this time next year. But God willing, *I'll* be different. Not perfect. Just a little more like Jesus than the day before. So buh-bye, Mr. Perfect! Mr. Real's surely more my type—and it's Ms. Real I'm hoping to more fully become. Because God loves me just that way.

As God's chosen people, holy and dearly loved, clothe yourselves with compassion, kindness, humility, gentleness and patience. Bear with each other and forgive one another if any of you has a grievance against someone. Forgive as the Lord forgave you.
COLOSSIANS 3:12-13, NIV

It's Not the Juice

A dear married friend shared a story that stayed with me for days. Even though I am not married. And I don't drink grapefruit juice or share grocery-buying responsibilities with anyone. It doesn't matter. Her story is mine, and I'll bet it's yours, too.

My friend likes grapefruit juice in the mornings. When she married her husband, he couldn't fathom how anyone could want grapefruit juice every morning. But his wife's habit has rubbed off, and now he likes it too! But they're on a budget. And she's responsible for the budget and the grocery shopping. So when he drinks the last of the juice, he doesn't replace it. And when she reaches into the fridge in the morning and finds the juice nearly gone (or worse, the empty bottle sitting on the counter), she isn't happy. At all. Now since there are two juice drinkers in the family, the agreed-upon budget doesn't stretch as far, meaning something else has to give if the current trend continues.

She says the juice became a source of persistent irritation in their household, but it wasn't really about the juice. The juice was just a trigger (or more positively a cue) for greater understanding or compromise or sacrifice or grace, hiding right there in her refrigerator! I get that. The "juicy" things that annoy me are cues too. They are reminders that I can be angry, resistant, or rude—or I can try to see beyond the immediate issue and move toward understanding. Because that's what love does.

I confess I felt grateful that the troublesome juice issue was my friend's and not my own, but I have a "juice problem" too. I am frequently too quick to take offense. I am often thin skinned and critical. I forget what I should remember and remember what I should forget. I struggle to forgive those who hurt me—even though I know I have been forgiven much. That's the state of things in my refrigerator. How are things in yours?

This love of which I speak is slow to lose patience—it looks for a way of being constructive. It is not possessive: it is neither anxious to impress nor does it cherish inflated ideas of its own importance.

I CORINTHIANS 13:4, PHILLIPS

I can't

I'm not good with "can't." It's hard for me to say and even harder to admit. For as long as I've lived, I've been conditioned to respond, "I can," even if I'm pretty sure I (really, truly) can't.

My trip to another city for a meeting was quick, logistically challenging, planned to the minute, and exhausting. If everything had gone right, it would have been difficult. And everything didn't. Because I can't make New Jersey transit trains run if the tracks are under repair. Or help "express" buses escape gridlock. Or command my own legs to move quickly up steep stairs when I'm carrying twenty pounds of gear. Say it after me, just for practice: "I'm sorry. That won't be possible. I can't."

It's probably no coincidence that God seems to have placed me lately in circumstances I have no power to change. The current list of things I cannot do by or for myself is looking as daunting as those three long flights of Penn Station stairs. Generally speaking (because generally is safer),

I can't heal disease or even mitigate its effects.
I can't multiply time or slow it down.
I can't keep the people I love safe from hurt or disappointment.
I can't make myself bulletproof to hurt or disappointment either.
I can't make someone love or want me who doesn't.
I can't save anyone at all. Not even myself.

There. I've said it. I can't. My needs are great, and my power is small. Very small. I know that. You know it too.

So here is my plan for today. I will not say "I can" when I know that I can't. I will say "I can't" more often—to others, to myself, and to God. Because I can't and he can, I will throw myself on his mercy, ask for his help, lean hard on his grace, and rejoice in his unfailing love.

I can't.
He can. He has. He will.
Amen.

Each time he said, "My grace is all you need. My power works best in weakness." So now I am glad to boast about my weaknesses, so that the power of Christ can work through me.
2 CORINTHIANS 12:9

Whose Battle?

Images from half a dozen global hot spots remind me that ours is not a world at peace. But I don't have to look any farther than my own block to know that. On my street, even in my own household of one, a wicked war rages.

There's the battlefront of sin and selfishness—skirmishes occur there daily. Artillery is launched with great regularity on behalf of and against pride. The struggle against halfheartedness and hard-heartedness is never entirely won. New combat zones are uncovered more often than I'd like. Negotiations are futile. My determined interests always crowd out reason and demand satisfaction. The old self just won't go down without a fight.

The question is, whose fight is it?

The apostle Paul confesses that even he finds himself in the thick of it: "The moment I decide to do good, sin is there to trip me up. I truly delight in God's commands, but it's pretty obvious that not all of me joins in that delight. Parts of me covertly rebel, and just when I least expect it, they take charge" (Romans 7:21-23, MSG).

You, too, Paul? If *you* can't win, then how can I? "Is there no one who can do anything for me?" he asks (Romans 7:24, MSG). Then, as if a light comes on, he answers his own question: "The answer . . . is that Jesus Christ can and does. He acted to set things right in this life of contradictions where I want to serve God with all my heart and mind, but am pulled by the influence of sin to do something totally different" (Romans 7:25, MSG).

Whose battle is it? It's the Son of God's battle—and he's won it already. My job is just to walk the conquered field in faith, trusting that he will keep an honest tally of the score.

So when I lose the struggle (and I've lost more than a few), it's good to know that someone else has long ago won the war.

Those who trust God's action in them find that God's Spirit is in them—living and breathing God! Obsession with self in these matters is a dead end; attention to God leads us out into the open, into a spacious, free life.
ROMANS 8:5-6, MSG

a Neighborly Gift

I met my neighbor Timothy while I was writing on my porch steps with sidewalk chalk. The four concrete steps up to my red wooden porch lure me like a white canvas tempts a painter. I see them and imagine ways to fill them up with words and color.

One morning I was busy lettering the words to a hymn on the steps and had my back to the sidewalk. I heard someone say, "Hello." I turned around and saw a middle-aged guy wearing shorts, a jersey, and a ball cap. "What are you writing?" he asked. And I showed him the stanza I had chosen to decorate the steps.

He seemed interested in the words, and we began to chat. Timothy lives nearby and does odd jobs in the neighborhood: landscaping, light construction, trash hauling. Because of the text I'd chosen for the day, we talked about faith. He believes in God, he told me, but he doesn't go to church much. I invited him to mine, and he seemed genuinely surprised. He knew of it, had driven by, but had never been inside.

"You should come," I told him. "It's a special place, full of sweet, caring people." He was hesitant and asked several questions to flush out just how "religious" I really was. "I just love Jesus," I finally said. "He's been really, really good to me."

Before he left, Timothy wrote his name and phone number on a scrap of paper and handed it to me. "I hope we get to talk again," he said. The next time he stopped by, he noticed the empty planter (which I'd been meaning to fill with flowers) on the porch. "Can I take this and put something in it for you?" he asked. "Well," I said, "it's attached. So it's not going anywhere." We both laughed, and he left, wishing me a happy Easter.

Two days later I came home in the middle of the day to a well-watered planter full of purple gnome. I don't know what motivated Timothy, and I confess I'm a little wary of his attention. But I want to know and love my neighbors in Jesus' name. And maybe, just maybe, Timothy does too.

If you give even a cup of cold water to one of the least of my followers, you will surely be rewarded.

MATTHEW 10:42

Watch Your Stuff

The Ace Hotel lobby in lower midtown Manhattan starts humming early with all sorts of business and creative types. Laptops and iPads glowing, phones buzzing, coffee brewing—you'd almost swear you can see ideas being born. If the Algonquin Round Table were reincarnated, it would be situated in the Ace. One long communal table anchors the cavernous space, and the energy there is quiet but palpable.

On one visit, I noticed a neatly lettered sign on that table. It read "Love your neighbor, but keep an eye on your stuff." That message was followed by the typical legalese about the hotel not being responsible if someone should walk off with your hardware.

Of all the interesting things there were to see in that lobby, it was the sign that captured my imagination. "Love your neighbor, but keep an eye on your stuff." Love your neighbor, but don't trust the nearest one not to take what's yours. Love your neighbor, but watch him or her carefully. Because you never know.

I confess: I live like that.

I *do* love my neighbor. But I'm careful about it. Cautious, even. I don't expect love back, really. Sometimes just the opposite. I may tell myself it's okay to let my guard down, but more often, I keep a wary eye on my stuff. I don't want to be proven naive or silly. I don't want to be caught with my heart unprotected. I know Jesus loves me and calls me to love others. I'm very sure of him . . . but not of them.

Am I the only one?

I wonder what would happen if I trusted just a little more? If I didn't keep such a close eye on my stuff? I wonder what things might be borne from the engagement that occurs as we muzzle our suspicions, open our hearts, and love one another?

I wonder if I have enough faith to leave my things on the table in plain sight and, for a moment, simply trust that they'll be safe?

If with heart and soul you're doing good, do you think you can be stopped? Even if you suffer for it, you're still better off. Don't give the opposition a second thought. Through thick and thin, keep your hearts at attention, in adoration before Christ, your Master.

I PETER 3:13-15, MSG

Bluebird

I stepped out the back door and heard it before I saw it: a tailless bluebird fluttering its wings against the sunporch screen—frantic but unable to fly. Tail feathers, it seems, provide essential lift for birds that mean to soar.

I moved closer; its wings flapped harder. I thought if I could position myself near enough, I might cup it in my hands and move it—before my curious dog went out for his first loop around the yard. Twice I tried to put my hands around the bird, and twice it flapped wildly, scaring me away. Then I saw a slim piece of branch broken from the pecan tree by the porch and scooted it under the bird's feet. It flapped as it grabbed hold, and I took a few hurried steps then flipped it—and the branch—over the waist-high fence dividing my yard from my neighbor's. (They have no dog.) It landed near their raised garden and, the next time I looked, was gone. I went back to the house, opened the door, and let Burley run.

For the rest of the day, I did reconnaissance in the yard before I let Burley out. I didn't want the morning's rescue to be in vain. But I also knew that, very likely, my bluebird friend would not survive for long. Not if it couldn't fly. And human hands—even careful, loving ones—could not long ensure its safety. It was missing something essential. It was beautiful, but deeply flawed.

So am I. So is almost everyone I meet. We need something beyond ourselves if we hope to do more than flap and squawk and bump along through life. We are hopelessly earthbound and fated to failure without the lift that comes from beyond ourselves. We were made to soar, but without intervention, our wounds will surely do us in.

God helps us. He saw our plight and sent his Son in a form that did not frighten yet was full of power to save. Now to those who are the Son's, he gives his Spirit: the lift we need to live the life we're made for. We're vulnerable, yes. But help is near. His hands mean to do the wounded good, and his scars say he knows well the price of doing so.

He heals the brokenhearted and binds up their wounds.
PSALM 147:3, ESV

anything for Me?

On an early-morning weekend stop at the doughnut shop, I watched a tiny drama unfold. The line was populated by several dads with kids in tow. As I shuffled toward the counter along with them, one little guy broke away from his dad and made a beeline for a row of gum-ball machines placed low to the ground to better appeal to their target market. While the dad bought doughnuts, his son crawled along the row of bright-red machines, lifting the metal flap on each one to see if he might find a stray coin or gum ball.

He came up empty, but he searched each one, getting low to the ground and peering up for possible pay dirt.

I admired his hopefulness and tenacity. It was as if he was asking, as he scooted along the dirty floor, "Anything for me?" He was about to have a mouthwatering hot doughnut—but he sensed there might be more. And if there was, he was going to find it.

I am rich. I have a heavenly Father who loves me beyond measure, good work to do, a loving family, and a circle of friends who surround me with care. I have a home I love, a church I adore, and a reasonable amount of health with which to enjoy and serve my God and others. But might there be more?

Don't get me wrong. The blessings that are mine I treasure. I do not count them as insignificant. But they don't negate the desire to be surprised by something more—even if it's small. The little boy in the doughnut shop must have once found a stray gum ball or a quarter behind one of those flaps . . . and he never forgot it.

My God keeps on surprising me, too, with small gifts too well timed and undeserved to be anything but providential. My task is to be in a posture to receive them. To stay low, humble, and expectant. To be unashamed to hope for his blessing.

I loved that little guy on the floor. I was rooting for him. He didn't find a gum ball. Not that Saturday. But that doesn't mean he won't look again. And so should I.

Everything comes from him and exists by his power and is intended for his glory. All glory to him forever!
ROMANS 11:36

My Starter Home

I never got the whole "starter home" concept. Until now. Years ago, when my friends were buying their first houses and calling them starter homes, I was moving from rental to rental and only vaguely concerned that I was not building equity. Every place I've lived in has felt like home to me, even the ones I didn't stay in long. They felt like home because friends and family gathered in them, my books were stowed in their bookshelves, and my dogs were happily in residence.

Then I took the plunge. Most of my friends are well down the road from their starter homes—but I just moved into mine. Through a series of God-kissed serendipities, I am living in a home I didn't expect and surely don't deserve.

Here's the sweetest part: no one will call one day and tell me it's time for me to move again. I've even given away my boxes this time. One dear friend termed this my "temporary-permanent" home, and on reflection, she's spot on. It's permanent. For now. Which makes it . . . temporary. It's home until I'm *really* home. So although I'm a little late for a starter home, that's exactly what I've got. That's what every other believer has too.

This earth is nothing but our starter home. It's not where we will dwell forever. God has planned a new heaven and a new earth that will have the comforting, sweet familiarity of an old pair of jeans or well-worn boots, but it will be brilliantly, audaciously shiny and new. He's planned our true, forever home, and he is bringing us to it in his perfect time.

I said no one will call and tell me it's time to move again, but that's not quite true. One day God will. He'll say, "Darling daughter—I love you. It's time to come to the place I've made for you. Close the door on that sweet starter home I gave you, and come with me to the place you were meant for all along." Then—and only then—I'll be at my final, permanent address and be fully, completely at home.

We know that if the earthly tent which is our house is torn down,
we have a building from God, a house not made with hands,
eternal in the heavens.
2 CORINTHIANS 5:1, NASB

Truth in the Checkout Line

All I needed was a morning paper and a carton of juice. I strode with purpose into the grocery store, grabbed the juice, swiped a paper off the stack, and queued up in the express line behind three other sleepy-eyed customers, none with more than a few items themselves.

And I waited. And waited.

Shifting from one foot to the other, I eyed the young cashier casually chatting up every customer as if she had all the time in the world. By the time she got to me, I was nearing a meltdown and in no mood to discuss anything. She scanned my juice and the *Chronicle*, which had been sitting on the belt for quite some time. Just when I thought we might be done, she placed my paper in front of her and began to read the headlines aloud to me. "'Rains Cause Local Flooding.' 'Inmate Escapes from County Jail.' *Did you see this?*"

I hadn't. Because what I really wanted was to read the paper at home, with a glass of orange juice. On my own.

"No," I said. "And I'd like to read it *first* if you don't mind." (Oh yes, I did.)

Her sweet face fell. Her smile disappeared. Although I instantly felt guilty for being short with her, I was sure *she* was about to apologize for being so slow and messing up my paper. Instead she looked at me with great concern and said, "You must be having a really bad day."

I was. I was so intent on my wants and so annoyed by having to wait longer than I thought necessary that I didn't consider her feelings at all. She wasn't checking my groceries inaccurately, and she didn't have a bad attitude. She wasn't lazy. She was just slow. And friendly. (And perhaps not best suited for the express line.) I, however, was rude and wrong. I mumbled something like "No, I'm fine" and exited as quickly as I could, my face flushed and my conscience burning. I hoped she didn't know me from anywhere. (Like church.) Then I sat for a while in my car, pondering the truth about myself that I learned from the checker in the express line.

The words of the reckless pierce like swords, but the tongue of the wise brings healing.

PROVERBS 12:18, NIV

What to Do with angels

When the house we grew up in was sold to my parents' neighbors across the street, my sister and I began the weeks-long, heart-tugging process of removing decades of memories hidden in ordinary things.

Two nieces who were (thankfully) still in the nest-feathering stage received tables and chairs, lamps and mirrors, cookware, linens, and a myriad of smaller treasures. Other things we gave away, glad that they could be used; still more we donated to a local mission. The most comfortable and familiar pieces furnished a new apartment for my dad and, even transported elsewhere, looked familiar and lovely reassembled. Still, we were left with much that no one claimed.

Nearly four months after my mother's funeral, three final bulging bags made their way to my own home. They were filled with Christmas decorations, including one tiny golden angel with a painted plaster face, pipe cleaner arms, and wings and a skirt of tulle. I remembered she had once held a songbook propped open on those outstretched arms—and she topped our family Christmas tree for more years than I can count. (I imagine she was benched when the tiny songbook went missing—or maybe when her right wing frayed and slipped its wire frame. Mother favored perfection.)

What to do with imperfect, aging angels? With those mementos whose luster has been lost? This one I chose to keep. I remembered her as the beauty she was once, and I could not part with that. I carried her from room to room, photographed her once, and tried to imagine what use she could possibly be in Christmases to come. Even now I can't quite assign her to service. Not yet. For the present, she simply acts as an odd portrait of myself: worn, frayed, song lost, wing wounded, unproductive but open armed, with maybe a bit of hope still hiding under her tiny, tired skirt.

What to do with angels? Hold on to them and hope. They may yet herald a brand-new coming with an age-old song.

He will send forth His angels with a great trumpet and they will gather together His elect from the four winds, from one end of the sky to the other.

MATTHEW 24:31, NASB

The Wrong Star

Years ago on a trip to Oxford, England, I met a man who had known author G. K. Chesterton. This chance encounter with an octogenarian book collector from London resulted in a most delightful conversation and the purchase of two treasured books. One is a first edition of *Orthodoxy* and the other a collection of Elizabeth Barrett Browning's poetry from Chesterton's own library, bearing his personal bookplate and his quirky, artistic signature.

Chesterton himself was something of a misfit: a Roman Catholic in a country of Anglicans, a bachelor until he was twenty-seven, and a large, heavy man easily identified, if not by his profile, then by the cape, small glasses, and cane that frequently enhanced his wardrobe.

Maybe that very oddness lies at the source of this Chesterton gem; one of my favorites: "We have come to the wrong star. . . . That is what makes life at once so splendid and so strange. . . . The true happiness is that we don't fit. We come from somewhere else."*

Do you ever feel like a misfit? At uncomfortable odds with the world—or maybe just slightly out of sync with its rhythms? I do. But perhaps I shouldn't mind so much. The apostle Paul felt it too. We are children of God, he said, waiting to be released from futility into glory. We are not misplaced, but we are not at home, either. We're destined for another home, and our true identity—mostly hidden now—will one day be made plain (see Romans 8:20-25).

The trick is to recognize our misfit, wrong-star status as the very thing that makes this passing life "so splendid and so strange." To embrace our Christ-born oddness as a glorious mark of sonship, in this our beautiful, awful, temporary exile—to see the fact that we don't fit in as our one true happiness.

How about you? Are you out of place too? Well then, blessings from one grateful, wandering alien to another. Let us always speak of our homeland with love.

His Spirit joins with our spirit to affirm that we are God's children.
ROMANS 8:16

---

* G. K. Chesterton, *Tremendous Trifles* (New York: Dodd, Mead, and Company, 1910), 314.

APRIL 25
The Power to Feel

Neuropathy is a term I was blissfully unaware of a few years ago. *Peripheral neuropathy* meant even less to me. It's more familiar now. Now I know that, at least in my case, it means a loss of sensation—especially in my feet—that affects me every day. Earlier this week it landed me in the shrubs by my back door after I missed the last step on a step stool. I couldn't feel where I'd placed my leading foot, and I didn't look. Next time I will.

In terms of walking and balance, it certainly helps to feel. But when I want to protect myself—my heart—against the stings the world quite naturally inflicts, I'd sometimes like to feel a little *less*. I'd like to be less sensitive to rejection or ridicule. A little less in tune to loss or loneliness. I wouldn't mind being more numb to *these* things, but I have to confess that feeling them (and feeling them acutely) nurtures empathy for others who feel them too.

The power to feel is a prickly blessing. A beautiful ache. A terrible joy. A paradox. Jesus knew it better than anyone. His power to feel was infinite: "He was pierced for our rebellion, crushed for our sins. He was beaten so we could be whole. He was whipped so we could be healed" (Isaiah 53:5).

It would be unwise for me to long for more physical sensation and for less heart feeling. To want more help and comfort for myself but to offer less of the same to others. The power to feel is not a parseable gift: I don't get to apply it where I want it and deny it where I don't. In every case, acute feeling shapes and sharpens me and makes me better able to see the hurts of others—and the amazing love of Jesus—with brand-new eyes.

Father, sharpen—and deepen—my power to feel!

He comforts us in all our troubles so that we can comfort others. When they are troubled, we will be able to give them the same comfort God has given us.

2 CORINTHIANS 1:4

APRIL 26

Cocaine Christ

Border patrol agents in Laredo, Texas, didn't notice anything unusual about a package containing a small religious icon, but drug-sniffing dogs did. And when the statue was examined more closely, agents discovered that the painted plaster figurine of Christ was made of nearly six pounds of cocaine valued at more than thirty thousand dollars on the street.

The woman carrying the figurines claimed she agreed to transport the statue to the Laredo bus station (in exchange for eighty dollars) for a man who couldn't fit it in his luggage. Authorities believe she did not know what she was transporting. They speculate that this may not have been an isolated incident—that unwitting tourists going back and forth between the United States and Mexico may have been trafficking small quantities of illegal substances under the guise of religious souvenirs.* But I'm not so sure. It seems like a lot of work (compared to bigger, more "traditional" shipments) for a smallish return.

Cocaine Christ seems like a dumb plot—but it makes a great story. Not because the content is uplifting, but because the contrast is jarring. Jarring enough to make a person think. It made *me* wonder what *I* may have hidden under the cover of Christ and passed off as "good." Like gossip masquerading as a prayer request, or animosity as righteous anger, or self-righteous judgment as caring concern. Come to think of it—maybe I could have hatched such a plan, after all!

The irony is, Christ means to cover me. Only he doesn't want to be a flimsy, painted disguise over my ugly, hidden flaws—he longs to cleanse me of them altogether, by the precious (not cheap) alchemy of his own blood-red sacrifice. I may try to cover my flaws with religiosity—but he stands waiting to do better than that, even before my smuggled "contraband" is sniffed out and exposed.

God's will was for us to be made holy by the sacrifice of the body of Jesus Christ, once for all time.
HEBREWS 10:10

---

* Dane Schiller, "Cocaine Jesus Statue Seized by Agents in Laredo," *Chron*, May 28, 2008, http://www.chron .com/life/houston-belief/article/Cocaine-Jesus-statue-seized-by-agents-in-Laredo-1777599.php.

The Little Things

Writing is not always glamorous or enticing work. Sometimes it requires more patience than outright skill. On a good day I take my place before an empty screen and stay put when I feel the urge to wander off.

I spent the first half of my working life looking for great things to do. But I believe I'll spend the second half doing little things as carefully and attentively as I can, with as much love as my heart can muster.

Like editing the memoir of a retired physician who is not a household name, written mostly to honor his recently deceased wife. Every time the two of us met, I was touched by their story and felt challenged to capture it with as much precision and poetry as it deserved. His book won't make the bestseller list (and in all likelihood, neither will mine). But his story is worth telling and telling well.

Not long ago I spent a Saturday volunteering at my church—but not in my area of expertise. No wordsmithery required. We did ordinary chores that had been neglected over time in favor of bigger things. I dug through a four-foot-deep lost-and-found bin and sorted items into three piles: to keep, to donate, and to throw away. I organized an office supply cabinet, rearranged and labeled staff mailboxes, and scrubbed bathroom sinks.

It could be argued that four years at a state college and a liberal arts degree prepared me to be a writer. Sort of. But no real curriculum exists for serving. There are no certificates to be earned by doing little things willingly and well. It is an honor and a pleasure to help a client "birth" a book. Because I love my church, it is an honor and a pleasure to serve it, too.

There is no shame in doing little things in God's economy. Ever. There is great joy to be found in doing them well. And when we are able to do the little things with love, well, that's as good as it gets, my friends.

As you learn more and more how God works, you will learn how to do *your* work.
COLOSSIANS 1:10, MSG

Mr. Irrelevant

In the National Football League draft, the final player picked in the final round is bestowed the title Mr. Irrelevant. Since 1976, NFL alumnus Paul Salata has announced this player, and the team selecting him has presented him with a jersey emblazoned with his three-digit draft number and the name Mr. Irrelevant.

Kalan Reed was chosen by the Tennessee Titans as the 253rd pick of the 2016 draft, making him Mr. Irrelevant XLI. Reed, who lived in Nashville as a child and still has family there, told reporters, "I couldn't be more excited. That's been my favorite team ever since I was little. It's a dream come true."

Some sportscasters deride the title Mr. Irrelevant as silly hype, insisting the last player chosen would have been better off going undrafted and becoming a free agent, so he could choose his own team and steer his own destiny. But Salata insists it's an honor to be chosen, celebrating the values of enduring effort and sportsmanship. Mr. Irrelevant is given a tour of Disneyland, takes part in a regatta, and receives the Lowsman Trophy, which pictures a player fumbling the ball. For a short time—perhaps for the only or last time in his life—he'll be the center of attention.

In our culture that prizes only the best, biggest, shiniest, youngest, smartest, most beautiful, and richest, Mr. Irrelevant is a winsome contrast. Every day, you and I meet people who *feel* irrelevant but are not. They are not because each of us is created in God's image, and he knows each of us by name. If God gave us jerseys, they'd all say "1" because we are all unique and precious in his sight. He knows what we are capable of and how we fit in the fabric of his creation. As his ambassadors in this world, we can give attention to the underdog and refuse to overlook the underhyped. We can love without regard to the culture's mixed-up values and instead see those we meet with God's perspective.

Every season a new player joins a brotherhood of Mr. Irrelevants. But he will never, ever be what the name on his jersey says. He can't be. God wouldn't have it. And neither should we.

We are God's masterpiece. He has created us anew in Christ Jesus, so we can do the good things he planned for us long ago.
EPHESIANS 2:10

The Deep End

For the record, I never cared for the wading pool. From the summer I first learned to swim, I've gravitated to the deeper end. I've done my share of treading water there—feeling for the firm bottom beneath me, willing my toes to brush against it.

In the deep end, you must eventually trust the water to buoy you, resting when you're too tired to keep moving your arms and legs. In the deep end, you don't shun floaties if they're offered. (Every little bit helps.) In the deep end, you don't worry so much if your suit is cute and colorful or your style is enviable. You're just thankful to keep your nose above the water.

In those earliest plunges into the deep end, the things I counted on for comfort seemed to float away. I knew the firm, wet tile around the pool existed, but I couldn't seem to reach it. The ladder was never near enough for my liking.

I can't command life's deep end either. It doesn't obey me. Its unpredictability demands my trust . . . insists upon it. All I can do in the deep end is cry out to the one who knows my whereabouts and has more than enough power to rescue me and those I love. He is strong to save. He knows the threats and hurts and fears of the deep and is not daunted by any of them. He has been there himself.

My God commands the wind and water. "Billows his will obey," the old hymn "Love Lifted Me" says. He's a carpenter who speaks waves into submission and calmly soothes the fears of seasoned fishermen. He's a storm chaser with a mighty reach and infinite love. And his is the kind of precious and prayed-for help that never arrives in the baby pool. It doesn't need to. We can stand there.

Whether we choose it or not, it's the deep end that makes us sure of him and better swimmers in the end.

God, the one and only—I'll wait as long as he says. Everything I need comes from him . . . He's solid rock under my feet, breathing room for my soul, an impregnable castle: I'm set for life.
PSALM 62:1-2, MSG

Stepping In

I once interviewed a retired pastor—a gifted evangelist with a shepherd's heart—for a book project. He recalled coming to his final pastorate as a much younger man and exploring his new church from top to bottom. In the basement he was shown an old, ornate pulpit and was asked if he might like to put it back into service.

The pulpit wasn't just a modest ledge on which to prop his Bible—it was a serious piece of walk-in furniture! "I realized," he said, "that this pulpit—and the pastorate it represented—wasn't something a preacher stepped *up* to—it was something he stepped *in* to."

The world might have viewed this neophyte pastor's ecclesiastic call as a challenge to "step up." But he rightly saw it as an invitation from Christ to "step in"—to enter and fully inhabit a role that required more—much more—than he humanly possessed.

Has God ever summoned you to a task or a season you were sure was bigger than your gifting—or even than your courage? To a space so formidable that you were awed by its vastness? Friends have told me they felt this weight the first time they held their infant child. I've felt it on the first day of a new job, in the dizzying seconds before opening my mouth to speak, and in the yawning emptiness of a new page, before one word is written on it. I may have even exhorted myself (or someone else) to step up in such circumstances as these.

I know better now.

The only appropriate response to the call of God is to *enter it* fully and in faith. Unreservedly. Sidling up to his charge is not obedience. Hedging our bets is no way to honor his trustworthiness. Happy is the man or woman who can step wholeheartedly into the path God opens, no matter how daunting or uncertain. No dallying. No teasing. No hiding. *All in.*

After all, that's what Jesus did—and he's the one we're called to imitate.

He set aside the privileges of deity and took on the status of a slave, became *human*! Having become human, he stayed human. It was an incredibly humbling process. He didn't claim special privileges. Instead, he lived a selfless, obedient life and then died a selfless, obedient death.
PHILIPPIANS 2:7-8, MSG

May

Small World

A stranger I spoke to on the phone turned out to be the mother of my oldest niece's classmate. A speaker I recently shared a platform with happens to be friends with an author whose book I enjoyed immensely—and he kindly connected us. A young pastor I did a project for graduated from my old high school several years after me and told me he rode his bicycle up and down the street I lived on as a child. I shared a literary agent with the husband of my sister's college roommate. (Twenty years earlier, this same agent was the Young Life leader of one of my former coworkers.) I could go on, but I won't.

It really *is* a small world, after all.

Scarcely a week goes by that I do not uncover some amazing, unseen connection between persons or events I had thought were completely unconnected. And God, of course, knows everybody.

In a universe too wide to imagine, we have a God whose hand is as evident in the smallest coincidence as it is in the stars or the sun or the sea. He's big. Very big. But he still does "small" with deft delight. In a world with far-flung corners, there's no place he hasn't been . . . and isn't still. He's somehow in between everything that is and all that will ever be. There's no one I can meet that he doesn't know down to their darkest secret and no secret of mine that is hidden from him.

He's the "one degree of separation" that connects me with eternity and the one common thread between me and everyone and everything that's here and now. In him, it really *is* a small, small world.

He is the image of the invisible God, the firstborn of all creation. For by Him all things were created, both in the heavens and on earth, visible and invisible . . . all things have been created through Him and for Him. He is before all things, and in Him all things hold together.
COLOSSIANS 1:15-17, NASB

Sandals and Snow

I should have watched the Weather Channel. Just because it's sweltering in Texas doesn't mean the rest of the country has obediently followed suit. For a spring trip to Colorado I had packed light: a pair of jeans. Black slacks. A couple of jackets. Two skirts. And three pairs of really cute sandals. Imagine my surprise to wake up the morning after my arrival, pull aside the drapes, and see white. Everywhere. Real, live flurries had covered everything as far as I could see, and the snow was still coming down. Tiny icicles clung to the rails of the balcony, and the steely gray sky showed no sign of clearing.

The slopes had closed the week before, but God wasn't done depositing fresh powder. I had imagined in my downtime I would walk through the smallish ski town in my sandals, jeans, and a T-shirt, but I had imagined wrong. In fact, I didn't leave the hotel once from the time I arrived to the morning I left again for the flight home. I simply wasn't dressed for it.

Inside at the conference, I was the idiot speaker from Texas who was very nearly barefoot. Colorado girls know better than to expect spring just because the calendar says April. They had boots and sweaters and layers of warm, fleecy shirts. I had sandals in the snow.

Sometimes life throws you an unexpected curve. Sometimes you arrive for your assignment laughably unprepared. Sometimes you trust your instincts, and your instincts are wrong. Sometimes you just fail to consult the experts to know what might be in store.

Regardless, God goes on ahead. He's ready for anything, even if I am not. I had conversations in my downtime at the hotel that I might have missed if the days had been sunny. Instead, I met some amazing women and listened unhurriedly to their stories—stories I might never have enjoyed had I been better prepared. I arrived with a set of expectations—and a suitcase full of clothes—that didn't exactly fit the occasion. But God knew what I'd need. He always does. In fact, sandals and snow might have been part of his plan all along.

The mind of man plans his way, but the LORD directs his steps.
PROVERBS 16:9, NASB

Push-up Pain

In the moments between sleeping and waking, I felt a painful squeezing in my chest. I think I might have groaned out loud. I ached with a deep soreness that I hadn't remembered the day before. I wondered if I might have slept awry or if maybe the soreness was a bad case of flu, arriving overnight like an unwelcome visitor.

Then it hit me. It *had* to have been the push-ups.

The day before, I'd done a fitness assessment, and push-ups were part of the drill. Only I never do them. As in never, ever. And so, nose to the floor, knees bent and feet up, I did a pitiful, paltry number of them before my arms began to quiver and then I melted into the mat.

As hard as it is to believe, that barely double-digit number of push-ups did me in. I recovered quickly enough from them *that* day, but I paid dearly the next. I was decidedly out of practice in the upper-body-strength department, and if one morning after was any indicator, getting better was going to hurt.

Getting better often requires a pass through the pain department. Pushing past the hurting point is usually where the real work begins, not ends. Have you noticed?

Maybe you've extended yourself beyond your usual comfort zone in a relationship, or pushed beyond the place in prayer where you might have given up, or persisted in loving someone whose unlovable actions all but begged you to quit. Maybe you've quietly been faithful to a cause no one could see, laboring far beyond the point that it started to hurt.

I'm counting on the fact that my push-up pain will point the way to a stronger body and that I'll be glad for the trouble it took to get there. In the same way, the day *will* come when you'll be glad you bothered to suffer! The payoff will be sweet, not in spite of the hurt, but because of it.

Momentary, light affliction is producing for us an eternal weight of glory far beyond all comparison, while we look not at the things which are seen, but at the things which are not seen.
2 CORINTHIANS 4:17-18, NASB

Fear and Fearing Not

I used to be fearless. I was. And even as a grown-up, I consider myself something of a risk taker and mostly brave. But maybe I don't *look* brave. Once my pastor asked from the pulpit if anyone in our congregation had gone skydiving. When I raised my hand, he looked shocked. "Leigh McLeroy! You?" Yes, me. And I loved every crazy, wind-rushing, heart-pounding second of it. So these days, when I find myself on firm ground with that odd, disoriented free-falling feeling in my gut, I am truly surprised. And I'm feeling it more and more.

What if I lose my very modest but hard-earned savings? What if I don't have enough work this week or month or year? What if I wake up one day and the words refuse to come, or a chronic ailment becomes acute and renders me helpless to help myself? What if lifelong friendships fade or loved ones die or no one really ever has my back? What if I open my heart again and it's manhandled or, worse, ignored?

I don't like my fear. At all. But God says a certain kind of fear is good. Fear him, he says, and wisdom can begin. But for any other cause he insists again and again, "Fear not." So I am to fear. And not to fear. C. S. Lewis weighs in: "It is very desirable that we should all advance to that perfection of love in which we shall fear no longer; but it is very undesirable, until we have reached that stage, that we should allow any inferior agent to cast out our fear."*

Fear. And fear not. Fear him, and in fear of him, fear nothing else.

God is love, and the man whose life is lived in love does, in fact, live in God, and God does, in fact, live in him. . . . Love contains no fear—indeed fully-developed love expels every particle of fear, for fear always contains some of the torture of feeling guilty. This means that the man who lives in fear has not yet had his love perfected.

1 JOHN 4:16, 18, PHILLIPS

---

* C. S. Lewis, "The World's Last Night," in *The World's Last Night and Other Essays* (New York: HarperCollins, 1960), 117.

Elvis's Ride

When in Paris, you see the Louvre and the Eiffel Tower. The Colosseum and the Vatican Museums are must-sees when visiting Rome. No one would come to New York and fail to at least *glance* Lady Liberty's way. So when I found myself in Nashville with a little time to spare, I did what any good tourist would do and took a turn through the Country Music Hall of Fame and Museum.

Growing up in Texas means I've done my share of two-stepping to country-and-western tunes, so I enjoyed the museum experience. I listened to audio of famous songwriters talking about their craft and saw at least a hundred fancy guitars. Porter Wagoner's sequined suits are displayed next to Dolly Parton's wasp-waisted dresses, and lyrics scrawled on legal pads hint at how humbly some songs are born.

But the oddest thing I saw in my pass through country music's historic hall was Elvis Presley's "Solid Gold" Cadillac. The car sits behind Plexiglas, its doors ajar and every surface gleaming. According to the literature, the car's hand-rubbed finish is made of crushed diamonds and fish scales—and its bumpers are plated in 24-karat gold. Its interior boasts a record player, a shoe buffer, a bar, a swivel-mounted television set, and two telephones.

The seats are crushed velvet, the drapes are gold lamé, and the roof is studded with gold records. But oddly enough, the King of Rock and Roll rarely drove his car once he tricked it out. Mobs surrounded it. The slightest bump or scratch required hours of repair. Finally, Elvis parked the car in Graceland's garage and then later sold it to his record label. It was better suited to display than it ever was for driving.

How many of us are in danger of accessorizing our lives to the point of uselessness? We are made to move—to be a people in transit from one world, one realm, to the next. But when maintaining our stuff becomes more demanding than obeying our Master, serious reflection is in order. I wasn't sure what to make of Elvis's gold-plated ride, but maybe it was a sermon on wheels. And I'm glad I heard it when I did.

I count all things to be loss in view of the surpassing value of knowing Christ Jesus my Lord.
PHILIPPIANS 3:8, NASB

Passion!

On a recent grocery store run, I witnessed a heart-stopping toddler meltdown: the kind of have-a-fit-and-fall-in-it moment every mother alive can probably identify with. This little boy's piercing screams made me wonder if he might be tangled in the shopping cart or experiencing some kind of excruciating torture. Then he found his words and through a barrage of tears bellowed, "*I want it! I want it!*"

Heads were turning. And he was *serious.*

As I pushed my cart out the door, I considered this mom and her unhinged little boy. I don't know what he wanted—probably something placed at a child's level (wicked marketers!) near the checkout, just when mom must have thought she was home free. But this little guy wasn't ambiguous about his wants. No sirree. His desire had some real passion behind it.

I thought about this kid long after I'd left the store. And I wondered, *Etiquette and adult decorum aside, is there anything I want that much? Anything I am that desperate about? Anything I might, in my most unguarded moments, plead for that passionately?*

If there is not, there should be. Big things like "Your kingdom come" and "Your will be done" (Matthew 6:10) and "Love the Lord your God with all your heart, all your soul, and all your mind" (Matthew 22:37) and "Be holy" (1 Peter 1:16). I should want these things—really want them—with a passion that gets the best of me at times and destroys my ability to keep my emotion in check for fear of alarming the neighbors. I shouldn't disdain such desperation. I should welcome it.

I don't know what the little guy at the grocery store wanted. By now he's surely over it, whatever *it* was. But I don't want to be over my longing for God and for his Kingdom, ever. I want it. I want it! I do! Help me, Lord Jesus, to always want more of you.

While following the way of Your judgments, O Lord, we have waited for You eagerly; Your name, even Your memory, is the desire of our souls. At night my soul longs for You, indeed, my spirit within me seeks You diligently.

ISAIAH 26:8-9, NASB

Compassion

I'd had a year. I mean, a *year*. It began with the unexpected death of my mother, followed by three other deaths, two more eulogies delivered, the slow and silent withering of a once-vital friendship, work challenges, financial storms, and health issues exacerbated by factors far beyond my control.

So when I found myself sitting in the doctor's office hoping to find a way to keep a chronic condition at bay without treatment I couldn't afford, I simply couldn't stop the tears. In that moment my very wise and kind physician met me with a compassion that was utterly Christlike. As I blubbered, she rolled her stool over in front of me, took both my hands in hers, and simply said, "Let's get to work."

I assumed she was about to take me through a series of familiar diagnostics related to my condition. But she didn't. She held my hands in hers and began to pray. She called on the name of Jesus. She prayed for my health and my heart and for my God to make a way for me to get the treatment that I needed. She prayed for wisdom, for peace, and for mercy. And she asked the Father to give me a boundless supply of hope and encouragement. I was crying even harder by the time we both whispered, "Amen" but feeling far better than before.

Leaving the hospital in a way I do not normally go, I noticed a sculpture I'd never seen before. I set down my coffee cup to examine it more closely. *Compassion's Touch*, the plaque below it read, and I stood for a long time looking at those two bronze hands—hands obviously belonging to two different people and softly touching in a way that communicated human love and mercy. I couldn't help touching them too and running my hands of flesh along those lovely hands of metal.

Sometimes, as my compassionate doctor demonstrated, human touch says more than words can. Sometimes, prayer is stronger than pernicious antibodies in my own blood gone rogue. I don't know how all of this will work out. But I know the Father knows—and that he has ready hands that stand in for his in places I cannot even imagine. None of us, no matter what, are beyond his compassionate touch.

Lord, don't hold back your tender mercies from me.
PSALM 40:11

MAY 8
Of Grackles and Grace

A sleek, golden-eyed blackbird scurried in front of my car as I pulled into the drive, hustling out of harm's way with iridescent wings flapping furiously. We missed each other but not by much. *Why don't you fly, you silly old thing?* I wondered. Flying would be so much simpler and more efficient than the awkward evasive movement he employed. I mean, the bird had shimmering wings for a reason!

He reminded me of me. Of the bluster and flapping about I do on a rather regular basis to try to keep safe from the threat of sin and to live a life worthy of Christ. As if I could do that for myself! "Morality," said C. S. Lewis, "is a mountain which we cannot climb by our own efforts; and if we could we should only perish in the ice and unbreathable air of the summit, lacking those wings with which the rest of the journey has to be accomplished. For it is *from* there that the real ascent begins. The ropes and axes are 'done away' and the rest is a matter of flying."*

My grackle friend was made to fly . . . to be gracefully airborne, not nervously earthbound. He had within him the stuff he needed to ride the cool lift of a current of air. So it's easy for me to see (and to say) that he should have been using it. But it's harder to understand that in the same way, I have what I need to live the Christian life in the person and power of *Christ himself.* Yet instead of relying on him to get me where I long to go, I pull out the "ropes and axes" of self-effort as if to drag myself along to glory inch by agonizing, ugly inch.

When, oh when, will I learn for good that the grace that saved me *is* the grace that sustains me and will indeed be the very grace that leads me home?

―――――――――

After starting your new lives in the Spirit, why are you now trying to become perfect by your own human effort?
GALATIANS 3:3

---

* C. S. Lewis, "Man or Rabbit?" in *God in the Dock: Essays on Theology and Ethics* (Grand Rapids, MI: Eerdmans, 2014), 113–14.

New Driver

As I waited in traffic for the light on a crowded city street to change, I noticed a handmade cardboard sign taped to the back of the very nice car just in front of me. "Caution," it said. "New Driver. Be Patient. Makes Sudden Stops. Thank You." The words were followed by a smiley face. I considered the uncommon humility of the driver—or the driver's parent—who made this sign. The sign said to other drivers *I'm new at this—and I might not be very good at it yet. Please show me grace.*

We don't often see or hear such honest confessions. More routinely, we claim more expertise than we actually possess. "Oh, sure, I know how to do that," we insist. Or "Yes, of course I'm familiar with ___." Or "Thanks, but I've got this. No worries." Except we don't always. Even if we've lived long enough to be proficient at a great many things, we are still amateurs in many other areas.

Maybe wearing hand-lettered signs around our necks would be a bit much, but it wouldn't hurt to admit that, young or old, we're still new at some rather important things. For example, I could truthfully say, "Please be patient with me. I'm new at asking for help, and I might pretend I don't need it—even if I do." Or "Caution: I'm prone to make critical comments when I'm angry or stressed. You might want to steer wide of me today." Or "I'm not great about saying I was wrong and asking forgiveness. Just so you know." There are plenty of things at which, even after years of following Christ, I am still a rank amateur. How about you?

There's no shame in letting others know we're still learning. I seek to follow my Savior, but I do badly at times. I'm inexperienced in holiness, although I desperately desire it. Please be patient with me. I stand in need of grace, and I would return the same to you, if you asked.

Unlike the culture around you, always dragging you down to its level of immaturity, God brings the best out of you, develops well-formed maturity in you.

ROMANS 12:2, MSG

Going Back the Way You Came

My rather addled sense of direction is well known among family and close friends. I've taken trains the wrong direction, gone to the wrong airport, overshot countless exits, and once famously managed to get lost between Bronte and Ballinger, Texas. (If you could refrain from looking these two towns up, my illusion of competency might remain intact for just a while longer.)

Sometimes I get lost because I'm not paying attention. Or things start looking familiar that actually are not. I'll imagine I've already been at an intersection or a wide space in the road and get a weird but unfounded sense of déjà vu.

Once I even managed to get lost hiking by myself. Not scary lost. Just annoying lost. I was in a familiar spot on trails I'd hiked before, but some of the old markers had been replaced. A mile and a half up to a bluff with a fabulous view I encountered no problems. But coming down I reached a three-way fork and could not, for the life of me, remember which way to turn to get back home, and I chose wrong. It was midmorning and very overcast. When I realized I'd made the wrong choice, there was only one surefire way to correct it: go back the way I came. So I did. And although my hike took far longer than I'd planned, I did find my way home.

Sometimes God in his mercy takes me back the way I came, letting me pick up where I turned awry or missed the marker I should have seen. This doesn't seem like progress, but it almost always is. When I go back the way I came, I can make a different choice and see a different outcome. And here's the other tender thing God has taught me: going back the way I came doesn't just make the desired destination possible, it allows me to see the way there with new eyes, alert to what I might have missed before.

Are you a little, or even a lot, lost? Could it be time to consider going back the way you came? The way may be long and tedious, but your Guide is very, very good, and he always means to lead you home.

———

Lead me down the path of truth.
PSALM 25:5, MSG

Making Crooked Things Straight

Sometimes the full effects of a storm don't become apparent until long after the wind has subsided. A category 3 storm pulled one huge tree down but not *into* my house, only resting on it. I had no power for nearly two weeks, but my little 1920s pier-and-beam cottage fared amazingly well—except for the garage.

I didn't notice at first that a large tree limb was leaning heavily on the garage roof. Or that the entire garage itself had begun to list slightly to the east. I finally noticed when I tried to open its doors and could not.

A crew of workers came to tackle the off-kilter garage. In a matter of hours, these men literally wrestled that old garage back into form, sawing away the offending tree and then attaching great straps to the frame to coax it back to square once more. The end result was good. I once again had a garage I could open (and was not afraid to go into.)

We are not always aware of our own storm casualties either. Perhaps we've suffered a loss or abuse or grief so strong that we're amazed to be standing at all in its aftermath. Only after a bit of time do we see that we are still bruised or bleeding or at the very least off balance. When daylight shows the damage, there is only one thing left to do: gather the mercy of God and the community of saints around us and wrestle for as long as it takes to get upright again.

A short time ago at a retreat I was asked to lead, I met a beautiful young woman who just two months before had buried her infant son. She told me her story, and as she did, I was awed by the weight of it and silenced by her loss. I had nothing to give her but my own tears, but in the providence of the Architect who loves her, I believe even those might be part of the shoring up that will help her get upright once again.

One day, all that was once crooked will be made straight. One day, the damaging results of every storm will be put right. Don't you long for that day? I do.

He heals the brokenhearted and bandages their wounds.
PSALM 147:3

Kindled

I never imagined I would read a book without turning its pages. Since I bought my first Whitman's children's classic at a five-and-dime store in Corpus Christi, Texas, I've been one hopeless, book-loving word nerd. I "heart" the feel of new covers, the smell of freshly printed pages, and the soft pop of a just-creased spine. I like writing in margins, underlining lovely phrases, and folding back pages I mean to visit again.

But then I received an e-book reader. I've learned that while nothing will replace the old, familiar way of reading for me, I enjoy the benefits of carrying around an ever-ready shelf of books in one slim case. Who cares if the *National Geographic* in the doctor's office is two years old, or the paper stand at the corner coffee shop is empty by seven in the morning? I have plenty of titles to choose from right here in my shoulder bag. In short, I've been "Kindled": reintroduced to a very old love in a brand-new way.

I have another love who has been surprising me in new ways for years. We met when I was eight, and I fell hard. He was (and still is) the best thing that ever happened to me. He fit my third-grade heart like a glove, and he's fit every day since just as perfectly. He found me first, loved me, and invited me in. We have years of history, yet he still surprises me with his kindness.

Lately he's been teaching me that weakness isn't repugnant, but pride is. That vulnerability isn't nearly as dangerous as I used to think. That I'm not as strong as I once believed and more comfortable with that fact than I ever imagined I might be. That the hard things I can't change might just be the very best tools at his disposal for shaping me into the image of his Son. And that even when I'm weary or angry or frightened or more than a little lost, he keeps right on tending the fire he first kindled in me such a long time ago. It never burns in quite the same way twice . . . and I am learning to love him for that, too.

I will refine them like silver and purify them like gold.
ZECHARIAH 13:9

Simultaneous Contrast

A few years ago I experienced a physical challenge that left me anemic, fatigued, and depressed. After six months of medication, I faced major surgery and another four months of recuperation and fatigue. But nearly a year after this puzzling storm began, the clouds cleared. I woke up one morning renewed. I wasn't achy or tired or sad. As wonderful as that morning felt, it would have seemed totally unremarkable if I hadn't been sick for so long. It was the dissimilarity that made my wellness clear.

A dear friend who is an artist once told me about a phenomenon she called simultaneous contrast. She could never be sure a color was the right one in the tube or alone on her palette. She could only assess and appreciate its true hue on the canvas next to the other colors in a painting. The simultaneous contrast gave the new color she was applying its real tone. In the same way, only when we see our new life in Christ up against the old color of our formerly dead state can we begin to embrace our identity and truly live.

We died with Christ to the old, sin-ruled self, and we are raised with him to a new, God-directed, God-infused, God-empowered life. In Christ Jesus we are forgiven, emancipated, made righteous, and fully loved. We are heirs with Christ, sons and daughters of the Lord God, indwelled by the Holy Spirit for good works that he has prepared for us (see Ephesians 2:1-10). That's who we are—and we come to see it by contrast. The glorious truth of our identity in Christ should help us sleep soundly tonight and wake up tomorrow hopeful, expectant, and full of unshakable joy.

Now in Christ Jesus you who formerly were far off have been brought near by the blood of Christ. For He Himself is our peace, who made both groups into one and broke down the barrier of the dividing wall, by abolishing in His flesh the enmity, which is the Law of commandments contained in ordinances, so that in Himself He might make the two into one new man, thus establishing peace, and might reconcile them both in one body to God through the cross, by it having put to death the enmity.
EPHESIANS 2:13-16, NASB

MAY 14
Impulsive Acts of Grace

Remember those bumper stickers advocating random acts of kindness? I think the idea was that if we all participate, we might collectively achieve some great sea change of goodness. Just recently I've begun a new and very personal campaign. For want of a name, I'm calling it Impulsive Acts of Grace. (Unplanned, Strongly Prompted, Non-merit-based Showings of Odd and Unsolicited Favor is too long.) I have been offering these acts with very little forethought on my part. Otherwise, I might have nixed them all.

Why give a charm off my favorite necklace to a rebellious, defiant eighteen-year-old who's running from goodness as fast as his skinny legs will carry him? Because, as I sealed up a letter to him, I felt a strong impulse to do so. Because its inscription, "Jer. 29:13," seemed to speak his name. Will it matter in the long run? I don't know. But it mattered *then*, so I did it.

It felt right, too, to push an elderly lady's grocery cart back to the store after she'd slowly loaded her car, trying to hold the cart, her hatchback, and her balance all at once. "Would you like me to get that?" I asked her as I approached. "Yes, thank you," she said. She looked startled. So was I. I don't usually slow down for that sort of thing.

It was even less like me to offer up a whole ziplock bag of homemade cookies (which I'd baked for therapeutic purposes and put in my car to take to work) to a man at a stoplight with a sign that said "Homeless, hungry, please help." But when a light stopped me not ten feet from him, I rolled down my window, leaned across the console, and asked if some chocolate chip cookies would be okay. I didn't have to ask twice. "Bless you," he said. And then the light changed.

Would five dollars have helped more? Maybe. But I didn't have cash. I had cookies. And the fleeting impulse to hand them over. Will any of these impulsive acts of grace change the world? No. But maybe, if I keep on responding to that still, small voice, they *will* change me.

A woman came in with a beautiful alabaster jar of expensive perfume made from essence of nard. She broke open the jar and poured the perfume over his head.
MARK 14:3

Weathered, Beautiful, and Full of Character

The e-mail in my in-box trumpeted this subject line: "Weathered, beautiful, and full of character." Honestly, how could I *not* open it?

The message was from a catalog retailer I'd ordered from before, and I believe the pitch of the day was for antique pub signs—something I could most certainly live without! But the phrase that had caught my eye also applied to my favorite previously purchased item from that seller: my trusty messenger bag.

The messenger bag is made of smooth, untreated leather. It has no tooling or trim, no plush lining or interior pockets. Several years old now, my bag bears the scuffed patina of age and wear: rain spots, coffee spills, and a stray pen mark or two. It has carried manuscripts, Moleskines, gel pens, a zipper-sleeved laptop, a phone, multiple paperbacks and Bibles, dog treats, lip balm, contact lens solution, and occasionally an extra pair of shoes.

It's deep. And nondescript. No bling. With every trip it just gets softer, more flawed, and more beloved.

In time, I'd like to become "weathered, beautiful, and full of character" too. I'd prefer my personal weathering process to be a gentle one, but I don't mean to hide its effects altogether. I've earned every one of my years, and almost all of them have been spent following the sweetest of Saviors. The weathering process he's engineered has smoothed away some of my rougher edges and taught me to pack wisely and well. I can't say that I feel *beautiful*, exactly, but I feel his beauty welling up and spilling over in the most unexpected ways. And I pray that the cuts and dings and scratches I do bear will indeed make me "full of character" one day.

If my good God can one day make me "weathered, beautiful, and full of character," he can do it for you, too. I'm sure of it. Our part in the process is really very small. We must be willing to be filled up like my messenger bag and carried along, anywhere, for any reason he might choose.

Are you ready? Me, too.

Though on the outside it often looks like things are falling apart on us, on the inside, where God is making new life, not a day goes by without his unfolding grace.

2 CORINTHIANS 4:16, MSG

Fifty Years from Now

My sister and I visited a local frame shop with my two diplomas in hand—degrees earned more than thirty years apart. She had offered to frame my new master's diploma as a graduation gift; I was planning to redo the old undergraduate certificate so it wouldn't look shabby next to the new one.

As we considered different combinations of mats and frames, the lady helping us noted that one kind of mat was more archival and would not fade as my old one had. In the moment, it occurred to me that in another thirty-five years, that fact won't matter to me at all. I won't likely be here—and if in God's providence I am, I don't imagine a little mat fade will be a bother.

The day after our frame shop visit, my home church celebrated its twentieth anniversary—and the title of the morning sermon gave me pause. "Fifty Years from Now," the bulletin read. And again, I thought, *I won't be here. I'll be home.* Although I have the sense that God still has much to do in me, I know I've spent more time in this place than I have left to spend. And that fact does not vex me. I like my final destination; it gets sweeter by the day.

While some folks with more miles behind them than before enjoy looking back, I am decidedly focused ahead—and the question I'm asking is this: *What can I leave behind that will be a joy to others in the years to come?* I want to steward my gifts so that someday someone I've never even met will be blessed by them. To assure my nieces and nephews, their children, and the children of my dearest friends that there is no better life to be had than a life of following hard after Jesus. Fifty years from now, I want what I've done with *this* day to glorify my King and point to him like a compass points north: beautifully, consistently, without apology or fail.

O nations of the world, recognize the LORD; recognize that the LORD is glorious and strong. Give to the LORD the glory he deserves!
PSALM 96:7-8

MAY 17
Twitter and Tweets

I'm no dinosaur, but I've warmed very slowly to the social media craze. I'd rather speak face-to-face or on the phone than text. If you have something to say to me, I'd prefer almost anything to a text. My Facebook page is not updated as often as the gurus recommend, and I rarely appear in my own Instagram photos. If you see a tweet from me, you can be relatively sure I've been kidnapped and held hostage.

I hope I have done enough, social network–wise, by maintaining as best I can the web of friendships that has grown through many years in mostly old-fashioned ways. But the pressure to "get with the program" only intensifies with each passing day.

I recently attended a conference for women in ministry where I was advised (multiple times) that I was remiss in not tweeting. "Twitter," one attendee said, "is so *now*. Everyone's on it." Facebook (I heard) is "so yesterday." (Too many older people on it was the explanation given for its decline.) Twitter allows me 140 characters to tell the world what I am doing *right now*. It invites me to follow the tweets of those whose lives I'm interested in, keeping up with them moment by moment.

But I might not have the energy to care, because most days I can barely keep up with my own life.

If I *did* tweet, here's what you might read:

I'm exhausted. Dead tired. I'm a morning person who frowned at this day's sunrise.

I'm worried about having enough work. About taxes going up. About the rattle in my car when I accelerate.

I don't think I've been a good friend lately. I want to do better but can't seem to find the time I need to try.

I fell asleep last night before I could pray. (Actually, before I could turn out the light.)

I need to "tweet" all right. But about the God who loves me and already knows where I am, what I am doing, and what thoughts are buzzing in my brain. So this morning, there's this—and it is enough: *Lord Jesus Christ, Son of God, have mercy on me. Lord Jesus Christ, have mercy on me. Have mercy on me. Amen.*

The LORD's lovingkindnesses indeed never cease, for His compassions never fail.

LAMENTATIONS 3:22, NASB

144

A Wacky-Good God

God is good. I've said that—and believed it—nearly all my life, but for a long time "God is good" meant he gave me just what I wanted or he gave me even more than I expected or believed I deserved. Now "God is good" means something different to me. It means his intent toward me is good, always. It means his best gift to me—Jesus—will never be topped. Ever. And it means his mercy never fails.

A short time ago, after a season of struggle on several fronts, he gave me resolution. Answers. Peace. And he didn't exactly answer *my* prayers. He answered the prayers of others—because fear and weariness and uncertainty mostly sabotaged mine. I could barely ask on my own. The elders of my church prayed. Loved ones prayed. Near and faraway friends prayed. And I took comfort in every single plea made on my behalf. They were as precious to me as a truckload of riches.

Written and hummed and whispered and silent, boldly stated and breathed in secret, they fell before the throne of a very good God, and he lovingly brought me through. A little roughed up by the ride, perhaps, but more sure of him than ever. A note from one friend made me laugh and cry in the space of a paragraph. Here is what it said, and it couldn't be any more true.

> Why, oh why, is our sweet Father so challenging in how he helps us grow in faith? Why do things have to seem so scary for us to grow? I am wondering, can you have strong faith without these hard challenges? I don't know. Can we know the love and provision of God if our lives are easy? I bet you can't. My, my, my what a wacky-good God he is.

He is indeed "wacky-good." (And I don't believe we should be offended by that phrase at all.) Whether the news is good or bad or the ship comes in or doesn't; whether what's lost is found or what's found is lost; whether desire is fulfilled or denied; whether in this life or the next (and it's closer than we think), my God is good, so good to me.

I will make all my goodness pass before you. . . . I will show mercy to anyone I choose.
EXODUS 33:19

Think Small (but Dream Big)

So many folks have big dreams. Big hopes. Big ideas. But they're convinced they can't do what God's put in their hearts to do because "other people" won't cooperate. So the dreamers keep dreaming, but after a while the very dream that used to seem like a sweet and tantalizing savor becomes a hard, bitter lump of resentment and regret. And eventually, those dreams wither.

I have two words for dreamers: think small.

I began writing a weekly devotional fifteen years ago, with fewer than twenty-five people on the receiving end. I did it because I'm a writer, and writers write. The numbers didn't matter then, and they don't now. Every devotional, every article, every book is read by one person—one very real person—at a time.

I started teaching over thirty years ago . . . in my own living room. I invited half a dozen friends over to study the Bible together, offered to lead, and never looked back. Those friends invited friends, and though there were never more than a dozen or so of us gathered at any given time, we kept it up for seven years of Monday nights. Those were some of the sweetest teaching experiences of my life.

Today I travel long distances to speak to groups far too large for my living room, being paid for what I still consider a privilege. But there's no place I'd rather teach than in my own church on any Sunday morning of the year. On a "big" Sunday there might be thirty of us in class—but don't be fooled. Important things happen when we gather in Jesus' name, no matter how many are there.

If you belong to God, then he has gifted you, put dreams in your heart, and equipped you to be his servant in the place he's set you down. You're not where you are by accident. Don't be fooled by the numbers game! We don't have to be the biggest, or the best known, or the most followed. We simply have to be faithful where we are. Defy the world today: dream big and think small.

Salvation is not a reward for the good things we have done, so none of us can boast about it.
EPHESIANS 2:9

MAY 20

Nothing Strong Enough

The storm that began plowing through a sleepy Oklahoma suburb at 2:45 on a Monday afternoon stretched seventeen miles long and over a mile wide, and for over forty-five minutes it separated houses, schools, and hospitals from their foundations; flung trucks and automobiles from the road; and uprooted trees, fences, and utility poles from the earth. Winds of up to two hundred miles per hour left a horrible, flat trail of rubble in their wake.

Storms come, turning ease to terror with the sound of a warning whistle—or without it. "God does not keep His child immune from trouble," writes Oswald Chambers. "He promises, 'I will be with him in trouble . . .' (Psalm 91:15). It doesn't matter how real or intense the adversities may be; nothing can ever separate him from his relationship to God."*

When the good people of Moore, Oklahoma, climbed from their storm cellars and hiding places, many had been separated from their homes. Their neighbors. Pets. Ordinary comforts they'd come to rely upon and expect. But no child of God was separated from his love.

Teachers spread their bodies over their students to spare them from the assault of flying debris. A woman with two boys—ages three years and six months—took shelter in her workplace while her children were in a day care a few miles away. They were safely reunited in a hospital emergency room.

Two network newsmen marveled at the kindness shown by neighbors and strangers, calling it "faith-based FEMA." One said, "If you're waiting for the government, you're going to be in for an awful long wait. The Baptist men, they're going to get it done tomorrow."† They reported cars and trucks on the edges of the highways into town, parked and open, their occupants handing out water, groceries, towels, and clothing. Ordinary people showing extraordinary kindness.

Because even the most terrible of storms is not strong enough to separate God's children from his love.

Neither death nor life, nor angels nor rulers, nor things present nor things to come, nor powers, nor height nor depth, nor anything else in all creation, will be able to separate us from the love of God in Christ Jesus our Lord.
ROMANS 8:38-39, ESV

---

* Oswald Chambers, *My Utmost for His Highest*, May 19.
† "In Okla.: 'Faith-based FEMA' to be 'huge part' of recovery effort," Baptist Press, May 22, 2013, http://www.bpnews.net/40357/in-okla-faithbased-fema-to-be-huge-part-of-recovery-effort.

The Same Hand

Nearly thirty years after my undergrad days, I again carry in my pocketbook a student ID. The back window of my car, much to my oldest niece's amusement, sports a student parking permit. I'm in school again, pursuing a hybrid master's degree in the disciplines I loved most as an undergrad: literature, theology, history, and philosophy.

Aside from the time demands graduate school makes on an already-full schedule, I love it. And I'm discovering that the undergrad who was content with a long string of Bs and a few As and Cs is no longer satisfied with any letter but A.

What I'm finding most delicious about school this time around is the way my faith informs every bit of my learning. If those four long-ago years at a state university were my first spiritual renaissance, this chapter of academic life is my second. Then I was learning to test a ten-year-old faith for its practical veracity, and it proved truer than true. Now I carry within me a relationship more than four decades old, and it doesn't just inform my own experiences, it also informs every ounce of literature, art, history, and philosophy I am exploring.

And I shouldn't be surprised. As John Owen wrote, "The same hand which laid this foundation, doth also finish the building."* (This time around, I knew enough to check Owen out of the library for fun—not because he was assigned reading!)

The same hand that laid the foundation is the hand that is finishing, and will one day completely finish, the building. The building of one individual follower (me), of every other follower, and of his great church.

Some things have changed. My classmates have dreadlocks and soul patches. A few have gray hair and soul. But one thing stays the same: the hand that laid the foundation will doubtless finish the building. And what a beautiful hand it is.

No one can lay a foundation other than that which is laid, which is Jesus Christ.

I CORINTHIANS 3:11, ESV

---

* John Owen, *A Treatise on the Holy Spirit and His Operations* (Xenia, OH: Board of the Calvinistic Book Concern, 1841), 102.

Obedience Class

We assembled one evening a week: seven of us with our dogs. Owen and me, then the rottweiler, the border collie, the shih tzu, the Labrador, the English springer spaniel, the pit bull, and their respective owners. We came to train our dogs—and to be trained—by a master trainer who knew the ropes. (Or more precisely, the leashes.) We learned basic commands and how to motivate our dogs to obey them. That meant food treats in return for obedience, at least to start with. But once the commands were learned, the treats were not automatically dispensed. "Good dog!" might be offered, or another word of praise, or a pat, or sometimes just more walking or playing.

As near as I could tell, that was when school ended and relationship began.

We started with *sit*—saying the word, giving a motion, then shaping the desired posture on our dogs with our hands. (Treats all around for doing it right.) Then we began to work on the no-hands sit, then on *stay*. We let our dogs know they were released from both sit and stay with an enthusiastic "Okay!" and a strong leading motion.

I learned a lot at obedience class. (Owen did well too.) I can't help but think of his lessons as a reminder to me of my own. I have a very good master. He loves me beyond reason. He proved it, once for all. He chose me, paid for me, and means to live with me and lead me all the way home. If my lessons go well, there will be more—much more—for me than treats for obedience. There will be real, satisfying, vibrant relationship. The kind that's built on reliability and trust. Not predictability. He doesn't promise that. But he will keep on doing the things he's promised, and I'll keep on believing he knows more than I do and does everything in love.

Each time our class was done, the instructor admonished us to go home and practice. To introduce distractions—the everyday kind our dogs might not experience in the classroom. Skateboarding children. Whizzing traffic. Other dogs. Lots of them. Taking obedience to the streets allows trust to strengthen and confidence to grow.

I'm off to obedience class. Are you coming too?

Those who obey God's word truly show how completely they love him.
I JOHN 2:5

The Man Who Knew Too Much

Two strangers—a man and a woman—met one day at an ordinary well. Their conversation stuttered along in fits and starts with the odd feel of an out-of-range cell call: pauses and missed cues, awkward "disconnects" between query and response. They needn't have spoken at all, but he broke the ice with a request it would have been impolite to ignore: "Give me a drink," he simply said. *Game on.*

Then, in a matter of a few swirling moments, they were speaking of mountains and worship and prophets and something he called living water, even though the water in the well seemed as ordinary to her as ever.

The man who stood before her was unlike any man she had ever encountered. For one thing, he knew too much. Knew things she'd rather have kept hidden. Knew things that caused her shame and required that she maintain vigilant defenses. He saw her soul as it truly was and did not turn away.

You and I play to our strengths and do our best to cover our flaws. We've read the relational playbook. We know that vulnerability is dangerous and that a protective veneer of toughness and confidence is a prophylactic against possible hurt. We don't roll over for anyone. Ever. So like this woman, we're more than a little undone when someone slips inside the armor and says, "I see your stuff. I'm not repelled. I'm still here. Now let's *really* talk."

I may hide my most shameful secrets from the world with some measure of success; I can pretend to be bulletproof in my actions and judgments, and I might get you to buy it. *But Jesus reads my mail.* He's seen me at my worst, and just when I believe he should reject me on principle (his!), he moves in closer still. I can't shake him. Not with diversionary God talk, not with peacock-like displays of the very gifts he's graciously given, not with puffed-up pretense or stiff-armed resistance.

He sees every flaw and draws closer, holding out his hand as if to say, "*Here, let me love that, too.*" And then lo and behold, he does.

If anyone is thirsty, let him come to Me and drink. He who believes in Me, as the Scripture said, "From his innermost being will flow rivers of living water."
JOHN 7:37-38, NASB

Broken by the Plow

I don't know much about plowing. I've certainly never walked behind a plow, although long ago I rode on a tractor with my grandfather as he dug deep furrows in West Texas earth for cottonseed to nestle in and grow. I remember the rich smell of turned-up earth and how good it felt to sit tucked up under his chin as we rumbled over broken soil.

The earth doesn't seem to mind its bruising, but oh, how I mind mine. A *no* when you've prayed for a *yes*, or slamming doors or angry words can jar the joy right out of your day. Little slights you're used to ignoring can become supersized when what you needed instead was kindness. Disappointment can seem as sharp as the point of any plow, and so can confusion and longing and waiting—and the quiet cuts they make.

It's no fun being broken by the plow. But such plowing is the very tool God often uses to turn me over and ready me for whatever good he means to give. I'd resist if I could, but he's bigger and stronger—and besides, I can't see past the row I'm on. He can. He is a wise and loving husbandman.

A. W. Tozer says, "The plowed life is the life that has . . . thrown down the protecting fences and sent the plow of confession into the soul. . . . Discontent, yearning, contrition, courageous obedience to the will of God: these have bruised and broken the soil till it is ready again for the seed. *And as always fruit follows the plow.*"*

I don't always love the plow. But I love the Tiller of my soul and the fruit he means to bring. And until the next harvest season, I can breathe in deep and find comfort in the smell of the rich and readied earth he turns . . . even when its rows are cut in me.

There is an appointed time for everything . . . a time to plant and a time to uproot what is planted. . . . He has made everything appropriate in its time.

ECCLESIASTES 3:1-2, 11 NASB

---

* A. W. Tozer, "Miracles Follow the Plow," in *Paths to Power* (Chicago: Moody, 2016); emphasis added.

The Long Hello

I'm no good at good-byes. I never have been. When most kids rejoiced on the last day of school, I silently grieved. I knew I would miss my teachers and that there were likely some students I would not see again when roll was called in the fall.

Now, as an adult, I've found that I dread good-byes even more. I do not want the circle of people I love broken. I just don't. I long for us to remain connected to one another. I long to keep seeing the faces and hearing the voices of those whose hearts are knit to mine. Every good-bye first stings like a cut and then aches like a bruise, and I am getting less and less graceful at receiving them.

As delighted as I was to hear my sweet great-niece say her first discernible words ("Uh-oh!"), my heart also broke a little to hear her chirp, "Bye-bye!" to me as I walked away. She reminded me that we learn early to say those words. We have to. And even with lots of practice, they don't get any easier. Every time I left the home of my mother's oldest sister as a child, I left crying—looking out the back window of the car until I could not see her face, her house, her street, her town. Only when I could no longer glimpse the top of the local water tower would I turn around, wet faced and resigned, and look toward home.

But praise be to God, there are at least two unexpected gifts in our unwanted, lifelong gathering up of good-byes. First, each painful good-bye is a sign that we have loved—and this is no small thing. For those of us who believe in the resurrection, our good-byes are a mournful prelude to a joyful day when parting will be no more. As songwriter Billy Sprague puts it, "Heaven is a long hello." Imagine it! Long hellos, hundreds, thousands of them, rolled into one eternal greeting with no dreaded good-bye. We won't need that skill, those words, ever again. Jesus made sure of it. In him we will know only hello, forever.

He will wipe every tear from their eyes, and there will be no more death or sorrow or crying or pain.
REVELATION 21:4

Struggle Well

The tent card displayed in my beachside hotel room advised me to keep my drapes closed at night and the light on the balcony off. But not for my own privacy or well-being: for the good of the sea turtles.

Sea turtles hatch on Florida beaches in late summer and early fall, and the hatchlings—once they crack open their buried shells and struggle up through packed sand—begin their nocturnal trek seaward. They move toward the shoreline by a combination of instinct and moonlight reflected on the waves. Man-made light distracts them, turning what should be a straight shot to freedom into a confused (and dangerous) wandering toward other, lesser lights.

This exodus in the dark is full of peril. The hatching is struggle enough. Then comes the arduous crawl from beach to sea, when the hatchling couldn't be more exhausted. Once in the water, a twenty-four- to forty-eight-hour swim frenzy ensues, moving the turtle to the deeper water where it can survive and thrive. The first year of its existence is known as "the lost year" because during this time it is rarely seen. An eighty-year life span is possible, and once the sea turtle reaches adulthood, it faces few predators. But 90 percent of the hatchlings do not survive their first year.

A dear counselor friend of mine once listened intently and with empathy to a litany of distress, then let a moment or two fill up with not-unkind silence. Then he smiled at me and said with great wisdom, "Struggle well, Leigh."

When did we hatch the misguided idea that our best life is free from struggle? When did we decide that the things we were made to seek should come to us easily instead? When did we imagine that our status as children of a great King meant a life of bodysurfing ease and not a harrowing swim for our very lives?

Yes, a great salvation is ours. Yes, a wonderful plan for our sanctification is in place. Yes, his victory over sin and death is full and final—but it is the beautiful struggle that proves to us this is so.

Struggle well.

Exhort one another every day, as long as it is called "today." . . . For we have come to share in Christ, if indeed we hold our original confidence firm to the end.

HEBREWS 3:13-14, ESV

So Sure

A few days ago a friend told me that her son, about to enter kindergarten, was anxious about his first day at a new school. He'd had a great time in preschool with friends, but this was a new routine and a place where he knew no one. On Sunday I walked by his Sunday school class and ducked in to say hello.

"Hey, B——," I said, "I hear your new school starts tomorrow." He nodded but not too enthusiastically.

"Did you know your new school is just around the corner from my house?" I asked him. He did.

"Well," I said, "Now every time I go past your school, I'm going to be thinking of you and hoping that you're having a good day." He smiled a little and continued putting away toys. I didn't give it another thought. Until his mom texted me to say that he'd told her later, "Miss Leigh said every time she passes by my school, she will wish I have a good day" and that it made him happy.

In fact, on the evening of his first day of school, B—— asked his mom what color my car was. When she asked why he wanted to know, he told her, "In case she is passing by wishing me a good day while I am outside at recess, I want to wave to her."

You know what I love about that? I made a simple promise, and the recipient of that promise took me at my word. I'm not sure what I've done to earn that trust, but you can bet I'm not about to squander it. B——'s school is not exactly on my normal route when I leave my house, but I've already driven the few blocks out of the way to see it and pray that he *was* having a good day. After all, I gave him my word.

My heavenly Father has promised to remember me. He's engraved my name on the palms of his hands. He's called me his own and adopted me forever through the blood-bought sacrifice of his only Son. He's as good as his word, and I am sure, so sure, of him.

We who have fled to him for refuge can have great confidence as we hold to the hope that lies before us.
HEBREWS 6:18

Mulched

Somewhere between late spring and early summer, the flower beds and tree borders of my yard receive a good cleaning and then a layer of dark, pungent, feathery mulch.

I didn't know to do this until I observed that the healthiest-looking landscaping in my neighborhood was covered each spring in a deep blanket of the smelly, organic stuff. Then I googled *why mulch?* and got on board.

In early May my beds smell like a ripe barnyard (the smell fades in a week or so), but the soil will hold its moisture and weeds will be kept (mostly) at bay for another year. By then, all the stuff that was spread on top will have worked its way into the soil and nourished it, and it will be time to mulch again.

The last time I swept away the stray bits of mulch from the sidewalks and driveway, I thought, *This is me.* Loads of stuff from elsewhere has been piled upon my heart in this emerging season and spread thick. It hasn't been pretty. But it could, and in the Father's sure providence *will*, turn out for my good. The mounds of trials and aches, together with the light of God's Spirit and enough time, will somehow feed my soul, discourage weeds of sin and selfishness, and help me hold in my heart the much-needed water of his Word.

In this paradox-rich world my Father has created, dead matter (like mulch) can actually nurture and protect what's living. And a layer of darkest brown can promise greener greens in days to come. I've seen the seasons change and observed his faithfulness through enough of them to believe that he's at work beneath the surface of my life. I can't see it yet. I don't have to. But I will trust and wait.

I've been mulched. And I pray I am the better for it.

God is my king from of old, who works deeds of deliverance in the midst of the earth. . . . You broke open springs and torrents; You dried up ever-flowing streams. Yours is the day, Yours also is the night; You have prepared the light and the sun. You have established all the boundaries of the earth; You have made summer and winter.

PSALM 74:12, 15-17, NASB

Scrabble or Jenga?

Board games may be making a comeback. If Americans are looking for more family-oriented entertainment, then classic games like Monopoly, Scrabble, and Life fit the bill. And I for one couldn't be happier. I love Scrabble. I love that the tiles—one hundred of them in all—are still made of wood and not plastic and that every game offers its players brand-new arrangements of seven letters to work with. Really good Scrabble players will tell you that they can "see" the words in their tiles from long experience of studying rack after rack of them, game after game. But the original one hundred tiles and their corresponding values never change.

Jenga, on the other hand, is *not* a game I particularly enjoy. Jenga players construct a tower of interlaced wooden slats, and then slat by slat, player by player, the tower is deconstructed. The aim of the game is to see how many (and which) slats can be removed before the tower is compromised and falls.

Scrabble is a game of rightly appropriating raw material. Jenga is a game of taking it away.

When it comes to the Bible—the holy, inspired word of God—are you a Scrabble person or a Jenga person? Do you, under the guidance of the Holy Spirit, strive to see the spiritual truth contained in its perfect wholeness and apply that truth correctly in the context of your life, or do you attempt to see which of its "slats" can be removed, leaving something that manages to stand?

The most joyful, infectious, compelling men and women I know are those who believe in the wholeness and mystery of the Word of God; submit their own thoughts and actions to its unchanging truth; and do not attempt to deny, remove, or disregard the parts of it that most offend or challenge them. I don't want to mishandle an instrument sharper "than the sharpest two-edged sword" (Hebrews 4:12). I want to study it carefully, day after day, year after year, until my eyes more easily see the truth that it holds, and I am able to faithfully apply it to the game board that is my life.

The word of God is living and active and sharper than any two-edged sword, and piercing as far as the division of soul and spirit, of both joints and marrow, and able to judge the thoughts and intentions of the heart.
HEBREWS 4:12, NASB

Reading the News

Lately it's been hard to read the news.

Far from me, injustice rages and chaos rules. Thirty children and their teachers are awakened at gunpoint and murdered at a boarding school in Nigeria. Insurrection, rape, and armed assault disrupt the streets of Egypt. A British soldier is beheaded on a London street in broad daylight, and his bloodied, delighted murderer celebrates on camera. *Lord, have mercy.*

Nearer to home, a media-soaked, incendiary murder trial comes to a fever-pitch end, politicians call each other names and angle for personal power while claiming to represent "the people," and nineteen brave firefighters die in a single blazing Arizona afternoon. *Christ, have mercy.*

Nearer still, at my house—in my family, my congregation, my community—sickness challenges stability, death lurks, relationships are broken, betrayal wounds, and hopes are shattered. *Lord, have mercy.*

I wonder how God means for me to read the news and what he means for me to do with the suffering I see and feel. I can't simply ignore reality written large in black and white. When I was little, my dad would let me sit on his lap as he read the paper. I would "read" with him, looking at the pictures or the occasional word he pointed to and helped me to sound out. Together, we read the news—and I am sure not all of it was good, even then. But I did not know it. I was shielded from the weight of the words in the crook of his arms. The news, in fact, was secondary. His presence was everything.

How should I read the news today? Perhaps in the same way: in my Father's arms, taking each story to him. Pray for this, Father? Praise you for this mercy, or that one? Bring this known or unknown person into our circle of love and simply hold their needs up to you? Ask for the wisdom and courage to comfort or confront, speak out or keep silent?

I read the news, and my heart fails. But his does not. He sounds out for me the truth behind the headlines and reminds me that the last word will be his.

I consider that the sufferings of this present time are not worth comparing with the glory that is to be revealed to us. For the creation waits with eager longing for the revealing of the sons of God.
ROMANS 8:18-19, ESV

Plans Change

"I never read fiction," my friend declared. "I only read stories that are true." The literary gauntlet was thrown down—and a challenge accepted. We agreed to swap books. He offered historical nonfiction in exchange for a novel of my choosing. I accepted his worn copy of *Endurance: Shackleton's Incredible Voyage* and handed him Ernest Gaines's *A Lesson Before Dying*.

The leap of faith was mostly his. I'm almost certain Gaines's novel was the first my friend had ever determined to tackle start to finish. But the pleasure, I fear, was mostly mine. *A Lesson Before Dying* is fiction that reads like fact and rings utterly true—even though its characters are born of imagination. *Endurance* is fact so unimaginable that it reads like fiction.

Sir Ernest Shackleton attempted, in 1914, to cross Antarctica. He'd wanted to be the first man to reach the South Pole, but two others beat him there. So he found a new dream, but he failed at that, too. Sort of. He never completed his intended 1,500-mile trek. But he kept twenty-seven men alive for two years after disaster struck, and ultimately brought them to safety. Plans change.

Shackleton began his voyage at age forty, setting sail from England. After five months at sea, his great ship became wedged in ice. Only a day's sail from their destination, he and his men were stranded for eleven months waiting for the ice to free them. It didn't. Instead, it crushed his ship until it gave way with a giant groan into a heap of wood and steel and wire. Plans change. Shackleton and his men were at the mercy of the wind and the water, and they knew it. Their captain never began the journey he intended—but he finished one he never might have started had the choice been left to him.

I'm not where I thought I might be today. Maybe you're not either. But God is writing a story with your life and with mine—one grounded in reality, yet as unpredictable and luminous as fiction. I am learning to let his hand have free reign with the manuscript, because thankfully, plans do change.

Jesus said to his disciples, "If any of you wants to be my follower, you must give up your own way, take up your cross, and follow me."
MATTHEW 16:24

June

Once upon a Time

I stood up and moved to the podium to face a room full of precious women gathered on retreat. I'd planned to talk about the Kingdom of God, and I was prepared and ready. But when I saw their faces, for a moment I was struck dumb. Not with fear. With a heart full of memories and images flickering across my mind's eye. It was as if God whispered, "Once upon a time" and then clicked the projector on.

I saw the church where I walked the aisle at eight to give my heart to Jesus. A hillside in New Mexico where I wept at nineteen and knew that yes would be forever. A tiny church in Brazil wet with rain and ringing with praise. Dozens of retreats, living room Bible studies, Young Life clubs, and Sunday school classrooms. I saw the faces of friends, teachers, mentors, and loved ones. I saw my own face as a little girl, a fresh-faced teenager, a grown-up woman in love, and an older, if not wiser, version of her, arms empty but heart full.

Then I did something I hadn't planned on. I told the women waiting to hear about the Kingdom what I'd just seen. And of how good God has been to me. Then I swallowed and blinked back the tears, opened my Bible, and followed him again to someplace new.

A week later I was back in the church I'd attended as a child, this time for a wedding. The sanctuary was redecorated, but the space was still the same. The aisle the bride walked on her father's arm, I walked once upon a time in white anklets and black patent shoes beside my own dad. The bride took her groom's hand at the altar; I took the pastor's at the same spot, and he smiled down at me.

I told someone once, "We have history, God and I." And we do. Once upon a time our love was shiny and new. But it's sweeter to me now than it was at the beginning. "Grow old along with me. The best is yet to be. . . ." That's my story. I believed it yesterday, and today I couldn't be more certain that it is true.

The LORD is my chosen portion and my cup.
PSALM 16:5, ESV

No Two Alike

Four hundred years ago, the Japanese perfected the art of raku, the ceramic firing technique where a clay piece is painted with glazes containing copper and other minerals and then fired in a kiln at high heat for a short time. In the more modern, Western raku style, once the glazes melt, the white-hot piece is removed from the kiln and placed in a metal can filled with combustible leaves, sawdust, and shredded paper. As these catch fire and blaze, a lid is placed on the container, cutting off oxygen to the fire. The loss of oxygen affects the glazes, resulting in various lusters and a smoky-gray patina where no glaze was applied. Spritzing the heated pieces with water can further affect their final appearance.

Because fire never burns the same way twice, no two raku pieces are alike. And because the elements of heat and oxygen and water are change agents, what goes into the fire often looks, save its original size and shape, nothing like what comes out. Some pieces are stunningly beautiful. Others are rather ordinary. Each is wonderfully unique, particular, and true to itself—just like people.

We come through life's fires made and remade in the image of God, but no two of us are alike. When I see the grace of well-lived decades, I wish it could be mine, now. When I see the fresh exuberance of youth, I remember it with sharp longing. I see gifts so different from mine—so shiny and fine—that I wish my own were less plain. When I tried my hand at raku, I sometimes wanted other people's ceramic pots to be my own when they emerged from the fire lovelier than mine. In the same way, I have wished for the shapes and colors and ways of others to become my own. But it was God's pleasure and joy to make me just as I am and to finish me as he sees fit.

We belong to him, in the fire and smoke and water. The process is his, and so are the results. May he make of us what he will in his good time.

Who are you, O man, who answers back to God? The thing molded will not say to the molder, "Why did you make me like this," will it? Or does not the potter have a right over the clay, to make from the same lump one vessel for honorable use and another for common use?

ROMANS 9:20-21, NASB

Me against the Snake

I recently did something I've never done before and hope to never do again. I killed a snake. By myself. With a garden hoe. The snake was a complete mess by the time it was over, and frankly, so was I. This particular snake had invaded my sister's backyard and was discovered by her fearless miniature dachshund, who mistook it for a chew toy.

I hate snakes. And I hate killing anything. Even a bug. But there was no one else to do the deed, so I charged in and tried to separate dog and snake with my foot. I thought I had, but the dog shot around me, grabbed the snake in his mouth, and began to shake it from side to side. I threw my car keys at the dog, and startled, he dropped his prey.

By then my sister had come outside. The snake seemed a little stunned and wasn't moving . . . much. I grabbed the dog, and my sister grabbed a garden hoe. "We've got to kill it," she said.

"Couldn't we just go inside and let it die on its own?" I asked. When I saw she wasn't giving in until Mr. Snake was dead, I handed her the dachshund, took the hoe, and went after the invader. When I'd finally prevailed, my sister and I went inside, and I collapsed in a chair.

Killing the snake reminded me that God has done battle with Satan and bruised him on the head—and that it took a great, messy, and terrible sacrifice to do away with my own sin. I didn't have to fight to win forgiveness. Jesus has already secured that, and it is mine. But I do have to fight for the turf he's already won. You see, Satan is a cunning snake. He won't just crawl away and die.

Since I killed the snake, I've been less able to take my own sin lightly. And I've fallen even more in love with my sin killer: the beautiful one who went to war on my behalf—and won.

If while we were enemies we were reconciled to God by the death of his Son, much more, now that we are reconciled, shall we be saved by his life. More than that, we also rejoice in God through our Lord Jesus Christ, through whom we have now received reconciliation.

ROMANS 5:10-11, ESV

Let It Go

Sometimes I'm such a slow learner that God patiently repeats my lessons, changing the scenery but not the subject matter. Lately, his curriculum has centered on letting go.

I'd stopped into a neighborhood deli for a box lunch and placed it on the passenger seat of my car. I was driving down a busy city street . . . hungry enough to eat my meal in the car, but heading home instead. The fellow on foot at the intersection held up a sign that said "Broke. Hungry." He had two pressing problems, and I had only one. I could solve his second problem. All it required was surrendering my neatly packaged tuna-on-wheat sandwich with salt-and-vinegar chips and a pickle. I rolled the window down just as the light was turning green again and held out the box. "Want my lunch?" I asked. He did. "God bless you," he said as the car behind me honked, and I let my sandwich go.

On another day and on a different street, I was stopped again at a light when I heard a woman shouting into her cell phone. Every other word she was screaming would have been bleeped if she'd been on television. I felt the walls of my heart go up in resistance to her spewing rage. But before the light changed, I looked again. She was still holding the phone, shaking her head from side to side and wiping away tears that were streaming down her cheeks. I hadn't planned to, but I whispered, "Help her, Jesus. Please help her." And as the words fell out, I let my judgment go.

Sandwiches and judgments are easier to surrender than my own pride or selfishness or plans. I'm learning to release my grip on those as well, as my Tutor bears down hard for my own good. Moment by moment, a trusting response to the Spirit is the kind of life I'm made for.

Maybe after a thousand more lessons, large and small, I will finally learn, no matter what I'm clinging to, to simply let it go.

May the Lord of peace Himself continually grant you peace in every circumstance. The Lord be with you all!
2 THESSALONIANS 3:16, NASB

In the Book

A friend phoned to tell me how she happened to connect with someone over a book of mine. This friend—a hairstylist—had a new client in her chair. They began to talk and discovered a strong thread ran between them: one had a sister-in-law with leukemia; the other had lost a daughter to it. They shared bits and pieces of their common experience; then—all cut and styled—the new client turned and saw a copy of my book in the corner of the studio. "We're in that book!" she exclaimed. "So am I!" the other reported. Both were friends of mine but had never met one another.

My friend Amanda is in the book and will quickly point you to the page. Karelyn squealed when she read about herself, and Denni's face went soft. Another friend reports that her young daughter proudly announces her presence in print, and (depending on the audience) both of my nieces own up easily too.

Leighton's there, and so is "Sam" (not his real name). So are Diane and Lynn and Charlie and Victor and one unnamed old boyfriend. Why? Because their stories are interwoven with mine in ways that make it impossible to tell my own story without them. Before they were in the book, they were solidly in my life.

Years ago, my name was written in a book too. It's called the Lamb's Book of Life, and it's a part of my permanent record for now and eternity. I'm in there. If you know Jesus, you are there too. Along with us are Moses and Enoch and Esther and Nicodemus. Matthew and Boaz and Nathan and Joshua and Job. Elizabeth and a Samaritan woman whose name I don't yet know but will. Peter, Paul, Timothy, and Titus are there. An Ethiopian. A prodigal.

Our books won't last. They are written in disappearing ink. Our names in them may connect us now—but it's the presence of our names in *his* book that connects us to one another forever. One day, we may run our fingers over the very page that bears our name. See who's there with us. Seek them out. Until then, may we savor the truth that we are in the book.

Don't rejoice because evil spirits obey you; rejoice because your names are registered in heaven.

LUKE 10:20

JUNE 6
He Knows

Good fathers know their children. They know who they are, down deep. They know what they need. My God is a very good Father. My hopes and dreams stand transparent before his eyes. The present condition of my heart is not hidden from him, nor is my future. He sees it all with great clarity and great love.

So perhaps I should not have been surprised when, browsing a cavernous antique shop's basement full of old books, I found the one meant just for me. Walking past the musty shelves and brushing the spines with their faded titles, I stopped before a ninety-year-old collection of Communion sermons titled *In the Breaking of the Bread* by James I. Vance. What first caught my eye was the book's publisher, the same one who also published two of my books. That was tender. But what took my breath away were the chapter titles of this book—the very subjects I had been reading and writing about for more than a year. My imagination had been wrapped up in the truth of the presence of Father, Son, and Holy Spirit, and in the rich metaphor of the table. So imagine how my heart fluttered when I turned to the book's contents page and glimpsed the words "The Mystical Friendship" and "Christ Liveth in Me" and "Inside the Cup."

These words showed me the book was mine, and even more, that my Father knows where my mind and heart and energies are focused. He knows even how to place my hands on a precious book written decades before I was born, at the exact moment I needed to find it. That day, in the dim light of that basement-turned-book-treasury, I read, "Jesus is not far away. He is with us. . . . He is here. We may not always realize His presence. We may not see Him. . . . [But] Christ is with us. Heaven is at our doorstep. Jesus is at the table. It is always so."*

Oh yes, he is indeed. And he knows.

O LORD, you have examined my heart and know everything about
me. . . . You know everything I do.
PSALM 139:1, 3

---

* James Isaac Vance, *In the Breaking of the Bread: A Volume of Communion Addresses* (New York: Revell, 1922), 15.

Flying Solo

On a recent full flight from San Diego to Houston, I chose the first-row window seat. Nodding at the businessman on my left as I took my seat, I waited to see who'd be buckling in beside me.

I didn't have to wait long.

A flight attendant leaned in and asked if she could seat an unaccompanied minor between my row mate and me. We both agreed, and a six-year-old boy with a Batman backpack and a rolled-up blue blanket plopped down. The flight attendant asked if he needed anything from the backpack before she stowed it overhead for takeoff, promising to retrieve it for him when we were at cruising altitude.

Myles was going to Texas to see his dad, he said. This wasn't his first time to fly, either, just his first time by himself. (But he wasn't scared.) Within moments of taking off, he began to fall asleep, clutching the blue blanket in his lap. Myles slept through beverage service and the captain's release of the seat belt sign. But when he woke up, he was ready to roll.

The attendant got him his backpack, and he pulled out a bottle with his name on it and a freezer bag so full of snacks I wondered what his mother had been thinking. Myles opened the bag and ate (in hurried order) a bag of cookies, a package of crackers, two packets of Starburst candies, and several bags of Goldfish crackers. With every item he opened, Myles asked, "Would you like some?" I declined as I looked around for the airsickness bag.

Myles was cute, confident, talkative, and self-aware. All was well with him, until we began to descend for landing. Then his ears began to pop and his head hurt. He wasn't brave anymore. He was scared and confused and began to cry. Myles's hurt was temporary (sucking a hard candy helped), and his father was the first person I saw waiting at the end of the Jetway.

I smiled and waved at them both, then thought, *One day my own mix of bravado and panic will be forgotten, and I will place my hand in the hand of the one who has both traveled every mile with me and waited for me to arrive at home.* None of us fly solo.

You have enclosed me behind and before, and laid Your hand upon me.
PSALM 139:5, NASB

Covered

For a season, and thankfully not a long one, I felt uncharacteristically vulnerable and a bit adrift. I couldn't trace my unease to any specific source, but a series of random challenges had left me isolated and alone.

Many reassuring, familiar things were changing, and I couldn't see what might take their place. "Faith," says the writer of Hebrews, "shows the reality of what we hope for; it is the evidence of things we cannot see" (11:1). How encouraging that evidence must be, especially when so little *can* be seen.

I wasn't at all sure that my forced march of faith was making me stronger. I never expected to be protected from the bumps and bruises of challenge and change, but still I longed for someone to have my back. Then a dear friend called and suggested lunch. "Dear friend" doesn't tell the half—she very nearly raised me in the faith and has been a source of wisdom and encouragement for more than half my life. Her own life had taken a sad and scary turn just a few short years before, but she emerged strong and sweet and lovelier than ever.

After a meal and a life-giving conversation, she pulled a gift bag from her side of the booth and placed it on the table. "I have something for you," she said. "When Bill died, a friend gave me this, and now I want you to have it." I pulled out a crocheted prayer shawl, still carrying its rumpled tag. "I used to put this around me and cry," she said, "until I couldn't cry anymore." Then she looked at me through tears and said, "I have your back. Even if we don't talk for weeks, and I don't see you, I have your back. I always will. Wrap yourself up in this and remember you are held, you are loved."

That shawl had hugged my friend's shoulders in hours of heaviness, and in the Father's care she is more beautiful for it. Now it has covered my lap as I read and write, and it has been draped about me as I pray and cry. A tangible reminder that I am loved and held.

I am leaving you with a gift—peace of mind and heart. And the peace I give is a gift the world cannot give. So don't be troubled or afraid.
JOHN 14:27

Even Still

Is it just me, or are the bullets coming faster these days? The sound of a breaking news bulletin on my local network station feels more ominously frequent of late, and I sometimes walk right past a screen or a newsstand without so much as a glance at the headlines. I don't *want* any more bad news, thank you. I'm already quite full.

And if these times don't seem dangerous enough—unspeakable acts of terrorism, terrible natural disasters, an anemic economy, high unemployment numbers, and utter disregard for the rule of law—there are rumblings of still more dangers to come. I recently completed *two* separate studies of the book of Revelation. (A coincidence, I assure you. I did not *mean* to bone up on the Apocalypse just now.) Neither study reassured me that our present troubles will soon be over. In fact, just the opposite.

Large-scale dramas we have plenty of. But every day I'm made aware of smaller yet just as daunting threats. The life-threatening illness of a friend. Infertility. The loss of a business, a home, a marriage, a mate. Sometimes I just want to cry out, "Who's running this show? And could we have just a little order in the house, please?"

Here's one thing my simultaneous end times studies are teaching me: whether I'm pre- or post- or amillennial, whether I'm pre- or post-Trib, whether I believe I'll be able to identify the Antichrist when he comes or not—the prince of this world can have no power over me or this world that the King of glory has not allowed. None. It may be hard to see God's sovereign hand when things go badly wrong (just ask Job!), but my limited vision proves neither the Almighty's absence nor his indifference.

Even in the midst of terrible things, my God is still at work. Even still he is sovereign over kings and rulers, events and history. Even still he is making all things new. The darkening backdrop of the times may appear frightening, but it is like a black velvet cloth laid out to make a single jewel—Jesus—shine ever more brightly than before. Even still.

I am the Alpha and the Omega, the First and the Last, the Beginning and the End.

REVELATION 22:13

Do It Again!

My friends Barney and Karen married one another again on their forty-fifth wedding anniversary—for the eleventh or twelfth time. (Barney can't remember exactly.) Barney keeps surprising Karen by renewing the commitment they made when they were two kids fresh out of college with their whole lives ahead of them. They did a good thing back then. Through ups and downs, they can see now that they chose well. So they just keep choosing to do it again.

For this particular hot June afternoon, Barney had invited family and a few friends down to their lake house and happened to include their minister among those gathered. After lunch we all headed down to the water to witness their nuptials. Karen half suspected. She even asked Barney early that morning if they were getting married again, and he said no. I'm not sure how that full disclosure thing works in marriage, but I think in this case it was probably okay not to give up the plan in advance.

The words my friends spoke that Sunday were very similar to the ones they vowed the first time. They promised to love, honor, and cherish one another "until death do us part." And they'll very likely promise again before that time comes— because delight almost begs repetition. Children know this. Some grown-ups do too. And when you love a God whose mercies are new every morning, sometimes the longing to "do it again" just can't be ignored. "It is possible," writes G. K. Chesterton, "that God says every morning, 'Do it again' to the sun; and every evening, 'Do it again' to the moon. It may not be automatic necessity that makes all daisies alike; it may be that God makes every daisy separately, but has never got tired of making them."*

Have you thanked God for his goodness today? Do it again. Told someone you love them? Do it again. Have you offered mercy, sung praises, given liberally, or sought forgiveness? Then by all means, do it again! The best things never get old, and our Father is forever making all things—even familiar things—brand new.

Love never gives up. Love cares more for others than for self. Love doesn't want what it doesn't have.
I CORINTHIANS 13:4, MSG

---

* G. K. Chesterton, *Orthodoxy* (Chicago: Moody, 2009), 92.

Where I Didn't Plan to Be

I'd never been to Arkansas before, but when a lovely woman from Texarkana, a friend of a friend, asked if I would come and speak to her church, I said yes. My trip happened to coincide with a nasty low-pressure system stalled over half the state of Texas, so not far into the drive I found myself stranded a long way from my destination.

I hadn't planned to spend half a day at a car dealership in Livingston, but that's where I pulled in when the road was closed. I spent an afternoon with Otis, Danny, and Shannon in the service department (and got two new tires while I waited). Shannon offered me the chips from his sack lunch; Danny found the tires I needed and dispatched a brave driver to pick them up. And Otis called the hotel next door and hooked me up with the last available room in case I had to spend the night—which ultimately, I did.

I never planned to bunk at this lakeside inn. There were crumbs on the telephone, and the carpet in front of the sink squished when I walked on it. The only food available was more chips from a half-empty vending machine. If I hadn't committed months before to this particular engagement, I might have turned back. But I'd promised, so I went . . . and prayed God would give *me* something to give *them*.

But what I really hadn't planned on was being the recipient of so much kindness at my destination from people I'd never met. A precious team of women whose efficiency and enthusiasm could probably have managed the invasion of a small country before lunch. The generosity of a pastor who offered her study for the few moments of calm I needed before standing up to speak. Hugs from strangers and the laughter and joy and goodness of being in the extended family of God for a few precious hours. I didn't plan on any of that, but God did.

I should know by now that my plans are subject to change, but his are true and perfect every time. I should count on that, but I don't always. That's why it's good to sometimes find yourself in places where you never planned to be.

The mind of a man plans his way, but the LORD directs his steps.
PROVERBS 16:9, NASB

JUNE 12
A Twenty-Two Dollar Lesson

Mohammad held open the door of his yellow cab to me, but when he heard my destination, he was visibly irritated. Everything about his body language quickly changed when I said, "Gaylord Texan." He slung my bag into the back and slammed the door. Now unsure that I was willing to be his passenger, I paused and said, "Your choice. We don't have to go." He corrected me in a huff: "Yes. I do. If I refuse you, I can lose my license."

All of a sudden I wasn't feeling at all warm and fuzzy about our transaction. If there had been another yellow cab right behind his, I might have taken it. But Mohammad had a corner on the market, so I climbed in. In the backseat, I read the fare rate, although my driver had already said, "Twenty-two dollar minimum" twice. For the first mile or two I considered offering a well-chosen word about the importance of good customer service. But I'm glad I didn't.

I decided to see what I might learn from Mohammad, instead of what I might teach him. I studied the inside of the cab. I watched the route he took. In a matter of just a few minutes we arrived at the hotel. He stopped the cab, and I reached for my credit card. "That's twenty-two dollars," he said for the third time. "It wasn't very far," I ventured. "I don't understand why you didn't want to take me."

He softened visibly. "I should apologize," he said. "I've been at the airport all morning. You were my first fare, and it was only twenty-two dollars. If it had been longer, I could have made more. I will barely break even."

Now I got it. "Apology accepted," I said. And I meant it.

As I signed the ticket, I added a tip that was at least three times more generous than the grudging twenty-two-dollar ride I'd received warranted. I didn't say anything more to Mohammad except, "I hope your day gets better." Then I pulled my bag into the hotel lobby and said a silent prayer of thanks for him. Without even trying, he taught me to love extravagantly. Give without demanding reciprocity. Understand that I, too, have been a recipient of unmerited grace.

And be grateful.

Of His fullness we have all received, and grace upon grace.
JOHN 1:16-17, NASB

What Can I Do for You?

The phone rang early on a Saturday morning, but I'm glad I answered it. The caller quickly introduced herself, then told me she had been at an event earlier in the week where I had spoken. Cutting to the chase, I asked her, "What can I do for you?"

"Oh," she said, "I remember you said something about baseball, so I wanted to offer you some tickets for a game later this month." She told me she and her husband had Astros tickets they had not used *once* in the current season. At field level. Behind the home dugout. With a parking pass and club-level access.

I was becoming really, really grateful I'd answered the phone. Because I *love* baseball. Especially September baseball. And particularly September baseball when my home team is making a run for the wild card thanks to a white-hot August. I don't often go, because it's not in my budget. But on a random Saturday morning, a person I'd never met offered me four tickets I could not afford and a choice of two dates on which to use them, and then she offered to bring them to me to boot! We made arrangements to meet, and I thanked her sincerely and profusely. She'd enjoyed the talk I'd given so much, she said, that she wanted to do something nice for me in return. And she certainly had.

Later I thought about my skeptical attitude toward the phone call and how quickly it had changed. I anticipated being asked for something—instead I was given something. I imagined there was something I might do for the caller, but instead she meant to do an unexpected, undeserved kindness for me. There was no work to be done on my part. A gift was extended with no strings attached.

My unknown caller that morning became to me a living example of grace. God does for me what I could never do for myself. He bestows on me things I cannot afford and do not deserve. Wonderful, deep, solid, eternal, irrevocable things. That's what he does for me, when I can do nothing for him.

It is not what you and I do. . . . It is what *God* is doing, and he is creating something totally new, a free life!
GALATIANS 6:15, MSG

along for the Ride

My dog Burley likes road trips. His crate fits perfectly in the back of my car, and he's always ready to hop in. He never begs to see an itinerary or questions my route. He doesn't ask if we're there yet or whine for a rest stop or water or a toy. He gets settled in his crate, I get behind the wheel, and off we go. I'm in charge of the driving, and my sweet, four-legged boy is along for the ride.

I usually put something interesting in the crate to occupy his attention—a rawhide or a beat-up toy—but before long Burley's lying down, his eyes drooping closed and his breathing even and slow. He's not afraid to sleep while I navigate; he trusts me to get us to our destination.

You see where this is going, right?

My dog's faith puts mine to shame. In contrast to Burley, I wonder often what the driver (let's call him God) is up to, questioning the destination, the route, or both. I feel the need for frequent updates to reassure me that we are, in fact, making good progress. And in no way do I relish being loaded in for travel facing backward, with no visibility and no control over the trip.

God means to get me from point A to point B and to mature me in the process. I find it difficult to give myself to traveling blind—to say yes to the journey and say nothing more. I struggle to relax, and I fear that if I close my eyes we may veer hopelessly off track.

Even writing these words, I feel ashamed. I've followed God long enough that I should have more confidence in his way-finding skills. I should relish the trip and be relieved to not be minding the map. I should feel free to sigh and sleep—to snore, even—knowing he is getting us where we need to be. After all, he is the navigator. And I'm just along for the ride.

Jesus responded, "Why are you afraid? You have so little faith!" Then he got up and rebuked the wind and waves, and suddenly there was a great calm.
MATTHEW 8:26

Untweetable

I once told a friend that he'd know the end was near if he ever saw a tweet from me. So far he hasn't. No one has. If you're a person who lives life 140 clever characters at a time, by all means tweet often and be happy. Or if Instagram or Pinterest is your social medium of choice, well then post or pin away.

Tweet or no tweet, most days my life is quite ordinary. But it is good. I work for a living. I try to be a caring daughter, sister, aunt, and friend to the people I love most. I worship. I pray. I study and write and read. I tend to what author Kathleen Norris has called "the quotidian mysteries"—a fancy way of saying I cook and clean and shop and keep house—all very ordinary but necessary things. I don't do any of these things in the company of celebrities while wearing fabulous outfits. Not every day for me is a stellar hair day, and I believe, given a choice, barefoot is usually best.

You might think I lead a boring life—but I see things. Hear things. Ordinary, amazing things. I may talk or write about them. Or not. But I try to be fully present and live them first. I'm not bulletproof. I fall. Literally and figuratively. I mess things up, ask for forgiveness, and if I can, try to make them right. I get hurt and cry real tears, just like you. But #uglycrybefore6am isn't likely to be trending—nor is #justburnedmysecondpanofoatmeal or #wowthatreallyhurt!

Know this: every person you see today leads a life that is in some way exceptional. Whether they've tweeted it or not, everyone has a story. Don't assume just because they haven't advertised they have nothing of value to say. Instead of promoting your own prettied-up narrative or perusing those of a dozen dazzling others, I dare you to try this: turn to someone near you, look them in the eye, and say, "Tell me about *your* day. And not just the pretty parts. I really want to know." You might be delighted by what you learn.

You know what I am going to say even before I say it, LORD.
PSALM 139:4

Beauty Exposed

True beauty is not always in-your-face obvious. Instead, beauty can be downright covert. Consider almost any fairy tale. *Cinderella*? Beauty in soot-covered, orphaned, impoverished disguise. *Beauty and the Beast*? Well, the most surprising beauty belonged not to Belle but to the Beast—who was quite something to behold when his brave and caring heart was exposed.

In my book-filled study, a chalk-written imperative exhorts, "Expose beauty!" It's a reminder that artists don't *create* beauty. But on our best days we uncover it, highlight it, or point out where it might be hiding. We tease out *existing* beauty and truth, laying bare what might have been hidden from the naked, untrained eye.

I often tell people that my work, whether teaching or writing or collaborating, is most like holding an empty picture frame over a given spot and insisting, "Look right here. Don't miss this!" Granted, I'm a novice tour guide. But my commitment runs deep. When I see something beautiful, I want you to see it too.

In the lobby of a local high-rise, a part-time photographer (who works in the building by day as a securities marketer) displayed his first-ever show of stunning photographs. I walked through the exhibit with him, marveling at his eye—and his ability to expose the beauty of very ordinary things. This artist's subject matter? Old oil storage tanks. Where one person might have only seen rusty steel and lifeless shapes, this artist's eye revealed the oddly beautiful hues and textures, bathed and shaded with dappled afternoon sunlight.

He exposed well-hidden beauty.

In *The Beautiful Ache* I write, "True beauty isn't manufactured. It's reflected. And his perfect heart is the mirror that shows us how lovely we were meant to be and will, by His grace, one day become."*

The secret is to keep watching . . . because every day exposes beauty. I can't tell you where to look. But I can invite you to keep your eyes open for God's presence and to be willing to be surprised at the wonders he has in store.

Blessed GOD, Israel's God, the one and only wonder-working God!
PSALM 72:18, MSG

---

* Leigh McLeroy, *The Beautiful Ache* (Brenham, TX: Lucid Books, 2010), 162.

Those Softener Sheets

My mom added fabric softener to the laundry the old-fashioned way: standing over the washer as its rinse cycle began and pouring bright blue liquid into the rising water from the cap of the softener bottle. When I began doing laundry on my own, the method had gotten a lot neater: you simply tore a small softener sheet from a roll and tossed it with your wet clothes into the dryer.

These days the sheets are folded and packaged precut, not perforated, and a sheet in the dryer leaves your clothes smelling fresh and clean.

Plucking two softener sheets from the box and tossing them into the dryer after my damp clothes, I remembered the old way and how much trouble it seemed to be. Listening for the washer's rinse-cycle sounds demanded attentiveness, and pouring the liquid into the premeasured cap did too. Screwing the cap back on to the bottle usually required wiping up the blue liquid that dribbled down the side. It was at least a three-step process; now it's only one. But the result is much the same.

So somewhere between the washer and the dryer, I wondered what unexamined efficiencies I've worked into my spiritual life. What three-step processes have I collapsed into a single toss for the sake of time or user-friendliness or both? Have handy prayer acronyms or formulaic discipleship strategies made me any softer or sharper or deeper—or any more trusting or caring or wise?

I'm not knocking efficiency. But I don't want to be fooled into thinking domestic advances apply more widely than they should. Conditioning a heart (as opposed to a pair of scratchy Levis) takes time. Plenty of it. And putting the Word of God into my life requires standing over countless "cycles" with the Book in hand, waiting for its Author to show me what it means and why it matters deeply.

Changed lives don't result from offhand applications of holiness. A quick tumble with the Word is not the same as being steeped in it. And where my heart is concerned, it's the process—messy, inconvenient, and time-consuming as it is—that makes me more like Jesus.

The things you have learned and received and heard and seen in me, practice these things, and the God of peace will be with you.
PHILIPPIANS 4:9, NASB

The Things She Loved

Yes, I do sometimes scan the obituaries printed in the drastically shrinking daily newspaper. Last week a photograph caught my eye, and I learned this about the dear woman who died: "She loved photography, Coca-Cola, and unicorns." Yes, that's what it said. But the two words *she loved* made me wonder, *What if we were known by what* other people *think we love?* What would someone who observed my life over time (or even over an afternoon) imagine that I love? And if I were to be proactive and painfully truthful, how would I answer that two-word prompt about myself? "She loved . . ."

Because someday someone will fill in the blank.

Once, an old boyfriend and I exchanged "I love" lists. It was a sweet exercise and a fun way to tell each other a few of the things we most enjoyed. I remember items like Sousa marches and flannel sheets, border towns and crossword puzzles. Wearing clothes still warm from the dryer, the smell of freshly mowed grass, hot baths, and peonies. But my deepest, truest loves weren't on there. I can't speak for him, but I left off several of the things I love most.

I love Jesus. I have since I was eight. And I love him more each day that goes by. I love my family and my friends, and I believe they know it and love me back. I love beauty and truth . . . and anything that combines them *really* makes me happy. (In her poem "I died for beauty," Emily Dickinson said "the two are one," and I'm not so sure they aren't.) But if I could only fill in one blank, there's no contest: "Oh, how I love Jesus, because he first loved me."

Paul said he purposed to "know" nothing among the Corinthians but "Jesus Christ, the one who was crucified" (1 Corinthians 2:2). That was his one thing. Know Paul for an hour and you would know *that*. His obituary would have easily written itself. So what do you love? How would those who know you best answer the question? How would you? Because even now, we're becoming known by the things we love.

I decided that while I was with you I would forget everything except Jesus Christ, the one who was crucified.

I CORINTHIANS 2:2

Canyon Birds

I'm a novice birder, but for several days I've been watching the hummingbirds practicing frenzied levitation before their hanging feeders, the vultures slowly surfing the currents above and between the canyon walls, and the indistinguishable wrens and sparrows flitting from limb to limb everywhere I look, morning or evening.

There are 156 bird names listed in my pamphlet, along with codes for the frequency of their sightings: *a* for abundant, *c* for common, *u* for uncommon, *o* for occasional, and *r* for rare. The seasons in which they usually appear are included too, along with space to record a birder's recognition of them.

Although I'm a novice, I've been mesmerized by their trills, their flight, their songs at night. How good of God to have made so many of them. And beyond making them, how good he is to care for them as well. These canyon birds are not so productive, and neither have I been for the last few days. The solitary minutes and hours have not yielded up more than a few dozen pages, all told—but I feel a shifting that says they will. The seeds are there.

The words are not abundant yet, and as I reread them they seem quite common (*c*), but my God is decidedly uncommon (*u*) and his beauty is more than occasionally (*o*) fine. There's time for what he'll do, and I trust that he will provide. I can wait. The provision will come.

Wendell Berry writes,

So, friends, every day do something
that won't compute. Love the Lord. . . . .
Love someone who does not deserve it. . . .
Laugh.
Laughter is immeasurable. Be joyful
though you have considered all the facts. . . .
Practice resurrection.*

Whatever plans I came here with have scattered to the wind. Just the songs remain, and they are enough. They will always be enough.

Look at the birds of the air: they neither sow nor reap nor gather into barns, and yet your heavenly Father feeds them. Are you not of more value than they?
MATTHEW 6:26, ESV

* Wendell Berry, "Manifesto: The Mad Farmer Liberation Front," in *The Country of Marriage* (Berkeley: Counterpoint, 2013), 14–15.

The Mystery Basket

Four chefs. Four wicker mystery baskets. One hot mess of ingredients. Welcome to *Chopped*, the Food Network fun house where four competing chefs attempt to make order from culinary chaos.

You know, easy stuff like "Whip up a little appetizer from shad roe, vodka, Cheerios, and pickled pigs' feet. Time starts . . . now!"

Honestly, the fact that the competitors don't freeze like deer in headlights or run away from their baskets screaming seems quite miraculous to me. But these cooks have got game. They make something from whatever they're given and serve it up for judgment from appetizer to entree to dessert. Those who falter in the face of the mystery-basket ingredients are "chopped," until one winning chef is named *Chopped* Champion.

Imagine coming face-to-face with Spam, macerated cherries, pork rinds, and peanut brittle and creating from them something (anything!) edible. But the contestants do. Episode after episode. The only ironclad rule is this: use every ingredient in the basket.

Watching *Chopped* I see that, where God's sovereignty is concerned, I'm the mystery basket, presenting him day in and day out with ridiculous combinations of stuff that couldn't possibly be made God honoring or useful. But somehow he consistently, miraculously does both.

Somehow he takes my stubbornness and my weak will, my cynicism and my smart mouth, my worst mistakes and my truest hopes, and he doesn't just make do; he makes something beautiful and true. While I would surrender in the face of my rotten mess of raw material, he does not. He is undaunted by my lack of sweetness or my smelly sin. He rolls up his sleeves and begins to do what only he can do: make art from emptiness, harmony from dissonance, good from "Oh, good grief."

What he never does is refuse to love or use me when I open the basket before him and surrender. He brings all of himself to all of me, and the result is a good and glorious mystery, indeed.

I entrust my spirit into your hand. Rescue me, LORD, for you are a faithful God.
PSALM 31:5

The Heart Stretches

The human heart is a wonder. I don't mean its chambers and its arteries or the intricate rhythms and flows that sustain life, although those are mysterious and majestic enough. I mean the heart's amazing capacity to stretch and hold what it must, to take in more than might seem possible, then expand to receive still more.

I knew this as I sat by the bedside of my oldest aunt, an eighty-four-year-old woman who never lived more than a few miles from where she was born, picked cotton and ginned it, married twice but had no children, cared for her own aging parents until their deaths, and loved my sister and me like we were her own. On her nightstand sat the only personal artifact in a small and sterile room: a photograph of her husband, my uncle, who had passed away the year before.

Her world had been small. Her heart was not. My sister and I drove nearly fifteen hours to spend less than five hours with her. But every mile was worth the trip. She hardly spoke and seldom smiled. Her hair was snowy white, and her body was little more than bones. But her face said she knew us and remembered. I couldn't stop smiling at her. She had always made my heart glad.

"What are you thinking?" I asked her as she slowly ate her breakfast, even though she'd barely said a word the day before. I waited. She waited. Then she said, looking me full in the face, "Just how good it is to be with you." My heart broke a little at that, and at the sound of her voice. And in the breaking, more room was made.

The heart stretches—just when you think it might break. Ask the mother of an adolescent son with cerebral palsy, enduring weeks of surgery and rehab when other kids his age are off at summer camp. Ask the man who holds his dying brother's hand, and whose comforting presence is the only medicine left to give. The heart stretches. Pain clears the way for still more love.

Hearts that are held by Jesus do not break. They stretch. And when they do, they hold more love, not less.

I will give them one heart, and put a new spirit within them. And I will take the heart of stone out of their flesh and give them a heart of flesh.
EZEKIEL 11:19, NASB

Surprised by What's Inside

You never know what something holds. Not even your own back door.

I tried to close mine for the fourth or fifth time in a day, and when it swung wide to accommodate my happy mutt, the bottom fell out. Literally. The metal bar on the bottom of the door dropped off, and chunks of rotten wood crumbled onto the floor. Which is strange, because it's a *metal door*.

After weeks of subfreezing cold and rain, the old stuff inside the door turned loose, and so did the plate that was holding it in. It took me nearly five minutes to figure out where the wood had come from. Because a metal door isn't supposed to shed rotten wood . . . unless rotten wood is what's inside.

Silly me for thinking it was empty.

Sometimes I'm just as surprised by the stuff that comes out of me. I think I've emptied my heart of old hurts or mean memories or pet sins, and then they fall out at my feet—living proof that, even after all these years, I don't fully know the contents of my own heart. When the stress of everyday living reaches a tipping point and the constraints that keep stuff in give way, I see rubble I don't recognize at first. Then I realize it escaped my own heart.

I have three times more history (in years) with Jesus than without him, and I'm still surprised by what's inside. The things I've kept far from him are the very things I want most to be rid of and that he wants most to heal.

The rubble from my door—annoying as it was—has served its purpose. It has sent me searching other interiors for more things that need to go, so that God's fresh goodness has more room to burrow deep in me.

Something has gone wrong deep within me and gets the better of me every time. Is there no one who can do anything for me? Isn't that the real question? The answer is that Jesus Christ can and does. He acted to set things right in this life of contradictions where I want to serve God with all my heart and mind, but am pulled by the influence of sin to do something totally different.

ROMANS 7:20, 24-25, MSG

That Old Eraser Magic

After scrubbing my old pedestal tub with every cleanser known to man, I'd almost given up on it ever gleaming again. I'd tried gritty bath cleaners. Frothy foams. Strong-smelling bleaches. But no matter what I used, the water stains and the dingy not-quite-white smudges refused to budge. I kept the shower curtain tucked into the tub and hoped any hall bathroom guests were polite enough not to peek.

But lo and behold, in the cleaning products aisle I noticed the image of an old bald friend with an earring and a promise. Mr. Clean: the man who shows up in strangers' kitchens with his own mop. When I saw the bright-blue box that said "Magic Eraser," I immediately thought of my tub and tossed the tiny sponge into my cart. Nothing ventured, nothing cleaned.

I confess I was skeptical. The bright-white eraser sponge didn't look magical at all. But I wet one as instructed, knelt beside the tub, and started scrubbing. In a few seconds, the stains I couldn't erase to save my life were disappearing. When I got up off my knees, my tub was spotless (although the sponge was wrecked). All day long I kept pulling the shower curtain back to look again—as if the spots were hiding and would return if I were not vigilant.

Something I didn't expect to work did. A problem I had resigned myself to live with was eradicated. And I couldn't help but think of my own sin-stained heart and the amazing "magic eraser" that is the blood of Christ. It's hard to imagine that blood could be an efficacious cleansing agent, but it is. It's hard to believe that something as filthy as the rags of my own attempted righteousness could be made white as snow. But they have been. They are.

By Jesus' perfect, sinless sacrifice offered once for all, my stubborn sin has been erased. And by that same sacrifice he keeps on cleansing me when I soil what his blood has made clean. It's better than magic. It's grace. And it's amazingly, desperately, wondrously good.

If we say we have no sin, we deceive ourselves, and the truth is not in us. If we confess our sins, he is faithful and just to forgive us our sins and to cleanse us from all unrighteousness.
1 JOHN 1:8-9, ESV

Dead Man Walking

"How are you?" is a question most of us ask or answer several times a day. A former boss of mine used to reply to the query with a blustery "Perfect and improving!" (He was either terribly optimistic, bluffing, or both.) When someone asks me, I typically answer, "Fine, thanks" without thinking. My hair could be on fire, and I wouldn't change my story as it blazed.

Even though our culture is obsessively self-focused, we are seldom fully self-aware. We're not really cognizant of how we are. We tend to answer "How are you?" as if we'd been asked "How do you feel?"—imagining that our feelings are a true barometer of our spiritual reality. They are not.

The apostle Paul offers any believer a marvelous answer to this question, tucked into his letter to the church at Ephesus: we were once dead in our transgressions, and now we have been made alive in Christ. *How am I?* I am alive in Christ. I am loved by a God who is rich in mercy. I used to be dead in my sin, but now I am made alive together with God's Son, raised up and—in an already-but-not-yet kind of way—seated in the heavenly places. But to fully embrace this magnificent state of being, I must first embrace the stark fact that without Christ, I was dead. Not just unconscious or unmoving or resistant to his love . . . but lifeless. Flatlined. Unable to respond.

It's hard to think that we were once dead men and women walking, isn't it? Some of us considered ourselves pretty vibrant before we were brought to life in Christ. We may have appeared confident, successful, or favored, but looks can deceive. Dead is dead. And that's what you and I were before grace quickened our hearts. We believed that we were independent, autonomous agents of self-rule and that what turns out to be bondage was life. But it wasn't life at all.

You were dead in your trespasses and sins. . . . But God, being rich in mercy, because of His great love with which He loved us, even when we were dead in our transgressions, made us alive together with Christ.
EPHESIANS 2:1, 4-5, NASB

JUNE 25
Sharing and Personal Fruit

At the grocery store entrance where selected sale items are displayed, I saw this sign: "Personal Watermelons $2.99 ea." *Personal* watermelons? What's so personal about a watermelon?

The personal fruit beneath the sign was smaller than a regular melon—the ten-plus-pounders destined for happy picnics and summer backyard barbecues. Each personal watermelon was no bigger than a small cantaloupe, the obvious cue that *personal* meant "watermelon for one."

But who eats a whole watermelon alone?

A watermelon is practically a party announcement in a shopping cart that takes something akin to a village to lug, balance, slice, and serve. And that's the point. The invasion of the "personal" adjective in the produce aisle was new for me. Personal-sized fruit has apparently now joined single-entrée frozen meals, tiny one-serving cans of veggies, and single-packaged cuts of meat as a shopping-for-just-myself option. When did things not for sharing become so desirable?

The odd option of purchasing personal fruit served to remind me just how prevalent this culture of *me* has become and how comfortable *I've* become with it. I work on a personal computer (almost a redundancy now) and carry a personal collection of apps and music on my iPhone. (Funny, I never noticed the glaringly obvious *i* before.) I have nearly a dozen personal identification numbers swimming in my brain and just as many personal preferences registered hither, thither, and yon.

Because I live—and work—alone, I need to consciously resist the pull of the personal. I don't need a personal watermelon; I need more reminders to share. Before Jesus surrendered his life once and for all, he shared it again and again—and so should I. So here's my plan: I will not personalize what I might, with a little fore-thought and deliberation, share. At least once a week I will place something in my grocery cart that I can't consume alone. I will look for new ways to share . . . not just produce, but the fruit of Jesus' sweet life in me. Because we're made for him and for each other . . . and we have Person-al love to give away.

Do not forget to do good and to share with others, for with such sacrifices God is pleased.
HEBREWS 13:16, NIV

Risky Business

"Of all arguments against love," writes C. S. Lewis, "none makes so strong an appeal to my nature as 'Careful! This might lead you to suffering.'"* Lewis readily admits his own preference for what he calls "safe investments and limited liabilities."† *If only it were that easy.* At the same time, he also sees the danger of nurturing a steadfastly cautious heart: "The only place outside Heaven where you can be perfectly safe from all the dangers and perturbations of love," he writes, "is Hell."‡

Not much of a choice, is it?

Once you've loved deeply and lost—a friend, a significant other, a mate, a child, or even a pet—you're undeniably vulnerable. To love again is no assignment for the weak or timid. Loving with abandon demands courage, but it is surely a risk worth taking. "Go after a life of love as if your life depended on it," writes the apostle Paul, "because it does" (1 Corinthians 14:1, MSG).

God's story abounds with courageous characters who went hard after love when it would have been easier to retreat. There is Mary, the unwed teenage mother of God-in-the-flesh who trusted God's plan. Then there is Ruth the Moabite, who lost her husband then forsook her homeland to travel with her also-widowed mother-in-law to a place she'd never seen. She came to Israel as an exile and a beggar and became grafted into the lineage of Christ himself! Don't even get me started on Abraham: asked to sacrifice his long-promised son, Isaac, on a bonfire of unquestioned devotion. I can't fathom that kind of risky love.

I've read the stories. This kind of beyond-human-limits love is possible—but only when we know we are loved beyond all limits by God himself. We can be sure we are loved in just this way because God did for us what he did not, in the end, require of Abraham: he sacrificed his Son on our behalf.

Love is not safe. But God has loved us anyway. Will you take on the risky business of loving as you've been loved?

Beloved, let us love one another, for love is from God.
I JOHN 4:7, NASB

---

* C. S. Lewis, *The Four Loves* (New York: Houghton Mifflin Harcourt, 1991), 120.
† Ibid.
‡ Ibid., 121.

Everything Bar

I'd stopped in at a favorite neighborhood coffee shop—one *without* a green awning—with plans to sit and cradle a skim latte in a hot, bowl-shaped mug. As I stood at the counter waiting to pay and perused the sampling of baked goods before me, something called an "everything bar" caught my eye.

The everything bar was a vegan creation whose label assured me that it was "sin without the guilt." I can't confirm or deny that culinary assertion. I didn't buy one. I'm not a vegan, and I wasn't particularly hungry. But I have to confess, the thought of that sinful but guiltless confection stuck.

In real terms, "sin without the guilt" couldn't *be* more harmful.

Sin without remorse, without guilt, without shame, is the mark of the living dead: breathing men and women who sin—but who sense no connection between their sin and their own spiritual demise. To experience sin without the guilt is to deaden the spirit to the infinite love of God in Christ. It is to deny both the personal and the corporate consequences of my misdeeds, imagining that the sin that seems to promise "everything" in the moment will not cause something good to die.

To want sin without the guilt is to want cancer without the warning signs. The sting of guilt I feel when I've consumed an "everything bar" of greed or bitterness or lust or selfishness is not something to be rid of, but something to be treasured. My sickness at my sin is the bittersweet symptom of Christ's presence in my soul. As long as he is in residence, my sin will not go down well with me—and its precious ill effects will point me to repentance every time.

The one who first promised sin without the guilt labeled his treat in just the same way—and he knew full well that he was lying. His line—and his offerings—haven't changed one bit.

If you are living according to the flesh, you must die; but if by the Spirit you are putting to death deeds of the body, you will live.
ROMANS 8:13, NASB

Our Unprofilable God

If you've watched the news networks for long, you're familiar with the cast of expert commentators they utilize to explain the day's events. I'm most curious about the profilers—the psychologists, attorneys, authors, and academics whose specialty it is to get inside the head of someone and explain his or her behavior.

Explaining past behavior with an eye toward predicting the future is apparently big business—especially when the person being profiled is powerful and their actions are impactful. Maybe it *is* possible to profile a world leader or a political kingpin or even a criminal, but one World Leader can't be neatly profiled. Even if you look for clues that will allow you to predict God's future behavior, you are likely to be surprised.

It is true that God's character never changes. He is "the same yesterday, today, and forever" (Hebrews 13:8). But his ways are inscrutable. They are higher than ours. He loves truth so much that he would strike dead a couple of converts who misrepresented their generosity, and he loves holiness so much that a man who mishandles his Ark must die. But he also loves mercy so much that he allowed his own Son's suffering, and grace so much that whoever believes may receive not his or her due punishment but Another's righteousness.

Go figure.

See if you can say why floods come or children die or marriages fail, or why some of the lame and sick and sad are made better and some are not. I can't. The God I love and serve and seek to follow is knowable but in no way predictable. He's utterly exacting and yet unbelievably merciful. He receives sinners and abhors sin.

The moment I begin to try to hem him in with my meager understanding, he explodes the cords of my reason like so much silly string, leaving me awed, speechless, and rather glad to have a God who strikes me dumb with ease. I dare not say I know him inside out—I cannot. I examine his ways not to predict but simply to praise.

I shall remember the deeds of the LORD; surely I will remember Your wonders of old. I will meditate on all Your work and muse on Your deeds. Your way, O God, is holy; what god is great like our God? You are the God who works wonders.

PSALM 77:11-14, NASB

Following the Trail

We gathered at my house—my small group of seven sisters in Christ and me. On that evening our focus was on one member, our youngest. She was preparing to leave in a few days' time for a six-month, three-thousand-mile hike—a journey she'd been planning for more than a year. As the circled date on the calendar neared, we peppered her with questions, listened to her hopes and concerns, and did our best to wrap her in prayers that would outpace her steps and carry her along.

We sounded like seven mothers as we asked about safety measures, vitamins, water, food, clothing, and communication. (And bears. And bees. And sunscreen.) I'm sure all of us were thinking the same thing: *I'd never do that.* (I haven't encountered a travel challenge in years that didn't involve a bad flight or an unfortunate hotel.) She'd reckoned with almost everything—even with the possibility of not finishing what she began. She was clearly as ready as she would ever be.

And she didn't have a clue what the journey would bring.

None of us do. Even those of us whose lives are insulated by central air-conditioning and ATMs, by the regular routines of job and family, by familiar neighbors and well-stocked grocery stores. Because tomorrow will come, fully packed—and not by us. The trail—any trail—has its own mysteries, its own demands, and its own surprises. The only sure thing is the one whose hand we hold and whose steps we follow.

May nothing on your trail today seem larger than his presence. May no threat—however real—disturb your peace. And may every turn hold some trace of him that points you onward . . . and home.

Jesus told his disciples, "If anyone would come after me, let him deny himself and take up his cross and follow me. For whoever would save his life will lose it, but whoever loses his life for my sake will find it. For what will it profit a man if he gains the whole world and forfeits his soul? Or what shall a man give in return for his soul?"
MATTHEW 16:24-26, ESV

JUNE 30
Pray!

When I see a situation that worries me, I first wonder what I can *do* to make it better. What I can best *do* is pray.

As I sat at my desk one morning, I heard the wailing cry of my neighbor's young daughter. She was sobbing in the driveway, and her dad was calmly telling her to get in the car so he could take her to school. The commotion went on for several minutes, and I wondered what I could do. Should I go outside and try to help? Then it hit me: pray. Just pray. So I did. I prayed for my neighbor, that he would not lose patience or become angry. (I might have.) I prayed for his daughter, that God's Spirit would calm her and that her agitation would somehow unwind. I prayed that God would care for her if there was something upsetting happening at school, and protect her from anything she might fear. And in a few moments, the crying stopped.

As soon as it did, I wondered why I didn't routinely pray for situations unfolding around me, instead of wishing I might help or wondering if I should intervene. I should. In prayer.

Later, at my favorite coffee shop, a couple at a nearby table spoke angrily to one another. They were quiet at first. Then it got loud. I don't know if they were divorced or separated, but they seemed as far apart as two people could be. They were arguing over their children, who (thankfully) were not there. They barked at one another for several minutes before I began to silently pray. *Help him to hear her. Help her to control her anger.* The harsh words escalated, and then she abruptly pushed her chair back and left him sitting alone, midsentence. He pushed his coffee cup away, folded a section of the paper on the table between them, and followed after she had cleared the door.

I don't know what effect, if any, my prayers had. But I prayed anyway. It was the best I could do for them in those moments I would rather not have witnessed. As I finished my coffee, it occurred to me that perhaps I was there that morning for one purpose: to pray. Just to pray.

The effective prayer of a righteous man can accomplish much.
JAMES 5:16, NASB

July

More than Enough

Jail, I've discovered, is pretty much the way it looks on television. It's not in the best part of town. It's not exactly clean. A crowd, mostly female, assembles long before visiting hours begin. But I didn't go to jail because I wanted to authenticate my picture of it—I went because I couldn't comfortably stay home. Someone I cared for was there.

The inmate visit is TV-drama-like too. A deputy calls your name, and you enter a short corridor with five plastic chairs and a glass wall separating those five chairs from five others. What is not like television—what is far too real and gut wrenching—is seeing a kid you love walk in wearing orange clothes and a plastic wristband, head shaved and shoulders sagging. What will break your heart in an instant is seeing him sit down in front of you, look you in the eyes, and mouth the words "I'm sorry."

The oddest thing to me about jail is how ordinary it seems for those visiting. I was crying during my visit, but the people on either side of me were having conversations about everyday things as if no glass were separating them from their loved ones, as if coming downtown to talk to someone you love while a deputy holds your belongings were *normal*.

The worst thing about jail is the knowledge that the *real* bars, the ones that will not be opened in thirty or forty-five or ninety days, are the ones that surround the human heart. And the real prisoners aren't the ones who can't walk out the door. The real prisoners are the ones who can't feel forgiveness and find hope. Because without an abundance of both, most of these prisoners will almost surely return to their physical cells.

I don't ache because no key to my lost sheep's personal jail exists. I ache because I hold the key that would bring freedom, and I would willingly give it to him if he would only reach out his hand to take it. It's a grace-shaped key, and it's more than enough.

Where sin increased, grace abounded all the more, so that, as sin reigned in death, even so grace might reign through righteousness to eternal life through Jesus Christ our Lord.
ROMANS 5:20-21, NASB

JULY 2

Free and Easy

As the seconds turned into minutes, I could feel my anxiety rising. Why would a giant truck drive down a barely passable residential street overhung by branches, with no room to spare on either side? And why did *this one*, now hopelessly jammed between branches and pavement, have to attempt such an ill-advised maneuver in front of me? I was sandwiched in, blocked ahead and behind, and not happy about it.

If I didn't know it before, I certainly knew it then: I don't like being constrained or stuck. I'm the person who drives her own car so she can leave the party when *she's* ready to go. Who has (thanks be to God!) the sort of job that allows her to work on Saturday instead of Tuesday if that's what seems best. I rarely have nightmares, but if I do, they almost always involve being trapped somewhere and unable to flee.

Sometimes I get confused about freedom, though. I think it's about control. But it's not. It's about surrender. About self-forgetfulness. About maintaining keen focus on a task, on others, on God. I am never more trapped than when I am bobbing and flailing in a sea of me. It's dark there. And deep. And I am never freer than when I lose myself in creating or listening or teaching or loving—when all my energy is aimed *elsewhere*.

Full of worry, focused on my own pain, anxious to have my own needs met, I live in an ever-tightening vise. But focused on others, I can give myself as an offering of love on one or a hundred small altars, anywhere, anytime.

Lilies bloom without coercion. Sparrows fly without Zoloft. The sunrise arrives on time—not a minute too late or too soon—whether I watch for it fitfully or go to sleep. *Consider* these, Jesus said, and find comfort.

The free and unencumbered life I long for I cannot get by striving, holding, manipulating, or micromanaging. Only by surrendering my own interests, ego, and anxiety again and again and again will I ever be unstuck. Whomever the Son sets free is free indeed.

If you grasp and cling to life on your terms, you'll lose it, but if you let that life go, you'll get life on God's terms.
LUKE 17:33, MSG

Helpless

Coming out of a neighborhood restaurant, I saw something odd lying on the one-hundred-plus-degree sidewalk. As I veered away to keep from stepping on the thing, I looked more closely—at a naked, pink, dying baby bird. There was no broken shell nearby, but the bird was not old or fully formed enough to survive without the egg's protection. This hardly-a-bird was helpless to fly, barely breathing, and dying on the blistering sidewalk.

I cried all the way to my car.

Helpless is hard to see. When the helplessness is not fixable, it's even worse. But this world we live in is fallen and flawed—on its way to redemption by a beautiful King, yes, but in the meantime harsh. Unforgiving. Inhospitable. Unfair. Relationships decay from the inside out. Bodies fail. Leaders lie. Promises are broken, and the evil prosper. And baby birds fall from safety and die.

I hate the helplessness I feel at times, and I know others feel it as well. I wish I could make more things right. But I can't. I can't eradicate injustice or cure disease or eliminate hunger. I would have an almost impossible time falling asleep at night if not for this: my God is merciful. He sees, really sees, the helpless—just like I saw that bird. And he has every resource at his disposal to put wrong things right. Sometimes he works miracles. Sometimes he works through us. And sometimes he works behind the scenes, slowly, in ways we do not see. But his mercies are everlasting. They survive every sorrow.

So when hardness of the world breaks my heart, I can do three things: I can stop and see the tragic thing, give it my attention, and not look away. I can ask God, "What would you have me to do?" and then do it. And I can thank him for embodying mercy in the form of a bleeding Son, by whose stripes you and I and a hurting world may be healed. Praise him. His mercy endures forever.

The LORD is king forever and ever; the nations perish from his land. O LORD, you hear the desire of the afflicted; you will strengthen their heart; you will incline your ear to do justice to the fatherless and the oppressed, so that man who is of the earth may strike terror no more.
PSALM 10:16-18, ESV

It's Not about the Book

An inveterate people watcher, I was delighted with the opportunity to attend a national publishing conference and observe writers interact with their world apart from the printed page. Some authors engaged the persons seeking their signature; others barely acknowledged their presence.

One ninety-year-old teacher/writer/theologian/author arrived alone a mere five minutes late for his signing, apologizing in a soft voice to the line of folks already snaking around the signing booth. "I'm a little slow," he said in a barely British accent. "So sorry." Then he removed the lid from his pen, smiled at the first person in line, and reached inside his tweed jacket for a decidedly untrendy pair of glasses. "I'm torn," he said to her. "If I put these on, my handwriting will look nicer, but I won't see your face as well." Then he began to inscribe her name in the book with much greater care than he wrote his own.

I witnessed another author sign half a dozen books before giving the first one away. He simply signed one book and pushed it down to the end of the desk, leaving it there to be retrieved while he efficiently signed the next. He seemed confident he had mastered a system for dealing with his public. It was all about the book for him, but for the people in line, it was about the *moment*.

A day earlier, I'd heard Eugene Peterson speak on the subject "What Are Writers Good For?" His conclusion was that writers are good for tending to things using revelatory language. Their calling is to a slow process not unlike gardening, he said, or spreading manure. "Manure is not a quick fix," he said, "but it's the stuff of resurrection, and God is not in a hurry."

If you're a God follower, hear this: it's not about what you do or what you work with. It's about the everyday moments in which you can embody Christ, bringing him into each human interaction with grace. Are you an accountant? It's not about the spreadsheet. A carpenter? It's not about the cabinet. A musician? It's not about the song. Today will offer a moment in which you can be present to another soul. In which you can incarnate the Word made flesh. It's not about the book.

He must become greater; I must become less.
JOHN 3:30, NIV

I am the Lion

I never used to be afraid. I've lived alone in a big city my entire adult life, traveled halfway across the world and back by myself, started a business from nothing with no safety net, skydived from thirteen thousand feet, and stepped up to speak in front of perfect strangers more times than I can count. For as long as I can remember, I've leaped first and panicked later.

But now I've begun to worry about the ordinary things that keep a person up at night (deadlines, illness, finances) and other, unknown things that seem to lurk about the edges of my consciousness. I'm more aware of evil than I've ever been, more uncertain about the future than I'd like. I am not fearless anymore.

Events of any given day can cause a tightening in my chest and a desperate feeling of anxiety. One reminded me of a passage from C. S. Lewis's *The Horse and His Boy*. Shasta, the protagonist, feels something following him. Frightened, he finally asks, "Who are you?" The presence answers, "One who has waited long for you to speak." When the presence invites him to share his sorrows, Shasta describes how he ran away and was chased by lions, how he swam for his life and then was chased by another lion in the desert. "Don't you think it was bad luck to meet so many lions?" he asks.

His companion answers, "There was only one lion." When Shasta questions this, his companion says, "I was the lion."* In every instance Shasta had felt fear, a lion had been near—not hunting him, but protecting him.

A lion sleeps beside my bed. Nothing can touch me when he is near. He guards my sleep and has shadowed me through every waking trial and victory of life. He is terrible and beautiful and full of light—and his very breath makes every other fear seem small.

One of the elders said to me, "Stop weeping; behold, the Lion that is from the tribe of Judah, the Root of David, has overcome so as to open the book and its seven seals."

REVELATION 5:5, NASB

---

* C. S. Lewis, *The Horse and His Boy* (New York: HarperCollins, 1954), 163–64.

Who's Your Daddy?

The phrase "Who's your daddy?" can mean, among other things, "Who's got your back?" The answer can make decisions more clear and calm countless anxieties. That's because our daddy bestows our identity.

Ages ago, long before anyone was coolly asking, "Who's your daddy?" someone was answering. His name was Paul, and he was telling dear friends of his—friends who seemed to have forgotten—who their daddy really was. "God sent his Son . . . to buy freedom for us who were slaves to the law, so that he could adopt us as his very own children. And because we are his children, God has sent the Spirit of his Son into our hearts, prompting us to call out, 'Abba, Father'" (Galatians 4:4-6).

Abba for Paul meant *daddy*. It's a child's word for his beloved father. Intimate. Connected. Familiar. Sweet. It reveals a sure and certain relationship, one that offers security and comfort. When our hearts cry out in confusion or pain or fear, the automatic response is "Abba!" or "Daddy!"

So who's *my* daddy? He's the one whose name I call when I need help or hope or healing. My daddy, and yours, is the one we run to when, as Martin Luther wrote, "the Law scolds us, sin screams at us, death thunders at us, the devil roars at us." Luther knew that "in the midst of the clamor the Spirit of Christ cries in our hearts: 'Abba, Father.' And this little cry of the Spirit transcends the hullabaloo of the Law, sin, death, and the devil, and finds a hearing with God."*

Abba may be a small word, but it speaks volumes. I may be in trouble, and help may seem far away, but when push comes to shove, I know I am his child. Who's my daddy? *He* is. And when I forget, my elder brother Paul reminds me that I am adopted and I belong. Who could ask for more?

Our Father who is in heaven, hallowed be Your name. Your kingdom come. Your will be done, on earth as it is in heaven.
MATTHEW 6:9-10, NASB

---

* Martin Luther, *A Commentary on St. Paul's Epistle to the Galatians* (1535), trans. Theodore Graebner (Grand Rapids, MI: Zondervan, 1949), chap. 4; available at https://www.ccel.org/ccel/luther/galatians.vii.html.

Waiting in the Dark

When I drove up the driveway in the early afternoon and hit the garage door opener, nothing happened. Thinking I hadn't pressed it hard enough, I pressed again. Nothing. Then I thought, *Power's out.* It was. And it would be for the next ten hours.

Because of the time of day, I couldn't be sure if my neighbors were affected or if the outage was my own special gift. I let Burley out in the yard for a run, grabbed my phone, and dialed the number on my last utility bill. Busy. Busy the next fifteen to twenty times I tried it. Finally it rang through to the phone-tree gauntlet, which recognized none of the identifying information I was prompted to give. Flunking out of Phone Tree 101, I was transferred to a breathing human.

The representative said she was sorry for the inconvenience, but her screen showed that power should be restored to my area by six o'clock that evening. I gathered up my candles and matches, looked for a flashlight, and then phoned a friend to see if she might meet me for an early dinner.

When I arrived back home at dusk, there was still no power. Burley wasn't bothered—he was just glad to see me. But I was beginning to be agitated. For the next six hours I tried phoning the utility company for an update. Nothing. When my call finally went through, I waited on hold for forty-five minutes, then hung up to go recharge the phone in the car.

It was dark outside. It was dark inside. And I was in the dark about when that might change. I read by flashlight. I called my sister. I walked outside a few times to see who else on my street was affected.

Here's what I learned waiting in the darkness: helplessness bothers me. Being ignored by your energy provider is no fun. Knowing that others are in the dark too doesn't make much difference. The moment that the lights go on (even if it's midnight) is satisfyingly sweet. And no matter how dark my house gets, I'm certain that somewhere, Someone sees.

If I say, "Surely the darkness shall cover me, and the light about me be night," even the darkness is not dark to you; the night is bright as the day, for darkness is as light with you.
PSALM 139:11-12, ESV

a Matter of Flying

I couldn't help but hear. And I really, *truly* didn't want to. But the two people seated near me did not keep their voices low. So I heard plenty. One phrase stopped me cold: "I could take the cheating. But not the lying about it." The other person quickly concurred that cheating was, well, inevitable. But lying was indeed abominable.

Isn't it interesting where we choose to draw the line when our morality is a self-constructed house of cards? If the partners of these two had cheated on them and then told the truth about it, would *that* have been perfectly fine?

I was saddened and repulsed and convicted all at once. Saddened by the darkness of the lives of these two. Repulsed by the coarseness of their conversation. But mostly I was convicted about my *own* propensity to make up ridiculous rules and try to live by them. I desperately need an outside-myself morality because my homemade one is hopelessly corrupt. I am thankful that I know this. I want to get better, but I can't on my own. C. S. Lewis writes,

> Morality is a mountain which we cannot climb by our own efforts; and if we could we should only perish in the ice and unbreathable air of the summit, lacking those wings with which the rest of the journey has to be accomplished. For it is *from* there that the real ascent begins. The ropes and axes are 'done away' and the rest is a matter of flying.*

I am bound by gravity and weighted down by Adam's sin and my own. But my God has bright wings of grace, and he swoops low and fast to rescue us when the ropes and axes of self-reliance and self-approval give way. Then the rest "is a matter of flying!"

> God made Christ, who never sinned, to be the offering for our sin, so that we could be made right with God through Christ.
>
> 2 CORINTHIANS 5:21

---

* C. S. Lewis, "Man or Rabbit?" in *God in the Dock: Essays on Theology and Ethics* (Grand Rapids, MI: Eerdmans, 2014), 113–14.

Truer Than I Feel

The importance of how I feel on any given day about any given subject is highly overrated. I'm a feeling person, yes, but the truest thing about me is not how I feel. There is something truer than my emotions. Years ago (when I suspected my feelings might be lying to me) I began a list. I made two columns on a single sheet of paper and labeled them "How I feel" and "What I know is true."

In the first column I recorded the half-truths, fears, and insecurities Satan frequently whispers to me. In the second I wrote promises, assurances, and assertions from God's Word, believing that what God says about me or my circumstances trumps how I feel when a discrepancy exists between the two. I don't deny my feelings. I air them like dirty laundry. Sometimes lies appear far weaker in my own handwriting than they sound rattling around my heart and head.

So an entry on the left-hand side of my list might say, "Forgotten." But the corresponding entry on the right would say, "Can a mother forget her nursing child? Can she feel no love for the child she has borne? But even if that were possible, I would not forget you!" (Isaiah 49:15). Or the right column might read, "Fearful of the future" and the left "For I know the plans I have for you," says the LORD. They are plans for good and not for disaster" (Jeremiah 29:11).

See how it works?

Mike Mason calls love "an earthquake that relocates the center of the universe."* Because of the great love with which God has loved me, I am able to relocate the center of my universe from my unreliable emotions to God's very reliable truth.

Someone asked me once if my list has changed over time. It has certainly grown longer. The way I feel—the left-hand column—changes with the wind. But that right-hand column, well, steady as she goes. Because no matter how I feel, I have chosen the way of truth and set my heart on God's law (see Psalm 119:30). And Jesus Christ is the same yesterday, today, and forever (see Hebrews 13:8).

Fix your thoughts on what is true, and honorable, and right, and pure, and lovely, and admirable. Think about things that are excellent and worthy of praise.

PHILIPPIANS 4:8

---

* Mike Mason, *The Mystery of Marriage: As Iron Sharpens Iron* (Portland, OR: Multnomah, 1985), 37.

The Word on the Street

Words are the raw material I shape each day to pay the mortgage, keep puppy chow in the pantry, and maintain a reasonably full gas tank. Sometimes those word duties are exciting and their end result beautiful; sometimes not. I've written books I've delighted in and books that were a chore. But all told, the books are just a tiny part of the word trade I dabble in each day. Much more ordinary (and frequent) are the functional, practical words that may not inspire anyone but are nonetheless useful to those who are, for instance, seeking to understand the intricacies of a health care plan.

On their own, viewed on a dictionary page, words don't mean much. But strung together and placed in context, they mean everything. In the right hands, using the right voice, everyday words can become something special.

I considered this the other day as I was reading my Bible. It's an extraordinary book full of ordinary words. But voice and context (and supernatural inspiration) make the book sing. Its main Father/Son/Spirit character gets most of the best lines, but lesser characters (Moses, David, Peter, Paul) make out pretty well with theirs, too.

And as I was thinking about how much more glamorous it seems to say, "I'm working on a new book" than "I'm working on a two-paragraph bio for a business plan," it hit me: Jesus never wrote a book. He didn't even make *that* many speeches. He simply went about his Father's business day by day, speaking common street words to the ordinary folks he met. Words like "Your faith has made you well" (Mark 5:34) and "I thirst" (John 19:28, ESV) and "A certain man had two sons" (Luke 15:11, KJV).

And every word was perfectly timed and chosen. Rightly spoken and full of meaning.

You and I might not *think* we're wordsmiths composing a story—but word on the street is, we are. We're building, blessing, correcting, comforting, instructing, asking, offering, and probably even offending word by word, sentence by sentence. The real story we have to tell is being written—not in books or speeches or carefully composed paragraphs—but on the most ordinary days of our lives.

A word fitly spoken is like apples of gold in a setting of silver.
PROVERBS 25:11, ESV

The Power of Suggestion

"Got any plans for this weekend?" my friend Sal asked.

I'm pretty sure I told him I'd be camped in front of a big screen with like-minded friends, wearing something maroon and watching the Aggies whip up on their opponent of the week.

"How about you?" I countered.

"Fayette County Fair in La Grange," he said, "to see ZZ Top." For those who are not of that era, ZZ Top is a rather eccentric and storied Texas band who began making music in the 1970s, and they haven't quit yet. Arguably their most famous song is a tune called "La Grange" about the tiny Texas town where they'd be playing.

As soon as Sal said the words *ZZ Top* and then *La Grange*, a guitar riff went off in my head and *kept on* playing. Just those few words were a powerful enough suggestion to keep me humming for the rest of the day. I went to bed that night with a healthier respect for the power of suggestion.

You and I are *created* with the power to suggest. We can remind ourselves. Speak to ourselves. Encourage ourselves. Fill our hearts and our ears and our eyes with more sensory input than our lifetimes could possibly catalog. So it makes sense, doesn't it, that we should be selective and wise about the "tracks" we fill our minds with?

The ancient Jews (along with some modern Orthodox Jews) had a practice of binding words—the words of God—to their foreheads and arms using strips of leather and tiny boxes called phylacteries. That may seem strange to Western eyes, but the Jews meant to remember what God had said—to keep his commands and his precepts at the ready.

I carry his words with me, too—but they're much less obviously stored. I hide them in my heart and let them suggest to me what counts, what matters, what to love, where to look, when to speak and to whom. All day, every day, they powerfully suggest that I am my Father's and that this is *his* world. I wouldn't have it any other way.

Summing it all up, friends, I'd say you'll do best by filling your minds and meditating on things true, noble, reputable, authentic, compelling, gracious—the best, not the worst; the beautiful, not the ugly; things to praise, not things to curse.

PHILIPPIANS 4:8, MSG

Bigger and Bigger

I held my first Bible in my hands, and it felt smaller—much smaller—than I remembered. My many adult-sized editions of the same book are stuffed to the brim with notes and maps and study helps, and most barely fit in the crook of my elbow, much less the palm of one hand. This one, by contrast, seemed minuscule. What is the odd phenomenon by which childhood things seem to shrink in contemporary light? So many souvenirs from the past seem to grow smaller with the years—all out of proportion to the woman I am today. But the God of my yesterdays never shrinks. He grows bigger and bigger with each passing year.

Once upon a time he was small enough to squeeze into my eight-year-old heart. Today I know that the sea and the sky cannot contain him. Way back when, I discovered he could be trusted with smallish disappointments and middle-sized fears; today I know he reconstitutes great big broken hearts and that there is no threat from within or without that can cow him.

I used to say when people asked to hear my testimony that I met my Savior young and simply grew up with him. But now I see that while I was growing up with him, he was outgrowing me at every turn.

What a relief that my God does not shrink as I grow older. Every year I find him bigger. Bigger than disasters and sickness, bigger than broken promises and bruised hearts. Bigger even than my own sin and selfishness. Hymn writer Frederick Faber says it this way in "The Eternal Spirit":

> *Ocean, wide-flowing Ocean, Thou, of uncreated love;*
> *I tremble as within my soul I feel Thy waters move.*
> *Thou art a sea without a shore; awful, immense, Thou art;*
> *A sea which can contract itself within my narrow heart.*

Time may play tricks on my perspective or make of my memory a flimsy scrim, but my God just keeps growing bigger. I'll never outpace him or outgrow my need for him, and he'll never prove smaller than I remember. That's a sure and certain mercy and a joy forevermore.

Mighty God! Far beyond our reach! Unsurpassable in power and justice! It's unthinkable that he'd treat anyone unfairly. So bow to him in deep reverence, one and all! If you're wise, you'll most certainly worship him.
JOB 37:23-24, MSG

angry Words

Leaving a local restaurant after a pleasant lunch, I noticed a scrap of paper pressed on my car's windshield, secured by one wiper blade. It was a handwritten note, and the greeting was not standard: "You stupid [bleep]," it began. "Learn how to park so I can get in my car, you [bleeping bleep]."

I didn't remember having difficulty getting into the spot I'd parked in, and clearly the vocabulary-limited writer was now gone, because the driver's side of the car next to mine was accessible. I can't count the number of times I've returned to my car only to have to climb in on the passenger's side. I'm surprised there was never a *Seinfeld* episode about it. Even so, I've never left an angry message like this in retaliation.

The note felt like an attack from an invisible assailant, and it hurt. I would have apologized, but I couldn't. My verbal assailant's act of "word rage" left me no room for response. And truth be told, it made me a little heartsick. I thought about the words off and on for the rest of the day and wondered about the person who left them. Did the person feel better after spewing profanity in my direction? Were they any less inconvenienced? Did they regret their outburst later or continue the day angry: snapping at others, flipping the bird in traffic, slamming doors, and squealing tires? How much anger vented is enough?

Words are strong, powerful things. They live longer than their spoken sound or their written ink or the recycle bin on my computer. They have staying power. And because I know I have left too many of the wrong sort behind and need to think before I do so again, I'm actually becoming sort of grateful for the message my unseen attacker left me. Their angry words weren't meant to remind me, but they did: "May the words of my mouth and the meditation of my heart be pleasing to you, O LORD, my rock and my redeemer" (Psalm 19:14).

And let me know when I, too, have said more than enough.

With the tongue we praise our Lord and Father, and with it we curse human beings, who have been made in God's likeness. Out of the same mouth come praise and cursing. My brothers and sisters, this should not be.

JAMES 3:9-10, NIV

The Life I Owe

Once, at a favorite coffee spot near my house, I participated in a job interview. I was a silent participant and an uninvited one, but when the person less than two feet from you takes a call and embarks on a nearly hour-long review of her career to date, you feel involved—whether you mean to be or not.

There were other things to do, of course: finish the cup of coffee sitting before me, review notes for a meeting of my own later in the day, or just gaze out the window at the neighborhood as it stretched itself awake. But even as I attended to these few things, I couldn't help but overhear.

For the record, I would have hired her after the first quarter hour. She was focused, articulate, and assertive on her own behalf, yet not annoyingly so. Her tone was crisp and engaging. She represented herself well. *This girl deserves a shot,* I thought. *Hire her.*

At some point during the interview, I looked down at the Moleskine open before me and at the marker kept inside to cue the day. My eyes fell on the words of the old hymn "O Love That Wilt Not Let Me Go": "I give Thee back the life I owe," the marker read. *The life I owe.* This life I have to offer up to God is flawed, unworthy, and woefully inexperienced in holiness or even good works. When God came looking for me, I didn't have the sense to search for him. And when Christ invited me to follow, there was nothing on my résumé to suggest that I would be an asset to his Kingdom! But he extended the offer nonetheless. *Come. Follow me. Receive as a gift my so-great salvation.*

I never deserved to be his disciple. Never. He "put his love on the line while . . . we were of no use whatsoever to him" (Romans 5:8, MSG). Yet the offer came. So my response is simple. I accept. Here, today, Jesus, is all I have for you: this ordinary life I owe. It's yours for whatever purpose you desire, to be spent in love and joy and gratitude, moment by moment, this day, for you.

God demonstrates His own love toward us, in that while we were still sinners, Christ died for us.
ROMANS 5:8, NKJV

The Death of Dabbling

I've never accomplished anything significant by dabbling. Have you? The list of things I've dabbled in is long, but I can assure you I am not even minimally proficient at any of it. For example, I'll never perform in *The Nutcracker* or attend a showing of my original oil paintings or win yard of the month. Trust me.

Dabbling is quite common these days, but persevering is not. In fact, perseverance is an alien concept in a culture that demands constant gratification in almost every realm. Because we don't wait for much, we don't know much about persevering. Instead we dabble, flitting from one thing to another, looking for the quick payoff.

To keep at one thing (as opposed to dabbling at everything) requires a belief that the process is at least as worthwhile as the goal, and that the results are in God's hands. King David knew about valuing the process. He learned early on that he would be Israel's ruler, but it took his predecessor a long time to get the memo. Walking the path as it unfolded was an exercise for David in forward-looking faith, and each step prepared him for the role he would one day assume.

Our spiritual forefathers learned to prepare for the unseen, to dwell in uncertainty, to live with unfinished dreams, to participate in miracles, to choose the hard road for eternal profit, and to follow God into any impossibility.

Sometimes as he fulfills his plans for me, God prunes a dream or allows suffering or failure or loss or disappointment. It's not the end. God's part is to steer my course; my part is to persevere in it: to daily commit to him all my works and ways, believing that he will establish me and accomplish what is right.

I've dabbled in a lot of things—but I don't want to dabble in my relationship with him. I want the real, delicious fruit that comes from following him all the way home.

Time will fail me if I tell of Gideon, Barak, Samson, Jephthah,
of David and Samuel and the prophets, who by faith conquered
kingdoms, performed acts of righteousness, obtained promises,
shut the mouths of lions, quenched the power of fire, escaped the
edge of the sword, from weakness were made strong, became mighty
in war, put foreign armies to flight.
HEBREWS 11:32-34, NASB

Ten Degrees

Sometime in 2008, a passenger boarded a Lufthansa jet traveling from Mumbai to Dallas. He chose the airline—and its first-class section—because he was told its seats would lie flat, and he planned to sleep through at least part of the twenty-hour journey.

He soon discovered he had been duped. The seat he purchased did not lie completely flat. Instead of the expected 180 degrees, he was only able to recline *170 degrees*, causing him considerable distress—so much that he sued the airline for damages, claiming "agony and mental anguish." (He also noted that his first-class seat reclined only *slightly* more than those in economy—a fact that no doubt contributed to his mental anguish.)

Seven years later, the passenger's claim was settled in his favor, although he was only reimbursed for the cost of his flight, and the airline was required to deposit a modest fine into a consumer redress account.

Seriously? Agony and mental anguish over ten lousy degrees? Seven years of legal wrangling for $1,000? At what point during those seven years did the passenger's anger finally subside? I secretly prided myself on not being the kind of person who gets her knickers in a serious knot over nothing.

At least until I asked myself, *So, Leigh—what's* your *ten degrees?*

What is the thing you cannot let go of, even though the offense is a distant memory, and in hindsight, the anguish was a mere blip on the radar? What still makes you seethe, thinking you were tricked or taken advantage of? What "lie-flat" promises were made to you that you believe were malicious or fraudulent? And— have you *really* forgiven and forgotten?

I scoffed at this traveler's ridiculous seven-year legal snit for all of five minutes. That's how long it took to realize my own, better-hidden sense of entitlement and outrage at being cheated out of ten degrees of *something*. Anything. Or having something I think I deserved withheld.

I'm all about the justice. Until *I* need some mercy.

Thankfully, Jesus has justly settled the account of my offenses against God and lavished upon me the mercy I need but have not earned. He's all about justice and mercy, too. And not just for ten degrees of my fatal "gone wrongness." For all of it. Always.

While we were still helpless, at the right time Christ died for the ungodly.
ROMANS 5:6, NASB

Chosen

I'm not always good at hope. Unless it's for someone else. In that case, I'm the most hopeful person on the planet. My hope for others is sincere and sometimes even contagious. But for myself, not so much. I *want* to hope. And sometimes I allow myself that secret luxury. But I mostly keep my longings to myself. Because disappointment and shame are so tightly woven together for me that when push comes to shove, it's almost impossible to separate the two. If I hope out loud and my hopes don't materialize, I'm embarrassed that I allowed myself to hope at all.

I'd been interviewing for a coveted job assignment and expected to hear soon whether I'd be selected. I wanted the work. I asked friends to pray. I'd updated family members who I knew were pulling for me. And when the wide field of candidates narrowed to two, I actually felt hopeful. Then I got the news I was waiting for, but I wasn't the one chosen. Suddenly, I was in junior high again, wishing I could have done better at basketball tryouts. Or in my late twenties, longing to be married and wondering why I wasn't chosen, *period.*

In times like these, I find comfort in knowing I was chosen by an all-or-nothing God. He didn't just want a little of my heart; he asked for the whole thing. And he doesn't just mean to use a speck of the gifts he's given. He means to tap them dry. He didn't pursue me and woo me to no purposeful end. He chased me and won me to make me his forever. *He picked me. I am chosen.* Now and then I forget what that means and let other, lesser decisions rack my heart and twist my thoughts into tight, confusing, shame-filled knots, but he doesn't let me go. Not now. Not ever. I'll be disappointed again if I dare again to hope. Everyone is at one time or another. But that cannot change this one, glorious, solid truth: I'm his. Always.

Long before he laid down the earth's foundations, he had us in mind, had settled on us as the focus of his love, to be made whole and holy by his love. Long, long ago he decided to adopt us into his family through Jesus Christ.

EPHESIANS 1:4-5, MSG

Small Things + Great Love = Mighty Impact

Cassie started working as a waitress at Avalon Diner when I was beginning grade school—and she retired after fifty years of faithful presence in the same job.

Nearly every Friday for twenty-five of those fifty years, my father and I sat across from one another at "Cassie's booth" for breakfast. And although she could write up orders, pour coffee, and balance plates with the best of them, she wasn't just our waitress. She was family.

When I found out Cassie was retiring, my heart sank. I simply couldn't imagine our Fridays at Avalon without Cassie's banter, her smile, her playful teasing of my dad, her questions about family and work and—finally—the "What you want this mornin', baby?" that I can just about hear in my sleep. No menus. She knew we didn't need them, and neither did she. And if dad couldn't always remember or decide what it was he wanted—she reminded him.

On Cassie's last day we were settled in our regular booth, and she was on her feet, moving through the morning crowd as cheerfully as always. But as person after person streamed in with cards and flowers and hugs, what I'd never realized became very clear: Cassie wasn't just our favorite. She was everyone's. She'd loved a lot of people year after year the very same way she'd loved us. Her son Rodney was there, and she pointed him out so I could say hello. He told me he'd walked his mama to the bus stop on her first day at Avalon and then walked to his own stop to catch the school bus. "I told her then that on her last day, I'd drive her to work and drive her home," he told me. "So here I am."

"We sure do love your mama," I told him.

"She loves you, too," he replied. And then he added, "She's my role model."

Cassie's my role model too: small things done with great love equal mighty impact over time—no matter where you find yourself. And it's the people you meet along the way that matter most of all.

———

Don't just do the minimum that will get you by. Do your best.
COLOSSIANS 3:23, MSG

Drive Through (or Not)

If you are young in the faith, and if the epic fail of one who is *not* young in the faith would in any way rock your world, stop reading now. Because this is not going to be pretty.

I drove through a fast-food establishment to get a cold drink, talked to the box, then pulled around the building to see three cars—two in an outside lane and one ahead of me in mine. I paid at the first window and was given my drink there too. Then a car pulled in behind me and I had no way to exit, so I waited. And waited. An employee came out and took money from a customer in the first car of the opposite lane. Smelling opportunity, I rolled my window down and asked him if he could help me get out, since I had paid and had my order. He looked at me and laughed. Then he went back inside.

I honked. Several times. No one came out. Nothing moved. I felt anger rising in me. I know my face was red. I might have been shaking a little. The next time the runner-employee came out, I opened my car door and yelled, "Get me OUT OF HERE!" He ignored me. So I followed him in the service door. (Yes. I did.) And I yelled at the nonplussed crew of workers: "I've paid my money. I have my drink. I've been here for fifteen minutes. GET. ME. OUT. OF. HERE." A manager told me they were busy filling other people's orders, and I would just have to wait. In my car, not in there. I slammed the door and went back outside, seriously considering just leaving my car in park and walking away.

The drive-through traffic jam was all it took for me to completely abandon my sanctification and make a total fool of myself. I'm telling you this because it's important to know that those of us who love Jesus deeply often fail him miserably. And because it never, ever ceases to humble and amaze me that *Jesus loves even badly behaved me.*

God made Christ, who never sinned, to be the offering for our sins, so that we could be made right with God through Christ.
2 CORINTHIANS 5:21

Proliferating Beauty

The city trail I like to walk stretches for miles along a winding bayou. It is surprisingly quiet, safe in daylight, and mostly flat. The views, however, are only average—until the wildflowers begin to bloom. Although they fade quickly in the summer's heat, they are lovely while they last.

On one early-morning walk, I noticed a sign posted along the trail by the city's parks department. The headline read, "Proliferating Beauty," and below it were pictures of several species of wildflowers. The sign noted that the wildflowers that "proliferate beauty" along the bayou are functional, too. They apparently save tax dollars by decreasing the need for mowing, and their roots deter erosion of the soil. So these flowers are not just for show. They're working, too.

The sign was probably erected to assure me that my tax dollars are being wisely spent. I get that. But I couldn't stop thinking about "proliferating beauty" as a metaphor for the gospel. It is, beyond doubt, the most beautiful story I know. Its narrative arc is nothing short of breathtaking. And the heart of the story, that "God so loved the world," never ceases to slay me with its simple power. But the gospel is a hardworking story too. It takes sin by the throat and wrestles it limp and lifeless. It makes strong saints out of weak and wayward men and women. It slowly, quietly, sometimes imperceptibly, is making all things new.

The gospel is not just beautiful. It is deeply powerful, productive, and transformative. I know, because it is transforming me. I'll admit I was taken at first by its wild beauty. But the longer I've lived with it, tarried with it, told and retold it to myself and others, the more I see that its beauty proliferates *life* everywhere it goes.

Teach me your decrees, O LORD; I will keep them to the end. Give me understanding and I will obey your instructions; I will put them into practice with all my heart. Make me walk along the path of your commands, for that is where my happiness is found. Give me an eagerness for your laws rather than a love for money! Turn my eyes from worthless things, and give me life through your word. . . . I long to obey your commandments! Renew my life with your goodness.

PSALM 119:33-37, 40

Fighting Words

Sometimes bad stuff happens, but I feel mostly insulated from the meanness I know exists in my hometown. Yes, I've been burglarized (once) and honked at (at least once a day), but I'd never experienced what it's like to be the target of blind hate—until just a few days ago.

Along with a few hundred other Houstonians, I'd lined up outside a local bookstore to have a former president sign a copy of his new memoir. This particular author happens to be a pretty polarizing public figure, even after his retirement to private life.

The crowd was friendly, and the line moved rather quickly.

The real "fun" came when I walked out of the store. I hadn't noticed the knot of protesters forming earlier, but about a dozen unhappy citizens were corralled on the sidewalk by a small police contingent, and what their group lacked in numbers they made up for in noisy venom. Their target? Anyone who'd purchased said president's book and exited the store with it. Including me.

When I was just a few yards from the group, a woman holding a painted sign screamed at me, spit flying, "Hater! Koran burner!" And those are just the words I can repeat. I was stunned. I was the last person she might expect to burn a book—any book. But the book under *my* arm, and that alone, was enough to make me the object of her fury. She'd decided what she believed about me, and it wasn't good. From one fact, she'd made a story.

I'm not a screamer, but I am a story crafter. My sidewalk accuser made me question whether I'd ever written anyone's story with as little data as she'd used to write mine. And I'm afraid I have. I've made quick judgments. Assumptions. I've been just as wrong about others as she was about me. Her fighting words made me sad for us both and determined to not repeat the mistake, with or without words.

There is one whose rash words are like sword thrusts, but the tongue of the wise brings healing.
PROVERBS 12:18, ESV

Sabbath Glory

It was an ordinary Sunday, and I followed my ordinary Sabbath routine: a mug of steaming coffee, a hot shower, a few minutes of quiet in my green "guest" chair with Burley stretched out nearby, and then preparation for church.

Dressed and ready, I fastened my watch on my wrist, stuffed my teaching notes in my Bible, grabbed my keys and an insulated cup, and opened the garage door with the remote. In the process I spilled a little coffee on my hand and shirt, giving thanks that I'd at least had the foresight not to wear white.

When I parked my car in my church's tiny parking lot, I heard the sound of singing upstairs. That muffled music made me glad to belong to a family of wounded saints who gather together in spite of the messy demands of everyday life.

I chatted my way through the downstairs hallway, jotted a brief outline on our classroom wall, and waited as the chairs filled. We're learning to love the Word, and it's the Word we come for.

From behind the lectern I saw them shine, these saints. I swear they did. This gathering of dear ones from different places and races and generations and families of origin, they dazzled me to no end. They always do.

Then we made our way into more glory: voices blended in worship and words of the Nicene Creed proclaimed together: "I believe in one God, the Father Almighty, Maker of heaven and earth, and of all things visible and invisible. And in one Lord Jesus Christ, the only-begotten Son of God . . ." When we began the solemn movement forward for Communion—couples, families, single moms with young children, teenagers, and young adults—I couldn't take my eyes away or stop the tears that slid down my cheeks. So much beauty at that table and beyond it.

"What did you do today?" a friend asked later. "Just went to church," I said, and my face burned at the way I'd shrunk so much glory into four small and ordinary words.

A terrible beauty, O God, streams from your sanctuary. It's Israel's strong God! He gives power and might to his people! O you, his people, bless God!
PSALM 68:35, MSG

Particular People

We are a culture of people who are very sure of what we want, at least in the coffee department. I thought I'd heard it all in terms of over-the-top beverage orders, but the fellow in line in front of me caused the meter to tilt. He ordered his coffee drink at—I am not kidding—140 degrees. And the barista didn't blink. Not even a hint.

As I walked away with my three-syllable order (in which *tall* actually means "small") I wondered if my discriminating coffee palate would have been able to discern the exact temperature of my drink down to the degree. (The answer to that question is no.)

I'm particular about getting the last word, or being judged right or fair or competent. I'm particular about finding the right word, not the almost-right one, and about keeping my word when I give it. But I'm surprisingly *un*particular with regard to things I should care much more deeply about. I don't worry enough that someone I know is spiritually lost. I don't lose sleep over a particular friend's heartbreak or fear, or because a particular ten-year-old boy's birthday gift from me is almost a month late. And I'm not particularly troubled that people less than three miles from me might have no dinner, when I have enough in my pantry to feed four other families on any given night. Isn't it strange what we're particular about?

One of the things I love most about Jesus is the particular way he loved. He focused on loving others one moment, one person at a time. May I show love to others through that kind of intentional presence as well.

They called to the blind man, "Cheer up! On your feet! He's calling you." Throwing his cloak aside, he jumped to his feet and came to Jesus. "What do you want me to do for you?" Jesus asked him. The blind man said, "Rabbi, I want to see."

"Go," said Jesus, "your faith has healed you." Immediately he received his sight and followed Jesus along the road.
MARK 10:49-52, NIV

Of Toes and Tuning Forks

Recently I found myself in a neurologist's office watching as she struck a tuning fork (with no musical instrument in sight) and held it to my big toe. "Do you feel a vibration?" she asked. I nodded my head up and down. "Tell me when you stop feeling it," she said.

So I concentrated on the slight buzz at my toe for a few seconds as it grew more and more faint, then reported, "It's gone." When she moved the fork higher and touched it to my ankle, I realized it hadn't stopped at all! The vibration was animating the fork, even if I no longer felt it in my foot. She repeated the tuning fork test on my other foot and ankle, with similar results.

When I asked what the test meant, she explained that the peripheral nerves in my lower feet weren't holding the vibration, indicating damage to the myelin sheath surrounding the nerves. I haven't stopped thinking about that vibrating tuning fork and its movement. The fork had not stopped vibrating, but I had stopped feeling it.

Once "struck" in time, the gospel story—creation, fall, redemption, and restoration—reverberates through eternity in myriad ways. It never stops, even if we stop feeling it. We can ignore the gospel story or deny it, but we cannot keep it from sounding forth.

The love of God in Christ resounds throughout creation. It can't *not* hum and buzz. If there is a tuning fork for the love of God in Christ, I want to feel its vibration in my chest forever. I want my heart and body and soul to ring with gospel beauty, always. I want my bones to reverberate with the truth that Jesus died to bring me into God's family—that I am his and he is mine.

So tap the fork, Father, and let it hum in me. "Come, thou Fount of every blessing, tune my heart to sing thy grace!"

All of this is a gift from God, who brought us back to himself through Christ. And God has given us this task of reconciling people to him. For God was in Christ, reconciling the world to himself, no longer counting people's sins against them. And he gave us this wonderful message of reconciliation.

2 CORINTHIANS 5:18-19

Naming Names

My sister and I go by our middle names. Both of us were named after our grand-mothers, but we were called Lynn and Leigh, never Alice and Nona. This, of course, caused all kinds of confusion on the first day of school, and it is still a pain when filling out forms. I will answer to Nona if need be, but every time I do I feel like an imposter. Technically, I bear her name, but it has always seemed more hers than mine.

Names specify. When the angel announced to Mary that she would bear the Messiah, he didn't say, "Name him whatever you like." He said instead, "You will name him Jesus" (Luke 1:31). It was a name that meant something: "He will be very great and will be called the Son of the Most High" (Luke 1:32).

A friend asked me once, "If the Lord had a name for you that embodied the new person he is making of you through his love, what would that name be?" I told him I thought he might lovingly call me "My unforgettable tattoo," because he says my identity is engraved on the palms of his hands.

Whatever his chosen name for me, it is one that both fits me and forms me.

In the flyleaf of one of the many books in his personal library, C. S. Lewis wrote, "All that you are . . . every fold and crease of your individuality was devised from all eternity to fit God as a glove fits a hand. All that intimate particularity which you can hardly grasp . . . is no mystery to Him. He made those ins and outs that He might fill them."*

"_____ is mine." Write your name, your true name, in the blank. He is ever naming names, and he loves the sound of yours.

I will not forget you! See, I have engraved you on the palms of my hands.
ISAIAH 49:15-16, NIV

---

* Quoted in Corbin Scott Carnell, *Bright Shadow of Reality: C. S. Lewis and the Feeling Intellect* (Grand Rapids, MI: Eerdmans, 1974), 163.

God Is Love

Someone had lettered the white sign by hand with a red Magic Marker and posted it on a busy street corner. As I pulled up to the light, I glanced out the window and saw its message: "God is love." That's all it said. No sales pitch, no phone number. Just "God is love." It was the last day of the year (and my birthday, to boot). I was on my way to an appointment, feeling slightly flu-ish and distracted by my own coughing. But when I saw the sign, I had to smile. "He is," I agreed out loud.

I don't know what that sign might have accomplished while on display. To me it was a reminder of a truth I've known for a long time but can never hear enough: that the Lord of the universe, the maker of all that is, is the one thing that we all want more than we want almost anything else—love.

Only not cheap love. Or flimsy love. Or fleeting love. No. He's the kind of long-suffering, deliberate, full-out love that scares you to death before it delivers you whole. The kind that means business and doesn't bluff or blink or fool around. He is the kind of love that dies to redeem its beloved and then kicks death in the teeth to make it stick. And any reminder of that—even a hastily scrawled and randomly placed one—is a welcome reminder indeed.

Because he is love, love is within my reach. Nearer than my next breath. More sure than the sunrise. Because I've seen his defining love, I have a pattern to follow. Because he is love, love is no mere vapor or feeling or idea. Because he is love, love has a name—and it's one that I know: *Jesus.*

God is love. When we take up permanent residence in a life of love, we live in God and God lives in us. This way, love has the run of the house, becomes at home and mature in us, so that we're free of worry on Judgment Day—our standing in the world is identical with Christ's. There is no room in love for fear. Well-formed love banishes fear. . . . First we were loved, now we love. He loved us first.

I JOHN 4:17-19, MSG

a Pillar in a Small Place

My uncle Dalton died in Abilene, Texas, but his life was firmly rooted in two smaller towns an hour or so away: Ballinger and Norton. In Ballinger, he married my mother's oldest sister and lived with her for fifty-two years. In Norton he farmed and owned and operated a cotton gin where other farmers from miles around brought the cotton from their own fields to be ginned and baled.

Both tiny towns are even smaller now; few of my aunt and uncle's old friends remain, and the gin was sold two decades ago. At the end of their life of love and family and friends, of cloud watching and domino shuffling, of dinners "in town," of grandkids and fishing and hymn singing on Sunday, they shared a twelve-by-twelve room in a nursing home with two twin beds and a linoleum floor. Their "home" got small. But their hearts never did.

On the Saturday my uncle's small town said its good-byes and buried him, the people he loved who loved him back were there. They filled a funeral home reception area to overflowing at visitation time and stood unmoving before a video screen that flashed old photographs, watching wordlessly as it cycled again and again. My uncle was strong. He was able to carry a lot, and he did. I am certain he carried all of us in his heart until the day he died.

As we drove away from my aunt and uncle's former home in one final caravan to the church, his neighbors stood on their front porches like soldiers at attention and silently watched until we passed. At his service, those gathered nodded their heads to "Amazing Grace" and recited together the Twenty-third Psalm. At his graveside, they sowed the words to the Lord's Prayer out into the hot West Texas wind, then slowly walked away.

My Uncle D. was a pillar in a small place. His name wasn't known far and wide, but his impact was deep and strong. I am the grateful recipient of the overflow of goodness and joy that streams from a small life well lived. May I leave so much behind!

Let love and faithfulness never leave you. . . . Then you will win favor and a good name in the sight of God and man.

PROVERBS 3:3-4, NIV

Loving His Fans

The car in front of mine on the freeway bore this jarring message on its bumper: "I love God. It's his fans I can't stand." Ouch. I actually sped up and pulled alongside the self-professed God lover who couldn't stand other God lovers, curious about what such a person might look like. What I saw (on a Sunday morning, no less) was a well-dressed, middle-aged woman who appeared to be on *her* way to church too. I guessed there were some "God fans" in her very near future. I hoped they were ready to be deplored.

I pondered that bumper sticker for the better part of the day. It mystified me. Because often, God's people compel me to love him *more*. Maybe because they're not just "fans" who can decide to like God one day and then unlike him with a keystroke the next. They're more committed than that. Their bond is the permanent kind, not a fleeting whim. They identify completely with the one they love, and he with them.

The God fans I'm thinking of act in ways that he has and does and would—and their loving actions bring him glory. They remind me of him. They coach and counsel and pray and encourage. God's people are flesh and blood carriers of God's love. He doesn't call them fans. He calls them friends. Sons. Daughters. And they look a lot like their Father to me.

I know folks who have been on the hurting end of Christianity. They've suffered unpleasant business in the context of the church. They've encountered hypocrisy where they had hoped for authenticity. God lovers don't always get it right. We mess up just like everyone else. But it's impossible, really, to love God and to loathe his people. He *is* his people. He dwells in them. And his Spirit quickens their hearts and moves their hands and feet.

So for the record, I *love* God. And his people—his true followers, not here-today, gone-tomorrow fans—only cause me to love him more and more.

God is love, and the man whose life is lived in love does, in fact, live in God, and God does, in fact, live in him.

1 JOHN 4:16, PHILLIPS

(Im)perfect Submission

I don't expect to lose, do you? I don't expect to be robbed of possessions, relationships, health, time, investments, or treasure. I expect what is mine will stay mine. But my expectations, I'm learning, are misguided.

Last week I filed a police report for stolen property. I answered various questions on the form. Was the value of the stolen property between $0 and $5,000? It was. Closer to $0, but yes, it was. Was it jewelry, a car, machinery, art, a bicycle, emeralds, rubies, or diamonds? (These were my choices. I'm not kidding.) And it wasn't. It was far more humble than that.

Lately, I've been visited by a plant thief. Plants I've nurtured and coaxed into bloom have begun disappearing from my front porch. It's a strange feeling to walk out on your porch with a watering can in the morning and wonder where your tended crop of beauty has gone. It's equally strange to imagine someone stealing from you less than one hundred feet from where you sleep.

In the wake of this weird rash of theft, God wove two more unexpected occurrences. First, I was robbed of a parking place in my neighborhood supermarket. The parking thief whipped around the corner from where I sat waiting for a slower-than-molasses shopper to back out of the spot I expected to take. I rolled down my window and stared at him. He didn't say, "Sorry." He looked right at me and said, "Too bad," then left me fuming because *that spot was mine.*

Later I chanced to meet a friend—Tom—who lives and works at a children's camp in Nigeria. He caught me up on his time Stateside and reminded me that he'd been in Africa for five years. Remembering his original commitment was for two years, I asked if he planned to stay indefinitely. He laughed and said, "I don't have anything left here. I've given it all away."

When he said that, smiling, I realized he couldn't possibly be the victim of theft. He didn't have anything he expected to keep, anything he'd permanently stamped with the word *mine.* And I realized he was a very, very rich man indeed.

Thank you, plant thief, rude grocery shopper, and Tom, for helping me slowly perfect my oh-so-imperfect submission.

If you give up your life for me, you will find it.
MATTHEW 10:39

Keeping Watch

We honor others by our willingness to stand near and remain present through life's inevitable twists and turns. Keeping watch makes us kin, whether waiting for the sun to rise or the test results to come, for the labor pains to begin or the long-unspoken prayer to be answered.

Jesus, before his arrest and crucifixion, asked his disciples only to stay near him and pray. "My soul is deeply grieved, to the point of death," he confessed. "Remain here and keep watch with Me" (Matthew 26:38, NASB). It seemed a small request; a shallow sip compared to the bottomless cup of sin and death that he would swallow. But they could not keep watch for long. Their sorrow and fear fell over them like a heavy fog, and watching soon gave way to slumber.

These events are history. We can't relive them, but we can read the written account and consider how it was to be invited. Can you imagine the Savior asking, now, for you to watch with him? "Watch and pray while your out-of-work neighbor looks for a job," he might say. Or "Watch while your child struggles to fit in at his new school." Or "Sit near that dying loved one. Be a fully present, watchful witness of their precious life and death."

I can passively sit before a television hour after hour with no purpose in mind. Labor dutifully over a computer until my work is done. But to watch and pray with Jesus? To honor him and others with my presence and attention in whatever circumstance may come? Not enough. Not nearly enough. Jesus doesn't ask us to right every wrong, free every captive, heal every hurt, win every battle. *He will.* He only asks us to be loving, faithful witnesses who will hear his invitation and keep watch with him over a small corner of the world he loves. Where will you keep watch with him today?

Jesus came with them to a place called Gethsemane, and said to His disciples, "Sit here while I go over there and pray." And He took with Him Peter and the two sons of Zebedee, and began to be grieved and distressed. Then He said to them, "My soul is deeply grieved, to the point of death; remain here and keep watch with Me."
MATTHEW 26:36-38, NASB

What's Inside

I spent the better part of a morning trying to locate a house I'd never visited in an inner-city neighborhood I hardly knew. I was sure I was in the vicinity, but I couldn't seem to locate the right section of the block. I didn't see any street numbers, and honestly, most of the houses looked more likely to be abandoned than inhabited. Frustrated, I dialed the number of the artist whose interview I'd edited some weeks ago and asked him for navigational assistance.

"Oh, yeah, you're close, you're close," he said.

"Is it past the vacant lot?" I asked him. He said it was.

"Past the church on the corner?" I wanted to know.

"Nah, nah," he said. "Look for the only house on the street with a blooming bush in the yard."

I waited in my car until I saw the artist's wife come out to meet me. She invited me in, even though I'd only come to pick up some edits that her husband hadn't been able to fax. She and I stepped onto the creaky porch just as he appeared at the door—a man in his seventies with twinkling eyes, a broad smile, and a white beard that barely grazed his chest.

"We call this our clapboard house," he said. "It was built in 1932." Even before I approached the doorway, I had decided that the inside would be just as unimpressive as the outside. And I couldn't have been more wrong.

The tiny living room was a gallery of bright paintings: still lifes, landscapes, watercolors, portraits. The cumulative effect of so many of them in one small space was overwhelming. Based on the house's ramshackle exterior, I had expected squalor—but the door had opened on an unlikely wonderland of color and story and creative riches.

I'm sure I've been just as wrong about countless people and situations as I was about that hard-to-find house. You simply can't know what's *inside* based on what's visible *outside*. The God who designed us is not that predictable. It's the contrasts that make life rich and surprising and real. I learned that at the only house on Saint Charles Street with a blooming bush in the yard. And I'm ever so glad I was asked to come inside.

Blessed be the LORD, the God of Israel, who alone does wondrous things.
PSALM 72:18, ESV

august

The Scent of Water

After a long, dry summer, much of what was green is turning brown, and what's still green is wilting. The azaleas in the front flower bed beg for watering, and I oblige as often as my conscience (and city watering prohibitions) allow. But every now and then, it rains. Last night it did. You could smell the rain before it fell: that damp, salty aroma of clouds pregnant with water. You could hear it as it neared, with the low grumble of thunder. And you could see the telltale lightning in the distance—a flickering lightbulb behind the clouds.

As the rain neared, every green thing began to murmur. The wind blew, and the treetops and the hedges began to twist and rustle in anticipation. Leaves fluttered as the drops began to fall. When the rain came down harder, it sounded like applause ringing out up and down the block.

Sometimes I get dry. Really dry. I can almost feel my soul shrivel and my heart wilt. I wonder that my skin doesn't grow as brittle as the heart it covers. Sometimes I need rain.

And then the winds begin to blow. The ones you can't see, only feel. A peculiar tremor of grace tells me it might be about to rain. I see a glimpse of light on my heart's horizon, and I think it may herald something wet and welcome. The low thunder of a well-timed word or a stray lyric or even a whispered prayer hints that what I need is coming on a different kind of cloud. And soon.

Is it a dry season? Do you need rain too?

My King says, "Anyone who believes in me may come and drink! For the Scriptures declare, 'Rivers of living water will flow from his heart'" (John 7:38). The world gets watered from the outside in. But the Christ follower is watered from the inside out. When I pray for the rain that my soul needs, somehow my God releases it. I can't say with authority how it works—but I've seen mostly lifeless things go green too often to doubt that it does.

Though its roots have grown old in the earth and its stump decays, at the scent of water it will bud and sprout again like a new seedling.
JOB 14:8-9

Ninety-Nine Names for God

She became a Christian eighteen months ago, she told us. My classmates and I were sitting seminar-style around a table in a graduate theology course, talking church councils, doctrine, and heresy. Most of us, I suspect, came to Christianity from no belief at all, or perhaps some vague, cultural belief in a benign but distant God. Not her. She converted from Islam.

Then she said something that made my heart ache and my eyes water: "There are ninety-nine names for God in Islam," she explained. "But not one of them is *Father*." What kind of God, after all, willingly adopts misfits and makes them heirs?

Well, mine does: "When the time arrived that was set by God the Father, God sent his Son, born among us of a woman, born under the conditions of the law so that he might redeem those of us who have been kidnapped by the law. Thus we have been set free to experience our rightful heritage. You can tell for sure that you are now fully adopted as his own children because God sent the Spirit of his Son into our lives crying out, 'Papa! Father!'" (Galatians 4:5-6, MSG).

A friend said her toddler son's cry—whether the issue is a broken crayon or a broken limb—is a loud and urgent "Dada! Dada!" He may be small, but he knows who his daddy is and where help comes from.

I thought of my own dad, past eighty now, who says without fail every time we part, "Call me if you need anything." Earthly fathers, even very good ones—ones who hear our cries and invite us to call out to them—will one day no longer hear us when we do. But in Christ, we have a Father who is eternal, constant, powerful, true, and near.

We are precious children—whatever our age—who are loved with an everlasting love.

My classmate who once worshiped a god who was no father is now adopted by a God who insists on being called Abba. That, she said, was a wonder to her. And it is to me, as well.

———

Doesn't that privilege of intimate conversation with God make it plain
that you are not a slave, but a child? And if you are a child, you're also
an heir, with complete access to the inheritance.
GALATIANS 4:7, MSG

Undeserving

Close to one hundred name tags were spread on the table near the door of the event. And although I'd almost rather be pushed out of an airplane at several thousand feet than walk into a room full of social "opportunity" alone, I approached the welcome table without excessive fear. I'd received an invitation, I'd RSVP'd, and I was confident that I could at least navigate the name-tag bit without much angst.

My bolstered confidence quickly vaporized when I scanned the table and didn't see my name.

The facts didn't matter so much anymore. Because I didn't have a preprinted name tag like all the others I saw, I suddenly felt awkward. Undeserving. Like my invitation had somehow been a mistake.

The hostess was very nice. She didn't seem at all bothered by my lack of an official tag. In fact, she had a roll of adhesive ones ready and a Sharpie nearby. She offered both with a smile, saying I could simply make my own. I didn't want to, but I did. The simple act of writing my name with a Sharpie solidly reinforced the nagging suspicion that I'd probably been carrying all along: that I didn't really deserve to be invited to the event to begin with.

I can't be certain how much a real name tag might have helped. Looking back I suspect that even with it, I would have felt uncomfortable and a little out of place. After all, I was shoulder to shoulder with many of the names that lined my own bookshelves, smiling politely at people whose words I had highlighted in yellow. And absolutely certain that no one recognized *my* name.

But I also realized that I, of all people, should be over the undeserving thing. I *am* undeserving. But for the one to whom it should have mattered most, it mattered not at all. And because I have received from him grace upon grace, every new grace should be not a reminder of my own unworthiness but a shout-out to his great goodness and mercy. It still amazes me. Thanks for skipping my name tag, just this once, God, so I could be amazed all over again at the glory of *your* name!

Blessed be the God and Father of our Lord Jesus Christ, who has blessed us with every spiritual blessing in the heavenly places in Christ.
EPHESIANS 1:3, NASB

Beautiful Body Parts

Faces line the long downstairs hallway of my home church. Even when it's empty. The artwork in our family of faith is its families of faith: children, grandparents, moms and dads, friends, and siblings, whose faces make the hallway come alive and never fail to stir my heart. I know their names. I know their stories. In seven years I've come to love them and to love being a family of one amid this larger family.

Some of my "relatives" have moved away, but their faces still greet me each Sunday. I'm glad. I miss them, and I need to be reminded that we still belong to one another. Ours is not a lavishly decorated family home. Its furnishings are simple and adequate but by no means fine. Still, they are enough. Our richest asset is displayed on and within and beyond our walls: the sweet saints who are the church. *His* church. His bride.

We've opened the Word together and been fed by the Spirit with its beautiful truth. We've celebrated birthdays and engagements and weddings, new jobs and babies and brand-new books. We've asked for and offered forgiveness, because sometimes—in the tight quarters of our fallen humanity—we've hurt one another without meaning to. We've prayed for one another with bold clarity in the crushing fog of uncertainty. And we've said good-byes to each other that felt like the tearing of flesh and were—because we are one body, tightly bound in love.

When I read the claim in Hebrews 12:1 that we are surrounded by "so great a cloud of witnesses" (NASB) as we run the race of life, I used to think those witnesses were high in heaven's grandstand, separated from the race by some vast, immeasurable chasm. And perhaps some of them were, and are. But others are close. Close enough to touch and rub shoulders with. Close enough to share a whispered prayer, or call when I am frightened or need wisdom. Close enough to weather with me a storm that comes from nowhere in an ordinary day.

This body we call the church is made up of some beautiful parts, and I am thankful—so thankful!—to be at home among them.

Now you are the body of Christ and individually members of it.
1 CORINTHIANS 12:27, ESV

Those Camera Angles

I'm hooked on the Olympics. But I recently noticed something about the coverage of these games that I hadn't before: the multiplicity of camera angles used to tell the story of any particular contest. Tumbling looks vastly different at floor level than it does from the bleachers. And swimming! The camera allows us armchair athletes to hover just above the bottom of the pool as the swimmers slash and glide a few feet above. How boring these games would be if they were shot by a single cameraman, with a single point of view.

As I've enjoyed these varying angles, I've imagined the angles used (and yet to be used) to tell the gospel story. The events surrounding Jesus' birth surely looked different to a shepherd than they did to a young pregnant girl from Galilee. The Crucifixion viewed from the foot of the cross was a world removed from the vantage point of the thief dying next to Jesus. And a former tax collector's version of the ministry of Christ is decidedly less poetic than the one written by the apostle John, but it, too, offers a true picture of the central character.

In the same way, the story of the gospel in your life looks different from mine. How Jesus first came to you will not mirror the way he first showed himself to me. A Palestinian Muslim-turned-Christian sees a different angle of the story than I do. But his experience is just as solid, just as true.

I wonder how much energy is wasted trying to steer others to our own perspective or experience of the gospel story when we might actually be enriched by their own? There are so many ways to receive the same truth, to watch the same story unfold. It is in no way diluted by these diverse perspectives. The focus of the "camera" is the same, but the angles—oh, the angles!—what a rich story they can tell.

There is one body and one Spirit, just as you were called to one hope when you were called; one Lord, one faith, one baptism; one God and Father of all, who is over all and through all and in all. But to each one of us grace has been given as Christ apportioned it.
EPHESIANS 4:4-7, NIV

AUGUST 6
Every Time I Turn Around

The days had been marked out on my calendar for weeks: "On-site/NYC." I had come to enjoy the city in small doses, but working there required a focus and energy quite different from my regular routine.

This time I was anxious about traveling alone and *being* alone in the city. Nothing I could put my finger on. Not quite fear. But close.

Before I left, I read these words from the Psalms in Eugene Peterson's *The Message*: "God-defiers are always in trouble; GOD-affirmers find themselves loved every time they turn around" (32:10). I read them but didn't think too much about them. Until . . .

I received a text the night I arrived from a dear friend, who said that he thought I might be in New York that evening and that he was praying for me. After a flurry of texts back and forth, "I've got your back" were the last words he said, and I felt every muscle in my body relax.

The next morning, in the hotel elevator (where no one smiles), an older couple rode with me, speaking German to each other in hushed tones. As I glanced their way, he winked, then touched his forehead to his wife's. She smiled too. And I felt seen. Included.

Later, during meetings with three colleagues, each one, individually and at different times, showed me kindness. One winked at an especially exasperating point in a meeting. Another asked about my ailing parents. The third, on our final day of meetings, asked, "How are you feeling about all of this?"

But it didn't end there. I relished an unexpected, arm-in-arm stroll up Broadway at night with an old friend who'd found time for dinner out. A man in a seat across the aisle on my flight home lifted my carry-on into the overhead bin when he saw me struggle. Then, after I arrived home, on my front porch sat a dinner ready to reheat, with a note on the container that said, "Welcome home, Leigh!" Through the kindness of strangers and of friends, I found myself loved—at home and away—every time I turned around. "There's no place you can go that I am not," God seemed to say. "Look around, and you'll see me everywhere."

God-defiers are always in trouble; GOD-affirmers find themselves loved every time they turn around.
PSALM 32:10, MSG

The Three That Count

By rep twelve of a fifteen-rep set of exquisite tortures devised by my half-my-age-but-twice-as-buff trainer, I was struggling. My arms were beginning to wobble, and I'm sure my face was turning red. "Come on," he said. "Breathe. Push through. It's the last three that count." I was in just enough pain to smartly reply, "If only the last three count, why couldn't we have skipped the first twelve?"

He laughed, and I did three more. When I'd finished, he said, "You're doing the first twelve to get to the three that really count. So you need them all." For the rest of the day I thought about those last three reps and my trainer's simple words. He's a kinesiology student, so I'm sure he could explain that "last three" bit in more detail than I would care to hear. But I'm a student of a different discipline, so my mind went in another direction altogether.

I thought about my Savior, who lived thirty years of relatively ordinary existence before he embarked on the three years that made the history books. Then I thought of the last few days of his thirty-third year and the Friday, Saturday, and Sunday that changed the world forever. They were grand. Glorious. Necessary! But without all that had come before, they would have been meaningless.

We often think of life in terms of attainment. But in truth, it's mostly preparation and perseverance. Moses lived some pretty mundane years on the back side of Jethro's farm before he got the "big job." Those years were preparation. Joseph languished in prison as an innocent man for years before his meteoric rise to power. Every day in his lonely cell was an exercise in perseverance. Neither man knew when he'd get to "the three that count," but the intervening time was making them ready.

I'm less and less tempted these days to skip the reps that come before "the three that count." Even when they hurt. The last three may change my body, but the unheralded, ordinary first twelve will most surely change my heart.

When all kinds of trials and temptations crowd into your lives my brothers, don't resent them as intruders, but welcome them as friends! Realise that they come to test your faith and to produce in you the quality of endurance.

JAMES 1:2-3, PHILLIPS

Found!

The oldest note in my dearest Bible was written in 1984. I can still remember where I was—and the circumstances in which I found myself—when I hastily scribbled it in the margin somewhere near Psalm 56. I discovered that touchstone again when that Bible, missing for more than seven years, was miraculously returned to me.

I'm not sure how, when, or where it was lost. One day I looked for it, and it was gone. Between three quick moves, a fire, and a burglary, I had no idea where it might be. And I mourned. I had bought it in my twenties—a slim, double-columned New American Standard that had been rebound when its original cover fell off. I seldom used it to study—it was too fragile. But I never meant to part with it.

Its front and back flyleaves held scores of handwritten notes, snippets of poetry and hymns, sermon points, and quotes from speakers. It recorded the history of my walk with God from early adulthood, and I missed it terribly.

So when I received a message through my website that said "I think I found your Bible in my company's warehouse," I was afraid to hope it might be *this* Bible. I asked no identifying questions. I simply contacted the sender—a man named Jack—and made arrangements to meet him at a construction warehouse not far from my home, then prepared myself to be disappointed. But I wasn't.

Jack came walking toward me carrying my old, dear friend in one hand, and I somehow resisted the urge to dance with joy in the parking lot. He explained he'd found it sitting on top of a cabinet after he'd asked a crew to rearrange a corner of the warehouse. Inside it he found my name (and a twenty-year-old phone number). Then his wife recognized my name because she'd read a devotional I'd written. I'm not making this up. I couldn't. Only God could swing this.

Now my old Bible is home. Found. And with every precious page I turn I hear its Author say, "Remember me. I have never forgotten you."

Guide me in your truth and teach me, for you are God my Savior, and my hope is in you all day long. Remember, LORD, your great mercy and love, for they are from of old.
PSALM 25:5-6, NIV

The Other Nine

I remember the story from Sunday school. I remember the characters—ten men plus Jesus—and watching my teacher press their fuzzy felt bodies onto a flannelgraph, one by one. Ten lepers. One healer. A mighty miracle. And only one thank-you.

Where were the other nine? Were they not ecstatic to spring from their prisons of rotting flesh? As they went on their way, it never occurred to them to turn around and praise the source of their good fortune. The Healer's words had made them whole, yet they had no words of gratitude for him.

We have so much in common, those other nine and me.

From that first mighty miracle that wrested me from death to life, to the dozens of daily graces that keep testifying to it with pitch-perfect echoes, I am healed. Helped. Loved with a love so wild it might break my bones with a whisper were it not so infinitely kind. Yet I, too, fail to turn to the Giver and say, "Thank you." So I'm saying it now, because his ear is ever tuned to his people's hallelujahs.

Thank you, Father: You saw me before I was born and predestined my place at your table. You have been my hiding place from old. You fix me so firmly in your truth, even in storms and uncertainty. You never change.

Thank you, Jesus: You came for me, wooed, and won me. You've been utterly faithful through every turn of life. You are each day's companion from first light to last waking thought. You are so, so good.

Thank you, Spirit: heart tuner, truth arrow, beauty bringer. You whispered, "Jesus" in my ear until I followed. You open my eyes each day to the Father and the Son—I see because you show me where to look.

One day we will sit together at the Lamb's table, where I will sing grateful hallelujahs to my Father-Son-Spirit God. Until then, glory, glory, glory!

Thank you.

Amen.

———

One of their number, when he saw that he was cured, turned round and praised God at the top of his voice, and then fell on his face before Jesus and thanked him. . . . Jesus remarked, "Weren't there ten men healed? Where are the other nine? Is nobody going to turn and praise God for what he has done, except this stranger?"
LUKE 17:15-18, PHILLIPS

Hothouse Flowers

I discovered the wholesale flower market in my city when I agreed to do the flowers for my two precious nieces' weddings—in the same year. That I am not formally trained in floral arranging speaks both of their sensible frugality and their unwavering trust in their aunt's aesthetic sense. The floral market ships blooms in from far-flung corners of the globe: roses from Australia and Argentina, peonies from New Zealand, orchids and lilies and tulips and dahlias from almost anywhere *but* Texas. These flowers, in and out of season, are often grown in hothouses to produce the fullest, most beautiful blooms. The results are stunning.

Hothouse flowers *are* beautiful. They're symmetrical, fragrant, and mostly blemish-free, but they don't just happen. They're coaxed—coddled and helped along by controlled temperatures and fertilizers and careful handling.

Christ followers aren't meant to be hothouse flowers. We're rooted in the saving power of the resurrected Savior, and we grow wild, nurtured by the indwelling Holy Spirit. Our beginning is supernatural, yes, but our surroundings are uncontrolled at best and sometimes downright hostile. We're not protected from automobile accidents or addictions, not immunized from cancer or chronic illness, not untouched by divorce or even death. It's a rough, unpredictable world God's placed us in, with the expectation that we will not be fleeting, flawless specimens but eternal, fruitful ones!

Contrasting human love (what we can do by our own contriving) and spiritual love (what God can do in and through us), German theologian and martyr Dietrich Bonhoeffer writes: "Human love breeds hothouse flowers; spiritual love creates the *fruits* that grow healthily in accord with God's good will in the rain and storm and sunshine of God's outdoors."* I like that.

You and I have been firmly planted in God's great outdoors. We're not pristine showcase blossoms; our risky growth is being steadily nurtured from the inside out. Our blooms may not be perfect, but in Christ—by the Spirit—we can defy the elements to produce real and lasting fruit. And when we do, our good Gardener-Husbandman will get the glory only he deserves.

May the God of peace . . . equip you with everything good for doing his will, and may he work in us what is pleasing to him, through Jesus Christ, to whom be glory for ever and ever. Amen.
HEBREWS 13:20-21, NIV

---

* Dietrich Bonhoeffer, *Life Together: A Discussion of Christian Fellowship* (New York: Harper & Row, 1954), 37.

The Hand That Feeds Me

Most people teach their dogs. I seem to keep learning from mine. When Owen the adorable Cavalier King Charles spaniel was just a pup, we attended obedience school. He really retained only two "obediences" learned there. He sits for his food, and he goes into his kennel when I say, "Kennel up."

When he's told to kennel up, Owen marches into his crate without coercion, then turns to face me and sits. He's come to expect a treat for this, and 99 percent of the time I oblige. By now he would go into his crate whether or not he received a reward for it—but when I see his upturned face and how expectantly he waits, it's hard for me to walk away without satisfying his desire. He's not starving. And he wouldn't whine (much) without a pinch of something good. But he sits and waits for what he hopes will come to him from my hand.

The gulf between Owen's essential nature and mine is wide. But the gulf between God's nature and mine is wider still. The truth is, Owen probably is a lot more like me than I am like God. Still, I wonder if my Master isn't pleased when I look to his hand to reward me and hope for his kindness to bless me. And I wonder if I eye the hand that feeds me even half as hopefully as Owen does.

God's been good to me. Very good. And he's done me good long enough for me to cease imagining that his goodness is an anomaly or a fluke. It is not. His is a steady, determined goodness toward me that I can count on. I can trust the hand that feeds me.

Even better—I don't need to worry about looking silly when I sit expectantly at my Father's feet. I know he is glad to find me there. And I believe it is not a hardship but a joy for him to feed me from his endless supply of loving-kindness. Because it really *is* better than life.

They all wait for You to give them their food in due season. You give to them, they gather it up; You open Your hand, they are satisfied with good.
PSALM 104:27-28, NASB

It Might Be Time to Twirl

Kara needed a grown-up helper for a little while, and thankfully that job was mine. One morning we met at a local department store to shop before the store opened. Local donors had made it possible for us to "buy" a set dollar amount of back-to-school clothes for Kara, who was starting first grade. As we waited for the other kids to arrive, we planned what she might need: new shoes, shorts, jeans, dresses, and shirts.

As Kara squirmed with anticipation, I was already tallying our list in my head, hoping I could stretch the allotted dollars by finding some good sale items. When the organizers gave the word, we stood up, and Kara took my hand. We fast-walked to the girls' department and began the hunt.

In less than twenty minutes, my arms were full of possibilities. Some I had selected; others Kara had chosen. We headed for the dressing rooms, but they were already jammed with other kids and their chaperones. Some kids were changing in the hallways, but Kara wanted a room. So we waited. Once inside I became the holder as Kara chose the first outfit. She dressed herself quickly, allowing me to adjust hems and smooth wrinkles. Then she looked in the mirror and smiled a megawatt smile. She liked what she saw! She looked back at me, and I nodded my approval. Then she opened the dressing room door and did a turn for another volunteer seated on the floor outside.

"Oh, look at you!" the woman cried. "That looks so pretty on you!"

We did this with each outfit. Kara dressed, smiled at herself in the mirror, twirled for me, then showed her new friend outside. After the third or fourth change, she came back in, threw herself across my lap, looked up shyly, and said, "I'm showing off."

I didn't mind at all. I would not have begrudged her one instant of feeling special and thrilled to be given so much at once.

Sometimes God blesses me, and I forget to twirl. Or I'm ashamed to openly celebrate, in case his goodness was accidental. I hide my delight as if it were wrong to be giddy in his sight. It is not. Let the twirling begin.

O taste and see that the LORD is good; how blessed is the man who takes refuge in Him!
PSALM 34:8, NASB

AUGUST 13
Taking His Sweet Time

My friend Steve is taking his sweet time. He's seizing small moments and making them count, because the time he has may well be short, and shortened time tastes strangely sweeter. He's savoring company, the sound of rain, kind words and kisses, books and memories, slow conversation, and meals he barely touches but deliberately, determinedly enjoys.

Yesterday we spent a morning in each other's company—me in jeans and no makeup, him in a plaid flannel bathrobe, and later, in what he calls his *American Gothic* uniform: baggy, suspendered denim and a faded T-shirt, with his familiar rimless spectacles perched on his nose. "I need a pitchfork," he said with a smile. Then I pulled up an image of Grant Wood's iconic painting on my phone, and we both laughed.

Never one for mindless chatter, he quickly presses into conversation that counts for something. Even when his words are quiet and labored, he's not about to waste a single one. He has a practiced writer's eye and speaks in images and metaphors that are hard and beautiful at once. His energy is focused on managing the simplest tasks, but his mercy is focused outward. During our visit, he asked about *my* family, *my* health, *my* heart, and then gifted me with words of blessing so painfully sweet and perfectly timed they made me weep. When he got up from his chair and padded into another room, I asked if he was okay, and he said, "I'm fine," padding back with a fat box of tissues for the tears rolling off my own cheeks and chin.

Why do we wait until time is almost gone to take our time with those we love? Why do we save the sweetest words until we have nothing left to lose by saying them? Why do we withhold what we could so easily give away, waiting for someone else to be the first to offer?

Steve is taking his sweet time. And teaching those he loves to take theirs, too.

We're not giving up. How could we! Even though on the outside it often looks like things are falling apart on us, on the inside, where God is making new life, not a day goes by without his unfolding grace.
2 CORINTHIANS 4:16, MSG

all the Time in the World

I expect to wait when I go to see the doctor—at least a reasonable amount of time. But on this day, my idea of *reasonable* was shortened by the fact that I felt lousy and had already waited nearly an hour to be called back to the examining room. Once I was inside, the nurse assured me that the doctor would see me "shortly." I settled in for however long it took.

After perusing three only slightly interesting magazines, I curled up on the exam table and tried to use my bicep as a pillow. In another minute or two, the door next to mine opened, and I heard the doctor go inside. Then (I confess) I heard every word said by the patient whose turn was before mine. And he talked—a lot. I imagined his time with the doctor might be similar to a typical appointment of mine, but it was not. He went on and on. In violation, I am sure, of every HIPAA standard written, I learned where he lived, where he worked, what his brother died from, what other doctors he'd seen, and what questions he had about a plethora of concerns from West Nile virus to early onset Alzheimer's.

At the beginning of each new gush of words, I waited for the doctor to cut him short. But she didn't. She listened. His appointment lasted nearly as long as my commute to the office, my time in the waiting room, and my exam-room-magazine-reading extravaganza combined. Then I heard the door close. I expected the doctor might take a few minutes to recover, but within seconds, the door to my room opened. She walked in, completely present as she apologized and hugged me. No empathy spent in the previous appointment was subtracted from mine. More time for my fellow patient did not mean less time for me.

When others are demanding more of God's attention, I sometimes imagine that he might lose sight of me. He does not. More grace for someone else is not less grace for me. And he has all the time in the world for me, no matter what's been spent.

GOD's a safe-house for the battered, a sanctuary during bad times. The moment you arrive, you relax; you're never sorry you knocked.
PSALM 9:9-10, MSG

Spending Big

I'm typically careful with money; I don't spend big without first considering both the need and my budget. But recently I spent more than I would have liked for the promise of an added return on investment. My splurge? Twelve months of a heartworm/flea preventive medication that my dog, Burley, takes monthly.

Why twelve months? Because the manufacturer offered a twenty-dollar rebate if I bought a twelve-month supply at once.

Since I had the money and knew I'd be buying it anyway, I thought I might as well go all in and save twenty dollars. But the website where I was supposed to apply for my rebate wasn't working properly, and I couldn't submit the completed form. If it *were* working, the fine print said I'd have to wait ten to twelve weeks for my twenty dollars. And, by applying for a rebate, I was also signing up for unwanted marketing e-mails from the drug company. Add those negatives up, and it was most definitely *not* worth the big onetime expense.

The more I thought about it, the madder I got. I wouldn't have spent so much money if I'd known how difficult redeeming my rebate would be and how long I'd have to *keep* paying with those marketing e-mails filling my inbox. I stayed mad for two days. Then I looked at Burley, he looked back at me, and I got over it. Because I love him, and I am committed to care for him no matter what.

Jesus spent big for love. He didn't die weighing his 100 percent investment in a world of sinners. (We weren't good bets.) He died—in complete agreement with the Father's plan—for love alone. He spent big out of love for the sons and daughters of Adam who had no other means of life but him.

Nothing spent for love alone is lost, ever.

God put his love on the line for us by offering his Son in sacrificial death while we were of no use whatever to him.
ROMANS 5:8, MSG

AUGUST 16
Set Free

I went to prison, but I wasn't forced to go. I traveled there freely with members of my church for a resurrection-week service with the residents of the Jester III unit of the Texas Department of Criminal Justice. Upon arrival, I dropped my driver's license in the red bucket at the guardhouse, passed through three sets of heavy electronic doors, and walked down a long corridor before arriving in the place where we would gather: a wide, hot, cement-floored room filled with three hundred or so men in white. Each of them was free to come and sing and pray, but not a single one was free to leave, as I was, when worship was done. All of us there had once been—or were still—prisoners. All of us had trespassed; all of us had broken rules designed to keep us safe and well; all of us had fallen—one way or another—into the grip of sin.

And some of us had been set free.

By a power greater than self-will or legal wrangling or time served, we'd been severed from our sin and its sentence and gloriously liberated. But the law didn't set us free. Love did.

Luck can keep a sinner from being caught. For a while. A loophole in the law can keep one from suffering the consequences of his or her sin. For a while. But only love can set a sinner free. Only perfect love can swallow sin whole, die, then live again to tell the tale. Only perfect love can cover our mighty multitude of sins. And only the life-giving Spirit can apply that perfect love to human hearts in a way that sets them free forever.

I left prison and crawled into my own bed later that night, free to sleep without fear and to wake without dread. Some of my nearest friends and neighbors are still prisoners, and some of the men who slept in Jester III that night are just as free as me. Because whomever the Son has set free is free indeed.

God did what the law could not do. He sent his own Son in a body like the bodies we sinners have. And in that body God declared an end to sin's control over us by giving us his Son as a sacrifice for our sins.
ROMANS 8:3

Burley's Bed (Is Me)

Eleven-week-old Burley plays hard. And when he's played long enough, he just quits. He sighs without subtlety, flops his 16.6 puppy pounds down wherever he happens to be, and burrows in to rest. His eyes flutter briefly, then close, his breathing gets soft and even, and he makes his bed where he finds it. For now, he likes my lap. And I let him rest there because when he's fully grown, he's going to be way more dog than I have lap.

I like to watch Burley while he sleeps. It's the only time I can really study him— see the satin smoothness of his coat and the white "Got Milk?" stain across his muzzle and silky throat. While he's asleep, I can examine to my heart's content his mismatched foot pads and the velvet tips of his ears. He quickly gets heavy, but I hesitate to shift his weight to the floor—both because I hate to wake him and because I know this sweet-boy stage will not last long. So I let my sleeping dog lie.

Burley's ability to rest is instructive to me. Rest is surrender. Rest is undefended release. To rest is to trust the bed on which you recline—and for now, Burley's bed is me. The place I go for rest is Jesus. His is the chest on which I lean hard in weariness or fear or trouble, and in his comforting presence, I sleep like a baby. He lets me linger there for as long as I need to, and his lap is never off limits. I'm never shooed or shoved away.

I didn't always run there the way I do today. I felt far too grown up to retreat to such a childish place. But every hour older I become, the more I need (and love) the tenderness and security of his arms. "Curl up here," he seems to say. "You're safe. And I won't make you move until you're ready, or put you down until you're sure you can stand."

In love and mercy, Christ Jesus lets his sleeping child lie. And unlike my Burley boy, I'll never outgrow the welcome of that precious space.

Are you tired? Worn out? Burned out on religion? Come to me. Get away with me and you'll recover your life. I'll show you how to take a real rest.
MATTHEW 11:28, MSG

AUGUST 18
Respecting the Storm

My city became the hub for victims of Hurricane Katrina when thousands of evacuees from Louisiana and Mississippi came to Houston for refuge. Many lost all that they had and came here looking to build new lives after that devastating storm. On the heels of Katrina, another storm gathered steam off the Texas Gulf Coast—and no one took it lightly. Stores were stripped of bottled water, batteries, and other items needed to prepare for and ride out a storm. Storm number two got more respect because of storm number one.

We're "show me" people, aren't we? We place great confidence in our own invincibility and in the resources we've amassed to make ourselves safe and comfortable. We believe in windows and walls and wheels, in ATMs and gasoline pumps and groceries. And until those things prove vulnerable, we keep on believing. But after one spectacular demonstration of the forces of nature, we're learning to respect the storm. Even so, I wonder how many millions are still denying the power of the storm's Maker?

Physical lives can be rebuilt. Spiritual lives must be rebirthed. We deny at our own peril the presence and power of the God who rides above the wind. He may appear indifferent, but he is not. He may seem removed from our insulated, day-to-day existence, but he is not. We may question whether he cares for us or sees our plight, but that question was answered once for all with the terrible death and glorious resurrection of his only Son.

His ways are beyond our scrutiny and far, far above our understanding. We are not as independent as we pretend. We need him more—much more—than we let on. And if we think that we will somehow stand against the winds of sin and the floodwaters of judgment without him, then we've simply failed to show him the fear, awe, and respect that is his due.

Physical storms teach a lesson about greater, invisible things: we are small and weak and lost and hopeless, no matter how well insulated we feel. And the only sure way to safety is to respect the one who commands every storm and to trust him to deliver us from what we cannot hope to conquer without him.

Those who cling to worthless idols turn away from God's love for them.
JONAH 2:8, NIV

Dance with Me

I've always been a bit clumsy. Ask my sister, who watched me walk out of a store one summer afternoon and wrestle a parked bicycle to the sidewalk. Clumsy or not, I spent four years of my childhood taking ballet, tap, and jazz lessons, and I danced on a high school drill team for another four years.

Today I don't often dance. A rare autoimmune condition has rendered my feet mostly numb, and some days I don't even walk with much confidence—much less glide or twirl. Trust me when I say toes are not extraneous cosmetic appendages. Actually *feeling* them goes a long way to keeping one steady and upright.

Still, there is something wonderful about dancing. I smile every time I hear a song I danced to in my teens or twenties. I still have (and wear) the slick-bottom boots that danced many of those carefree steps. "If we are indifferent to the art of dancing," says Havelock Ellis, "we have failed to understand, not merely the supreme manifestation of physical life, but also the supreme symbol of spiritual life."*

Once, a long time ago, a King asked me to dance. He extended his hand to me and called me by name, saying, "Dance with me." I couldn't refuse. I didn't *want* to say no, even though I wasn't sure I could match his steps or keep time with the music I heard. "The Christian life," writes Ken Gire, "is about following Christ's lead, not about him following ours. . . . He asks us merely to take his hand and follow him. To move when he moves. To speed up when he speeds up. To slow down when he slows down. And to stop when he stops. . . . We are relinquishing the lead. But look who we are relinquishing it to."†

"Dance with me," he whispers. And clumsy or compromised, shy or ashamed, unsteady or uncertain, I still say yes. And I dance.

Whoever has the Son has life; whoever does not have the Son of God does not have life.

1 JOHN 5:12, ESV

---

* Havelock Ellis, "The Philosophy of Dancing," *Atlantic Monthly*, February 1914, 197.
† Ken Gire, *The Divine Embrace* (Wheaton, IL: Tyndale, 2003), 89.

Pocket Change and Poetry

It had been there all along—that artless origami of dollar bills and one stray penny. It traveled who-knows-where with me, undisturbed, until I slipped my hand into my pocket and felt its tiny crush. I had with me something I'd forgotten.

The denomination of those bills in no way dimmed the delight of having found them. When seasons change and we slip into things we haven't lately worn, who knows what good those silent pockets hold?

Seasons do change. A season of threat or challenge ends like a sigh—so imperceptibly that the crease of time is never felt or seen. A season of quiet joy is interrupted rudely with an awful surge of shock or pain impossible to foretell. Even so, someone has been there, all along. He is surprised by nothing. He is, and was, and is yet to be—everlastingly present.

> O Lord, you have examined my heart
> > and know everything about me.
> You know when I sit down or stand up.
> > You know my thoughts even when I'm far away.
> You see me when I travel and when I rest at home.
> > You know everything I do.
> PSALM 139:1-3

I may be as unaware of his presence as I am of a secret stash of pocket change, but he is never unaware of me. I couldn't run if I wanted to . . . and sometimes, I do. No matter. He would find me under any imaginary invisibility cloak and gladly press me home again. His guiding hand never leaves the small of my back.

> If I ride the wings of the morning,
> > if I dwell by the farthest oceans,
> even there your hand will guide me,
> > and your strength will support me.
> PSALM 139:9-10

He's closer than the loose change in my pocket. Not seeing him won't make him disappear. In every season, through every change, *he is there.*

> You go before me and follow me. You place your hand of blessing on my head.
> PSALM 139:5

Living on My Knees

I studied his T-shirt for nearly three hours. An orange security alert put me in the airport well ahead of my scheduled departure, leaving plenty of time for people watching at the gate. Across from me sat a stocky, middle-aged man with one silver earring. He wore a black T-shirt that boldly proclaimed "I'd rather die standing than live on my knees."

I got the drift. His was a rough-and-ready credo—one that bespoke toughness and a fierce attitude. But the more I looked at it, the more it struck me as absurd. First (all modifiers aside) this fellow was saying he preferred death to life. To die standing, in this fellow's book at least, was a noble death. (And one much preferred to a life of meekness or servitude.)

But what's so awful about living on your knees? In the time I had to wait and ponder his emblazoned proclamation, I became more and more certain that a life spent on my knees was actually a great deal better than one spent standing in defiance. Then I thought for a longer time about what it would look like to live "on my knees."

If I lived on my knees, it would be impossible to look down upon others. If I lived on my knees, humility would come more naturally. From knee level, I could easily consider others more important than myself and serve them better than I might when standing tall. If I lived on my knees, I might be more ready to pray.

One day, the bold dude in the T-shirt *will* hit his knees. And I and the rest of earth's sons and daughters will join him. Regardless of how he lives or dies, this man will eventually find himself in a kneeling position before the King of all kings. It will be a far, far better day for him if he has practiced that posture in advance.

If I wore my heart on my T-shirt sleeve, I think it would read, "I'd rather live on my knees than die standing." And I would. Wouldn't you?

God elevated him to the place of highest honor and gave him the name above all other names, that at the name of Jesus every knee should bow.
PHILIPPIANS 2:9-10

AUGUST 22
Other People's Stories

For many years now, God has allowed me to be the teller of other people's stories. I tell my own story too. I tell it in teaching and in writing. (Maybe I tell too much: when my mother read my second book and I asked her what she thought, she said—after quite a long pause—"Well . . . it's very personal." And I guess it was.)

Years ago, when I had published nothing but the occasional poem or article, I was asked by my boss if I thought I could write a book for him. In delightful ignorance, I said, "Yes, I think so." To this day I'm not certain why he trusted me to tell his stories, but in the next six years I wrote five books, crafting and reshaping and adding to and subtracting from words he had spoken, as if I were him. It was his voice that spoke from the printed pages of each one and his name on the cover—not mine. And, although in time I would come to feel less than comfortable with the arrangement, it was a tremendous gift. I listened. I learned. And I fell in love with the art of telling.

I have midwifed in large and small ways the stories of more than a few persons of note. Their stories teach things I would never otherwise learn. They inspire, encourage, chasten, humble, and motivate me. Each time I sit down with someone and begin asking questions, I am blessed.

But I shouldn't be surprised. My favorite book is full of other people's stories: Moses, David, Solomon, Joseph, Jeremiah, Job, Nehemiah, Ruth, Esther, Samuel, John the Baptist, Mark, Matthew, Luke, John—and my favorite story of all—the story of Jesus. There are, John says, more stories of Jesus than have yet been told—stories which, if they were known and told one by one, we could not begin to count. I'm waiting (breathlessly!) for heaven's library. Until then, there are more stories to tell. Ask someone to tell you his or hers today.

Jesus also did many other things. If they were all written down, I suppose the whole world could not contain the books that would be written.
JOHN 21:25

Misunderstood

When I was thirteen, a boy named Phil asked me to go steady. I said an emphatic, expressive, dismissive no. That's because he was whispering when he asked, and we were in the middle of a science test. He said, "Do you want to go steady with me?" But I heard, "Do you have the answer to number three?" I wasn't interested in cheating, even though Phil was pretty cute. If I'd understood the question, I might have said yes. But I misunderstood.

Don't you hate being misunderstood? I do. I hate it most of all when my intentions are good and my words are carefully selected, but the wires get crossed somehow and communication falls flat. After I waved Phil off in science class, I learned that I hadn't properly understood his request. But no amount of fixing could get the moment back. Not only did he now think I wasn't girlfriend material, he also had reason to believe I thought he was a cheater!

I could have helped myself by asking, "What did you just say?" But I thought I'd understood. As a grown-up I've experienced plenty of times when clarification could have been just as useful, when it might have been good to step back and say, "What did you mean by that? I'm not sure I understood you." But I don't always ask. And others don't either.

As frustrated as I am at times by my own inability to communicate, I can't begin to imagine how Jesus must have felt. His words and actions were nothing but good. He came to seek and to save the lost. And those who should have been most open to his good news rejected it outright. He was kissed by a friend and betrayed to his enemies. Misunderstood. He was charged as an insurrectionist because he agreed that he was indeed a king. Misunderstood. He was put to death as a common criminal because he didn't behave like people thought the Messiah should. Misunderstood.

Christ was misunderstood, but God made no mistake. He knew exactly what he meant to do and why.

———

He was despised and forsaken of men, a man of sorrows and acquainted with grief; and like one from whom men hide their face He was despised, and we did not esteem Him.
ISAIAH 53:3, NASB

Branches Down

Nearly two weeks after Hurricane Ike ripped through Houston, Galveston, and the surrounding areas, streets in almost every neighborhood in my town were still littered with branches. Ike tore trees limb from limb, leaving tons of debris in its wake. The tiny tree lawn in front of my house was stacked head high with broken branches— most of them from the enormous oak in my backyard that split down the middle all the way to its roots. And next to my stack stood my neighbor's stack and her neighbor's stack and so on—all the way down the street.

On the first day after the storm, the downed branches all of us were cutting and dragging to the curb were still green. But as each day passed, fewer and fewer glimpses of green were visible. In a very short time, every downed branch was brittle and brown. Each one. Separated from the trunks and roots that gave them life-giving nutrients, they quickly died. The resulting stacks of dead branches hardly resembled the trees from which they'd been separated by howling winds and rain.

How is it, then, that I expect to thrive apart from the vine of Jesus Christ? How do I imagine that I might keep my soul fresh and fragrant apart from his quickening Spirit? How can I hope to bloom and bear fruit separated for even a day from him?

City contractors would eventually come and haul all those dead branches away. But with each day that passed, they became a stronger and stronger reminder to me to *abide*. I need the Spirit of the living God like those branches needed the life that comes from within, and apart from him, I really can do nothing.

Stripped from the support of his strong and steadying trunk, I am fit for nothing but the trash heap, but connected to him—engrafted to him—there is life: green, growing, vibrant, fresh life. One look at the downed branches made it easy to see where I belong.

Remain in me, as I also remain in you. No branch can bear fruit by itself; it must remain in the vine. Neither can you bear fruit unless you remain in me. I am the vine; you are the branches. If you remain in me and I in you, you will bear much fruit.
JOHN 15:4-5, NIV

White Dishes and Memory

Years ago while my friends were registering for their everyday dishes and fancy china, I bought myself eight place settings of unadorned white dinnerware. It was a practical purchase. At the time, eight place settings were enough to serve my parents, my sister's family, and me.

Some time after I purchased the dinnerware, my mom began replacing *her* old dishes with the same pattern. I don't remember if she liked my choice of dishes (our tastes were rarely similar) or if she, also practical, decided that her place settings plus mine would be enough to feed a larger, future version of our family at holiday time, should the need arise.

Either way, her white dishes together with mine could cover almost any dining possibility.

After my Mom's passing, we slowly parsed out her things. Furniture and other favorite items went to my sister's daughters, functional and sentimental pieces furnished my dad's new apartment, and I received the dishes that match my own.

Now my kitchen cabinet holds enough white dishes to feed a small regiment. I don't have a table large enough to host twenty-plus people at once—but I have the dishes, even if I don't have the room. I stacked Mom's inherited plates, bowls, cups, and saucers on top of my own so that they'll be used—if not all at once, at least one or two at a time.

Now each time I open the cabinet for a cup or a salad plate, I'm reminded that she's gone—and that I have stacks of memories yet unprocessed, just as I have stacks of dishes yet unused. Sometimes I'm still not sure what parts of my heart are my own and which are inherited from her. Our lives were as intermingled and impossible to cleanly delineate as these white dishes.

I don't expect to use the dishes all at once. And I imagine, too, that I will long be uncovering and examining what I carry inside that was once my mother's. I am, and will always be, her daughter. But I am God's one-of-a-kind creation and my own woman as well. May he make something beautiful, in his time, of the dishes and of me.

I will give to each one a white stone, and on the stone will be engraved a new name that no one understands except the one who receives it.
REVELATION 2:17

a little Piece of Home

Travel used to seem so glamorous to me. Sometimes, depending on where I'm headed and why, it still is. But more often, travel is simply work—and I'm as eager to get back to my home as some folks are to leave theirs. I miss my own bed. I miss my routine. And I miss the solid comfort of old, familiar things.

Every now and then, though, I'm given a little piece of home in a faraway place. Like the southern accent of a stranger or a familiar tune in an elevator or lobby. (Thanks, Lyle Lovett. I sure did enjoy the sweet surprise of those few bars from "The Road to Ensenada" heard in midtown Manhattan.)

Even better was the long lunch with one not-often-seen friend and a short road trip with another. (Joys really are multiplied when shared.) And tonight, more miles from home, I spent an evening with yet another precious friend who made room for me at the end of a very full day—the only time either of us could carve out for a visit. My surroundings might have been unfamiliar, but the company was not. Being with people I love never fails to make me feel at home.

Repacking my bags again, I'm almost certain that wherever I go, I'll discover reminders of home. And not just my God-bless-Texas home. My real, forever one. Every day, I feel the persistent tug of eternity. Of friends and family who have slipped off beyond time, of fleeting glimpses of supernatural beauty or blazing love or improbable peace. These are winsome postcards from another world—one my heart is tuned for but my eyes have not yet seen. And they confirm for me that my traveling will one day come to an end.

I'll finally arrive. I will be known. And I will perceive in full what today are only short, momentary fragments of recognition. My Savior has gone to prepare a place for me. How could I long for less? The best roads are filled with familiar signposts, and they always lead you home.

They desire a better country, that is, a heavenly one. Therefore God is not ashamed to be called their God; for He has prepared a city for them.
HEBREWS 11:16, NASB

Waiting for the Grade

I started graduate school almost thirty years after receiving my undergraduate degree, and more than once I asked myself what made me think I could ever do such a thing. My first degree in journalism is so old, I think its proof is stored on microfiche.

As an undergrad, I made mostly average grades and graduated with more gratitude than honors. But in the decades between degrees, I became one of those people who really cares how she does, who sweats twenty-page papers even though she's been quite comfortable writing three-hundred-page manuscripts. I was no longer content with just passing. I wanted to excel.

I once waited over two weeks for my first paper's grade in a class I loved on a subject I adored (the apologetic writings of C. S. Lewis). I couldn't skate on skill alone. My very knowledgeable professor wrote the textbook, for Pete's sake, so there was no fooling him. He was reputed to be a rigorous, demanding grader. I wanted to do well, but I didn't know where the bar was set or how I might measure up.

I was where I've rarely been, at least in a bookish sense: I was waiting for the grade.

It's human to want to know how we've done, and even to hope that we've done well. It's natural to need both affirmation and correction. I've felt all of this, but these days I'm feeling more: I'm feeling a sharper gratitude for grace. God's grace. On that count, the grades are in. By the so-great sacrifice of Jesus Christ, I've passed with flying colors. (On his coattails, yes. On my merit, no.) I've been conferred a status that stuns me, more than forty years after receiving it. Only one assessment is still to come, and it is the one I'm most keenly longing for: "Well done, thou good and faithful servant" (Matthew 25:21, KJV). Every mark I'm striving for today is for that honor. Those words.

I want to use up all I have. To spend everything I've got to honor the one I love best. I want to make my Father proud. That's the grade I'm waiting for.

Now the prize awaits me—the crown of righteousness, which the Lord, the righteous Judge, will give me on the day of his return. And the prize is not just for me but for all who eagerly look forward to his appearing.
2 TIMOTHY 4:8

An Invisible Thread

I spied it out of the corner of my eye as I stepped through the back door: a brown leaf, suspended in midair, spinning in the breeze in a singular, impossible dance. It seemed to defy gravity, but when I came closer, I saw that it hung from an invisible thread—the thinnest of filaments spun by an unseen, industrious spider.

I grabbed my phone and began snapping away. Honestly, who wants to shoot selfies when ordinary miracles abound right in your own backyard?

After lining up a few shots, I tucked the phone away, but I thought about that leaf all day—and about the invisible threads that hold us, too. About the filaments of faith that keep us aloft and help us to spin and dance, even against impossible odds.

"Now faith," said the writer of Hebrews, "is the assurance of things hoped for; the conviction of things not seen" (11:1, ESV). While I couldn't see the spider's thread, I was certain the leaf was attached to something. (Gravity is an absolute, after all.) But my faith is *also* attached to something: the solid, unseen weight of God's eternal power and glory.

Poet Emily Dickinson discovered the "conviction of things not seen" in nature, too—and extrapolated from it a divine apologetic:

> *I never saw a moor,*
> *I never saw the sea;*
> *Yet know I how the heather looks,*
> *And what a wave must be.*
>
> *I never spoke with God,*
> *Nor visited in heaven;*
> *Yet certain am I of the spot*
> *As if the chart were given.*

The thread that holds us may be invisible at times, but we *are* held nonetheless. The leaf I saw appeared fragile—and at the mercy of the unpredictable wind. But its dance was lovely, and its connection to something fixed and unmoving was utterly undeniable. And so it is with you and me.

By faith we understand that the worlds were framed by the word of God, so that the things which are seen were not made of things which are visible.
HEBREWS 11:3, NKJV

The Weight of the World

"They've got the weight of the world on their shoulders." I've heard that phrase used to describe those persons who seem burdened with sorrow for others. Whose empathy makes them emotionally vulnerable to the struggles they witness around them, and who grieve as if those struggles were their own.

In Sue Monk Kidd's *The Secret Life of Bees*, sister May Boatwright is just that sort of heavy lifter. When her sorrow feels most acute, May steals away to an old stone wall, where she tucks notes into its crevices to document the pain. This place beside a shallow river becomes her own private wailing wall and, ultimately, the scene of her drowning. The weight of the world is too much for May. She cannot carry it in her heart any longer.

"Share each other's burdens," the apostle Paul wrote to his friends in Galatia, "and in this way obey the law of Christ" (Galatians 6:2). But for how long? And to what degree? Until they become so heavy that all hope is lost? Surely not.

I'm no May, but I see the hurts of others piling up higher and higher all around me. A crumbling marriage. A menacing diagnosis. An abandoned child found by the side of the road. A widow improvising another day without the love of her life. A husband in need of a job and weary of being told no. The world weighs an awful lot. Too much.

So where do we take these burdens? Not far. I've barely held each one and whispered a prayer over it before I let the strong hands of Jesus take it from me. Why? Because he's the only one who can handle the weight of the world. I cannot.

Oh, how glad I am for that! I'm only expected to hand off these heavy hurts, casting all my cares on him because he cares for me. Jesus himself is my wailing wall. He is near to the brokenhearted, and he saves those who are crushed in spirit.

He's enough—more than enough—for the weight of the world.

Come to me, all of you who are weary and carry heavy burdens, and I will give you rest.

MATTHEW 11:28

AUGUST 30
Betrayed

After the world found out that Lance Armstrong lied about doping, he told all on Oprah's famous couch. When Oprah asked about one individual whom he sued into ruin for suggesting he had cheated, Lance said he couldn't remember the details. "We sued a lot of people," he told her.[*]

Celebrities, athletes, politicians, heads of state—not all are forthcoming with the truth. We may be disappointed in them, but we are not personally wounded by their lies. We may trust them, want to believe they are good, look up to them, even. But we don't *know* the Lance Armstrongs of the world, and they don't know us. They're not family or friends.

The real wounds come when the lies live closer to home. Down the hall, in the next pew or cubicle—or even on the other side of the bed. Then it's personal. Then the betrayal is tougher to bear. Sin stains everything. There's no Tide to Go pen or magic wipe to clean up the ancillary mess of betrayal. We're broken, all of us. And we have within our broken hearts more than enough potential to break others, too. If we think a smooth facade or a shiny exterior is enough to hide the darkness within the betrayer *or* the betrayed, we are sorely mistaken. "What's inside defiles the man," Jesus said (see Mark 7:20).

I don't know who celebrities like Lance Armstrong follow—but Christ followers should be true to the core. True inside out. Yet hypervigilance won't make that so. Religious rule-keeping won't either. We will be changed only by acknowledging the wretchedness of our prideful independence and clinging in dependence to Christ's righteousness. Only he transforms, heals, and makes new.

We in the family of faith must forgive one another. Betrayal—especially in the family—causes terrible pain and has the power to divide. But forgiveness is a form of voluntary suffering. We can choose it—and we must—because our own forgiveness has been bought by the voluntary suffering of God himself.

> He heals the brokenhearted and binds up their wounds. He counts the number of the stars; he gives names to all of them. Great is our Lord and abundant in strength; his understanding is infinite.
>
> PSALM 147:3-5, NASB

---

[*] Gordon Farquhar, "Lance Armstrong: Seven Unanswered Questions," BBC: Sport, January 18, 2013, http://www.bbc.com/sport/cycling/21085940.

The Power of Standing Still

All my life, I've wanted to move. I rode my childhood hobbyhorse to death in record time, springs worn and sprung from mile after imagined, stationary mile. I was the green-eyed girl who was ready to go. Even now I jiggle my foot or leg when my wait exceeds my wish to be in motion.

Lately, though, I'm learning the power of standing still.

Some of the things I once could do with ease—climbing, running, lifting, leaping—are not so easy now. Never really graceful in motion, I'm even less so now. So I surrender grudgingly to stillness and curse my weakness.

What's more, the stillness goes deeper than muscle and bone. By this age, I'm expected to hold my tongue and not let words fly fast and loose. To tell myself, *Hush now—be still*, when I know just the phrase I wish to hurl and where I'd like to aim it. I'm asked to hold my ground and not be swayed by whims or fads, or pushed beyond propriety or kindness. Sometimes I am able; sometimes I am not. But I have the power within me to be still. At my core there lies a fixed and steady center, even when I flail about and fall.

A piece of sad news yesterday held a snippet of a poem I'd long forgotten: Robert Frost's lovely "The Master Speed." He wrote it for his daughter's wedding day, and its most-oft quoted lines are the final ones: "That life is only life forever more / Together wing to wing and oar to oar."

Those are strong lines full of sweeping motion, but the ones that haunt my mind today are these:

And you were given this swiftness, not for haste
Nor chiefly that you may go where you will,
But in the rush of everything to waste
That you may have the power of standing still.

Father who knit my cells together and keeps my heart in metronome-steady time, let me grow to love the power, the glorious power, of standing still and resting quietly in you.

Don't be afraid. Just stand still and watch the LORD rescue you today. The Egyptians you see today will never be seen again. The LORD himself will fight for you. Just stay calm.

EXODUS 14:13-14

September

True

Ever since I first wrote about watching a horse whisperer in *The Beautiful Ache*, something about that mysterious dynamic between human and horse has stayed with me. The simple beauty of call and response, of compelling and connection, keeps inviting me back again and again.

Not long ago I found the notes I took the *second* time I watched a cowboy who knew his stuff work with a skittish horse, and the four years that have passed since I wrote them fell away as I read.

> "The more you get the emotional part of your horse, the less technique you need."
> "Confidence is knowledge challenged and found to be good."
> "Courage is being scared and doing it anyway."

I talked for a good while with this cowboy, listening to his unconventional training philosophy and well aware it wasn't just about horses. I have no idea what the man believes or doesn't believe about God, or if he could begin to see the parallels between the equine knowledge he was sharing and the ways of God with his children. But I could.

When God reached out to me, it was the purest, fullest, most uncomplicated overture I've ever known. Since then I've tested him over and over and found him to be unbelievably good. And the stuff he calls out of me isn't demanded by force of power; instead it's his love that compels me to give him the best I've got. Knowing he loves me makes me brave in ways I've never been brave before.

There was one stray word scribbled at the bottom of my last page of notes: *true*. The trainer's assistant confided to me that the two of them chose a single word to describe each person who attended this clinic, and the word they'd both agreed on for me was *true*. It might have been the nicest compliment I've ever received. After all, the one who loves me is truer than true, and because I'm his, that's what I long to be too.

I saw heaven opened, and a white horse was standing there. Its rider was named Faithful and True.
REVELATION 19:11

SEPTEMBER 2
My Silhouette, My Legacy

"Let your silhouette be your legacy." That's what the electronic sign advised. I spotted it on my way to a meeting, with no time to do more than guess at its likely connection to some high-end spa treatment. But even then, I was struck by the message's utter incongruity.

silhouette (noun): outline, contour, shape, form
legacy (noun): inheritance, heritage, endowment, gift

In other words, let your outline be your inheritance. Your contour, your heritage. Your shape, your endowment. Your form, your gift. Let your external configuration be what you strive to bestow to others and be remembered by.

There's another obvious incongruity: my legacy is bestowed when I'm dead. So I'm being asked to leave behind nothing but an empty form when I'm gone, in the hope that it will be said of me, "She had a great shape."

Later I did some digging. The line from the sign *is* connected to a trademarked portfolio of "medical aesthetics" that claim to "reshape and tighten without surgery or downtime." In other words, let my legacy be that I was "tight" and "reduced"!

I'm glad I saw the sign. It reminded me that the legacy I'm aiming for is not a legacy of form or outline. It's an endowment of content. A heritage of meaning. An inheritance of love. Father, when I take leave of this imperfect and very temporary form, let me leave behind thousands of acts of kindness, countless whispered prayers, hours of listening, scores of words upon scores of pages that point to you and your infinite goodness. Let me leave with others the memory of being seen and heard, loved and cherished, in your name and by your grace. I beg of you, don't let my silhouette be my legacy!

When he had left, Jesus said, "Now the Son of Man is seen for who he is, and God seen for who he is in him. The moment God is seen in him, God's glory will be on display. In glorifying him, he himself is glorified—glory all around!"
JOHN 13:31-32, MSG

The Mystery of Turning

I love to watch the seasons change. When summer's edges bleed into fall, the days become shorter. The leaves turn amber and rust and brown, then let go altogether in showers of color-rich confetti. The temperature drops, making sweaters seem reasonable again. One evening very soon, I'm certain to step outside and smell smoke rising from a neighbor's chimney. There's a turning afoot, and it's a wonder to behold.

Last week on my walk, a flock of birds flew past, so low I could hear the beating of their wings. And as if on cue, they changed direction—hundreds of them as one—moving east to west in a wide and graceful arc that took my breath away.

I'm turning too. In ways both seen and unseen, I'm becoming more of the woman God made me to be. I'm no more responsible for the good changes in my own soul than the leaves are for their glorious changes in hue. An invisible hand shapes us both, a hand that engineers every turning, from a season to a sigh; that makes possible every resurrection in every heart that ever beat.

God changes things. He changes us. When I forget that, my hope dies a little. But it needn't. There's enough evidence of turning in a single autumn afternoon to make me a believer for life. My God makes all things new. Sometimes the road to "new" runs through sorrow that looks permanent but is not. Sometimes the turning is a hard hairpin curve of repentance, pure and simple; other times it's a gentle drift into deeper, more dependent love. Every time it is a gift—something to be treasured for its surprise, not dimmed by explanation.

Are you thinking of a change that is impossible? Think again. There is no change that God cannot effect—no matter how unlikely it may seem. The tomb is empty. The ultimate turning has been executed, and its echoes never end. The only wonder is that we've embraced it once and still question, day by day, if he could do it all again. He can. He will. Watch expectantly for the lovely mystery of turning.

As you do not know the path of the wind, or how the body is formed in a mother's womb, so you cannot understand the work of God, the Maker of all things.

ECCLESIASTES 11:5, NIV

The Case of the Flame-Retardant Teller

I barely survived a three-alarm meltdown in lane two of the bank drive-through, and I was the one who started the fire. I had endorsed two checks and recorded them on my deposit slip. No other cars were waiting, yet the teller seemed to be taking an unusual amount of time on my transaction. When I glanced at the window, I noticed that she had called in a supervisor to help her.

"We can't deposit this check," the supervisor said. "It's not made out correctly." It was made out to the name on my freelance business account, which was on the account (along with my name) but not officially registered. It had happened a few times before and was always remedied by a quick phone call to the bank officer who helped me set up the account (and who now, after twenty years, worked for another bank). I explained all of this in a loud, agitated voice, but the supervisor didn't budge. When the teller asked if there was a bank officer she could call, I told her he now worked for a competitor. Then I asked if she'd rather I drive two blocks up the street and deposit it with them. (Yes. I did.)

"Are you going to deposit the check or not?" I asked her.

"I can't without the registration," she replied. "Would you like an application for it? The fee is fifteen dollars."

"I fail to see how that is going to help me today," I responded.

If I'd been in her position, I would not have offered. Not after a response like that. Once I was inside, she filled out the application, notarized it, and told me she would deliver it herself that afternoon if I made out a check to the county clerk. She proved the truth that a soft answer turns away wrath, because she turned away mine. Her calm was like a fire extinguisher that doused my rage.

I was much more humble when I left the bank than when I entered. And I went back the next day to apologize in person for my bad behavior. The teller was just as gracious then as she had been the day before.

By our speech we can ruin the world.
JAMES 3:6, MSG

Step-by-Step

I spied the two of them leaving the Washington County Courthouse together. They looked to be well into their eighties: he wore a jacket and a soft hat; she was in a simple skirt and blouse, her boxy handbag swinging from the crook of her arm. As they moved toward a short flight of steps leading down to the street, I noticed both of them were limping. She walked as if perhaps she'd had a stroke. He moved with a definite hitch that mirrored hers. I feared what might happen when they attempted their descent, but I needn't have.

As he approached the first step, he grasped both of her hands firmly in his. Then he planted his good leg below him, and she followed suit with her weaker one, trusting him with her weight. As soon as she was steady, he swung his other leg down and she carefully slid hers to meet his own.

Their movements were perfectly choreographed, and each person knew their part in the dance. They repeated their careful pattern to the bottom of the steps, then shuffled down the sidewalk together arm in arm. Their noontime errand was done, their dance was sweet, and the lesson they taught without knowing it was not lost on me.

We're all a little hobbled in one way or another. We need each other to get where we're going. Your calm can bolster my fear. My steady belief can encourage you in your next challenge. Alternating strengths for weaknesses, step-by-step, we all can achieve far more together for our Father—and his Kingdom—than any of us might hope to do alone.

The ease with which these two partners navigated their course gave them away as longtime collaborators. They'd obviously done this before. But most of us are not so at ease with revealing our weaknesses or being helped by another's strengths. Our world does not celebrate the vulnerability of interdependence. But maybe it should. After all, there is beauty in the quiet dance of compensating flaws—a sweetness to hands grasped in a common task. All that's required of us is that we let our shortcomings be balanced by another's help. Step-by-step, side by side, we can make it. Shouldn't we swallow our pride and *try*?

Bear one another's burdens, and thereby fulfill the law of Christ.
GALATIANS 6:2, NASB

In the Wee, Small Hours

An avalanche of deadlines has had me scrambling, moving constantly from morning until night from one insistent task to the next. Even so, I'm finding myself awake hours before dawn. If you want to know what three o'clock in the morning looks like, I can tell you. Or three thirty. Or four. It's crazy to be stirring at such hours when rest is at a premium, but I am. For a few days I was frustrated by this odd wakefulness, but now I've made peace with it. I know it won't last.

Sometimes I simply pray for a little while, remembering the day just past or the one ahead, then go back to sleep. But more often I rise, walk through the silent house, or even step outside to see the uncommon stillness of my street at that hour. Burley may stir too—or he may not. I try not to wake him, observing his loose-limbed repose and letting his peacefulness be a balm to my unease.

I don't understand why these watchful interludes in the wee, small hours should come now, when my plate is already so full, but I don't resent them. I'm embracing them. God is there, and it's just the two of us at three in the morning. No distractions, no other demands, no chirping phone or pinging e-mail or chiming texts.

In the wee hours, we meet and I listen; I tell him everything or nothing at all. This season will pass. I'm certain the sleep-like-a-rock-for-seven-hours pattern typically reported on my Fitbit will resume one day soon. But for now, we're up long before the sun, my God and me. And I'm certain I'm the better for it.

Lord Jesus, you were born among us in the stillness of the night. As we journey to you in faith, help us to welcome you in darkness, and we will become children of light, to the glory of your Father. We ask you this, who are our Savior, now and for ever.

CONCLUDING PRAYER FOR VIGILS, *Benedictine Daily Prayer: A Short Breviary*

When I remember You on my bed, I meditate on You in the night watches, For You have been my help, And in the shadow of Your wings I sing for joy.

PSALM 63:6-7, NASB

Running on Empty

A gauge on my car's dashboard tells me how close to empty its fuel tank has become. If I don't notice the gauge, a tiny blue icon lights up when I've got five miles' worth of gas left. And if the bright-blue light doesn't trigger action on my part, a digital readout counts the miles remaining until the tank is down to fumes. I don't believe it would be easy to run out of gas in this car, but one day I might prove myself wrong.

My body and soul don't have the bells and whistles of my Ford, but they can still let me know when I'm running on empty. After working two sixty-hour weeks for a client, I was dangerously near the big E. I broke out in hives twice. There were other signals too. I was too tired to eat. My neck and shoulders ached. I sat through a red light and then a green one (hard to do in my city with other drivers behind you, honking). When I finally did crawl into bed, I fell asleep before I could reach over and turn out my bedside light.

My body was saying, "Enough!" And my spirit was too. My prayers became little more than whispered *thank you*s and desperate *help me*s. Because I hadn't read my Bible, or prayed, or sung for the sheer joy of it in days, there was nothing in the tank: no truth, no hope, no beauty, no life. No deep well from which to draw. Just emptiness and bone-tired fatigue.

Then one night as I started home, I noticed that when I turned the key in my car's ignition, the word *Escape* appeared. (My car is a Ford Escape.) And that night, *escape* was just the invitation I needed.

Life will conspire to make us run on empty. But when it does, we need to remember to escape—even just for a few stolen moments—and do those things that give us life. An early-morning walk. An intimate conversation with a friend. A meandering prayer, a quiet meal, or a slow stroll through the pages of a favorite book. These are the things that fill us up, and they are waiting, no matter the hour or the day.

You're my place of quiet retreat; I wait for your Word to renew me.
PSALM 119:114, MSG

SEPTEMBER 8
Albumin (and Other Tiny Miracles)

Unless you are a medical student or a scientist or someone well versed in biochemistry, chances are you don't think much—or at all—about albumin. Sometimes referred to as the molecular taxi system of the body, albumin serum is a water-soluble, heart-shaped protein. The human version of it normally constitutes more than half of our blood plasma.

Suffice it to say I've come to appreciate albumin serum more than some and respect the folks whose job it is to collect, reintroduce, and recycle the stuff. I've even learned that some of these dedicated workers donate their own blood plasma to make substitute tears for those whose eyes can't produce enough of them!

This substance, with its heart-shaped infrastructure, performs some of the most essential functions of life—and we can't even see it work! It moves chemicals from one place to another. It carries certain medications where they need to go, all with very little fanfare: we are unaware of its value as long as it keeps working correctly.

Isn't that how most of us treat the intricate structure of our faith? Untested, we don't think of it much. Unchallenged, we don't consider its deep, rock-solid essence. As long as it keeps working correctly, that is, as long as we remain comfortable and relatively confident that our inherited righteousness will insulate us from harm, we don't bother to examine the complex system of miracles on which our lives rest. The whole Trinity has been at work around and within us to bring us into a community of cruciform love, and we rarely stop to bow our heads in awe.

Albumin, this invisible human serum, has made me more achingly aware of other things I cannot see—things just as real, essential, and miraculous.

There are quiet, tiny miracles at work on our behalf, even now. And belief is still the biggest miracle of all.

I will exalt you, my God the King; I will praise your name for ever and ever. Every day I will praise you and extol your name for ever and ever. Great is the LORD and most worthy of praise; his greatness no one can fathom.

PSALM 145:1-3, NIV

Prodigal Kindness

The word *prodigal* is a funny one. I'd always thought of it as an unflattering adjective, as in the *Prodigal* Son: the spendthrift, the high roller, the squanderer. But it has another nuance. It can also mean lavish, exuberant, profuse, opulent, or luxuriant.

I can testify to the surprise and delight of unexpected prodigal kindness. I attended a fund-raising luncheon that featured a well-known speaker, a lovely meal at a table full of friends, and a silent auction with some of the most amazing needlepoint items imaginable. (Seriously—who knew cuff bracelets, Christmas ornaments, and a full standing Nativity set were stitchable?)

Before the luncheon began, I spotted a friend whose contribution to the auction was a tiny blue Tiffany box ornament, beautifully stitched and finished with a small beaded clasp. It even opened! I told her that my oldest niece just a few weeks ago had received a similar box (with an engagement ring inside), and I thought she might like the needlepoint version quite a lot. I jotted down a quick bid, but it was early, and I never made it back to the table to rebid.

On the way out of the event, I spotted my friend again. "I bid," I told her, "but I didn't get it." Then she held out to me a bag containing the ornament she'd made: "Oh, yes, you did," she said. "It's yours."

Prodigal kindness. She purchased her own offering and gave it to me. I didn't win it, deserve it, or pay for it. She did. Twice. First with her time and then with her love. But her gift didn't end there. The cause we'd both come to support received her over-the-top kindness, and a half hour later so did my niece, when I drove to her office and handed her the little blue box, along with the story of how it was given to me.

You see where this is going, right?

This was not the first time I've been the recipient of such outlandish, prodigal kindness. Not the first time, thankfully, I've received what I did not earn.

———

God, being rich in mercy, because of the great love with which he loved us, even when we were dead in our trespasses, made us alive together with Christ.

EPHESIANS 2:4-5, ESV

With Water and with Words

I didn't mean to watch the ceremony commemorating the anniversary of 9/11, but for some reason I did what I rarely do on a Sunday morning: I turned on the television. When I did, I saw thousands solemnly gathered at Ground Zero and heard the litany of victims' names read by still-grieving sons, daughters, wives, husbands, siblings, mothers, and fathers. Those same names scrolled across the bottom of the screen; it would take more than four hours for the list of the dead to run from beginning to end.

Not only were the names read—interspersed with tributes from two presidents, a governor, and a mayor, anthems from a children's choir, and a haunting cello solo from Yo-Yo Ma—they were etched in bronze around an inverted fountain, framing nearly an acre of rushing water with a strange music of its own.

Along with flowing tears, the morning was awash with water and with words.

The water gave life and movement to what was for so long an ugly, unhealed scar. And the words—the names—made the place even more hallowed than it might have seemed before. With water and words, the space was set apart and put to use again. Slowly, families made their way around the perimeter of the fountain and searched for the names that mattered most to them. Some stretched out hands to trace one by one the letters that they loved; others knelt and wept; still others rubbed impressions onto paper with crayons or with chalk. Flowers, small American flags, teddy bears, notes, and photos were lingered over and then left behind.

Like this precious space at the lower end of Manhattan, I've been sanctified and set apart with water and with words. Christ himself has washed me, for he is living water. With his beautiful words of life he has wooed and won my heart. He doesn't mean to erase my past or eradicate my memory of it—his aim is higher: he cleanses and transforms it so that in his eyes I am radiant in the reflected beauty of his own splendor.

He makes all things gloriously new. Even me.

Christ loved the church. He gave up his life for her to make her holy and clean, washed by the cleaning of God's word.
EPHESIANS 5:25-26

Made to Remember

On a bitterly cold January morning, I visited a public storehouse of memory: an enormous cache of collective human consciousness and achingly personal artifacts. Together with hundreds of others bundled against the chill, I remembered the day we call 9/11 at the newly opened National September 11 Memorial and Museum.

Visitors moved into a vast space full of light and were strongly urged to watch a short introductory film before advancing through the exhibits. We queued up and quietly entered a small auditorium, and without being asked, sat shoulder to shoulder with strangers and waited.

For the next four hours, we wound around and down into the excavated site of unthinkable destruction, seven stories below ground. We heard the recorded voices of survivors, the wail of sirens, the urgent pleas of public officials, and the strangely calm reports of air traffic controllers. We saw crumpled trucks, twisted steel girders, and pieces of the planes once used as weapons.

The lower we descended, the smaller and more personal the artifacts became: crushed spectacles, an unused MetroCard, a melted cell phone, a single shoe, a printed page of instructions from a flight attendant's manual. An insistent, internal voice begged, *Remember this. Don't forget.*

The museum held only one piece of art: Spencer Finch's *Trying to Remember the Color of the Sky on That September Morning*. It covered the breadth of one vast interior wall, and behind it rested the unidentified remains of those who perished at the World Trade Center that day. What looked like a stone mosaic was actually 2,983 pieces of paper, each colored a different shade of blue.

When Jesus knew that he would be crucified and his disciples would be left without the physical presence of their beloved teacher and friend, he created a memory with them. He gathered them at a table, blessed a cup, broke some bread, spoke mysterious words about their meaning, and ingested both with them. "Do this," he said, "and remember" (see Luke 22:19). Try to remember today the color of grace and mercy, of holiness and hope, of justice and faithfulness and love. We are made to remember. Try.

Yours, O LORD, is the greatness, the power, the glory, the victory, and the majesty. Everything in the heavens and on earth is yours, O LORD, and this is your kingdom.

1 CHRONICLES 29:11

Not What I Expected

I'd arranged to meet a friend for dinner and was looking forward to our visit, but her last-minute message said she was under the weather and couldn't make it. So instead of hurrying back from an afternoon of errands, I stopped in at a favorite flower market and spent nearly an hour fingering and smelling luscious, autumn-colored blooms. Then I wandered through a half acre of pumpkins in a city churchyard, taking in the sprawling sea of orange. It wasn't the evening I'd expected, but it was lovely just the same.

Expectations are tricky things. As soon as we get our minds or hearts firmly fixed on something—whether it's a tantalizing menu option the kitchen is out of, or a choice work opportunity that fails to materialize—we set ourselves up for disappointment. When we decide what is best, we judge anything less to be undesirable. But the answer is not to avoid longing, to abandon striving, or to become numb and indifferent to loss. The answer is to hold our expectations loosely, believing that God's surprises—even the most confusing ones—have the capacity to delight. And maybe, just maybe, we don't know best what it is we need most.

Joseph probably didn't think a stint in an Egyptian prison was a good career move. But it was. And when the wandering Israelites' mouths watered for meat and fresh fruits and vegetables, they must have looked at the heaps of morning manna surrounding them and said, "Really, God?" Because if I expect freedom, I chafe at limits. Even constructive ones. If I believe death is the final word, I'll be deaf to the Savior's compelling promise of life. And if I expect meat, I am destined to be forever dissatisfied with the mercy that is manna.

In truth, the blessing is that God gives us what he knows we need, even when we've told him in no uncertain terms what it is we'd rather have. He's so very good that way. May I have the grace to trust him all the way to joy when what I get is not what I expected.

Oh, how great are God's riches and wisdom and knowledge! How impossible it is for us to understand his decisions and his ways!
ROMANS 11:33

Page Proofs

I received (by FedEx) the page proofs for my long-gestating second "baby"—two fat envelopes each stuffed with a hundred or so pages of clean, ordered type.

The page-proof stage of the publishing process may be my favorite. The almost-but-not-quite pages I leaf through are close—so close—to the secret ideas I've carried for so long in my head and my heart.

I know to treasure this "almost there" time. I know that holding the finished product in my hands and brushing the cover with my palm will be a fleeting moment. That I can only open a book's cover and pop its stiff spine for the first time *once*. That the freshly printed smell of new pages will quickly disappear and that no matter how careful we've all been, there *will* be a typo (and I will find it).

Now, almost made, the book is still no one's but mine. In a short time my long-cherished secret will be out, and I'll have no say over where it goes or what it says. It will no longer belong to just me, and I won't be sitting at the shoulder of every reader (thank goodness!) saying, "Oh, no—*this* is what I meant—not *that*!"

My time for creating is done, but the book's promise is just beginning.

I fumble my way through the stories I tell, trying to hold the thread of their original inspiration, fighting to keep it, losing my place. But God never loses his place in my story. I can't see more than vaguely into the next chapter, or even the next page. And even if I've planned well, sometimes a story takes me places I never meant to go.

Not so with him. He is an omnipotent, omniscient storyteller. He skips the page proofs altogether and moves from invisible to everlasting in one perfect thought.

If I say, "Surely the darkness shall cover me, and the light about me be night," even the darkness is not dark to you; the night is bright as the day, for darkness is as light with you. . . . Wonderful are your works; my soul knows it very well.
PSALM 139:11-12, 14, ESV

SEPTEMBER 14
Dressed Down

I had recently taught a Bible study lesson on pride and was also feeling encouraged about a pitch presentation some colleagues and I had made to an organization we all hoped to work with. I wasn't thinking of either of those things when I agreed to meet my sister for lunch and left the house decidedly underdressed. The restaurant we'd chosen was casual—but not T-shirt, jeans, sandals, and a ponytail casual.

I'd barely greeted my sister when I walked in the door and into one of the gentlemen who'd been seated around the conference table for the aforementioned pitch. The last time he'd seen me, I had looked decidedly different: sleek hair, earrings, skirt, jacket, polished pumps. Our eyes met, and for a split second I hoped he hadn't recognized the "new" me. But as soon as he caught my eye, he smiled.

I did what the moment required. I smiled back, said it was good to see him, and introduced him to my sister. Then I noticed the two other men in business suits with him. I knew them both, and it's safe to say they saw a side of me neither of them had seen before. After some upbeat small talk and greetings all around, we said good-bye.

I began to berate myself. How could I have gone out of the house looking so sloppy? What was I thinking? When we got to the table, I continued my self-thrashing: *How awful was that? Can you believe they saw me looking like this? How humiliating!* To my sister's credit she did not try to tell me I looked fine. (Truth telling has always been a hallmark of our relationship.) She simply said it probably didn't change things much, which was true except for this: it changed in an instant my estimation of how much pride I take in appearing put together. It reminded me of how much more I like the idea of "executive" me than everyday, unadorned me.

I hadn't bothered to dress up for a quick lunch with a family member. As a result, I was made to recognize how much pride still lurks in my dressed-down heart. Maybe it was a good thing, after all.

As in water face reflects face, so the heart of man reflects man.
PROVERBS 27:19, NASB

SEPTEMBER 15

Off the Map

I like maps. And because I'm a word person, I also like having written directions with my map. But sometimes even both of these are not enough.

Driving on a Texas ranch road, I was looking for a cutoff at an even smaller byway. I'd never been on either road before, and I was driving alone. Just as the light was fading, I found my small bed-and-breakfast, checked in, and changed my clothes. Then I got back in the car to search for my real destination—a small ranch in the Texas Hill Country where I was attending a living room concert that began in ten minutes.

The sun had disappeared, leaving a reddish tint on the western horizon. Three right turns (theoretically) and I was there. But which turns were they? I checked the map again and noticed these words: *Not to scale.* Not only was I unsure about where the turns were, but I had no idea how far apart they might be. I had the sinking feeling that I might have to turn around and trace back the way I came, missing the music I'd come for.

Passing a well-lit home that looked inviting, I pulled in to ask directions. As I stood on the porch and peered inside, I discovered I'd been there before! Nearly eight years earlier, I'd visited this very home. I knew its occupants. They didn't answer the door, but as I stood where I'd stood once before, I realized that while I might have been off the map, I was well within God's precise radar. He knew my whereabouts, even if I did not.

And I knew the turn I needed to make next. At the next crossroads, I turned toward a stone gate with two people standing at either side. I rolled down my window and breathed a sigh of relief as one said, "Welcome to Blue Rock." I walked up the path and went inside, falling into a rich space of hospitality, warmth, and music.

While I might feel lost from time to time, I am never beyond God's radar. I'll find the way home, and so will those I cherish. At the end of the road, we're sure to find Love waiting—doors open and lights on, ready to take us in.

How lovely is your dwelling place, LORD Almighty!
PSALM 84:1, NIV

My Stand-Up Jesus

I have a four-foot concrete statue of Jesus I purchased in a junk shop a decade ago. When I asked the shop's owner if it was for sale, she replied that everything was for sale but that she was partial to "Jesus" because he was a gift from an old boyfriend.

An old cemetery-robbing boyfriend, I thought, but I didn't say it. When I asked her the statue's price, she gave me an outrageous number. I said thank-you and moved on—but each time I returned to her shop, the statue was still standing near the door.

When I stopped in one rainy afternoon, the owner I'd previously met was gone. Two cowboy-looking fellows were casually presiding over the junk at hand, and I smelled opportunity.

"Is that statue outside for sale?" I asked. "The one of Jesus?"

"All this stuff is for sale," one of them answered with a vague wave of his hand.

"How much do you want for it?" I asked.

The cowboy drawled a price that was less than a quarter of the one originally quoted by the absentee owner. In less than five minutes, stand-up Jesus was being loaded into my trunk.

While I still have a bit of residual guilt about the manner in which he was acquired, I treasure my statue. Having a four-foot Jesus is a constant reminder of the one whom I offer my love and owe allegiance to, and he's started many interesting conversations.

Moving stand-up Jesus is not great fun. (Last time I moved, it took two grown men and a dolly to relocate him.) But I can't imagine my home without him. I've come to count on my statue's visual reminder that Christ is present with me every day. I've come to appreciate that the palm of one hand is scarred (I know!) and that he wears his heart openly on the front of his robe. Simply by standing in plain sight, my concrete Jesus prompts me to open my own hands and heart (and risk their scarring) to everyone who enters my home.

For a long time I thought I was the one moving Jesus, but now I see that it is Jesus always moving me.

He is actually not far from each one of us, for "In him we live and move and have our being."
ACTS 17:27-28, ESV

SEPTEMBER 17
Lost in Wonder

I was never a fan of the television series *Lost*. As near as I could tell without ever having watched an entire episode, the show followed the survivors of a plane crash on an unknown island—a place that was mysterious and a little scary, and where generally speaking, things were not what they seemed. Call me crazy, but their invented reality sounds an awful lot like mine.

Granted, I didn't crash here. I'm more of a natural-born citizen whose entrance into her "lost" world was far less traumatic. Because this is the only place I've ever known, I don't always comprehend its strangeness. I assume that I understand everything I see, because I've seen it so often and for so long. I imagine that life here is predictable and routine and ordinary. But it is not. Not at all.

Just yesterday I watched half a season's yellow leaves fall in one golden afternoon on my street. They descended in a long, slow, sustained flurry—as if God took a deep breath and sighed just above my front yard. And I was lost. In wonder. I've lived on this planet every day of my life and never witnessed such a moment before. Not even once. How often do I miss God's presence and the wonders he brings, simply because I'm distracted or preoccupied?

On Sunday, our hymn of the week was "Be Thou My Vision," sung beginning to end in morning worship by the gathered congregation I've come to love. And although I've heard the melody hundreds of times, it never sounded so achingly lovely as it did that day:

Be Thou my Breastplate, my sword for the fight;
Be Thou my armor, and be Thou my might;
Thou my soul's Shelter, Thou my high Tower:
Raise Thou me heavenward, O Power of my power.

It was exquisite. And I was lost.

You haven't seen it all friend, and neither have I. This world has ample surprises in store because the one who created and sustains it is ever full of them. And I'll be watching. Because you just never know. A girl could learn to love being lost.

I pray that your hearts will be flooded with light so that you can understand the confident hope he has given to those he called—his holy people who are his rich and glorious inheritance.
EPHESIANS 1:18

The "afters" Inside

A good friend of mine is an architect; he dreams up, designs, and builds beautiful things. Exploring vocation in general and his own vocation in particular, he says, "You've probably seen photos in magazines of 'before' and 'after' buildings or rooms. The 'befores' are a little worn, a little frayed around the edges, perhaps not quite right. But there are 'afters' in there, waiting to be released."

Feeling a little worn myself, a little frayed around the edges, I found my friend's words to be life-giving: "There are 'afters' in there." No matter how in need of restoration I may be, no matter how unrenovated I may feel, it is also true of me that my current state is not the entire picture. There are afters inside.

Ambrose of Milan wrote, "You must always be journeying: from decay to incorruptibility, from mortality to immortality, from turbulence to peace. Do not be alarmed by the word 'death' but rejoice at the good that the journey will bring. For what is death except the burial of vice and the raising up of virtue?"*

Our natural response when we observe decline or death—even change of any sort—is sorrow. Dread. Fear. But for new things to live, old things must die. Jobs end. Once-vibrant friendships fade. Teachers come and go. Addresses change. Loyalties do too. Adorable babies become strong-willed children. (And then those children learn to drive!) But in every instance, there are afters in there, waiting to be released.

For the believer, this is doubly true—because we carry within us the resurrection life of Jesus Christ. No matter how undone we feel, the story isn't over yet. No matter how limited our view, a fuller, richer picture exists. No matter how still the strings of our heart may be, unsung music stirs and will be sung. We are a people with afters inside, and we follow a God who makes them true.

We have this treasure in jars of clay to show that this all-surpassing power is from God and not from us. We are hard pressed on every side, but not crushed; perplexed, but not in despair; persecuted, but not abandoned; struck down, but not destroyed. We always carry around in our body the death of Jesus, so that the life of Jesus may also be revealed in our body.
2 CORINTHIANS 4:7-10, NIV

---

* Ambrose, *De Bono Mortis*, 4.15.

Just the Package, Please

Stores have begun to stock packages with no product. Have you noticed? Reach for an antihistamine, and you are likely to find an empty sleeve which must be taken to the pharmacist in exchange for the goods. The packages are simply ads for the real thing, which must be acquired elsewhere. I imagine these packages themselves are incentive enough for consumers to keep demanding their contents, but I'm struck by the fact that many of us, when shopping for something to believe in, buy just the packaging of faith and are satisfied to leave without the goods.

We buy the trappings of religion—stirring music, a certain worship style, or a charismatic teacher—and manage to content ourselves with these. We equate demonstration with devotion, and liturgy with love. I know because I've done it. We find the package enough and miss the God inside. The Bible records that even God's chosen people preferred to keep him at arm's length, dealing with him through a human go-between. In Jesus' day, the ritual obedience of the religious powers that be completely satisfied their appetite for holiness, to the point where they wanted nothing to do with the very holy God-in-the-flesh who stood before them!

But God's got our number. Or at least he's got mine. If I manage to leave church content without having encountered him, he is not deterred. He sidles up to me while I'm pumping gas or eating lunch, or he confronts me in the words of a stranger or in the kiss of a friend. "He sockets into everything that is," writes Annie Dillard. "Loud as music, filling the grasses and skies, his day spreads rising at home in the hundred senses. He rises, new and surrounding . . . wholly here and emptied—flung and flowing, sowing, unseen, and flown."*

There you go. I might be satisfied with his empty package, but he is not satisfied with my half-filled heart. He means to own it—and will use whatever means he finds at hand to do just that. Given my weakness for pretty wrappings and trappings, I'm exceedingly thankful that he does.

These people come near me with their mouth and honor me with their lips, but their hearts are far from me.
ISAIAH 29:13, NIV

---

* Annie Dillard, *The Annie Dillard Reader* (New York: HarperCollins, 2009), 436.

Glory-Saying

"Let's sing the doxology!"

The meeting was over, and my client—an octogenarian businessman, lay theologian, and philanthropist—was requesting a song. I'd never had a client or colleague or supervisor suggest that praise to God was the appropriate response to the culmination of our business together. But this man did.

So at his request, six of us who had just labored for a few hours after lunch sang these words in chorus:

Praise God from whom all blessings flow;
Praise him, all creatures here below;
Praise him above, ye heavenly host;
Praise Father, Son, and Holy Ghost. Amen.

This brief hymn of praise to the Trinity—known colloquially in Protestant tradition as *the* doxology—is actually *a* doxology, one of many composed for and sung in the church. The term itself is a mash-up of two Greek words: *doxa*, meaning "glory," and *logia*, meaning "saying." In my particular denomination, the words are typically sung in response to the receiving of the offering in Sunday worship. But we were not in worship that day, and we certainly hadn't taken up an offering.

Or perhaps we were . . . and had. Maybe work well done is worship, the mingling of myriad gifts for the creation of something greater is an offering, and the right response to both is "Glory!"

After that day, the doxology was regularly the final punctuation mark on our time together. The practice that had so startled me at his first suggestion quickly became the most natural thing in the world.

He has since gone home to the Father, but I can still hear his voice singing words of praise and thanksgiving. He was a good man, a man who long served God—and others—with unfailing humility and kindness. And he was the man who taught me that there is no wrong time to "say glory" in response to the one who is above all things and ever with us.

So today with you I sing, "Praise God from whom all blessings flow."

Remember your leaders, those who spoke to you the word of God. Consider the outcome of their way of life, and imitate their faith. Jesus Christ is the same yesterday and today and forever.
HEBREWS 13:7-8, ESV

Iggie and Me

For months I've been meeting a sixteenth-century Spanish monk every day for a half hour of morning prayer. We were introduced by a trusted spiritual friend and director who offered—twice—to connect us. At first I declined, because I couldn't imagine cramming another thing into my day. But months later, I said yes, because I had good reason to believe that this odd fix up was God's invitation.

Technically, I am making the 19th Annotation of the Spiritual Exercises of Saint Ignatius of Loyola. Through systematic, daily times of prayer and reflection on selected Scriptures, I am seeking a greater awareness of the presence of Christ in my everyday life.

If you were to peek at my calendar, you would see the notation "Iggie", morning, noon, and night (an extended morning prayer, plus a brief check-in called Examen at midday and in the evening). *Iggie* seemed like a cryptic shorthand for something hard to explain and even a little awkward to confess: "Yes. I'm meeting regularly with a monk. Who founded the Jesuits. And no, I haven't become Catholic." A brief litany of beeps on my phone reminds me that it's Iggie time: time to center my thoughts on the God I love, to listen, and to love him back.

Sometimes I read the Word and cry. Sometimes I confess. Sometimes I praise. Question. Plead. Give thanks. But it's not really Iggie I'm with—although his words are a wise and winsome guide. I'm with Jesus. And he's with me. What I discover about myself in the sometimes too-bright light of Word and Spirit *isn't* always a comfort. But he is. Every time.

I've no need to be afraid of meeting Jesus—even when he illuminates my sin. Because he loves his own and I am his. My dog-eared guidebook invites me to respond to what I read and experience in prayer with little conversations between God and me called *colloquies*. Some days I journal my thoughts, baring my soul and then praying that no one sees my words but him. I'm feeling less and less afraid of what Perfect Love will do with me when next we meet. He's so, so good that way.

Listen to the LORD who created you. O Israel, the one who formed you says, "Do not be afraid, for I have ransomed you. I have called you by name; you are mine."

ISAIAH 43:1

The art of Staying Open

After all these years, I still get a lump in my throat when I hear the words, "Now forming at the north end of Kyle Field," along with the whoops and whistles preceding the first few notes of the "Aggie War Hymn." (Other schools have fight songs; my alma mater has a *war hymn*.) When the Texas A&M University Ags left the Big 12 Conference for the reliably fierce SEC (Southeastern Conference), I suspect I was not alone in anticipating a rather bleak and bruising season of big-time college football. Was I ever surprised!

These "Rough tough! Real stuff!" guys just didn't lie down. Ever. At the end of twelve weeks, less than ten points separated them from an undefeated season. There was no game they were out of. And with a scrambling, not-so-big, and very green freshman at quarterback, even busted plays could end well if the receivers stayed open long enough. This made me appreciate the art of staying open in other ways too—ways that had nothing to do with football.

Instead of despairing when God closes the door on a piece of work, a coveted project, or a potential relationship, I would be wise to remind myself who is calling the plays and quarterbacking our tight team of two. Instead of resigning myself to a future of numbing sameness and routine, I might instead expect the unexpected at any moment. After all, my God is great at this kind of stuff.

He's the God who confounded the Canaanite armies and caused a fortified city's walls to collapse on a cue from a marching band. He made a king of a simple shepherd boy, spoke from a bush that burned, gave orders through a donkey's mouth, and even made the sun stand still to aid a struggling army. Rain or drought? No problem. Stay open. Believe. Redemption through an unwed mother, carrying a child *from* God, who *was* God? Stay open. Believe. And a living, breathing Savior who spent two days dead and buried? Stay open and believe. He has you in his sights.

But when the time arrived that was set by God the Father, God sent his Son, born among us of a woman, born under the conditions of the law so that he might redeem those of us who have been kidnapped by the law. Thus we have been set free to experience our rightful heritage.
GALATIANS 4:4-5, MSG

What's Going on Inside

I live in a city neighborhood that can be noisy. Sometimes, mostly at night, I hear music booming from the speakers of a passing car and think, *Good grief—what must that sound like to someone* inside *that car?*

I consider this about passing traffic, yet I hardly ever think about what it might be like to be inside someone else's skin. "You never really understand a person until you consider things from his point of view—until you climb into his skin and walk around in it," says wise Atticus Finch in Harper Lee's *To Kill a Mockingbird.*[*]

What's going on with the colleague whose husband I know lost his job—who has two kids and a mortgage and no easy way to make ends meet? What's going on inside the heart of the boy who carries the Diet Dr Pepper to my car in the drive-through, the one who greets me with a gold-toothed smile and likes to say, "See you next time"? What's it like to be him? What's going on inside?

I don't ponder this much, but I believe Jesus did. I believe he studied the centurion whose son was on his deathbed and felt the dry-mouthed fear of every father's worst nightmare. I believe he crawled inside the skin of a Samaritan woman at high noon and felt how it was to be shunned by the neighbors but dying for love. I believe he inhabited the heart of Peter each time Peter blurted the words, "I know him not!" and imagined what every traitor longs for most: the trust of the betrayed, undeserved but sure.

How many people do I pass in a day whose stories could use an infusion of hope? How many times do I ache for someone to pause long enough to ask *me*, "What's going on inside?" I don't know how it is in someone else's world unless I ask. Not any more than I know what's going on behind the lighted windows of my street or the car in the next lane.

Don't you ever wonder what's going on inside?

Seek the welfare of the city where I have sent you into exile, and pray to the LORD on its behalf; for in its welfare you will have welfare.
JEREMIAH 29:7, NASB

---

[*] Harper Lee, *To Kill a Mockingbird* (Philadelphia: J. B. Lippincott, 1960), 30.

Thirty-Five Thousand Loaves

I haven't started reading the obituaries. I swear. But one day at lunch I opened the paper, and the sections I usually read first (front page, sports, editorials) didn't last through the second half of my sandwich. So I opened the city section, which includes the local obits. The longest one caught my eye, so I read it through—and I'm glad I did. If I hadn't, I would have never known about Dr. Joe, and he deserves a nod.

This scholar, university professor, scientist, and researcher apparently had quite a notable academic career. But he was proudest of a nonprofit he began nearly fifty years ago that provided shelter for those visiting the city for extended medical treatment. For these more than seven thousand families—from forty-nine states and sixty-plus foreign countries—this scientist baked bread. That's right. Bread.

"He used his chemistry skills," I read, "to bake sourdough bread, which he gave to welcome guests, to encourage volunteers, and to thank donors." How much bread? Thirty-five thousand loaves, give or take. That's a lot of baking for an amateur.

Dr. Joe's story made me wonder, *Couldn't someone* else *have done that?* A local bakery, maybe? And they certainly could have. But they hadn't. He had. I imagined all the lives he must have touched with those loaves of bread. Bread for strangers. Bread for friends. Loaf after loaf after loaf. An inauspicious legacy of freshly baked love.

He had other things, important things, to offer. But I'll bet every person who received one of Dr. Joe's loaves remembers it.

What are you giving away? What ordinary thing are you willing to do over and over again for love? What simple thing can you offer? Will you? Baking is ordinary. Writing is too. Over the years, I've written more than seven hundred devotionals like this one and, week by week, sent them off to more strangers than friends. That sounded like a lot to me until I read Dr. Joe's obituary. Seven hundred? Meh. Times ten, girl—then we'll talk.

There's an exquisite beauty in a habit of small offerings made with great love. Anyone can . . . but not everyone does. Joe did. Will you? Will I?

———

Your kingdom come. Your will be done, on earth as it is in heaven.
Give us this day our daily bread.
MATTHEW 6:10-11, NASB

The Boys of (Late) Summer

April baseball is all about expectation. June baseball is ripe with possibility. By August (according to a friend of mine who is a sportswriter), unless you are within ten games of the division leader, you're as good as done. September baseball often holds a surprise or two—and my hometown team is one of them.

In August the boys of summer were languishing in the most disappointing way. If someone had told me then that by September these sleepwalking underachievers would be a game and half out of first place, I might have produced a very unladylike snort. But that is exactly where they are today.

Even in a game that is managed by statistics and analyzed into oblivion, there are intangibles. No one is unbeatable, and no long shot is unwinnable. That's why they play all the games on the schedule. Even when the odds are narrowing, they suit up, go to the park, and play ball.

My hometown team is on a hot streak. I don't know how far they'll ride it, or what the ultimate outcome of this improbable season will be—but their heart is impossible to deny. They're in the hunt, just days from October. And isn't that exactly where you'd want to be? Because beyond expectation and possibility and promise lies what *is*. The present is where the game is played. That's where the glory lies. That's where anything can happen, where hearts can catch fire and blaze in the most unexpected ways.

From the hometown boys I've learned that discouragement isn't fatal, that defeat isn't destined to repeat itself. That the long schedule has more twists and turns than you can imagine, and it is unlikely to play out according to any careful preseason plan. But mostly I've learned that each day's game is the opportunity of that day alone and must be met.

It's almost October. Even in my southern city, the air is getting cooler. And the game is getting harder, not easier. It counts more now. Not less. What is there to do today but take the field and play?

For nothing will be impossible with God.
LUKE 1:37, HCSB

Well-Watered

Three mornings a week, just before five in the morning, my lawn and flower beds are watered—but not by me. I am almost always asleep when the watering takes place, but through a programmed design more consistent than rain, refreshing comes. It happens whether I am awake or asleep, at home or away, anticipating or being surprised by it.

The first time I heard the watering, I was still adjusting to the sounds of a new house. I didn't expect to hear gurgling and hissing in the predawn darkness, and it startled me awake. Was something amiss?

A bleary-eyed, barefoot reconnaissance led me to the front lawn, where a fine mist was settling on the grass. The paving stones in the flower beds were glistening too. Drops were clinging to the towering magnolia, the just-bloomed agapanthus, and the knockout roses, and I could smell the wet earth embracing their roots. They were being watered—and watered well—while I was sleeping a few feet away, oblivious to the goodness going on when I wasn't looking.

I've just recently become aware of this watering by an unseen hand, but it's been going on much longer than I have been in residence here. Every dark night of my life—literal or figurative—I am being watered. God is giving rest and dreams and relief from the stress of daily living while I slumber. He is refreshing me through the hours of darkness with a living water I cannot conjure or command. He is bringing life to my sleeping soul in ways I do not expect or comprehend. I don't often recognize his watering when it takes place. More often, I arise and see its evidence: freshness where there was decay; hope where there was despair; nourishment where my heart's cupboard was growing bare.

This morning, if I walk outside early enough and take notice, the grass will be glistening, the stones and sidewalk will be wet, and the earth will hold enough water to withstand the blistering heat of another day. And because my God is the source and supply of all refreshing springs, my soul will be well watered too.

He split open the rocks in the wilderness to give them water, as from a gushing spring. He made streams pour from the rock, making the waters flow down like a river!"
PSALM 78:15-16

Underwhelmed

Sometimes, a Texas girl just wants a chicken-fried steak.

A while back, after thinking about it for several days, my resolve to abstain from such artery-clogging food weakened. My choice was deliberate. I called a place in my neighborhood that is known for the popular menu item and ordered one for pickup.

Out of guilt, I ordered a half-sized portion. I still felt bad about it but hoped that after eating it I might have only half-sized regret, too.

Turns out I had hardly any regret at all. When I picked up my order, it smelled bewitching. I noticed that the container I was handed seemed a little light, but I didn't think much of it. When I arrived home and opened the container to plate my long-savored entrée, however, I was sorely disappointed. The bag contained the smallest, most minuscule chicken-fried steak in all of Texas. My cookie-cutter-sized portion was an embarrassment to chicken-fried steaks everywhere—and certainly to the establishment that boasted about theirs!

How small was it? It easily fit in the palm of my hand. A slice of Spam would have dwarfed it. It in no way lived up to its promise *or* satisfied my craving. It was a chicken-fried impostor. I was utterly underwhelmed.

So what does a Barbie-sized portion of chicken-fried steak have to do with the gospel claim that Jesus saves? Just this: the promise is not only true as advertised, but the reality far exceeds all expectations of it.

Jesus saves. *And Jesus satisfies.* The first reality can be realized in a heartbeat. Salvation is an in-time event with eternal significance. It takes but a moment to place your faith in Jesus Christ's so-great sacrifice, but a lifetime is not long enough to understand (or to enjoy!) the gracious benefits of that surrender. Jesus saves sinners like me from the sure judgment of a holy God. And Jesus satisfies saved sinners with the riches of his goodness and mercy again and again and again.

You will not be underwhelmed by him. His grace will never disappoint. Every longing awakened by his promises will be richly, deeply, wildly satisfied in him. Because the gospel story doesn't *end* with the claim that Jesus saves. It begins there.

Oh, taste and see that the LORD is good!
PSALM 34:8, ESV

Baggage-Claim Carousel 6

I've been separated from my luggage a time or two by airline error, but I still check it at the curb. I've never understood why anyone would drag more gear than they absolutely must onto a plane. My policy is, if I can't wear my pajamas in flight, they don't need a spot in the overhead bin. While this belief saves my back some wear and tear, it also assures that I spend my share of time in baggage claim.

Precisely because I *have* come up empty there before, I'm never certain that I'll see my own bag tumble off the chute and onto the conveyor belt when I arrive at my destination. I'm hopeful, yes, but I don't necessarily trust that what's gone in will indeed come out.

On one such trip it occurred to me (while waiting at baggage-claim carousel 6) that my following-Christ life bears similar uncertainties. I know that I am his and he is mine. I know his Spirit resides in me. I'm just not always sure it's going to come *out*. I'd like to be more merciful. More kind. More patient. And these qualities are his very nature, so it's reasonable to expect they might emerge from me. But they don't always.

Sometimes they get lost in transit and arrive later than I'd like or not at all. Sometimes what comes out of me is not his nature but my own fleshly bent toward meanness or sloth or pettiness. My own baggage, in other words. Not the better stuff of his beautiful heart. It's in there, though.

Maybe I should not be surprised when I *don't* see it, but simply more grateful when I *do*. When what's gone into my heart by virtue of his great substitutionary sacrifice comes out with some measure of clarity and consistency. That's more than reason enough to believe that it can—and will—do so again.

In the meantime I'll be waiting expectantly for his indwelling goodness to come forth from me, trip by trip, bag by bag, day by day.

What the law code asked for but we couldn't deliver is accomplished as we, instead of redoubling our own efforts, simply embrace what the Spirit is doing in us.
ROMANS 8:4, MSG

Those Last Five Boxes

If you've relocated lately, maybe you've wondered the same thing I did after my third move in little more than a year: *Where in the world did all this stuff come from?* I didn't imagine my two-bedroom apartment had *that* much in it, but I can't exactly say that I've been living a pared-down existence.

Now, after reselling one hundred books and giving away clothes, a few small pieces of furniture, and even items I had multiples of (vacuums, coffeemakers, clothes baskets, blow-dryers), I am still a little more full than I would like. And nearly a month after the movers have been paid, there are five boxes sitting in the guest room that I can't quite reckon with. They contain items I don't need on a day-to-day basis but simply can't motivate myself to sort or store or throw away. If it's this challenging to simplify my exterior life, I'm wondering how much stuff I'm hoarding on the inside, and why.

Isn't it the last lingering bit of anything that challenges us most? The last few days of school. The last five pounds of a diet, or the last stubborn smidgen of unforgiveness? Why is it so hard to finish things off? Why, when I've unpacked sixty or so boxes, am I still looking at five? And why, when it would take only a few minutes of wrestling before God, do I refuse to open my heart and deal with what's inside?

Thankfully, there is a ray of hope for spiritual procrastinators and our stagnation of the heart. Jesus stands ready to help me with what I am too sad or afraid or disappointed in myself to face. He insists that he will never leave me nor forsake me, that it is his full intent to abide with me, and that his death-defying power is perfected in my weakness. How good is that? Best of all, he won't give up on me, even when I've exhausted my own resources and lack the will to finish the good work that he, in his mercy, has begun.

I am confident of this very thing, that He who began a good work in you will perfect it until the day of Christ Jesus.
PHILIPPIANS 1:6, NASB

The Sweet Smell of Suffering

Smell is one of our most powerful senses, connected to our subconscious memory in a way that our other senses are not.

Maybe like me, you can remember cherished smells from childhood—scents from places you've not visited in years. My grandmother's bathroom had the sweet, cherry-and-almonds scent of Jergen's skin lotion, which she applied liberally after every bath. The church I grew up in smelled to me like polished wood and Jungle Gardenia perfume—the signature scent of the woman who always seemed to sit in the pew just in front of us.

When Paul calls the Corinthian Christians "the fragrance of Christ," (2 Corinthians 2:15, NASB) I marvel at his metaphor. Although their relationships were difficult and their circumstances trying, he envisioned them as a victorious parade wafting the incense of grace wherever they went.

Maybe today you're thinking that you would be the fragrance of Christ, except you're heartbroken. Or you're longing for something that isn't and may never be. Or you're sick. Or someone you love is. Or you've lost someone immeasurably precious to you. Or you've messed up. Big-time.

If that's what you're thinking, the gospel contains better news for you than you could ever imagine: through the triumph of Christ, our emptiness can become abundance; our helplessness can become hope; and our failures can be exchanged for forgiveness, time and time again.

Peter denied Jesus right *after* he boasted to his Master, "I would die for you." What kind of God would accept such miserable failure? I'll tell you: *a God like ours.* Through the sacrificial blood of Jesus Christ, our failures become acceptable, and our shame survivable.

Like Peter, we can move from failure to forgiveness. Because *we* are the fragrance of Christ. Empty, helpless, ashamed . . . we are the fragrance of Christ. His presence is the divine alchemy that makes a beautiful aroma of our suffering and shame and spreads the sweet knowledge of him in every place.

Today, may his presence create an unforgettable fragrance in you.

Through us, he brings knowledge of Christ. Everywhere we go, people breathe in the exquisite fragrance. Because of Christ, we give off a sweet scent rising to God, which is recognized by those on the way of salvation—an aroma redolent with life.

2 CORINTHIANS 2:14-16, MSG

October

Write This Down

The question I'm asked most often when I go somewhere to speak or I'm meeting new folks is this: "How do you become a writer?"

There are more instructive answers, of course, but I usually just say, "Writers write." Writers process their world by writing it down—from the mundane to the profound. It's what we *do* because it's who we *are*.

Once, in the process of packing up my parents' home of nearly fifty years, I stumbled onto a small, very seventies-looking notebook filled with my handwriting. In the summer of my thirteenth year, I had apparently already begun the practice of recording stuff. Flipping through page after page, I read that the Indians won the Little League baseball championship, defeating the Braves. I read who I'd met at the neighborhood pool for a swim, where I'd ridden my bike, and what books I'd read and records I'd listened to in my more solitary, happy hours. I know this now because I wrote it down.

By the time I arrived at college, I had filled page after page of journals; I'd written nothing marketable or deeply profound—but the life I had lived to that point I had written down. Pleading prayers. Answered ones. Hurts. Dreams. Everyday happenings. I had not yet called (or even considered myself) a writer. But I was. Because writers write.

Writer or not, everyone has a story. And that story is solidified by writing things down. "Write down what you have seen," the apostle John hears just before he witnesses the apocalyptic vision, "both the things that are now happening and the things that will happen" (Revelation 1:19). Why? So that others will know the story of God—and of his everlasting love.

There are things you really should write down—so that you will remember too. "Don't be afraid! I am the First and the Last. I am the living one. I died, but look— I am alive forever and ever! And I hold the keys of death and the grave" (Revelation 1:17-18). He is God and there is no other. Write this down.

He who sits on the throne said, "Behold, I am making all things new."
And He said, "Write, for these words are faithful and true."
REVELATION 21:5, NASB

Buried Truth

The first time I saw the art installation on the esplanade, I did a double take. Driving south on Houston's Heights Boulevard, I passed something that looked like a half-buried church steeple. I recognized it as art (I'd already passed a neon beagle and a baby carriage made to look like an Airstream), but it looked more like the odd result of a small urban twister, neatly landscaped and strangely unscarred.

Several miles past the buried steeple, I was still wondering, *Why?*

It troubled me to see the church pictured as vulnerable and compromised. But she is. She is vulnerable to the flaws of the human persons who serve her. She is vulnerable to the preferences and prejudices of culture. And she is compromised. By the choice to peddle feel-good, pop encouragement and call it gospel. By every decision to insulate rather than risk. By the presence of charlatans and impostors in places of power.

Whether you believe Christ's church is winning or waning in public opinion, is wooing souls or repelling them, is contextually relevant or hopelessly out of touch . . . she remains the bride of Christ. G. K. Chesterton once described her as a figure reeling but upright through the ages.[*]

On the boulevard, she seems to be going down into the earth for good. But the whole arc of the Christian story leads us to this unflinching conclusion: *buried things rise*. Nothing is as it seems. And no matter how dark the horizon gets, the sun *will* rise on the day of the Lord and the trumpet *will* sound. As the Nicene Creed proclaims, "He shall come again, with glory, to judge the quick and the dead; whose kingdom shall have no end."

Now when I drive past this sculpture, I adjust my eyes to see the true reality: the church is not sinking into oblivion; she is rising as a bride from sleep to meet her Beloved. Her steeple ascends from the earth and points heavenward while the saints of all the ages gaze upward and the Risen One beckons her up and on.

Be on guard for yourselves and for all the flock, among which the Holy Spirit has made you overseers, to shepherd the church of God which He purchased with His own blood.

ACTS 20:28, NASB

---

[*] G. K. Chesterton, *Orthodoxy* (Chicago: Moody, 2009), 153.

The Gift of Groaning

I used to greet every new day by springing out of bed with ridiculous energy, but now my morning routine includes a minute or two of quiet groaning as I stretch and flex and coax my body into the movement the day will demand. When I lie back down at night, I groan myself into a position comfortable enough to welcome sleep.

I am coming to understand the longing with which the apostle Paul spoke when he said,

> We know that if the earthly tent which is our house is torn down, we have a building from God, a house not made with hands, eternal in the heavens. For indeed in this house we groan, longing to be clothed with our dwelling. . . . For indeed while we are in this tent, we groan, being burdened.
>
> 2 CORINTHIANS 5:1-2, 4, NASB

Perhaps more than any of his peers, Paul "got" groaning. He experienced the wear and tear of an itinerant preacher's life, and he had the physical scars to prove it. No doubt he longed for a resilient, resurrected body like that of the risen Savior he followed. But he also longed for an entire world made new with the glory of redemption. "The whole creation has been groaning . . ." he insisted, "right up to the present time" (Romans 8:22, NIV).

But there is grace in every groan. Momentary light affliction is producing within us an eternal glory that outweighs any trouble we might experience in the here and now. We don't lose heart, because in our waiting, we are becoming richer than we might have ever imagined.

I remember pain-free mornings with sharp longing. I have not abandoned the hope that I will experience them again. But I am learning to love my days bookended with groaning for the steady reminder that they give. My God is making all things new. Slowly. In his time. And whether he completes the change here or in the world to come, we must not lose heart. He is good, even when we groan.

> With eager hope, the creation looks forward to the day when it will join God's children in glorious freedom from death and decay.
>
> ROMANS 8:20-21

Tale as Old as Time

There's a scene from Walt Disney's *Beauty and the Beast* that causes a hard lump to form in my throat every time I see it. Tough but tender heroine Belle is dancing with the ugly, hulking beast, and she's smiling up into his hideous face, her eyes aglow.

It's one of those perfect moments where love creeps in against all odds and insists on staying put. Where beauty is utterly and completely in the eye of the beholder and not about to budge.

Apparently the appeal of that particular movie moment has nothing at all to do with age. I took my two nieces to see the animated film when they were seven and eleven, and on the way home asked them which part they liked most. Seven-year-old Victoria piped up from the backseat without hesitation: "Oh, Aunt Leigh—I loved it when she danced with him and he was still the beast."

So did I, baby girl. So did I.

Beauty and the Beast really is a tale as old as time. And the oldest, truest version of it goes something like this:

> You see, at just the right time, when we were still powerless, Christ
> died for the ungodly. Very rarely will anyone die for a righteous person,
> though for a good person someone might possibly dare to die. But God
> demonstrates his own love for us in this: While we were still sinners,
> Christ died for us.
> ROMANS 5:6-8, NIV

Who doesn't want to be loved when they're hopelessly unlovely? Who doesn't hope for a savior who sees them at their very worst and steadfastly refuses to be repulsed? Belle loved the beast before she had even an inkling of the prince he might become. And when she demonstrated that love, he became something altogether beautiful. Not before.

Not only did Christ love me when I was—by his righteous standards—quite beastly, he loved me enough to die for me so that I could become—again by his standards—altogether beautiful.

Just thinking of it makes me feel like waltzing to a song as old as rhyme, the Father-Son-Spirit melody of loving communion that never ends.

> Instead of your shame you will receive a double portion, and instead of
> disgrace you will rejoice in your inheritance.
> ISAIAH 61:7, NIV

cupcake ATM

On the back side of a cupcake store in my town, I saw a bright-pink "ATM" that claimed to dispense its frosted wares the way a regular one spits out cash. Truthfully, I was afraid to test the machine to see if it worked; it looked too much like an invitation to be "punked." Besides, those cupcakes are diet killers.

I did a little web research when I got home, though—just to satisfy my curiosity. Turns out, the cupcake ATM *is* real. You touch the screen, select your cupcake, swipe your credit card, and wait for the magic door to open, revealing the delectable and perfectly boxed evidence of your transgression.

So promising, that bright-pink machine. So tantalizing with its lure of instant, automated gratification. And so much like this world we live in. How many messages do we receive each day that insist the next delight is ours for the taking? That life is just one sweet cupcake after another if we swipe the right card and wait a mere second or two? That if we pray the right prayer, God will answer as we wish him to, and when? Or that if we are faithful church attenders or we tithe or support missions or volunteer in the nursery, God will be so pleased he will rain blessings down on our heads in return? If we're honest, we may have been duped at times into thinking, *That's the real gospel.* But it's not.

We follow Jesus Christ, the living stone who was rejected by men. Goodness didn't ensure ease for him, and it won't for us, either. He was ridiculed, mocked, persecuted, and murdered. He came to die, and he bade his disciples to take up their own crosses and follow him. His call to us is the same.

Don't fall for the pink facade that promises ease and satisfaction for a song—or a cupcake for $4.25. We can expect hardship; we can expect to suffer if we follow our Savior for long. Because he did. But we can also expect to be sanctified, glorified, and eternally satisfied in him. Just not here. 'Cause this world ain't no cupcake ATM, no matter what it promises. And it was never meant to be.

Suffer hardship with me, as a good soldier of Jesus Christ.
2 TIMOTHY 2:3, NASB

Celebrating Unpredictable Fruit

Where I live it's raining acorns. They pelt the roof like the fat drops of a summer thunderstorm. They cover the driveway like marbles and crack under my feet in the yard. Burley insists on selecting one to carry back inside like an after-dinner mint each time he goes out.

Even though I sweep often, I can't brush them to the curb fast enough to eradicate the crunchy carpet of brown. The gardening gurus say we're having a "masting year" and that the proliferation of acorns—some five to ten times the normal amount—is unrelated to any one weather factor or soil condition and totally unpredictable.

One might think that the acorns abound because conditions are perfectly aligned for fruit making, but that's not necessarily the case. Drought can trigger acorn over-production just as easily as optimal rainfall. During a masting year, the trees are working extra hard, expending more energy on the creation of fruit than in lengthening or strengthening their limbs or roots.

Will next year be the same? No one knows. An unseen hand bids them to be fruitful neither because of nor in spite of their surroundings. An invisible husband-man says, "Multiply," and they obey. By any measure, this season for me is a less-than-nurturing one. Conditions are in many ways harsh—not at all conducive to fruit bearing. Yet if I pay attention to the lessons I see illustrated in my yard and on my roof, anything could happen. My heart could reverberate with the unpredictable tuning fork of the Father and overproduce in ridiculous fruitfulness. I could have a masting year on the heels of the worst drought imaginable. It could be so. And I should not be surprised. The one who made the oaks and speaks to them has made my heart and rules it. He can multiply unpredictable fruit for no good reason— daring me to burst forth with productivity just when I feel most seedless and small.

You must go on growing in me and I will grow in you. For just as the branch cannot bear any fruit unless it shares the life of the vine, so you can produce nothing unless you go on growing in me. I am the vine itself, you are the branches. It is the man who shares my life and whose life I share who proves fruitful.

JOHN 15:4-5, PHILLIPS

The Art of Noticing

I once spent a day with a dozen seventh graders. They were part of an academic adventures program for accelerated students, and I was their creative writing instructor.

I was more than a little nervous—seventh graders aren't exactly my strong suit, and I don't believe writers can be forcefully made. Even so, I'd prepared a full array of visual instruction, reading, and writing exercises that I hoped would help us to at least discover what gifts might be lurking underneath, without anyone falling asleep.

When I learned the two pediatric dental residents across the hall were going to teach their would-be dentists to make impressions of their own teeth, I felt sure my budding writers would bolt. To the casual observer, writing is more than a little like watching wet paint dry.

For our first exercise, I placed several random items from my kitchen junk drawer in the center of each table, asked the students to select one thing each, and gave them two minutes to write a detailed description of the item they chose. It was fun to watch them turn the items over in their hands, shake and sniff them, then pick up their pencils and begin to write.

For the next six and a half hours, we created characters. Described settings. Examined the elements of plot using children's books. As we gathered for our last reading, one boy asked when we'd begun that morning. I told him 9:45. "It's gone by so fast," he said. "I'm not ready to leave." I could have kissed his untied tennis shoes!

Because they were looking to me (and to each other) for a glimmer of affirmation, I listened more carefully that day than I have in a long time. My seventh-grade scribes reminded me that we all long to be heard. And we hope for someone to acknowledge our efforts, even the tentative, unpolished ones.

Could someone in your world be pining for a thoughtful word or a spark of encouragement? Could you give them the gift of noticing?

A wise person gets known for insight; gracious words add to one's reputation. . . . Gracious speech is like clover honey—good taste to the soul, quick energy for the body.

PROVERBS 16:21, 24, MSG

Every Little Thing

"Jesus loves me, this I know," I used to sing. "For the Bible tells me so." It did. It still does. But love is communicated in myriad ways and must be recognized, received, and attended to in order to grow.

Not many mornings ago, I saw an array of clouds spread and layered across the sky in a pattern I'd never witnessed before. I thought, *How giving and good you are, God, that you could surprise me on an ordinary morning through clouds, in a way that makes me feel afresh your love for me.*

Don't get me wrong. He's done plenty of big stuff—cosmic, eternity-altering stuff—for all of us. But it's the little things that testify he always meant to love me and keeps on loving me still.

It's the phrase I stumbled upon in a children's book that echoed the exact words resonating in my heart the day before. It's the kindness of the clinician who held my hand longer than just a quick squeeze when he saw I wasn't hurt but still anxious and unsure. It's the ready forgiveness of a friend whose birthday I forgot, even though she always remembers mine. It's the unexpected answers to those seemingly impossible prayers that arrive just in time and yes, sometimes oddly packaged. And it's the blessing of waking in the wee hours of the morning with the sense that all will be well, even if—in the moment—it is not.

I need the promises of God that remind me of his great love for me. I need his Word to "tell me so" and to keep on telling me over and over again. I rely on it. I believe it. I have staked my life on its claims. But every little thing he does affirms that my God loves me. Every little thing he does is good for my soul, somehow. Every little thing he does keeps on echoing the truth of his precious, precious Word. Every. Little. Thing.

Blessed is the one whom You choose and bring near to You to dwell in Your courts. We will be satisfied with the goodness of Your house, Your holy temple.
PSALM 65:4, NASB

Selfie Nation

I was on a long flight, seated across the aisle from two ten- or eleven-year-old girls. I imagined their parents were sitting nearby, but the third seat in their row was empty, and they huddled together in the center with the armrests up, giggling.

A few minutes in, they began taking photographs of themselves, a diversion that went on for almost the whole flight. I was slightly jealous; I'd read the in-flight magazine and completed the crossword in less than half an hour and was bored silly. But they weren't.

They took photos of themselves together and individually. They posed with their hoodies up, then down; their tongues out, then in; their eyes wide, then feigning sleep. After every few photos, they looked at what they'd taken; discarded some, cropped others and added special effects, posted a few to whatever social media they were partial to, and then started all over again. They were completely amused and entertained by their own images.

I remembered traveling in the backseat of my parents' car when I was ten or eleven. I was glad to have a *Weekly Reader*, a deck of cards, or a Barbie doll for entertainment. Picture taking was reserved for Christmas or the first day of school or Easter, and someone else always did the honors.

But now camera-assisted self-portraits are the rage. Does that seem a little narcissistic to you? It does to me. How many selfies can one create without beginning to feel an inflated sense of importance? How much posing on one side of the camera does it take to deter lens-free living on the other side? I can't help thinking how hard it is to observe and enjoy and discover life while you're cataloging your experience of it for others to see.

We're a selfie nation, not simply when we take our own picture, but when we put ourselves in the center of our lives. I'm not slamming the exercise—or fun— of an occasional self-portrait. (Hello and thank you, van Gogh, Rembrandt, and Michelangelo.) I'm simply saying that there's infinitely more life to be lived looking outward than looking back through the lens at myself. Any world with me at its center is too small.

What good is an idol carved by man, or a cast image that deceives you?
HABAKKUK 2:18

Recessionary Spending

During a recession, things are tight everywhere. When we're not sure of our resources, we tend to draw back. We ask ourselves, *Do I really need that now?* or *Do I really need that ever?* These are questions worth asking, recession or no. But a voice in my head keeps calling out for spending, and not the kind you might imagine.

I'm hearing a line one of my parents must have said more than once in my growing-up years, because it stuck: "It doesn't cost you anything to be kind." That's the sort of recessionary spending I could get behind, and lately, it's been modeled for me.

Not long ago I sat in a coffee shop with a friend who wanted to show me something on her laptop, but the Wi-Fi was not cooperating. A fellow sitting next to us observed our frustration and called over a suggestion. As we continued to try to log in, he got up, walked over to our table, and tried it himself. When that didn't work, he logged off his own computer so that we could log on—as him! Turns out he was a regional supervisor for the coffeehouse chain, sitting in the store doing some paperwork. He was kind, and he spent some of that kindness on us.

On a recent trip from Portland to Houston I had accidentally gone on a mini fast. It never occurred to me that after a cup of oatmeal at six in the morning, I wouldn't be eating anything but peanuts until six in the evening! On the next-to-last leg, my seatmate (who learned I'd been flying all day) reached into his briefcase as we were preparing to land at *his* destination, pulled out two small packages of cookies, and said with a wink, "Here. Dinner's on me."

It doesn't cost us anything to be kind. And these two kind spenders have encouraged me to spend my way out of recession in as many ways as I can—one crazy act of love at a time. Will you join me?

You're here to be light, bringing out the God-colors of the world. God is not a secret to be kept. We're going public with this, as public as a city on a hill.

MATTHEW 5:14, MSG

For the Love of Crumbs

We're creatures of desire, made to long for that out-of-reach something, made to ache for what we sense but cannot see. C. S. Lewis called that inconsolable longing by its German name, *sehnsucht*, and a keen sense of it infused his writing and his life. "If I find in myself a desire which no experience in this world can satisfy," he wrote, "the most probable explanation is that I was made for another world."*

What Lewis discovered is that in ignorance of the true object of our hardwired longing—God—we substitute other things. We settle for less because we cannot imagine more or trouble ourselves to wait or to press on for the promise of that "other world." Especially when we are so hopelessly mired in this one.

We take crumbs when God would offer a feast. We substitute food or sex or worldly beauty or shallow friendships when we know they will not ultimately satisfy. Maybe we reckon that such meager pleasures are all that we can have—all that we deserve. In the latter we may be right, but in the former, we could not be more wrong.

God made us for himself—with the capacity to enjoy him forever. The Fall made us beggars for crumbs that will not—cannot—fully satisfy. But the table is set for us. It is groaning with good things. Any delight or pleasure that this world can offer is but a foretaste of the great, great feast that lies before us.

Still . . . we are not there yet. This wide place we are traveling through is mean and harsh and most unwelcoming at times—but that is no reason to imagine it is not crammed with hints of the glory that will one day be ours. And while we hope for what we cannot see, there is more than enough room and reason to delight in what our eyes can already comprehend: the daily, fleeting glimpses (crumbs?) of his goodness that are everywhere, always. We are made for just that kind of joy.

You will make known to me the path of life; in Your presence is fullness of joy; in Your right hand there are pleasures forever.
PSALM 16:11, NASB

---

* C. S. Lewis, *Mere Christianity* (New York: HarperCollins, 1980), 137–38.

Please Help

Her hand-lettered sign said "Please help." No added information about needing work or being hungry or homeless or disabled. Just two simple, direct words. She did not walk along the line of cars waiting at the intersection. She just shifted her weight from one leg to the other a time or two. The light changed before I could clearly see her face and whatever story it told, but I could read her sign and read it clearly. "Please help."

For blocks past the intersection where she stood, I wondered, *How?* What particular sort of help did this woman most need? Five dollars? Ten? Twenty? Although I'm sure currency of any denomination would not have been refused, what real difference would it have made? And how much currency would it take for her to abandon the sign and the street corner where it was displayed?

She held her sign, I'm presuming, because she wanted something specific. Something that might trigger change in her life. But what she triggered in me was a question—"How?"—and this conviction: I don't say "Please help" near enough. I am proud and more prone to give help unasked than to confess that I need it myself. When I could no longer see the woman at the corner, I pictured myself holding her sign and letting it be read by strangers.

And I pictured myself saying those two confessional words to my heavenly Father, over and over: *Please help.*

Please help me to love you more. Please help me to love my family and friends in ways that mean love to them. Please help me to love my neighbors well. Please help me to see the world the way you see it, Father, and respond to what I see as Jesus would. Please help me to listen to the still, small voice of the Spirit that beckons me and teaches me the way of love. Please help me to slay pride and selfishness and apathy and cynicism. They are ugly and do not honor you. Please help me to say "Please help" as often as I feel my need for your help. And please help me to bear a strong family resemblance to you and to your beautiful Son. Please help.

I lift up my eyes to the hills. From where does my help come?
PSALM 121:1, ESV

Open Windows

I had a window issue. My car's back driver's side window wouldn't stay up. No matter how many times I raised it, as soon as the car started moving, it would slip down again. When the weather was good, this meant only a slight bit of wind noise. But my slip-sliding window made rainy days a potential recipe for disaster and rendered trips to the car wash all but impossible.

While the car window was slipping, the windows of my little 1920s rental bungalow were shut tight and hadn't been open for ages. I couldn't catch a breeze for love or money. Funny, no? Rolling, I couldn't keep my windows shut, and sitting still, I couldn't open them!

My heart has windows as well. Is it any surprise that I'd like to either shut them when they fly open against my better judgment or pry them loose when the longing for air outweighs my fear of exposure? In theory, of course, the choice is mine. But windows, it seems, have a mind of their own.

Looking through an old journal, I read the recorded words of a friend who opined, "Leigh, from the front you're like a fortified city with a moat, but around back there's a screen door barely hanging on its hinges." He didn't quit there. "God help the man who tries to scale the front, but bless the one who bothers to try the back door instead."

I thought hard about those words. He was right. But since he spoke them, I've discovered more: I can't open my heart to God on the one hand and shut it to the world. Nor can I shut my heart to the world (even when I'm afraid) and expect to hold it open to God. Same windows. The challenge is to trust my Father with the rain and noise and heat that are beyond my power to control. Open windows are risky, yes. But nailing them shut, well, that's a kind of living death.

Give me open windows every time.

The moment I called out and you stepped in; you made my life large with strength. . . . Finish what you started in me, GOD. Your love is eternal— don't quit on me now.
PSALM 138:3, 8, MSG

OCTOBER 14
His to Give Away

Every time I go to a new place and meet new folks, I'm always a little ill prepared for the predictable questions strangers ask one another.

"How many children do you have?"

"What does your husband do?"

After these two awkward social hurdles are cleared, a third almost always follows: "You mean you've *never* been married?"

Usually this ends the quiz, but occasionally I'll get a final query: "Really! Why not?"

I've stopped saying I haven't found a dress I like. I've found dozens. Now I'm more prone to say that so far, God has not seen fit to give me away. My heart belongs to him. It's his to give—and if anyone *has* asked him for it, he hasn't yet agreed. Sometimes I am asked by younger women if I have the gift of singleness, knowing they hope I will say yes because they are sure they *don't*. And I *do* say yes, with this caveat: I have the gift because today I am single—and *this* day, all of it, is a gift from God. I don't know what gifts tomorrow will bring. But I plan to enjoy the gifts of this day and use them well.

My singleness is a present tense fact of my life, just like the fact that I am green eyed and Scotch-Irish, five feet seven inches and brown haired, that I live in the city but dream of the country, that I love baseball and dogs and Scrabble and can't whistle or tan to save my life. My check-the-box marital status is only one fact about me, and not the defining one. Not by a long shot.

Here's what defines me: *God loves me. I am his.* And I'll be his forever, no matter whom else I might belong to in the shorter term. That identity suits me. It fits. It's a role I'll spend eternity growing into. And now and forever, I am his to keep, and his to give away.

As for me, I am like a green olive tree in the house of God; I trust in the lovingkindness of God forever and ever. I will give You thanks forever, because You have done it, And I will wait on Your name, for it is good, in the presence of Your godly ones.

PSALM 52:8-9, NASB

Not Everybody Wins

A friend of mine is a former college and professional athlete. He knows what it is to compete at the highest levels: he was integral in one of the greatest comebacks in pro-football history. The same year he experienced that unlikely, glorious, come-from-behind win, he also experienced a very humbling Super Bowl drubbing. This friend likes to say that we are created to compete. But he doesn't believe for a minute that everybody wins or that everybody should.

If we are indeed created to compete, what kind of message are we sending our kids when we insist that everyone wins? When a mom friend told me that in her kid's soccer league they don't even keep score, my first reaction was "Why bother playing?" The "everybody wins" mind-set sends out ripples that extend far beyond the sporting world. I even wonder if our culture's obsession with pseudo-reality shows like *Survivor* or *American Idol* or *Top Chef* might reveal that abandoning real competition draws us to the unreal kind as remote-control–clutching spectators.

I think my friend is right. I think we are created to compete. And we live in a culture as uncomfortable with real winners and losers as it is with a God who doesn't give everyone a trophy just because they're sincere. Instead, he unflinchingly points out two roads. One leads to life, he says, the other to destruction (see Matthew 7:13-14). He insists we cannot serve two masters (see Matthew 6:24).

Not everybody wins. And (news flash!) no one gets out of here alive. But Jesus' victory over sin and death means that the one who believes in him *does* ultimately win, even if he or she dies. Someone's keeping score all right. But not always in the way we think. In the meantime, we are created to run so as to win, to fight the good fight, and to finish the race. Abundant, vibrant, God-honoring, soul-satisfying life is the game you and I were made for, and there are prizes to be had for the men and women who compete for their own joy and God's glory and to taste with him the victory that he won for us.

In all these things we overwhelmingly conquer through Him who loved us.
ROMANS 8:37, NASB

Missing Owen

There are two things I've said "never again" to more than once. Every time I've moved, packing up hundreds upon hundreds of books, I've said, "Never again," vowing to die in whatever four walls currently surround me. And every time I've buried a dog, I've promised, tears streaming, to never love—to risk losing—another.

Owen came to live with me as a ten-week-old pup when I wasn't certain I was done grieving another four-legged friend named Chester. Owen was a beautiful boy: well behaved, affectionate, a great companion, and an ever-ready traveler. He was a fixture on the back of the sofa. I didn't mind.

I wrote two books with him curled up under my desk, and he appeared in a video, too, at the producer's invitation. Off duty, Owen slept—and snored—on the foot of the bed each night, eventually migrating up to the pillow next to my head and settling there. His big brown eyes were the first thing I saw each morning.

For the last three months of his life, Owen suffered hurt after hurt, indignity after indignity. He retreated in pain, becoming less and less himself. Then we reached the point of no return. Resigned to the fact that I could no longer help him, I promised not to let him hurt anymore.

As we sat waiting for the end in the vet's exam room, he crawled up in my lap and licked the tears off my face. It was the most engaged he'd been in weeks. Minutes later he stopped breathing with my face right next to his. "Good boy," I whispered to him. "You're *such* a good boy."

I loved Owen every day he was mine, whether he was sick or well, playful or played out, scruffy or sleek, convenient or inconvenient. I loved him because he was mine. Maybe, just maybe, I loved him with the faintest resemblance to the determined, no-matter-what way that God loves me.

I pray that on Owen's last day I loved him rightly and well, even doing what it broke my heart to do. Even so, I'm missing Owen, and I don't think that will change anytime soon.

Never again? I'll never say it again. And I mean it this time.

***

We love each other because he loved us first.
1 JOHN 4:19

Little Trinkets

Just past the front doors of the discount store I frequent sits a section of ever-changing random stuff—all priced at a dollar or less. Mini notepads. Doggie treats. Tiny vases. Plastic pencil cases. Refrigerator magnets. I'm sure no one who visits the store regularly arrives with a shopping list that says "Four mini notepads, one fridge magnet, and a vase too small for more than one flower." They're coming for more practical items, but I'll bet many of them, like me, get caught in the sticky web of the trinket section.

The dollar section sprang to mind as I read this searing sentence by Calvin Miller: "To desire only what Christ gives and not to desire Christ Himself is to be bought off by little trinkets, never to own the greater treasure of His indwelling presence."*

I wonder how many times I've failed to get very far past the front door of my spiritual life because I've been "bought off" by the immediately gratifying gifts of God and ceased to pursue him? What a tragedy it would be if I allowed good health or a mate or money to satiate my hunger for the Holy One. What a waste to "fill my cart" with things that will only temporarily satisfy—as good as they might be—and fail to cultivate a true and abiding oneness with the Giver of all good things.

What steers me past the dollar aisle at the discount store when I *don't* stop? Sometimes I have one thing in mind when I arrive and little desire to tarry over less. Like a plunger because the kitchen sink is clogged. But it doesn't have to be an urgent need that pushes me on. It can also be the knowledge that there are other, more lasting and beautiful things stocked further in. And I want to discover them.

Little trinkets are fine, just not fine enough. And they can all too easily divert me from my real and true purpose: to know the greater treasure who is Christ, and to delight not in what he gives but in him and him alone.

I look upon everything as loss compared with the overwhelming gain of knowing Jesus Christ my Lord.
PHILIPPIANS 3:7, PHILLIPS

---

* Calvin Miller, *Into the Depths of God* (Minneapolis: Bethany House, 2000), 82.

OCTOBER 18
Worlds Away

"There is no frigate like a book to take us lands away," writes Emily Dickinson in her poem "The Book." And even before I knew those words of hers, I believed them.

Books have been my favorite mode of travel since I could tie my own shoes. They've carried me from Oz to Narnia, through caves and bogs and seas and forests, and even through wrinkles in time.

Of all the books I've known and loved since childhood, one has carried me farther than all the others combined: the Holy Bible. Its stories and characters are the ones most deeply ingrained in memory: Jonah swallowed up by the great fish, Noah building an ark and floating above the mountain peaks in it. Baby Moses, found in the river by an Egyptian princess, and shepherd boy David, whose slingshot and fearlessness slew giants.

Then there are the Gospel stories—the most magical ones of all—where Jesus walked and talked, and water became wine, and fish and loaves multiplied in one great picnic with leftovers galore. Where blind men got their sight back and where the wildest waves imaginable were tamed by a word from the one who made them.

In my childhood home we had a big coffee-table Bible that I remember being drawn to, not for reading, but for its elaborate cover and colored pictures. My own tiny first Bible with my name stamped in gold was more portable and child friendly. It had pictures too—a comforting one of the Nativity and a dark, brooding one of three crosses on a hill.

My other books did indeed take me worlds away, but only the Bible had the power to bring its Protagonist into my world and change it—and me—by his presence. Other books were for a time, and that time has come and gone. But I can't imagine a day when I won't ask *this* book to tell me its old, old story all over again.

The Word became flesh and blood, and moved into the neighborhood. We saw the glory with our own eyes, the one-of-a-kind glory, like Father, like Son, generous inside and out, true from start to finish.
JOHN 1:14, MSG

Is Anybody Home?

In the ten months I've lived in my little rental bungalow, I've seen my next-door neighbor on the west side exactly twice. The yard is neat. The front porch light comes on every night. I've even knocked on the front door a few times with a piece of misplaced mail—but there's never anyone home. We spoke briefly one day after Hurricane Ike, when almost everyone was outdoors and assessing damage. And we exchanged greetings once over our backyard fences.

If I simply went by how neat the house looks, by the appearance of the surroundings, I'd say the owner is often in residence. But if I was asked to verify this suspicion, well, I couldn't.

Each day I read the headlines and learn of a natural disaster destroying, another illness flirting with pandemic status, and foreign sabers rattling. Then it gets personal. Couples I thought were rock solid are separating. A friend's mother is dying. Another's sister is being challenged by an insidious disease that has no cure. Several friends are deeply concerned about their financial futures.

Some mornings I almost feel like looking toward heaven and asking, "Is anybody home?" But to judge whether or not God is in residence by the state of my circumstances would be a mistake.

So I rely on what I know for sure. God lives. He is here, and he is not silent. I may be more attuned to my immediate surroundings than I am to his presence, his people, or the small voice of the Spirit, but that myopic focus does not verify his absence. C. S. Lewis once said, "I believe in Christianity as I believe the sun has risen, not only because I see it, but because by it I see everything else."*

Someone is most definitely at home. The house is not unattended. Even in the half light of fear and sorrow and uncertainty, someone is always at home.

The Lord your God is in your midst, a mighty one who will save; he will rejoice over you with gladness; he will quiet you by his love; he will exult over you with loud singing.
ZEPHANIAH 3:17, ESV

---

* C. S. Lewis, "Is Theology Poetry?" in *The Weight of Glory* (New York: HarperCollins, 2001), 140.

When the answer Is No

The funny thing about *no* is that it never gets any easier to hear. I wasn't fond of it when I was seven or eleven or twenty-one. And I don't like it any better today. I learned early on to ask politely and to direct my request to the one who was most able (and likely) to grant it. I said, "May I please," and I said it to the parent I thought might answer yes. I learned there's a fine line between persistence and annoyance. And I walked it like a tightrope.

I've been hearing no a lot lately. If I didn't know better, I'd think vandals had stripped God's messaging system of its full alphabet—his yeses have been few and far between. I don't believe my requests have been unreasonable or even selfish as far as I've been able to discern. And I've asked respectfully, and as often as I dare. I've offered up to God what Spurgeon called "order and argument in prayer," and I've prayed believing that the things I've asked are well within God's power. I still believe it. And I'm still hearing no.

When I heard it over and over as a kid, I eventually relented. I moved on. I abandoned my unmet requests and began to focus my desires elsewhere. That doesn't work anymore. There are some desires that, for whatever reason, you simply cannot abandon, even when holding on to them hurts more than ditching them might. And the one who hears my requests these days cannot be easily abandoned or ignored. I need him too much, and I love him too deeply for that.

Even when he tells me no, it's him I want, him I trust, him I bring my wants and hopes and needs to. Because whether the answer is yes or no, he is the one I want to hear it from. And in case you're wondering, I'm still asking. And unless or until you hear otherwise from him, I think you should be too.

Ask, and it will be given to you; seek, and you will find; knock, and it will be opened to you.
MATTHEW 7:7, NASB

Wait Here, Please

I once recorded a snippet of Dr. Seuss's *Oh, the Places You'll Go!* on my voice mail greeting. It was a clever bit about "the waiting place . . . where everyone is just waiting." I liked the message. But I am sure after the first time or two, friends would have much preferred a simple, "This is Leigh. Leave a message." Waiting rather quickly loses whatever romance it might have had early on, but even so, I know very few people who are not, at any given time, waiting for something. Test results. A loved one's return. Someone to marry. A child to hold.

The Bible is a book full of waiters. Sarai. Elizabeth. Hannah. Moses. Job. David. Hosea. Jonah. What might we have heard if *their* voices had been recorded?

"It's no use."

"I'll never have a child."

"Why should I be stuck herding someone else's sheep for the rest of my life?"

"I've lost everything. When will you turn this thing around, God?"

"Samuel must have been mistaken about that king thing. Saul will kill me before he lets me take the throne."

Or maybe just, "Help, Lord!"

Some waiters wallowed in self-doubt and pity. For a while. But more often than not, these God followers learned to linger in their waiting places, seeing all that there was to see. And what there usually was to see was evidence of a great, patient, provident God at work—in the smallest of circumstances and in the hidden places of the human heart.

A wise friend once told me that we are never alone in the cold, dim cave of uncertainty. When our eyes adjust to the half-light, he said, we will see that there are tens, hundreds, thousands even, waiting with us. And maybe, he said, waiting for a word *from* us that injects hope or humor or sense into what makes no immediate sense at all.

Are you waiting? Me, too. Here's a meantime word for us both:

The LORD is the everlasting God, the Creator of all the earth. He never grows weak or weary. No one can measure the depths of his understanding. He gives power to the weak and strength to the powerless.

ISAIAH 40:28-29

a Church Girl Confesses

I was probably in my teens before I realized God might not be a Baptist. (Kidding there, but not by much.) Shortly thereafter, I discovered he wasn't constrained to being Protestant, either, or English speaking. God's family is remarkably diverse. Its members have a single common denominator: Jesus. Our allegiance should not be to any person, country, or creed but to a King and a Kingdom.

The scarlet thread that declares our allegiance to that King and his Kingdom is the blood of Jesus Christ. The key to inclusion in the family of God is nothing more and nothing less than the shed blood of his sacrifice applied to sinners of every ilk. "God," says John Piper, "is no respecter of persons in salvation or in damnation. The human race—and every ethnic group in it—is united in this great reality: we are all depraved and condemned. We are all lost in the woods together, sinking on the same boat, dying of the same disease. . . . If I am among God's elect, it is owing entirely to God's free grace, not to my distinctives."*

In a climate where many would seek to divide us, I conscientiously object. I don't mean to ignore our differences. They exist. But for the church, what binds us is infinitely stronger than what might segregate us into superficial camps. One great day we'll be united in a single, overriding allegiance that will make our differences not divisive but lovely, rich, and true.

Christ is our common ground. We are his body. Because I'm a church girl from way back, I've experienced the richness of the body of Christ at work there. But not just there. I've seen his body united in vacant lots and makeshift clinics and backyard barbecues. I've seen it around my own dinner table too. In Jesus, we're all grafted into a big, multifaceted, diverse (and yes, occasionally dysfunctional) family. Let's spite the devil, confound the world, and glorify the Lord together. Let's love one another, whatever the cost.

In one Spirit we were all baptized into one body—Jews or Greeks, slaves or free.

I CORINTHIANS 12:13, ESV

---

* John Piper, *Bloodlines: Race, Cross, and the Christian* (Wheaton, IL: Crossway, 2011), 135, 144.

Love Chooses

Love is something miraculous. Something miraculous that I *do* based on something miraculous already done for me. We are loved by a crazy-good God. And then we decide to love in imitation of his good and gracious example. "We love," writes the apostle John, "because he first loved us" (1 John 4:19, NIV). My God empowers my feeble attempts at proactive love, infusing them with his beauty and fierce loving-kindness. But I have to try. I have to choose to love with his kind of love.

As I write this, a favorite aunt is growing feeble and her husband even feebler. A few months ago, when my aunt and uncle could no longer take care of each other, their children moved him into a nursing home. She lasted less than a week in her comfortable, familiar home without him. Then she left it, closing the door behind her to share a small, bare room with him, no more than a mile away. She chose. Love chooses.

A good friend's sister has Alzheimer's. In the evenings, after my friend has worked a full day and the caregiver she has hired has gone home, she sits on the sofa with her sister and holds her hand. "I like this," her sister told her recently. "I like it too," my friend said. She is choosing. Love chooses.

My two precious nieces married last year—one in January and one in October. Their young lives stretched out wide before them like an open road, but they both willingly narrowed the boundaries with spoken *I do*s. The youngest one's voice quivered as she said the words; her older sister's rang out clear as a bell. But they both chose. Love chooses.

Love chooses the moments, and those moments become days and months and years. Love chooses—and by choosing, knowingly forfeits other choices. It is even glad to do so. Love chooses when it is afraid or hurt or fears rejection. When it is tired or uncertain or empty. The heart-rattling power of love is perfected in weakness, and it blooms bright and irresistible and wild every time it chooses.

Dear children, let us not love with words or speech but with actions and in truth. This is how we know that we belong to the truth and how we set our hearts at rest in his presence.
1 JOHN 3:18-19, NIV

Trouble in a White Impala

The e-mails from my neighborhood's volunteer watch captain were troubling. (His infrequent e-mails alert those neighbors who've asked to be informed of any suspicious goings-on in our area.)

Two men in a white Chevy Impala had been seen parking in neighborhood driveways when no one was home, kicking in the doors, and executing a series of snatch-and-grab robberies. It had happened almost half a dozen times—even though folks (including the police) had been made aware of what was going on.

Sometimes you know trouble is out there, but you can't tell when it's going to strike. It can still catch you off guard, even if you know what it drives. "If your house has an alarm," the e-mail said, "set it when you leave. Even if you're just going out for a ten-minute grocery store run." I do that. "These guys are brazen," it added.

Trouble is brazen. A few years ago, the little house I was renting (with no alarm) was robbed—the thief escaping out a broken window in the back as I was putting my key into the front door. I didn't hear him, but when I walked into my bedroom and saw my drawers and closet doors open and my mattress askew, I knew. A broken window, a broken back gate, and one broken plate were my only losses. The gate and window were repaired that evening, and as robberies go, it was a bust for the robber and only a slight inconvenience for me. But it made me aware that trouble is out there—with no way to know when it might visit.

We shouldn't be surprised by difficulties. "You will find trouble in the world," Jesus said, "but never lose heart—I have conquered the world" (see John 16:33). Whether we are prepared or unprepared, fortified or vulnerable, savvy or naive, we can't stop the white Impala from cruising the streets where we live. But we also have help, for "God is our refuge and strength, a very present help in [times of] trouble" (Psalm 46:1, NASB).

May the LORD answer you in the day of trouble! May the name of the God of Jacob set you securely on high!

PSALM 20:1, NASB

Bells and Whistles

I don't always hear the bells and whistles of my neighborhood, but then I don't always listen.

The bells chime on the hour or for special occasions, ringing out from one of the churches near my home. The notes they peal tumble over one another on the wind, their tones mingled with the noise of the day. Sometimes I detect a melody, sometimes not. But they make lovely music just the same.

The whistles make long and plaintive moans, each more like a lament than a song. I hear the whistles most often in the dark: faraway sighs that become louder and longer as they travel toward me on unseen tracks.

I sometimes fail to hear the bells and whistles of my life, too. I miss the bells of joy that well up and spill over into ordinary moments, but that doesn't mean they don't exist. It just means I've begun to take them for granted—to overlook the joyful ringing of a spectacular sunrise or an unexpected embrace from a friend.

There are whistles, too. Echoing reminders of things I should let go of, even when I'd rather not. Regrets that I can't redress or undo. Losses that don't seem to dim with time. It aches to hear them, but it's good to listen just the same.

Together, bells and whistles sound the story of my life. Yours, too. And it's the combination of them that keeps us clinging to the author of both. It's their strange and subtle intertwining that makes for a fuller, deeper, more percussive, and more precious existence.

Bells and whistles balance and bookend the days of our lives. Sometimes God throws a party in our presence, and the bells drown out the whistles. Sometimes he plays a dirge, and all we can hear are notes in a minor key. But it's all music from him, written note by precious note and line by glorious line.

———

There is a time for every event under heaven—a time to give birth and a time to die; a time to plant and a time to uproot what is planted. A time to kill and a time to heal; a time to tear down and a time to build up. A time to weep and a time to laugh; a time to mourn and a time to dance.
ECCLESIASTES 3:1-4, NASB

OCTOBER 26
ambidextrous

In all my years of teaching, in numerous rotations and schedules, I'd never once missed an assignment. But streaks are made to be broken. I arrived in my adult Bible study classroom one Sunday, five minutes late but eager to hear one of my gifted coteachers share a lesson from Nehemiah. Imagine my surprise when I entered the room and saw *neither* of my two coteachers—but instead a slightly bewildered room of learners staring at an empty podium.

Gulp.

Someone goofed. And that someone was me. We'd altered the schedule two weeks before, and apparently I misunderstood the new plan. So I confessed my already-apparent confusion and my soon-to-be-apparent unpreparedness, borrowed a pair of reading glasses to see the hopelessly tiny print of the pocket Bible I carry in my purse, and invited the class to pray, asking God to guide us as we opened his Word.

Together we read the text of Nehemiah 4, lingering over each section to consider its content. We read how the builders of the wall around Jerusalem faced ugly mocking and shame. How they became discouraged by threats and humiliation, and how their servant-leader Nehemiah responded. And we read how Nehemiah instructed the builders to work: with a trowel in one hand and a sword in the other.

He asked for ambidextrous workers. Men who could mend walls and also duel—choosing one tool over another in an instant, but ever ready with both. Some of his builders were no doubt experts with the trowel. Others excelled with the sword. But each carried both and at the sound of the trumpet, would lay down one and run toward the noise of battle with the other.

I favor the hand that builds over the hand that duels, but Satan is on the prowl, so I must be vigilant. I want him to go away and leave me to my tasks, but he has not. Thankfully, God is more than able to help us in the battle. Our God will fight for us when we are weak, unprepared, or fearful. He is ready, even when we are not.

Those who were rebuilding the wall and those who carried burdens took their load with one hand doing the work and the other holding a weapon.
NEHEMIAH 4:17, NASB

The Ugly Editor

I'd sat in this exact spot before—an old, velvet-covered club chair in a neighborhood coffee shop—and placed my mug more than once on the same table. So I must have seen the box before. But on this day it caught my eye, and as I fingered the tiny latch near the top, I was curious enough to open it.

Inside I found a stash of handwritten notes, some confessional, some philosophical, some hopeful, some sad. It seems I'd been having coffee for some time right next to a kind of rambling, stream of consciousness collective that was surprisingly frank. But here's the weird thing: an "editor" with a blue pen had seen fit to scratch remarks on every single one. The editorial comments were sarcastic, critical, accusatory, crude, and in a few cases, downright mean.

I tried to picture someone sitting down in the velvet chair and discovering the box in much the same way I had. But I couldn't fathom a person with enough venom (and time) to hypercritically edit each note. This person must have been having a really bad day, or life, or something. But I recognized the ugly editor's judging voice; I hear it all the time. It wants me to believe God's mercy toward me is limited and his love for me is conditional. It argues against grace and questions my every motive.

As I held the scraps of paper in my hands, I found myself wanting to go back over each one with a different color ink and refute everything the ugly editor had penned, replacing it with words Jesus might have said. Like "Go, and sin no more" (John 8:11). And "I will never leave you nor forsake you" (Hebrews 13:5, ESV).

Are you hearing the voice of the ugly editor? Don't cover your ears. Open them instead to the words of life from the author and perfecter of your faith: "The thief does not come except to steal, and to kill, and to destroy. I have come that they may have life, and that they may have it more abundantly" (John 10:10, NKJV).

We know that we are of God, and the whole world lies under the sway of the wicked one. And we know that the Son of God has come and has given us an understanding, that we may know Him who is true.
I JOHN 5:19-20, NKJV

The Pleasure of His Company

I'm an introvert at heart. I give this disclaimer often, because my work sometimes requires that I masquerade as the sort of extrovert I am not. I teach. Travel. Speak to groups of all sizes and meet strangers with regularity. But I'm always a little apprehensive at the mix-and-mingle stuff that's expected of me. Honestly, I'd rather be out with just a few good friends or curled up at home with a cup of tea and a good book.

A few months ago I traveled to another state for a client event where I knew only the hosts and none of the two hundred or so attendees, most of whom I expected to have little in common with. The sprawling resort was perfect for golf or tennis, but I play neither. And the first evening was a steep challenge: a large cocktail reception, then an entire ballroom full of dinner tables to navigate. The thought of both left me feeling like a seventh grader approaching the lunchroom on the first day of junior high: where would I sit? Who would I talk to? What would I say?

As I checked in to the hotel that afternoon, the desk clerk handed me my room key, then said, "Oh, I have something here for you." She produced a cream-colored envelope with my name handwritten on it. I opened it and read: "Mr. and Mrs. _____ and Mr. _____ request the pleasure of your company for dinner at 8 p.m." I could have cried with relief. I had a place to go and three of the few people I knew there to share a meal with. I was included.

I kept the envelope and the blue card it contained. They remind me that my heavenly Father has also made a place for me at his table. That I always have somewhere to go, a place where fellowship, familiarity, and God's presence await. In spite of my feelings of unworthiness or awareness of my meager pedigree, there is a place where I am always welcomed, wanted, and loved.

The pleasure of his company is never far away.

I stand at the door and knock. If anyone hears my voice and opens the door, I will come in and eat with that person, and they with me.
REVELATION 3:20, NIV

OCTOBER 29

Caught

I'm not usually caught. I have the reasoning power, the resources, the connections, and the creativity to work my way out of whatever difficult spot I might be in. Usually. But lately, I've found myself caught—and when I am truly caught, it's almost always because of something I cannot change. I can't change another person's mind or heart or past. I can't change illness or the economy. I can't change which people my heart goes out to; I only choose whether and when I will bend to its inconvenient leanings or deny them.

But caught isn't necessarily the worst place I can find myself. Once caught I am slower to act, more prone to reflect, more aware of others, and less sure of myself. When caught I am a thousand times more likely to fall on my knees and plead to the one who is not.

Are you caught? In a marriage that isn't working anymore? In a lie that no one's discovered yet? In a heartbreak that stays fresh, even as its genesis grows more distant? In a sickness a pill or time won't fix? A rift that words alone won't mend?

Paul said he was caught by a thorn in the flesh—an ailment of some sort he considered "a messenger from Satan to torment me and keep me from becoming proud" (2 Corinthians 12:7). He asked for God to take his thorn away. But God did not. Not the first time or the second or the third.

So Paul, being caught, made friends with his captor. He heard God's answer: "My grace is all you need. My power works best in weakness" (2 Corinthians 12:9). And he began to look at the things he could not change in a new way. I'm new at this caught thing, and I'm not as graceful as Paul. I'd welcome change, but God is not budging. I'm caught, but I'm holding on to his strength and praying to see glory. I want him to put my fears to shame and bring me to the day when I can point to him and say, "Look at my God! Isn't he good? And didn't he know all along what was best for me?"

I quit focusing on the handicap and began appreciating the gift. It was a case of Christ's strength moving in on my own weakness.

2 CORINTHIANS 12:9, MSG

The Inner Ring

One of the simplest, most basic desires of the human heart is to belong. Whether it's the cool lunch table in junior high or the best grown-up neighborhood, we long to be in the inner ring—not somewhere on the periphery.

I thought I was over this; I'm not, entirely. I still feel thirteen and not quite cool enough when I don't get the girls' trip invites or when I hear about the party after the fact. I pretend I'm fine with it. But it still stings.

Spending time with three hundred high school kids who've traveled a long way from home for camp, I see the inner-ring drama unfold in tiny ways. I see the boy who hangs back and hides his eyes under a hat indoors and out; the girl whose clothes are long outgrown; the young woman whose walker slows her from every churning clump of kids she might enjoy and keeps her moving cautiously along with a counselor by her side. I see the six-foot-four athlete who flounders in the deep end of the swimming pool yet spurns the hands of those who reach out to help him. They're all outside—and they know it. But they must long with all their hearts to be in.

We're human. We want in.

The good news is this: the God who is in himself Father, Son, and Holy Spirit welcomes us. He wants us to live in the inner ring of his perfect love. He asks, and we need no other invitation. He befriends, and we need no other patron. In truth, the tightest circle, the sweetest clan, the finest fellowship is open to us, not closed, by the gracious invitation of Jesus.

Are you lonely, in need of grace, dying to be known and loved? Come. Are you unsure of which way to turn, longing for tenderness, ready for adventure? Come. The table is set. The invitation is extended. Father, Son, and Holy Spirit form the one true and perfect ring that opens to welcome you inside.

God is faithful, who has called you into fellowship with his Son, Jesus Christ our Lord.

I CORINTHIANS 1:9, NIV

The Camera Doesn't Lie

Few would suspect that I worked my way through college as a television news reporter. For four hours each Monday through Friday I was a journalism student, then for another four I was a fledgling journalist, writing, interviewing, taping, doing stand-ups, and editing B-roll for the local evening news.

I got the job because I *thought* I was interviewing for a different one. The flyer posted in the journalism-school offices said "news writer." I was too green to realize that a news writer at a television station might actually have to read—on camera—whatever news she wrote!

I was shy. (Still am, somewhat.) When I was asked by my interviewer to read on camera, I was too stunned to refuse. So I read, got out of there as fast as I could, and went home and told my roommate how embarrassed and humiliated (and mistaken about the true nature of the job) I had been. To my great shock, they called four hours later and said, "You're hired."

I only did news part-time in college. I never learned to love the camera, and truthfully, it didn't love me much either. I gave up any ideas I might have harbored about becoming a *Today Show* coanchor and decided my journalism calling was definitely in print, or at least on the production end of the camera.

Years later, circumstances put me in front of the camera again. I worried. I fretted. I tried to remember if I have a "best" side. (I'm pretty sure I don't.) And for one excruciating afternoon, I recalled what it was like to look into the eye of the camera and try not to let my discomfort show. Those few hours reminded me of what I *never* liked about the camera: it doesn't lie. Not even a little. Impartially focused on its object, it simply renders what it sees.

And I remembered, too, that I live 24-7 before the truth-telling lens of one who never blinks. His inscrutable gaze misses nothing. His piercing eyes see past my carefully tended surface. And here's the hidden joy of what would otherwise be terror to me: he forgets nothing but the sin that I've confessed. And all that he sees, *he loves*.

As far as the east is from the west, so far has He removed our transgressions from us.
PSALM 103:12, NASB

November

That Innocent Age

The 45 rpm record dropped to the spinning turntable, and the needle found its groove. There were some scratches, but the music came through loud and clear: "A, B, C / Easy as one, two, three . . ."

My sister and I listened to this song and countless others like it in the living room of our suburban house throughout our elementary and junior high school years. It was, by and large, happy music, and the singers who performed it did not seem tormented. This was when the people behind the music performed it on TV variety shows, not in multimillion-dollar music videos. The artists seemed real then, almost like ordinary people.

When we listened to the Jackson 5 sing "ABC" or any of their other hits, we danced—and imagined we danced like Michael. We didn't, of course—nobody could dance like that. But we had fun trying. It was an age of innocence, and to this day the first few notes of these songs can still cause an involuntary smile to creep across my face.

I wish that innocence could have lasted. I think maybe the man who made the music wished it could have too. It looks as if he tried for the rest of his life to bring it back—but the clock keeps moving forward. Isn't it a wonder, then, that Jesus told a grown man he must be born again? That phrase has become a cliché at best, or at worst a defamatory grenade lobbed with a sneer. But I'll bet it would have had an almost irresistible appeal to the pop star who died a mere shell of the clear-eyed child he once was.

"You must be born again," Jesus said. You must come clean and start anew, wiping the slate clear. You must go back to the beginning, back to the age of innocence, he seemed to say. And he claimed to be the one to take us there. Forget nostalgia, antiaging serums, wrinkle creams, and grainy Ed Sullivan videos. There's only one way back to the age of innocence: a true innocence, not an imaginary one. He's it. There is no other.

Jesus answered, "Truly, truly, I say to you, unless one is born of water and the Spirit he cannot enter into the kingdom of God."
JOHN 3:5, NASB

What I Can Do

Some greet the morning after an important election dejected and angry. Some awaken to it jubilant and glad. Many are simply relieved that the bruising discord of another political mud-wrestling contest is finally done. Ballots are cast and counted every November. It is not new. We shake ourselves off and begin again.

Assignments may change in the halls of power, constitutional duties may be transferred and seats rearranged, but as followers of Christ, *our* assignment never changes, no matter who occupies the White House, the statehouse, the judicial bench, or the corner office. I am thankful that ours is a straightforward, unwavering assignment. And I am humbled by how simple and yet impossibly challenging it can be to put into practice.

When asked by experts in the law to state the greatest commandment, Jesus gave them a compound command, one whose two parts are ultimately toothless unless they are permanently joined. "You must love the LORD your God with all your heart, all your soul, and all your mind," he said. "[And] love your neighbor as yourself." (Matthew 22:37, 39). And he meant it.

Love God with every part of your being. And love your neighbor as yourself. No loopholes. No excuses. No insistence that the neighbor look like you, agree with you, or even like you. And in case his hearers were already internally calculating how to limit the size of that expansive universe, the Son of God told a story that first shattered, then expanded their definition of *neighbor* from "nearest only" to "immediately present and neediest also." Who is my neighbor? My neighbor is the one near me—in this moment—who is in need.

I have been instructed—by the one who first loved me—exactly whom I should love and how. I know what I can do, and you do too. I can love by seeing, by embracing, and by meeting the needs of those whose paths cross mine, in Jesus' name—ever grateful for the way he keeps on providing for me.

Grace, mercy and peace will be with us, from God the Father and from Jesus Christ, the Son of the Father, in truth and love.
2 JOHN 1:3, NASB

Gathered at the Table

Two weeks before Thanksgiving, at a tiny table in the dining room of a run-down rest home, five women of my family gathered. We represented three generations: my mother's oldest sister, my sister and me (her nieces), and my sister's two daughters (my own nieces). We were there to celebrate my aunt's eighty-seventh birthday, and she was not expecting us. We weren't sure she would know us, but by God's mercy she did. And she was glad we had come. She did not, however, remember that it was her birthday. No matter. We were celebrating her, not the day.

Long ago my aunt's house had been the destination of countless family holidays and gatherings. We were embraced in every sense of the word, every time we came. When I think of my aunt and uncle's home, I remember the comfy corduroy couches, slamming screen doors, sweating glasses of iced tea, fish fries, card games, and laughter. This time the world—and the table we gathered around—seemed much smaller and more grim. But my aunt knew us, and she knew we loved her. Although the table was small, the gathering was not. "Have y'all seen Memaw?" she asked once, referring to her mother who'd been gone more than twenty years. We hadn't, we told her. Not this time. Later she asked where "the little ones" were. The "littlest" ones in our immediate family—my nieces—were with us at the table, both solidly in their twenties.

Later, thinking of her questions, I realized that for her, we were all still present. The table was full. Her. Us. Us as we used to be (young girls), and the girls as even littler ones. Memaw was there, and I imagine our uncle was too. Maybe one of the gifts of old age and a dimming memory is that all of those you love are never far away. In Christ and in our hearts, the table is full, and not a one is missing.

———

Where two or three have gathered together in My name, I am there in their midst.
MATTHEW 18:20, NASB

Daddy's Got You

As kids go, I was only an average risk taker. But I was ready for almost any challenge that was preceded by these three words: *Daddy's got you!*

I heard them as I rode down the driveway on my training-wheel-less bike for the first time or leaped (eyes and nose squeezed shut) into the deep end of the swimming pool. The words weren't audible at other fear-inducing events, but I was still certain of them when I stood at the free throw line in junior high basketball games, bawled my way through a newly broken heart at sixteen, and watched my parents drive away from my college dorm at the beginning of my freshman year.

Knowing that someone who loves you has your back can go a long way in making you brave.

I wonder how many things I might have never tried without my dad's encouraging presence. I wonder how often I would have waited in the shadows and hoped for someone else to lead if he hadn't told me I could. My dad who often made me brave did the bravest thing for me when I turned thirteen. He wrote me a letter (delivered with a long-stemmed red rose) that celebrated my short life with typical parental enthusiasm and ended it with words something like this:

> Your mother and I will always be proud of you, but it is your Maker you must answer to, and yourself you will face in the mirror each day. Many things may change, but one will remain constant: your dad's love for his daughter.

Early on, Dad set me free from pleasing him so that I might fully follow Jesus and the dreams *he* had placed in my very young heart. That is why it has been no great leap of faith for me, in the days since, to believe the bold promises and commands from my heavenly Father. He says he will never forsake me. I count on that. He says I am justified and have peace with him. I rest there. He says I can do all things through Christ who strengthens me, so I am confident this is so. His promises make me better and braver than I would otherwise be. My Abba Father's got me. I am so grateful he has.

Many waters cannot quench love, nor will rivers overflow it.
SONG OF SOLOMON 8:7, NASB

Router Failure

A wireless router connects my desktop, laptop, and printer, allowing me to share and print files and access the Internet from any place within its reach. Until it failed, I didn't pay much attention to how it worked. But in the handful of days it has been on the blink, it has been more instructive to me than it ever was fully operational. The router always conducted its business in the background. It had no independent agenda or purpose—it just maintained connections to what was already operating. It was a conduit. A link. A liaison of sorts. But when the router stopped working, I was forced to think about how much I've come to depend upon its "covert" operation.

I wondered, too, if in some cases *I'm* not the ad hoc router between what God is saying and what someone else is straining to hear. Between what a struggling soul wants to pray but can't find words for and the father who listens attentively. Between real, tangible resources and a real, tangible need. Between another's request and God's ample provision. If I *am* meant to be that kind of router (and I suspect I might be), what allows that to happen—and what keeps it from happening?

Simply put (forgive me, any technically astute person who might be reading), I'm pretty certain three things must occur. The power must be on. I must be connected to the power source. And I must be connected to the intended recipient of that power. Because my router failed, I've begun to troubleshoot each of these things more conscientiously. And I've noticed a funny thing. When, in my mind's eye, I grasp the hand of God and grasp another's hand in order to love or help or intercede, I'm stretched out, cruciform style. Of course. Because that's just the way Jesus has done it for me.

Since we have a great priest over the house of God, let us draw near with a sincere heart in full assurance of faith. . . . Let us hold fast the confession of our hope without wavering . . . and let us consider how to stimulate one another to love and good deeds.

HEBREWS 10:21-24, NASB

Pressed Down, Shaken Together, Running Over

My doorbell rang in the early afternoon—at the same time my phone dinged with this text from a friend: "You home? Open your front door." She was standing on my porch with a case of my favorite sparkling water. I'd asked her earlier in the week to remind me of the name of the tiny market near her house that sold *this beverage* by the case; she'd decided to go me one better.

Fast-forward to a weekly women's Bible study I've attended for years. Before the lecture began, another friend sat down next to me for a hug and a quick catch-up. Her darling pair of earrings caught my eye. "Those are great," I told her. "They look so pretty on you!" Almost before I could get the compliment out, she had the first one off. I thought she was handing it to me to admire up close, so I held out my hand. Then she took out the other earring, and placed them both in my hand. "You take them," she said. "Really. A friend sells them, I can get another pair." I put them on right there on the spot, wowed and humbled by her spontaneous generosity.

Later that week, at church, another precious friend who noted my uncharacteristic-for-Sunday flats (for balance) pointed to her own flat, sturdy shoes and said, "These are great. What size do you wear?" When I told her, she slipped her foot out of one, saying, "Just try it." They were great. "I'm gonna give you these," she said. "No, you're not," I told her. "You can't go home barefoot. I'll get a pair. Just tell me where you got them." She did—but the next week she came to church in tennis shoes and handed me her comfy flats.

Sometimes the gifts come in a crazy, unexpected flurry—and you're left breathless at God's demonstration of his own great grace and mercy. "See," he seems to say, "I can bless you anywhere, anytime. And you can do the same to others." Together, pressed down, shaken together, running over, we can put flesh on our great, invisible, everlasting treasure.

Give away your life; you'll find life given back, but not merely given back—given back with bonus and blessing. Giving, not getting, is the way. Generosity begets generosity.
LUKE 6:38, MSG

This Beautiful Desert

"I feel so untethered and ungrounded," I told a trusted friend. "None of the things I've counted on seem certain anymore. The only thing I'm still sure of is God." He didn't shrink back or fall away in a dead faint. My confession didn't rock his world one bit. He just nodded knowingly and said, "That's good enough." And he was right.

This isn't a season of plenty. My barns are not full, and I am certainly not thinking of building new ones. My surest comforts aren't so comforting anymore, and my sweetest dreams seem silly when I name them—so I don't. But even in this desert, even in this odd, unsettling wilderness, my God keeps coming at me, relentless in his love.

He keeps turning up: in an unexpected bouquet of tulips and daisies left with a handmade card on my doorstep. In a friend's well-timed e-mail, brimming with love. In the first pink rose on the hedge out back, defying any frost to set spring back another hour. In a long-distance prayer, spoken as I held the phone to my ear and wept. In the exquisite sliver of moon that hung low enough on the horizon on a recent night that I almost reached for it.

How can I be sure it's him? Who else makes the desert bloom? Who else causes rivers to run in dry places and the wilderness to bear fruit? I am not sure about tomorrow. I am not even sure about this afternoon. I am not sure that "the check is in the mail" or that dreams will come true or that happily ever after even exists. What I *am* sure about is this: he can make joy out of almost nothing. "Joy," says Stanley Hauerwas, "is the disposition that comes from our realization that we can trust in surprises for the sustaining of our lives."*

He still surprises me. I believe he always will.

"Indeed, the LORD will comfort Zion; He will comfort all her waste places. And her wilderness He will make like Eden, and her desert like the garden of the LORD; joy and gladness will be found in her, thanksgiving and sound of a melody."

ISAIAH 51:3, NASB

---

* Stanley Hauerwas, *The Peaceable Kingdom: A Primer in Christian Ethics* (South Bend, IN: University of Notre Dame Press, 1991).

Overheard

I'd stopped for a bite at a local café and slipped into a small booth by the window. My back was inches from the diner on the other side of the bench, and I was less than six feet from his companion. I had figured them for coworkers when I sat down and wasn't paying attention to their words at all until I heard the woman say, "I'm really into spirituality now. I think each of us has a soul." Then she surprised me by announcing that she'd been doing a lot of reading and had concluded that Satan was a myth. God, she insisted, was behind most of the evil in the Bible. When people got out of line, he obliterated them.

Then the conversation took an unexpected turn: "I really didn't know what I was doing when I had you," the woman said. "I was too young. We shouldn't have kids when we're that young. I mean, Mary was, like, fifteen or something. (I assumed she was talking about Mary the mother of Christ but couldn't ask.) "When you're old enough to do a good job of it," she added, "you don't have the stamina anymore."

There was silence, then the man she was with said, "You did okay. I had food to eat, and you checked on whether or not I went to school. I turned out all right."

What I had first heard jarred my apologetics-fixed brain into gear. But the real destination of the conversation broke my heart. The two people I'd thought were coworkers were mother and son. And they hardly knew each other.

Here's what separates me from the woman I overheard: I believe I've been rescued, not punished, and that the same one who rescues is able to keep, help, and heal me in any circumstance of life. I believe he heals the brokenhearted and binds up their wounds, restores the years the locusts have eaten, and pleads my case before the throne of God. And what I heard that day at lunch only made me more sure. Not less.

Since this is the kind of life we have chosen, the life of the Spirit, let us make sure that we do not just hold it as an idea in our heads or a sentiment in our hearts, but work out its implications in every detail of our lives.

GALATIANS 5:25, MSG

OJ and Me

Making my way to a departing flight, I stopped at the newsstand to pick up a paper and something to drink. Normally I would have grabbed a coffee, but I'd already had two cups, so I chose orange juice instead. I bought a *USA Today* and a plastic bottle of Florida sunshine with a twist-off lid. Before boarding, I took a sip or two, twisted the top back on, and dropped the bottle in the bottom of my bag.

A few minutes later I found my seat and, with my carry-on sitting in my lap, recognized the distinct smell of oranges. I tipped the bag to peer inside and saw twenty ounces of juice sloshing and swishing over my cell phone, pocketbook, hairbrush, sunglasses, and several pages of lecture notes. The bottle cap was bobbing in the lake of vitamin C, and the flight attendants were preparing for takeoff.

I caught one attendant's eye and tried to explain my dilemma quietly enough so that my seatmate would not hear. The attendant granted my plea and allowed me to dash to the lavatory to empty the sticky contents of my bag, turning it upside down over the toilet. The flight had not yet taken off, and I was already a mess. A gaggle of four-year-olds at a Chuck E. Cheese's birthday party could not have been as disordered as I was, and it was barely nine in the morning.

I have an imaginary vision of myself as someone whose clothes never wrinkle, whose hair is never out of place, who is always on time and who is never frustrated by life's unexpected zingers. But that is not the woman I am in real life. In real life I am the woman who runs late, whose keys are often missing, whose day frequently (and quickly) degenerates into chaos, and whose bag is full of orange juice.

But I am also the woman with at least a million reasons to rejoice anyway.

I don't mean to say that I have already achieved these things or that I have already reached perfection. But I press on to possess that perfection for which Christ Jesus first possessed me.
PHILIPPIANS 3:12

Fitting Me to Fly

Perhaps since Adam saw the first bird soar, we have wondered what it might be like to fly. Leonardo sketched hundreds of fantastical machines that might lift a man heavenward, but nothing his complex mind could conjure ever flew. The dynamics of flight—evidenced in the ease of everyday sparrows and finches—are more easily imagined than imitated.

There's a retreat center I love where opportunities to observe flight abound. From everyday canyon birds—sparrow, titmouse, robin, and mockingbird—to the occasional owl or hawk or fiery cardinal, the air of the place flutters and snaps with able wings.

On one visit, in a third of the time it took the God of the universe to make everything that is, I crafted a gross approximation of . . . a single feather. Coached by a patient, self-taught artist, I chose a rough tongue of tupelo wood and kept sanding more and more of it away, following the pencil marks he'd sketched. Lower here. Higher here. Thinner. And thinner. Still thinner? Yes.

When the sanding had left a soft layer of dust over my jeans and hands and under my fingernails, a feather did emerge. "You're ready to burn," my teacher said. I liked the sound of that. I'm a city girl and don't often play with smoking tools.

Again, following his marks, I cut and burned groove after thin groove into the smooth wood, working from the shaft outward. Then I primed and painted and repainted my single feather until a fast-flying owl at two hundred feet might be momentarily fooled that he'd lost a part of himself. (Maybe.)

In all that shaping and burning and coloring, I imagined the patient, loving work God does in *me*. Not content to let me plod along in grim duty or determined obedience, he means to let me lose myself in grace and truly soar. I'm made for more than a tight punch list of dos and don'ts. He's carving and smoothing my clumsy soul for the wind of the Spirit to ripple through and give me lift where I was once leaden.

With every nick and brush and burn, my still-creating Father is at work, fitting me to fly.

We who live by the Spirit eagerly wait to receive by faith the righteousness God has promised to us.

GALATIANS 5:5

My Pint-Sized Tutor

The cute blond in the waiting room was flirting with me. Shamelessly. I had buried my nose in my book, but he was cheerily persistent. He sidled closer, making no sound. Then he flung his plastic cup of Cheerios onto the empty seat next to me and stared until I looked his way. When I did, he broke into a toothy grin and moved closer still. I winked. He giggled. Good stuff sometimes starts that way.

Although we didn't introduce ourselves, his name was Jack. I know because his diaper bag said so. His mom watched him carefully and clucked a warning when it appeared he might deposit a few Cheerios in my purse. Jack didn't seem at all intimidated by meeting a full-grown stranger. He expected his overtures to be well received and seemed to delight in being noticed. We played peekaboo until his mother's name was called and the two of them followed a nurse into the exam area.

I heard my own name a few moments later, and I went in as well—standing at the desk to answer a question from the receptionist. As I stood there, I felt a gentle bump to my calf, then a little blond wrapped his arms around my knees. Jack was back.

His mom spoke from the open door behind me: "He found you again. So sorry." But honestly, I didn't mind. I hardly knew Jack, but I wasn't offended by his sneak attack. I was charmed by his enthusiasm. He was not afraid of rejection. He expected nothing but kindness from a stranger.

Jack taught me a giant lesson in approaching one who is greater than I am—say, God. I can approach him with confidence, expectantly, and without fear. I can be sure of his welcome because he is a good Father, whose only Son has vouched for me. My hope of being received is entirely reasonable based on these things.

I admired Jack's confidence. I welcomed his persistence. I appreciated his desire to be near me. And he wasn't even mine!

Let us then approach God's throne of grace with confidence, so that we may receive mercy and find grace to help us in our time of need.
HEBREWS 4:16, NIV

Love Lab 101

Remember those science classes in school that had a lecture and a lab? In the lecture, you heard the theory and hopefully took good notes. In lab, you put those theories to the test. Examples became experiments. Facts became findings. Learning was "fleshed out" in the lab.

There are hundreds of places recorded in history where God's lectures were brought to life in the lab of human experience, but few are as dramatic as the story of an Old Testament prophet named Hosea. His life-altering course of study could have been called Love Lab 101.

What a command God gave to Hosea: "Go, take to yourself a wife of harlotry" (Hosea 1:2, NASB). What an experiment! What happens when you mix the love of a good man with the repeated straying of an unfaithful woman?

In this love lab, Gomer was more than Hosea's harlot wife. She's you and me. She's anyone who belongs to God and cheats. Hosea felt that pain. God chose for him a bride who was flawed, fallen, and human. And that bride did what flawed, fallen, and human persons are prone to do: she spurned the love of her good husband and gave herself away to strangers instead.

But while Gomer was out with other men, her brokenhearted husband was quietly moving on her behalf. At God's direction he built a fence around her to keep her from destroying herself. Hosea protected and provided for her during her very public indiscretions. Then he did an even more unthinkable thing: he wooed back his cheating wife! He didn't *allow* her back; he determined to *win* her back!

Just like Hosea, God doesn't drag us cheaters to the woodshed—he lures us to the wilderness, where undistracted and alone, he can win our hearts all over again. He invites us out of the crowded ballroom of life and onto a quiet balcony, where he can whisper sweet, forgiving things in our ear.

That is the gospel. We are more desperately wicked and lost than we could ever imagine. And he is more loving and merciful than we could ever hope. You've heard the lecture. Maybe you even believe it. But have you taken the lab?

There is no fear in love; but perfect love casts out fear, because fear involves punishment, and the one who fears is not perfected in love. We love, because He first loved us.

1 JOHN 4:18-19, NASB

Journey and Camp

It's taken me years to figure it out: we're an end-result, hunker-down people, and we follow a process-happy, move-it-along God.

I've thought countless times if I could just get to my destination, God and I could rest. We could make ourselves comfortable and stay put.

Fat chance.

My God is forever moving me. Out of complacency and into passion. Out of fear and into faith. Out of comfort and into unplanned adventure. I'm a nester he's called to be a nomad. A homebody he keeps on coaxing out the front door. He moves me. He always has.

When the sons of Israel came out of Egypt led by Moses and Aaron, God commanded them to record their travels, which are capsulized in Numbers 33, from Egypt to the plains of Moab. They journeyed from one place, they camped in another, and then they journeyed and camped again. And again.

God was taking them somewhere and seemingly taking his own sweet time. But there were miracles large and small along the way and no doubt something to see at each journeying and camping place.

I could say the same. The glories and graces I've seen as I've journeyed and camped with my God could fill a book and then some—literally! Just when I think I've seen a good-enough place like Elim with twelve springs and seventy palm trees, just when I start to unpack and set up housekeeping, he says, "Let's go on." I'd stop and pull the covers up to my chin at the first cozy corner, but he's got something else in mind. We're moving.

I may be a good ways from home. But he's here. He's never called me to a place he's not. My bag is not fully unpacked. This is just a campsite. There's more journey ahead. And I'm learning that wherever he leads, I'd be crazy *not* to go.

Then they left Succoth and camped at Etham on the edge of the wilderness. They left Etham and turned back toward Pi-hahiroth, opposite Baal-zephon, and camped near Migdol. They left Pi-hahiroth and crossed the Red Sea into the wilderness beyond. Then they traveled for three days into the Etham wilderness and camped at Marah. They left Marah and camped at Elim, where there were twelve springs of water and seventy palm trees. They left Elim and camped beside the Red Sea.

NUMBERS 33:6-10

NOVEMBER 14

Give Us a King!

Most of us feel safer with some kind of ruler. We want a higher power to give us guidance, to advocate for us, and to protect us. (But not someone too high or too powerful.)

When the Israelites begged for a king like the other nations, they were really asking to separate God's rule from the whole fabric of their lives and to relegate him to the Tabernacle only. They sought to marginalize what was meant only to be magnified. They believed they knew best, and they wanted a king they could see and bargain with.

Like them, we live more comfortably with a king. That's why we're so quick to bow the knee to power, beauty, control, lust, or money. But Israel learned what some of us who belong to God are still trying to settle: to the extent that we seek another ruler, we seek our own heartbreak. When we plead for something less than God himself, we plead for our own demise, however slowly it may come.

London heard its first performance of George Frederick Handel's oratorio *Messiah* in 1743. As the story goes, the crowd watched in hushed expectation for the response of England's reigning monarch, George II, to Handel's great "Hallelujah" chorus, with its proclamation of the "King of kings and Lord of lords" who "shall reign for ever and ever." Reverently, quietly, the temporary king of a temporary kingdom rose to his feet as the words and music resounded. One by one, his subjects stood in tribute to their king's King.

Have you looked for a king who is like other kings? Are you pleading in your heart for something smaller to worship than the One True King? Do you believe you know better than this King what is really best for you? I have. And sometimes, God help me, I still do. But what I should be doing instead is paying tribute with my very life to the only King worth honoring. Because he *shall* reign forever and ever.

They shall speak of the glory of Your kingdom and talk of Your power;
to make known to the sons of men Your mighty acts and the glory of the
majesty of Your kingdom. Your kingdom is an everlasting kingdom, and
Your dominion endures throughout all generations.

PSALM 145:11-13, NASB

What to Do with Good News

We're not so very accustomed to good news. In fact, it is usually just the opposite. We're bombarded with not-so-good news—so much of it that we've almost become numb. The market is falling? Unemployment is rising? Wars or rumors of wars abound? Gridlock seizes Washington? No kidding. It's the norm. On a personal front, I've realized that I don't often expect the news to be good—and I am likely to be mistrusting of it when it appears to be. Even so, a recent trip to the mailbox turned up two unlikely pieces of good news. My local energy provider sent me a check (resulting from a class action lawsuit for overcharging thousands of customers), and an insurance premium actually went down. Neither windfall amounted to much, granted, but I viewed both as good news!

The best thing we can do with good news is to receive it, and the best news I've ever heard and received is this: "Since we have been made right in God's sight by faith, we have peace with God because of what Jesus Christ our Lord has done for us" (Romans 5:1). Does that sound too good to be true? It's not. "You see, at just the right time, when we were still powerless, Christ died for the ungodly. Very rarely will anyone die for a righteous person, though for a good person someone might" (Romans 5:6-7, NIV). Maybe. "But God showed his great love for us by sending Christ to die for us while we were still sinners" (Romans 5:8).

That's *the* Good News. And my heart tells me that even though it sounds more far fetched than an overpayment reimbursement or a favorably adjusted premium, I can believe it. So I've done what is rightly done with good news: I've received it. And every single day of my life I mean to demonstrate my unwavering belief in God's great Good News by what I say and by how I live and love.

Because the gospel is not too good to be true. It's too true to be anything *but* good.

God made Christ, who never sinned, to be the offering for our sin, so that we could be made right with God through Christ.

2 CORINTHIANS 5:21

a New Driver

The line at the local DMV was out the door and snaking around the building by nine o'clock in the morning. Although twenty-four stations for service lined the perimeter of the interior, only eight employees were helping customers at any given time. (Yes, I counted.)

Each of us in line had been given a number, and those numbers were not being called in any sort of sequential order. The whole system defied understanding—or at least it defied mine. Most of us were not excited to be there. But at least one of us was. One teenage boy and his father appeared quite happy to shuffle forward in line, then linger for an undetermined time in the sea of plastic chairs that spanned the width of the room. In fact, this young man was practically bouncing on the balls of his tennis-shoed feet in giddy anticipation, chattering happily with his dad.

While we were there to renew our licenses, he was clearly there to get his for the first time. We had plenty of driving history behind us and were annoyed at the chore of having to renew. But this young man was not annoyed. Not in the least. The thrill of the open road and the promise of a driver's license not marked "provisional" made his own wait seem like nothing.

It's been years since I first got behind the wheel of my brand-new faith in Christ. My relationship with God the Father, God the Son, and God the Holy Spirit cannot be called "new" by any linear measure of time. But what a tragedy it would be if I simply lined up each day and trudged along with grim determination to reach some unseen finish line! What a waste to become so numb to the joy of following Jesus that I resent time spent in his company.

This day is brand new, even if my faith is not. I cannot know what it might hold, nor will I see it again when it is done. Dear God, surprise me! In whatever way you see fit, answer my prayers and disturb my plans. Let me be giddy with expectation of what we might do together, today. After all, you, precious Father, make *all* things new!

Because of the LORD's great love we are not consumed, for his compassions never fail. They are new every morning.
LAMENTATIONS 3:22-23, NIV

Under the Bell Jar

"I feel like I am under glass," I told a wise and trusted friend, "and the rest of the world is on the outside." He responded to my analogy with a question: "Are you there to be quarantined—or nurtured?" Maybe my prison was really a kind of greenhouse. I hadn't thought of that.

The French developed the garden cloche, or bell jar, to nurture young seedlings in hostile weather environments. The cloche protected the plant from cold and frost and—with the sun's light—hastened it to maturity. Under the bell jar, it could grow unimpeded.

I'm no fragile seedling. But I am still growing—daily—into the image of the one who designed me for his garden. And if he sees that I need some nurturing protection of *his* design, who am I to resent the glass?

It feels a little lonely here, but I am not alone. It's a bit warm and confining, but it's beginning to feel more like a hothouse than a holding cell. And you'd be surprised by the light that finds its way inside. Every day I notice some well-placed reminder that God knows my whereabouts. Like the friend who offered to help me with the flowers for a niece's wedding about the time I was wondering how I might manage four hand-tied bouquets with only two hands to do the tying. Or the busy mom friend who offered me the only three free hours in her crazy schedule to teach me to make homemade rolls and filled the waiting time between steps with mugs of warm coffee and good conversation. I must not be invisible after all.

Do you feel as if you're under glass? Could it be that instead of your prison, it's a tiny garden paradise filled with the light and love God knows you need to grow? My life begins to change when I cease to deny or simplify its challenges, choosing instead to receive what the Father gives—trusting him to make from my trials something God honoring, pleasing to him, and good for me as well.

There are far, far worse places to be than under the bell jar.

Bless the LORD, O my soul: and all that is within me, bless his holy name.
Bless the LORD, O my soul, and forget not all his benefits.
PSALM 103:1-2, KJV

Doubling Down on My Mistakes

Have you ever doubled down when something was clearly not working, making meaningless microcorrections along the way but still aiming wrong? Have you stayed on your chosen course despite frustration and failure and as a result lost time, hope, integrity, or joy?

During one holiday season, I made three consecutive pans of gingerbread, each almost inedible in a different way. Pan one was too sticky. Pan two didn't rise. The contents of pan three had to be chiseled into the sink. I was certain I knew the recipe, which I never bothered to look up because I'd made it dozens of times. So I kept tweaking the amounts of the individual ingredients. But my errors weren't merely a matter of degree. I was missing ingredients fundamental to the gingerbread-making process. My intentions were good, and my confidence was high—but I wasn't going to get it right until I swallowed my pride and revisited the recipe.

Gingerbread's not life or death. Failing to get it right after three tries was annoying, although doubling down on my baking mistakes didn't hurt anyone. It just wasted time. But in some areas of life, doubling down does real damage. Like continuing in the same persistent sin, just changing the scenery around it. Or repeating relational patterns that have already proven toxic, just substituting new characters. Or worst of all, placing our faith again and again in anything but Christ and expecting God to bless and prosper us. German theologian Dietrich Bonhoeffer once famously said, "If you board the wrong train, it is no use running along the corridor in the opposite direction." (He certainly didn't mince words, did he?)

"Repent," Jesus said, "for the Kingdom of Heaven is near" (Matthew 3:2). In other words, get off that death train you're riding and let me give you life. Real life. Starting here and now. Stop course correcting on your bullet train to nowhere, and go where I'm going. Get off your self-selected ride (and your self-righteous high horse!) and follow me, instead.

Thankfully, although we double down in stubborn pride before him, God has already doubled down in faithfulness to us. His plan for us has been, is, and will forever be good.

He who did not spare His own Son, but delivered Him up for us all, how shall He not with Him also freely give us all things?
ROMANS 8:32, NKJV

Twenty-Five Million Reasons

A professional football player with a penchant for outrageous behavior takes too many pills and becomes unresponsive. The authorities are called, and police reports categorize the incident as an attempted suicide. Later his publicist (the same woman who called 911 on his behalf) argues that he never tried to take his own life. Why? "He has twenty-five million reasons why he should be alive," she answers, referencing the player's annual salary.*

If this famous athlete had twenty-five million reasons to live, does it follow that a penniless person has zero? Or would an infant, whose earning power is undetermined, have no reason to keep breathing another day? Is there anyone who believes that money inspires us to live life—or makes it more precious than it already is? And who needs twenty-five *million* reasons to live, anyway? Isn't one good reason enough?

God has given you another day. There's your reason.

Today I saw a combination of colors in the afternoon sky I'd never seen before. That's reason enough for me to want to taste tomorrow. A dear friend reports that her baby daughter has begun to smile. I haven't witnessed it yet, but I hope to very soon. I washed fresh blackberries today, and tomorrow morning I may taste a handful of them, standing at the kitchen sink and looking at the sunrise. As I do, a song might come on the radio that I've never heard before but won't be able to forget. I might see an old friend or meet a new one who will enrich my life forever. The possibilities of any day are endless and fine, and I am hungry to taste them.

Now that I think of it, I am richer than a crazily compensated NFL star. The one who is my reason for living never stops making arguments on life's behalf, and only a fool would get bogged down by sheer arithmetic when there is even a sliver of daylight left to savor. So what are you waiting for? Breathe. Say thank you. Embrace the Giver and the gift . . . and *live*.

See, I set before you today life and prosperity, death and destruction. For I command you today to love the LORD your God, to walk in obedience to him, and to keep his commands, decrees and laws.

DEUTERONOMY 30:15-16, NIV

---

* "Owens Fires Publicist Etheredge," ESPN, January 9, 2007, http://www.espn.com/nfl/news/story?id=2725205.

Unfolding

I've got a plan. Do you? I've got a plan for Thanksgiving prep, a writing plan for the remainder of my grad school semester, and a food plan for what I will and will not eat during the upcoming calorie-rich holidays. I have a plan for the flowers I'll do for my niece's upcoming wedding, a plan for systematically purging the paper in my study, and a plan for sending out the Christmas cards I wrote last week (hopefully well in advance of Christmas).

But what I think I need is a plan to stop planning. At least for a little while.

Every time I spend a few days at my favorite place of retreat, I come away awed at how good stillness feels. And I wish I could become better at letting my minutes and hours and days simply unfold. Not every day. I do have work that must be done to pay bills. But I don't have to fill every available slot on my calendar with swift and surgical deliberation. I'm not that essential to the operation of the universe.

I normally justify my busyness by saying I don't want to miss anything. But I see that I could easily justify my stillness with the same phrase. I wonder what I've already missed in my hurry to get it all done.

A devotional given last weekend by a friend recommended what he called "focal practice." Being present in the moment. This is how he said he could know he was there: "There's no place I'd rather be. There is nothing I'd rather be doing. There is no one else I'd rather be with. I will remember this day/moment/sight/conversation for a long, long time."

As this day unfolds, I mean to be present in it. And I mean to let that good, unhurried unfolding teach, heal, restore, encourage, and direct me to specific and heartfelt thankfulness.

My God is good. This day is his. And there is no place I'd rather be.

The LORD is the portion of my inheritance and my cup.
PSALM 16:5, NASB

Getting to Grateful

Any trainer worth his or her salt will tell you this: the muscles we use are the ones that grow stronger. The ones we ignore tend to move toward atrophy.

My thankfulness muscle has been getting a little flabby. Somehow, without my awareness, I've been working out my negativity muscles. Mentally, I've been keeping a list of woes and adding to it daily. But none has threatened the life of anyone I love or my own. None has caused me to sleep one single night on the street or miss even one meal I hoped to eat. None is permanent. Not one is beyond God's awareness.

That's what I've been remembering. Here's what I've been forgetting: I've been forgetting small acts of kindness by friends and strangers. I've been forgetting the full weight of God's history on my behalf. Forgetting that I'm called and equipped and empowered by the God of Abraham, Isaac, and Jacob. Forgetting that this part of my story is only *part* of my story. Forgetting that God is still writing the rest and that it will prove not only flawless but beautiful.

A friend of mine is facing an enormous trial with great grace. Her future is uncertain. Her present is challenging. When someone remarked that she looked lovely, almost radiant, she smiled and said these words: "Cancer becomes me."

I am humbled and haunted by her confession. To all those who see her shine and wonder if she's had "something done," the answer is yes. She has. She's had a work of supernatural grace done in her heart that has produced, against all odds, thankfulness. And it's quite lovely.

So as I commence a new kind of workout, I need to say some thank-yous: Thank you, Father, for the overdue check that is sixty days and counting. For the funny random hiccup in my car when I accelerate. For the job that didn't pan out, the plan that fizzled, and the imminent arrival of the third child of the man I once thought I would marry. Thank you for who you are in all of this, and who I am in you.

Let us continually offer up a sacrifice of praise to God, that is, the fruit of lips that give thanks to His name.
HEBREWS 13:15, NASB

Grateful, Grateful

John Bucchino is a talented composer and lyricist whose songs I stumbled on several years ago. My favorite tune of his is one called "Grateful." "I've got a heart that can hold love," it says, "I've got a mind that can think." It's impossible to stay depressed, writes Bucchino, when he remembers how he's blessed. I get it. I am truly blessed and duly grateful, too.

I'm grateful for any day of late that feels more like fall than summer. And for the pink sunrises I see every morning now that my bedroom windows face east. Grateful for the work that is waiting for me each day: good work that I enjoy; work that consistently puts gas in the car and groceries in the pantry and gives my heart and mind a workout in the process. Grateful for the friends whose questions keep me honest and whose prayers keep me close. For a lifelong best friend who happens to be my sister and for two beautiful nieces (and their husbands) whom I am crazy about. For parents who believed in me no matter what goofy thing I did. For big stuff like life and health and small stuff like blackberries on sale at the grocery store and blood-red peonies abloom in November. For things hoped for and things unexpected.

Mostly, though, I'm grateful that my heart knows whom to thank for all the goodness that is mine. Sure, the list of things is gratifying, but it's the Giver who really makes my heart sing. Any gift divorced from its giver is a lifeless thing; I'm grateful God "leaves the tags on" for me so I can see where all the best stuff comes from.

What are you grateful for—and for whom? What satisfies your soul and makes your heart sing? Whose presence blesses you like crazy? What beauties threaten to take your breath away? You really should thank Someone, don't you think?

Every generous act and every perfect gift is from above, coming down from the Father of lights; with Him there is no variation or shadow cast by turning. By His own choice, He gave us a new birth by the message of truth so that we would be the firstfruits of His creatures.
JAMES 1:17-18, HCSB

The Space Between

I've spent more time than I'd like to admit wrestling in a space so small you can't see it. It's that space no wider than a breath between faith and fear. Between faith in a God who loves me beyond reason, and fear of whatever force or feeling I've allowed to become bigger than that love.

You'd think after all this time I'd be less cowed by Satan's lies. But the evil one never stops whispering them, and sometimes, even against my better judgment, he suckers me again. Sometimes I believe him when he says, "You're not good enough" or "You can't have what your heart most desires." Sometimes I still expect the worst, although I know God's intentions for me—even in the most difficult of circumstances—are nothing but good.

But then I spent two days watching the good that can happen in that mysterious space between faith and fear. I went to see a cowboy work with horses whose fear kept them from the kind of relationship their owners hoped to forge with them. This cowboy didn't avoid the horses' fears; he worked through them, moving in until he somehow sensed a horse's confidence had overcome its need to run. Several times he held his hand close enough to touch a skittish horse but didn't. Not until he knew his touch would be welcomed and received. "Put your heart in your hand when you touch your horse," he instructed. I've thought a lot about those words.

Jesus came to me with his heart in his hand. His love felt utterly overwhelming yet completely safe. And day after day he helps my cautious, halting unbelief. He helps me believe that he works all things together for good as I love him and see his purpose. He helps me believe that he will never leave me or forsake me, even if I disappoint him badly. And he helps me believe that he is living water and life-giving bread and the kind of shepherd who did not hesitate to lay down his life for his sheep.

Mostly, he helps me believe that I, too, can move toward fear with my heart in my hand—closing that sliver of space between with settled confidence in nothing less than his own everlasting love.

As the Father has loved me, so I have loved you.
JOHN 15:9, NIV

The Free Stuff

Trust me: you appear a bit out of place when you attend a horsemanship clinic with no horse—but no matter. I'd watched a horse whisperer do his magic before and written about it in my book *The Beautiful Ache*. I found the whole thing so moving and instructive that several years later, I wanted to see it again. Thanks to the story-telling and teaching skills of this particular horseman, I came away with my trusty Moleskine brimming with relational truisms

One comment in particular rang like a bell for me. The trainer said, "The real measure of a horse is not what it gives you when you ask for it—it's *what it gives you for free*. Your job is to allow it and receive it." He was describing a relationship of trust that offered more than rote obedience or technique or hyperattentive rule keeping. One that included the possibility of amazement, fluid collaboration, and even surprise.

As a former champion rule keeper, I've been far too satisfied with my own out-ward compliance. I've hidden my heart (as if I could!) from God when I believed all he really wanted was for me to mind him. But that kind of relationship isn't what satisfies him, any more than it satisfies me. It's the free stuff that tells our story: it's the moments I steal to be with him, just because. It's the prayer breathed on the fly for the person he's just brought to mind. It's getting lost in his Word because it's just so beautiful and good. And it's lying down at night glad for another sweet day in his care, and telling him so. That's the free stuff.

In my relationship with my heavenly Father, and in every other relationship in my life, it's the free stuff that spells the difference between good and great. And it's the free stuff that binds us in the best way, as I respond to his endless grace with more love, over and over again.

I love the LORD, because he has heard my voice and my pleas for mercy. . . . Gracious is the LORD, and righteous; our God is merciful. The LORD preserves the simple; when I was brought low, he saved me. Return, O my soul, to your rest; for the LORD has dealt bountifully with you.
PSALM 116:1, 5-7, ESV

You Smell

They named her Lois, and for two weeks she was the toast of my town. She drew rock-star-worthy crowds, who lined up with cameras in hopes of catching her in an over-the-top pose. And like a true celebrity, she teased them for a long time before she obliged.

Lois the corpse flower (a.k.a., *amorphophallus titanium*), an endangered Sumatran species, boasted a rather spectacular six-foot bloom that gave off the smell of rotting flesh when fully opened. In its natural habitat, the plant's powerful odor attracts pollinating carrion beetles that come from near and far to lay their eggs in its stinking petals.

Horticulturists at the Houston Museum of Natural Science bought the bulb for seventy-five dollars from a North Carolina nursery specializing in exotic flowers. When it became clear six years later that the plant might actually bloom (not all of them do), they moved her out of the greenhouse, set up a twenty-four-hour webcam, opened the Museum around the clock, and sold buttons that boasted "I came, I saw, I smelled." No kidding.

Zac, Lois's caretaker, became something of a celebrity too, filling a Facebook page with his insights and tweeting updates about his smelly friend. But here's what amazes me: people were quite literally captivated by this gigantic, stinking flower and her powerful, awful odor. One woman who stood in line to see Lois in bloom said, "It's not a smell I was expecting . . . it's like garbage, rotting garbage. *It's beautiful and it's atrocious at the same time.*"

Did you know Christ followers smell? They do. And apparently it's a smell that is beautiful and atrocious at the same time, depending on whose nose is doing the smelling. To those whom God's Spirit has enlivened, it's a sweet, compelling odor. To those still in darkness, it reeks. It's either uncannily inviting or terribly off putting. But it's always there. And it's powerful.

And just like Lois, it's sure to draw out a strong reaction from anyone drawing close enough to its bloom.

We are to God the pleasing aroma of Christ among those who are being saved and those who are perishing. To the one we are an aroma that brings death; to the other, an aroma that brings life. And who is equal to such a task?

2 CORINTHIANS 2:15-16, NIV

Superglue

I have solid faith in superglue. Ever since I first glued my thumb and forefinger together with it in record time, the sticky stuff has been a powerful thing in my mind.

In its resting state, superglue looks a lot like water. Too clear and runny to really cement two opposing bodies together. But somehow when it comes in contact with those opposing bodies, well, ladies and gentlemen, look out.

I don't take the properties of superglue lightly. I know what the stuff can do. If superglue is in the equation somewhere, chances are very good that *something* is going to get stuck to something else.

I know even less about the mind of God than I do about chemistry, but here's something else I'm assured is true: I am stuck to God, and he is stuck to me by a kind of divine superglue. Because of the sacrifice of his Son Jesus Christ, and my faith in him, neither one of us is going anywhere. Falling markets can't break our bond. Electoral outcomes can't come between us. Sorrow can't drive a wedge. We're connected, and we're not coming apart. What the apostle Paul calls "the love of God that is in Christ Jesus our Lord" (Romans 8:39, NIV) is permanent. Period.

Thumbing through an old hymnal, I found these words by George Matheson that comfort in their certainty and beauty:

> *O Love that wilt not let me go,*
> *I rest my weary soul in thee;*
> *I give thee back the life I owe,*
> *That in thine ocean depths its flow*
> *May richer, fuller be.*

There's only one thing strong enough to keep me bonded to God, no matter what I do or what the world does to me. Christ's own saving, sanctifying love is glue than cannot, and will not, let me go.

I am convinced that neither death nor life, neither angels nor demons, neither the present nor the future, nor any powers, neither height nor depth, nor anything else in all creation, will be able to separate us from the love of God that is in Christ Jesus our Lord.

ROMANS 8:38-39, NIV

adopted

I know someone who wants to be adopted. He's past the age where that is likely to happen, but when this brown-eyed waif of a seventeen-year-old dreams, he dreams of having a family who wants him. Even though I know the odds aren't with him, I tell him to hold on to that dream. And I dream it for him too.

He's not cuddly and innocent. He's seen too much and done things he regrets. But I love him for reasons I cannot begin to explain, not the least of which is because I can. The system does not work in his favor. The law will not save him. Only love can do that. Only love of the unlikeliest kind.

I have friends who were adopted when they were small. Today they are strong, vibrant, productive adults. Once upon a time, when they were most vulnerable, someone who could love them did. It's as simple as that.

I also have friends who've recently adopted children. A beautiful daughter from China. Another from India. An adorable son from Russia. These parents love their children fiercely, and I'm certain they can no longer imagine life without them. They traveled a very long way to bring their children home.

When I was younger, I used to wonder if I was adopted. My sister is, from a purely physical standpoint, most obviously my mother's daughter. I am not. I don't even look that much like my dad, although there's a picture of *his* mother as a teenager that could be of me at the same age if you squint just right.

I used to wonder if I was adopted. Now I know I am.

Someone wanted me, even though I gave him no good reason to. Someone came from a very long way to bring me home. I didn't even know enough to dream of the thing I needed most, and it came to me just the same.

I know someone who wants to be adopted. I'll bet you do too.

———

God sent forth His Son, born of a woman, born under the Law, so that He might redeem those who were under the Law, that we might receive the adoption as sons.
GALATIANS 4:4-5, NASB

NOVEMBER 28
Awaiting New Wine

It's time for a new Bible, but I don't *want* a new one. The one I've most often used for years now is comfortably familiar. But its cover has detached from the spine, and pages are coming unhinged, sections at a time. The concordance has several folded pages stashed in the back, the way my grandmother used to keep folded tissues in her purse. If I don't turn the pages gently and coddle it carefully in my lap, it might not last another week.

But I don't want to let it go.

A new Bible always feels like starting over, and one glance at this one reminds me I've come a very long way. I know its tearstained pages, and those that have been like sweet balm to wounds the world made. I know where to turn to verses that have shaped my life. I know where the promises are that feed my soul, and I need them no less now than I did when this Bible was new.

This is not just any book, or even any Bible. It's a record of my most recent history with Jesus, and it's unspeakably sweet to me. It occurs to me that my reluctance to replace my old Bible is in some ways like my reluctance to leave whatever comfort God has given me and venture into the newness of the unknown. But he didn't call me to a faith that stalls out in the first place it finds that feels like home.

There is infinitely more ahead with him than there ever was behind. The past, as hard fought and precious as it was, is not where I'm meant to live. Every day with him is a clean white page waiting for old words to be applied in a new way. He will bring new wine, teach new lessons—if I will let go of the old.

So when no one's looking, one day soon, I'll kiss the cover of this dear old friend and put it away. I'll crack a new spine and breathe in the smell of new pages and wait again for brand-new wine.

No one puts new wine into old wineskins; otherwise the wine will burst the skins, and the wine is lost and the skins as well; but one puts new wine into fresh wineskins.

MARK 2:22, NASB

Spanx and Shame

Our ancestors Adam and Eve were created by a loving God and given free rein of the most lavishly beautiful resort imaginable. In Eden, they had all that they needed, but they wanted more. They disobeyed God by eating the one thing forbidden. Immediately they were made self-aware. They'd always been naked, but now they were naked and *ashamed*. This painful emotion drove them to seek cover. They hid, creating for themselves some pretty ridiculous camouflage: scratchy fig leaves sewn together as primitive undergarments.

If you think shame isn't still driving us into hiding—then you've never met a pair of Spanx. These twenty-first-century industrial-strength fig leaves are an industry unto themselves—promising to smoothly cover every physical shortcoming imaginable. Tummy rolls. Thigh dimples. Even "bat wings" and back fat. (I am not kidding.) I haven't seen it yet, but I imagine one day a full-body "glove" will exist that covers *everything*. Maybe it already does.

We've never stopped covering up. Sin and shame have not gone out of business. But God didn't leave Adam and Eve in their flimsy fig leaves—and he won't leave us in our Spanx. He covered the first couple, and he covers us, too. He replaced their sad and ineffective "camo" gear with animal skins in the Garden—the first record of bloodshed. But not the last:

> This is real love—not that we loved God, but that he loved us and sent his Son as a sacrifice to take away our sins.
> 1 JOHN 4:10

In other words, our God sees all that we would hide, and in love, covers us. No sin, no shame. And no Spanx required.

I sought the LORD, and He answered me, and delivered me from all my fears. They looked to Him and were radiant, and their faces will never be ashamed.
PSALM 34:4-5, NASB

Second Chances

One spring afternoon, Marva rang my doorbell. She explained that she had done some work for other folks in my neighborhood and wondered if I might have something for her. She was sick, she said, and needed money for medicine. She did not look well.

I asked her what kinds of jobs she'd done for my neighbors. "I could clean your windows," she offered. So we circled my house, counting the windows and agreeing on a price. But Marva didn't have her supplies with her. It was too hard for her to carry them every day, she said, because she had a lot of pain. I asked if she could come the next day, and she said she could. So I put some cash in an envelope and waited.

But she didn't come the next day. Or the next. She didn't return to my door for two weeks. When Marva rang the bell again, I offered the same deal we'd agreed upon the first day we met. When she'd been cleaning a little while, I left and drove to a nearby spot to get her a hamburger. (She still looked very thin and frail.) I was afraid she might be offended that I'd bought her lunch, so I asked her if she wanted to share a burger with me. She did. But we didn't exactly eat together. I took her a plate and a drink, and she sat down on my porch steps to eat.

I fixed my plate but stayed in the house. I wanted to go outside, sit down, and ask her to tell me her story. But I didn't. And I still don't know why not.

Marva cleaned my windows last week. I fed her lunch and paid her well, but I didn't do what I should have done. I didn't love her as a neighbor. I didn't listen to her and honor her bravery to come and ask again for work. Marva got a second chance, and she made good on it. I hope she'll give me another chance one day soon, so that I can do the same.

"You shall love the LORD your God with all your heart, and with all your soul, and with all your mind." This is the great and foremost commandment. The second is like it, "You shall love your neighbor as yourself."

MATTHEW 22:37-39, NASB

December

Spending It all

Several years ago a friend and I wandered through a palazzo in Florence, Italy, killing an hour or so before our return flight home. We'd been in Italy for nearly a week and were feeling pretty confident we could navigate the peculiar traffic, strange money, and communication mazes with some measure of ease. We decided to spend every lira in our pockets and headed for the nearest gelato stand.

Using a combination of gestures and words, we ordered—we thought—two single-scoop cones of gelato. What we got was two double-scoop cones for twice the price we'd planned. We emptied the contents of our purses and pockets and still came up short. The gelato vendor looked at us with pity and waved us out of his store.

I was reminded of that spend-it-all spree when I attended a Bible conference to hear a noted teacher. Prof, as he was affectionately called, was nearing his eighties. Cancer had claimed his right eye, and he wore a black eye patch against his softly aging face. His gait was slow, and his hands trembled—but when he began to teach from Scripture, he was ageless.

His voice was full of delight, and I swear his good eye twinkled. He challenged us to live intentionally for Christ in a dying world—and he did it with passion, clarity, and power. As he did, I thought, *He's spending it all. He's spending every last bit of himself doing the thing he was made to do, to the glory of the one who made him. This man means to go out empty.*

Some of us are savers, and some are spenders. After watching Prof teach for a handful of hours, I was more sure than ever that I want to be a spender. Right now is a slice of time so thin it can barely be measured, but we live like this world is everything we've got. In time my own body will age and slow and falter, too, but it's not the best of what I have to offer. I'm made for spending from the inside out, and the heart held fast by Jesus is *always* young. Prof taught me that.

Always work enthusiastically for the Lord, for you know that nothing you do for the Lord is ever useless.

1 CORINTHIANS 15:58

Check

While cleaning and organizing recently, I uncovered a treasure I didn't know I still possessed. Some years back I purchased a mostly blank book and filled its pages with pure, unfiltered desire. Or more appropriately, desires. Like a third grader gone wild, I drew, wrote, and made outrageous lists of things I'd dreamed of but had never said out loud to anyone. I spilled out in fuchsia and berry-blue ink a whole trove of hopes and wishes, and then I quietly put the book away.

Until just the other day.

I found it, opened its cover, and began thumbing through its pages. When I did, I discovered that my heavenly Father has brought many of those forgotten dreams to pass, most of them without any help from me.

I dreamed of a house with a porch swing. (Check.) A tiny study with floor-to-ceiling books. (Check.) A good horse. (Not just yet.) A godly husband. (Ditto.) A book written in my name, not someone else's. (Check, check, and check.) Opportunities to teach God's Word to women. (Check.) The chance to skydive. (Check.) A trip to Paris. (Check.)

As I ran my fingers over line after line, I blinked back tears. God had literally given me the desires of my heart. Not just made my halfhearted *wishes* come true but placed strong, specific desires deep in my heart that he meant all along to fulfill—to remind me of his love and to show his power. To cause my lips to praise him and my happy tears to bless his name. To remind me that he knows the good plans he has for me.

Are there some longings I'm still waiting for his hand to fill? Oh yes, there are. But they pale (truly!) in comparison with what he has already done. He knows me. He knows my heart. And he's not offended when I go childlike on him and hope wildly for his eyes only. He welcomes my wanting. Designs it even. For my own good and for his great glory.

Because even when I've forgotten my dreams, he remembers. (*Check.*)

I'm thanking you, GOD, out loud in the streets, singing your praises in town and country. The deeper your love, the higher it goes; every cloud is a flag to your faithfulness.

PSALM 57:9-10, MSG

Rearranging Things

I'm not sure if you could call it home improvement, but change is underway. I'm rearranging my study and its books, trying to assess what should stay and what should go (no easy task for a book-loving, literary nerd).

Less than half the books have been reshelved; the others stand in hip-high stacks around the dining room, forming a kind of ad hoc, uneven wainscoting that's growing on me although it's only temporary. But the change hasn't stopped there. Within a week of the book purge, my furniture got in on the deal as well.

My sofa of nearly twenty years (and whatever coins were underneath its cushions), together with my dining table and four chairs, have made their way to a new home across town. They'll soon provide seating for six young urban missionaries in a rented town house, combined with other odds and ends furnished by members of my church. When the call went out for furniture, I thought, *Why not? There are six of them and only one of me. I have other places to sit.* When one of our pastors shared with me the amount of their weekly individual allowance for food, I realized I'd spent it that day—on lunch.

Hopefully in the next few weeks I'll meet the girls who are settling in and maybe bring a meal to fill that old, familiar table. Oddly enough, I don't miss it much. And that fact makes me wonder if my rearranging is anywhere near done. I've questioned lately if I'm living rightly: whether I have just enough or too much, if abundance has become the expectation and my own comfort the rule of thumb for acquiring more. Do I share willingly what is mine? Am *I* a good neighbor? A generous friend?

I pray so. Because God has been very good to me. I don't know where the tipping point lies between too much and not enough, but I hope I find it. Until then, I invite the one who owns it all to gracefully rearrange what is mine in any way that pleases him, in the name of love.

Give me neither poverty nor riches, but give me only my daily bread.
PROVERBS 30:8, NIV

Playing My Song

"Please throw me a bone, God," I remember praying during a particularly tough season. "I just need a little something good to know you're still with me and you haven't temporarily forgotten my whereabouts."

If that sounds ungrateful, let me assure you I am not. I know my life is rich with blessings. But sometimes I *ache* for an intimate touch, a sign, and a timely word of encouragement from my heavenly Father. I don't doubt his existence or his love. But when the hard stuff of life sucker punches with unnerving aim and regularity, what's a girl to do? And where else would she go?

Later that same week, driving to an early breakfast meeting, I synced my phone to the car's stereo to distract from the slow crawl of commuter traffic. My tunes were on shuffle; I was only half listening to the random mix when a song written by a friend came on, which made me think of *another* of his songs—so perfect for my present season.

"Please, God," I whispered out loud, "I need to hear that one. Could you play it for me now?"

As soon as the sound of the first song faded, the chords of the next one—*the one I'd just asked for*—began. Oh yes, it did. And my tears fell hard at the loving-kindness of my very near—and listening—God. You can call it a coincidence if you like. I know better. Someone good was playing my song with perfect timing. Just so I'd know I am loved. Just so I'd know he hears. And just because I'd asked.

One day we'll look back
and see how this road
wound like a drunk man
stumbling home
how every whisper of joy
every bellow of pain
*made us beautiful again.**

Things may look messy now, but one day we will *all* be beautiful again. And we have a God who loves us enough to remind us this is so.

Sing psalms and hymns and spiritual songs to God with thankful hearts.
COLOSSIANS 3:16

---

* Nathan Tasker, "Beautiful Again," *Home* (Luxtone Records, 2015).

Only One

I've been in my new home for several months, but I continue to learn things about this tiny 1950s ranch—the kinds of things one only learns by living in a place over time. I've learned that the back door is impossible to jimmy if I've walked out without my keys, and after paying a locksmith $129 for my mistake, I decided this is probably a good thing, after all. I've learned where the gutters drip and which fence boards need replacing; I know the sounds the air conditioner and furnace make as they cycle off and on and where water pools on the driveway after a heavy rain.

I've also learned that when I only have one of something, I pay special attention to it. This is the only home I've ever purchased. I have no plans to purchase any other. I treat my one home with attentive care. I tend to it and love doing so. Having only one of something sharpens my focus on that thing. It increases my care of it.

I have only one life. I will not have another. It's *this* life I must cultivate, invest, steward, spend. And I have only one Savior—my Father's only Son. If all goes as I pray it does, I will spend every bit of this life I've been given bringing honor and glory to the only begotten Son of God. But the offering up of this one life (while it may have been decided decades ago) is not done once for all time but in increments of minutes, hours, and days. That means every decision counts. Every word counts. Every seemingly insignificant interaction is ripe with opportunity, for good or for ill.

Mary Oliver, in her poem "The Summer Day," presents the challenge this way: "Tell me, what is it you plan to do with your one wild and precious life?"

I plan to spend my only one, on my Only One. What about you?

I'm asking GOD for one thing, only one thing: to live with him in his house my whole life long. I'll contemplate his beauty; I'll study at his feet.
PSALM 27:4, MSG

Not by Me

Grace means that something good was done *for* me but not *by* me—something uncoerced and undeserved. How do I recognize grace? It is difficult to receive, and its beautiful sting almost always wrecks my pride.

When I am forgiven—that is grace.

When I am accepted solely on the basis of another's generous invitation or goodwill—that is grace.

When I am blessed—that is grace.

When my response to a challenge or slight or difficulty is better than I know I am, that is grace.

Grace is a houseguest who cleans out your refrigerator, top to bottom, and disposes of the stuff you were afraid to open for fear of what you'd find. It sets your things in order while you are away, without mentioning it or expecting a reward.

I felt the sting of this concrete example myself when a house-sitting friend not only watched my home and wrangled my darling dog, but returned my neglected fridge to its rightful, pristine state without a word. As I did a mental inventory of the things she'd disposed of, I felt a telltale sense of shame and wounded pride: as much as I *want* to be that person whose insides are as carefully kept and curated as her outsides, I am most assuredly not. Not even close. My messy fridge was undeniable proof—just as its now-gleaming inside proves the power of love to change what most needs changing. Even when the process is not pretty.

I was beyond delighted for my refrigerator makeover. Truly. But I was also humbled that it needed doing and more than aware that I was the one responsible for its woeful *before* state—but not its beautiful *after*.

May it ever be so, too, with the insides of my soul—rearranged forever for my good, but not by me.

When we were still without strength, in due time Christ died for the ungodly. For scarcely for a righteous man will one die; yet perhaps for a good man someone would even dare to die. But God demonstrates His own love toward us, in that while we were still sinners, Christ died for us.
ROMANS 5:6-8, NKJV

Me and Nanny McPhee

I felt someone looking over my shoulder. I was in Barnes & Noble late on a weekday afternoon, reading a book I was thinking of buying. (Yes, I do that.) I was also trying to ignore the small lurker nearby, imagining that she was only interested in the book in my lap. Then her young voice asked, "What's that?" I ignored the girl at first, thinking she was speaking to someone else. She wasn't. She was speaking to me and gesturing. "It's a book," I said, confused.

"No," she answered, pointing at my face now. "What's *that*?" I wondered if I'd marked on myself with a pen when she said, "On your *cheek*."

Well. There is a mole on my left cheek. I've always had it. I don't even notice it anymore. But she did. Geesh.

"It's a mole," I said, now feeling the furtive stares of the shoppers nearby. And I began to feel a little freakish. I'd never considered the mole a glaring defect or a cosmetic flaw, but this child surely did. "A what?" she asked again. "A mole," I repeated, now wishing to drop through the floor. *Whose kid was this?*

I felt bad for the rest of the day. Like there was something grotesquely wrong with me. And there is. But it's not a mole. It's not anything external at all. My heart is flawed and more than a little sick. I was born that way. Yet in spite of my flaws I have been loved with an everlasting love. My God, who could easily (and with pinpoint accuracy) name my every defect, instead chooses to see in me his only Son's righteousness. I am robed in it. Covered by it. He does not see my sin sickness any longer. He sees goodness, truth, and beauty, while I see mostly Nanny McPhee.

So if you were to point to me and ask, "What's that?"—I would hope with all my heart you were seeing Jesus. He's the lovelier of the two of us, by far.

See how great a love the Father has bestowed on us, that we would be called children of God.

1 JOHN 3:1, NASB

Listening for the Voice

Four red-upholstered, mechanized chairs sit in a row facing a stage. At the moment before a contestant steps up to perform, all four judges' chairs rotate 180 degrees. They are unable to see the singer they're judging. They can only listen for "the voice." If they like what they hear, they press the button on the chair's console, and a lighted sign on its base says "I want you." The chair turns again and reveals to the judge the owner of the voice.

It's a television gimmick, but it works—even though choosing something sight unseen is risky. The contrast between the look of the singer and the sound of his or her voice is often striking. This show reminds me that I sometimes struggle to discern the voice of God. I want to hear it, but I'm not always certain I have. I strain to pick up the nuanced leadings of his Spirit, the whispers and the warnings. I cannot see him, but I long to hear from him, to know he's with me.

I've never seen God's face, but I've come to recognize and love his voice. It causes me to turn and listen, turn and notice, turn and *choose*, every day. How could it not? It's his voice that turned water into wine, calmed waves, and healed hurt people. It has become as familiar to me over time as the first voices I heard as a child, and there is never a time when it is not speaking.

Truthfully, I most often hear his "echo"—I know in retrospect that the voice I heard was his. But there are times—oh, those precious times!—when I recognize him in the moment, and we are able to communicate as friends.

I want to become a better listener. I want to turn and keep on turning at the sound of his voice. There is no sweeter sound.

The voice of the LORD hews out flames of fire. The voice of the LORD shakes the wilderness; the LORD shakes the wilderness of Kadesh. The voice of the LORD makes the deer to calve and strips the forests bare; and in His temple everything says, "Glory!"
PSALM 29:7-9, NASB

Something to Say

I'd been invited to an industry awards ceremony—a gathering for those whose business it is to promote the businesses of others. Before the hardware was dispensed, a half dozen or so people mounted the rotating stage (an *American Ninja Warrior* feat in itself) to make various announcements. Then one fellow, dressed in decidedly noncocktail attire from head to foot, mounted the stage and began a monologue I still can't quite describe. His existential rambling included a boat (I think) and lots of stars. He lost me within seconds, and everyone else, too. No one knew what he was saying or why. The two emcees of the evening stood helplessly by the rotating stage as the man went on about his own interior journey, unaware of the confusion of the audience or the incoherence of his words.

Not everyone deserves a platform, I thought in that moment. Not everyone has something worthwhile to say. Not everyone who is miked and onstage has considered the responsibility of that particular space and time. We live in an age when microphones and well-lit stages confer importance, if not honor. An age when platforms are built to serve a person and his or her agenda, rather than demanding a person fit to occupy them. I suspect we have it backward. Perhaps we should consider not the window dressing of communication but the meaning of the words themselves and the reliability of the one offering them. Perhaps we should weigh them carefully and not be fooled by the sophistication of their context.

I am sure I have spoken, and may still speak, when I really have nothing to say. I am equally certain that some occasion has required speech and I have kept silent. I have spoken and written empty words when I might have used life-giving words instead if I had only taken more time to consider the moment and the needs of those reading or listening. And I'm sure I've stood on a platform that added weight to words of mine when their substance was less than weighty.

It's best to speak only when we truly have something to say.

———

The heart of the godly thinks carefully before speaking; the mouth of the wicked overflows with evil words.
PROVERBS 15:28

Looking for Overland

It is a wise professor who, after assigning her class *The Portable Atheist* by Christopher Hitchens, follows that literary millstone with *The Silver Chair*. C. S. Lewis is an apt remedy for too much darkness. My favorite bit of monologue from *The Silver Chair* comes from a Marsh-wiggle named Puddleglum. He's odd and slimy and sometimes rude, but he has a very brave heart. He and his traveling companions are trapped in a place called Underland—a dark place. The queen of Underland hopes to trick them into believing that Underland is all there is, and even though they've seen light before, she comes *this close* to succeeding. Then Puddleglum pushes hard against her spell and makes the claim that rallies my own heart against the darkness every time I read it:

> One word, Ma'am. . . . One word. All you've been saying is quite right, I shouldn't wonder. I'm a chap who always liked to know the worst and then put the best face I can on it. So I won't deny any of what you said. But there's one more thing to be said, even so. Suppose we *have* only dreamed, or made up, all those things—trees and grass and sun and moon and stars and Aslan himself. Suppose we have. Then all I can say is that, in that case, the made-up things seem a good deal more important than the real ones. Suppose this black pit of a kingdom of yours *is* the only world. Well, it strikes me as a pretty poor one. . . . So, thanking you kindly for our supper, if these two gentlemen and the young lady are ready, we're leaving your court at once and setting out in the dark to spend our lives looking for Overland.[*]

I'm no fool. I see the darkness. I smell the fear and hate and evil. But even so, I remember something different. Something beautiful and true and full of light. Better to set out in the dark in its direction than to deny it ever was, and is, and will be. I'm looking for Overland. Aren't you?

My soul yearns for you in the night; my spirit within me earnestly seeks you.

ISAIAH 26:9, ESV

---

[*] C. S. Lewis, *The Silver Chair* (New York: Macmillan, 1953), 154–155.

For Love or Money

Not everyone loves their job. I know. I didn't always love mine.

For more than two-thirds of my working life, I was employed by someone else and received a predictable every-other-week paycheck for my efforts. Occasionally I did jobs I loved, but mostly, I worked for the money. All that ended with an unexpected corporate rightsizing that left me with a modest severance and a cardboard box filled with the personal items from my corner office. It was the only job I've ever been asked to leave and the best day yet of my career.

It launched me into what some call entrepreneurship, which is just a fancy word for the vocation known as "living by faith." I'm self-employed. But I work for the God who is love. Together, we write books, magazine articles, newsletters, web content, speeches, reports, scripts, and the occasional bit of poetry (no money *there*). I create things with words—work that I *do* get paid for but would still do even if I did not. Telling stories is what I love, and the gospel story is the one I love telling most of all.

When I was younger, I could hardly envision this life that is mine. Perhaps I caught glimmers of what God had in store, but mostly I was looking to anyone and anything *but him* for love or money. No more.

My goal is to do good work and to do it in a way that brings him glory, because my God deserves every bit of praise and honor that comes his way. Mine is not a household name. My books aren't on the *New York Times* bestseller list or among Amazon's top sellers. I don't always know when—or from where—the next assignment will come. But I do work I love every day, and usually I get paid for it. Don't tell, but it is such a joy to me that I think I'd do it for love alone.

Make a careful exploration of who you are and the work you have been given, and then sink yourself into that. Don't be impressed with yourself. Don't compare yourself with others. Each of you must take responsibility for doing the creative best you can with your own life.
GALATIANS 6:4-5, MSG

Everlasting

Several years ago a precious, thirty-year-old Bible was mysteriously lost to me. This battered, twice rebound, long-loved book had seen me through so many joys, doubts, struggles, and triumphs of my Christ-following life! To hold it was to hold a well-marked road map of the way God had led me so far. I celebrated like crazy when it came home to me through a set of circumstances only he could have engineered. Then just a few months later, I wailed like a baby when it was destroyed.

During a stretch of days that involved longer-than-normal absences from home, my beloved Bible proved too great a temptation for my teething pup Burley to resist. I left one morning for the hospital and ended up staying most of the day and late into the evening. Unfortunately, I also left Burley and the Bible alone together. When I arrived home, my normally enthusiastic dog was strangely shy. When I looked into my study, I saw the reason why. Scattered on the rug were pieces of cover and spine, wads of gnarled text, maps with strange new borders, and hand-lettered notes turned into soggy hieroglyphics.

I was heartbroken. I fell to the floor and sobbed, gathering the pages back together and holding the whole mess to my chest. I screamed at Burley. He cowered in his crate. I hit the floor with the heel of my hand so hard I had a bruise for a week. Finally I placed the whole mess into a box and stored it out of sight. But not out of mind.

Then I read a quote from Michael Downey in his book *Altogether Gift* that pulled me up short: "Human life, all of it, is the precinct of epiphany—of God's showing, of God's constant speaking and breathing."* My life—not the pages of my old Bible—contains my spiritual history. So does yours. Monuments of faith are not everlasting, not even the dearest ones. God is. His love is. By his great sacrifice those things belong to me, and I can never lose them. They are incorruptible, immutable, everlasting . . . and mine.

———

I saw another angel flying in mid-heaven, holding the everlasting Gospel
to proclaim to the inhabitants of the earth.
REVELATION 14:6, PHILLIPS

---

* Michael Downey, *Altogether Gift: A Trinitarian Spirituality* (Maryknoll, NY: Orbis Books, 2000), 35.

Crazy Hope

I am cautious with hope. I always have been. My heart leaps to it quickly, but my head says, "Careful there, missy. That hope you're fooling with is dangerous stuff. You don't want to get hurt or look foolish, do you?" I don't. And because my head can argue longer (and louder) than my heart, I've spent a lifetime carefully reigning in my hope—and I've done a pretty good job of it.

Even so, my heart still sometimes gets the best of me.

I've fallen off the functional stoic's wagon a time or two of late. I've hoped, and I haven't exactly hoped in secret, either. And sure enough, I've been disappointed—and even a little ashamed that I didn't manage my longings with a firmer hand.

Creative projects that looked promising at first didn't pan out in the end, and I feel silly that I actually believed they would. Fledgling friendships that seemed they might flutter and take wing have fallen with a tiny thud. And the old, familiar things I've counted on in the past to comfort me simply haven't, and don't much anymore.

I've dared my heart enough to hope, and it seems that hope is having the last laugh. The modest home I hoped I might buy, I can't. The numbers don't quite add up. (While "self-employed" is a wonderful, unpredictable, faith-stretching way to live, it apparently fails to impress the mortgage lenders.) And the elegant dress I *did* buy for an anticipated celebratory event was never worn; I returned the purchase, tags still attached, handing it and the receipt to a quizzical clerk with a shrug and a quiet "Didn't work," although the dress itself worked just fine.

Hope is not for the fainthearted. It requires no small amount of bravery to keep at it and to risk disappointment. But even when I doubt the wisdom of cracking my heart open one more time for anything at all, I know I surely will. I will because the opposite of a hopeful heart is a hardened one, and *that* would be the death of me.

And I will because my truer-than-true Father holds every crazy hope of mine. He bids me come and ask again, and he never makes me ashamed for having done so, whether his answer hurts or heals.

———

Hope does not disappoint.
ROMANS 5:5, NASB

Broken Things

Lately I've been confronted with broken things. A broken gate. A broken window. A broken paisley plate that fell from the top shelf of a wobbly bookcase. And just this week, a fifteen-foot limb that broke away from my neighbor's tree one night and landed with a loud crash not two feet from my front steps.

The gate and window were quickly repaired. The plate broke into three almost-neat sections, although I can't locate a few small edge pieces needed to glue it back together. The branch I dragged over to the side of the yard between our two houses, and my neighbor kindly sawed it into kindling and stacked it away. But I can't quite escape the feeling that I'm in the vortex of some invisible wind that is swirling wildly around me. And breaking things apart.

"Things fall apart; the centre cannot hold," writes Irish poet W. B. Yeats in "The Second Coming." But I challenge his conclusion. I believe it can and does. The center holds because the beautiful Son is at the center, holding all things together: "For by Him all things were created, both in the heavens and on earth, visible and invisible, whether thrones or dominions or rulers or authorities—all things have been created through Him and for Him. He is before all things, and in Him all things hold together" (Colossians 1:16-17, NASB).

Circumstances at the edges can be perilous, yes. Things are broken. They crash and fall and shatter. But the center is strong. The center holds. Or better, *it is held*.

The challenge is to celebrate the mending, not mourn the pieces. To be thankful for the repairs and not lament (at least not for long) the breaking. The challenge is to believe—even before things are put right—that *rightness* is near and possible and that it will come. Broken things *will* be mended: one day even our own hearts' cracks and fault lines will be flawlessly fixed and stronger for it.

Because my God loves broken things. Even me.

Although you were formerly alienated and hostile in mind, engaged in evil deeds, yet He has now reconciled you in His fleshly body through death, in order to present you before Him holy and blameless and beyond reproach.

COLOSSIANS 1:21-22, NASB

I See the Moon

Every night before bedtime when we were small, my sister and I said our God-blesses with our parents close by. "I see the moon and the moon sees me," we'd begin together. "God bless the moon and God bless me." Then we'd leave the moon for still more distant lights: "I see the stars and the stars see me; God bless the stars and God bless me."

Our God-blesses started big (the heavens!) then got sweetly small as one by one we'd name every member of our extended family—grandparents, aunts, uncles, and cousins—and ask God to bless them, too. It was the surest liturgy of my childhood, and I can't remember more than a handful of nights that it was missed.

I don't say my God-blesses anymore. My prayers these days are less scheduled and a lot more complex. But they're not any more profound or true. Those child-hood prayers were the alphabet that taught me to piece together prayer's language, and although I add more words today, the subject/verb/object structure of yesterday is still at the very heart of it all.

God is, and should be, the subject of my devotion, the recipient of my requests, and the acknowledged one who blesses all that is (and who are) blessed. It's just that simple. Even now. So when my mind is jumbled or my heart is troubled, when I can't find the words to order my grown-up prayers to God, I'm thinking that "I see the moon . . ." might not be a bad way to start.

Oh, I know the *moon* doesn't really see me. But the moon's Maker does. Tonight his moon is waning just a shade past full, and as it sits low and golden in the autumn sky, I plan to whisper, "I see the moon and the moon sees me; God bless the moon and God bless me." Then, because he really *is* the one who sees us all and holds within himself the power to bless us, I'm going to name as many names as I can call to mind and ask him to do just that.

Maybe I'll even be saying yours.

In times of trouble, may the LORD answer your cry. May the name of the God of Jacob keep you safe from all harm.

PSALM 20:1

Silver and Gold

The weather in my town isn't reminding me of Christmas; yesterday afternoon was a balmy eighty-three degrees. But superstore parking lots are full of fresh-cut trees, lights are up on neighborhood streets and shopping centers, and the red kettles of the Salvation Army can be seen outside grocery stores across the city.

Each red bucket is attended by a bell ringer wishing passersby a Merry Christmas, whether they leave a donation or not. It's hard for me to walk past without dropping at least my wallet's latest loose coins into the kettle. But others leave more than spare change.

Already twice this season, the local army bell ringers have received gold coins wrapped in dollar bills, one with the message "A Child Is Born—Jesus. Merry Christmas!" and another reading, "Glory to God in the Highest!" It happens every year. And every year it makes the news. Gold coins worth thousands of dollars are dropped anonymously like nickels or pennies from persons who have more than gold to give: they are reflecting the love of the Christmas Child, Jesus. They don't ask for receipts for tax purposes or stop to have their picture taken as they drop in their donation. They give in secret, in gratitude for the greatest gift ever.

I don't have much silver and no gold to speak of. But the phantom red-kettle givers remind me that what I have is worth far more. I have Jesus. And I can give him away in the name of love. I've been given the gospel. I've received the Christ child. I have all that I need and far, far more than I deserve. I am rich, and I live among the poor in spirit. I possess what the world needs most, and I know—because I need it too. By giving what is mine by grace, I celebrate God's great gift to me.

A child was born, and he is worth more to me than silver or gold. Glory to God in the highest!

Thus says the LORD, "Let not a wise man boast of his wisdom, and let not the mighty man boast of his might."
JEREMIAH 9:23, NASB

Wrestling the Tree

Every year, envisioning a tall, fresh-smelling fir tucked in the corner of my living room, I do serious recon on where the most reasonably priced, healthy specimen can be found and make the annual expedition to the tree lot. Then, after looking at and handling no less than a dozen viable candidates, I select one tree to take home with me. I choose a lot that will trim the trunk, hoist it to the top of my car, and tie it down, but after that it's a do-it-yourself deal all the way home and beyond.

At some point every year, I also acknowledge this universal truth: setting up a Christmas tree is no one-man (or in my case, one-woman) job. I could ask for help. But there's something about the maddening me-and-the-tree duel that suckers me in almost every time. I see no reason why I *shouldn't* be able to outmaneuver and outmuscle the process and the tree, whose size I almost always regret as soon as I've gotten it home.

I wrestle a Christmas tree only once a year. But it's really about the tree and me all year long. The tree I wrestle daily is my own cross, which I've been commanded to take up and carry with me, allowing myself, my wants, my will to die. The cross is a tree I both love and struggle against. I love its complex beauty, and I struggle against its simple invitation. I love its power and struggle against its grace. It's not easy, this wrestling with the tree.

I may resist much-needed help with my Christmas tree. But I'd be a fool to resist much-needed help with my cross. (Even Jesus had help to carry his.) And thankfully, when I've overestimated my own ability or strength or resolve, or when the whole cross-carrying process has left me exhausted and scraped up and scarred, the one who's gone before me sees my struggle and says with patience and empathy, "Won't you let me help you with that?"

I will. Oh yes, I will.

He forgave us all our sins, having canceled the charge of our legal indebtedness, which stood against us and condemned us; he has taken it away, nailing it to the cross.
COLOSSIANS 2:13-14, NIV

DECEMBER 18
My Egg-Carton Advent

Last spring I spent many weeks working on my master's thesis: an apologetic of the role words play in coming to faith and growing in it. It was a nontraditional sort of fulfillment of a traditional requirement. And it was much more difficult than I ever imagined it might be.

For example, to demonstrate how affected I was as a child by the poetry of Emily Dickinson, I had to remember myself as that child to rediscover the condition of my heart and the particulars of my life when I first encountered her work. But once I managed to put myself emotionally in the past, I couldn't remain there. I wasn't writing in a child's voice or a young adult's voice—I was writing as the woman I am today.

As challenging as my thesis was, the single emotion that dominated this process for me was gratitude. I saw, all over again, the providence of God in my life as he brought each of my literary guides and their words to me just in time. I needed Emily as a child. Her poetry was food for a heart that was starving for something *other* and for the assurance of a deeper, wider world. I needed C. S. Lewis as a college student, coming into my faith apart from my family of origin, learning how to love, and beginning to make my way in the world. Most recently, I have needed Ignatius of Loyola to understand and experience anew the nearness of God, to encounter him in a place beyond words.

So this Advent season, instead of the typical calendar that emphasizes *waiting* for the Messiah, a wise friend suggested I create a different sort of calendar that adds a reminder each day of how Christ has *come*, and is *coming*, to me. You might think the egg carton on my kitchen counter looks a little plain and strange, but each odd artifact or rolled scrap of paper tells a story of its own—of how the Word keeps coming to me. When I take the time to breathe in his presence, the richness of his love never stops amazing me. Even so, Lord Jesus . . . *come*.

Do you think lightly of the riches of His kindness and tolerance and patience, not knowing that the kindness of God leads you to repentance?
ROMANS 2:4, NASB

Comfort and Joy

The bright tin caught my eye on the grocery aisle—its shiny, red lid seemed to call out, "Pick me! Pick me!" from a full shelf of teas. Its label read "Comfort and Joy," and honestly, who couldn't use a little of that?

My mind went quickly to the odd English carol in a minor key, whose only verse I could remember was this:

God rest ye merry, gentlemen
Let nothing you dismay
Remember Christ our Savior
Was born on Christmas day
To save us all from Satan's power
When we were gone astray.
O tidings of comfort and joy,
comfort and joy,
O tidings of comfort and joy.

I bought the tea. Like I said, who couldn't use a little comfort and joy? It makes a good, fragrant cup, and the happy container brightens *my* shelf too. I'm still puzzling about the slow refrain of "comfort and joy" wrapped in a minor key—but isn't life like that? Pressures and fears and sorrows and hurts compound, then a slow, deep tide of joy rolls up from a place you didn't know existed.

Christ our Savior was born for me and for you. In the midst of minor-key life, he is a sure and steady comfort. The powers of this world have been soundly beaten by him, and the lingering wounds we feel from his enemy's blows are not fatal. Not anymore.

My comfort and joy is in this holy, rolling tide of Christmas—Immanuel, God with us!—this eternity-deep wave of truth and beauty that defaces, surpasses, outshines, and eclipses every minor-key squall of life. So I will sip from my cup of comfort and joy . . . and sing.

The LORD will comfort Israel again and have pity on her ruins. Her desert will blossom like Eden, her barren wilderness like the garden of the LORD. Joy and gladness will be found there. Songs of thanksgiving will fill the air.
ISAIAH 51:3

DECEMBER 20

and Wonders of His Love

Thousands filled the streets for the annual Christmas tree lighting at Rockefeller Center in New York. Tuning in to the made-for-television spectacle, I saw a glamorous pop singer step to the microphone, bejeweled and sporting a long white fur coat over a sequined gown. She sang "Joy to the Word" in a syncopated beat as the camera cut to children clustered near the stage, awestruck at her glittering image. *Joy to the world! The Lord is come; let earth receive her King!*

I wished there had been someone in my living room with me so I could have poked them and said, "Did you hear that? She said 'Lord'! She said 'King'!" The singer's star power overshot the real message of the song, but she sang the words just as they were written. Cynical me imagined she'd just repeat the first verse a dozen times or so until the next performer was cued for the camera, but I was wrong. She trilled right into the next verse, and then the next: *He rules the world with truth and grace, and makes the nations prove the glories of his righteousness and wonders of his love. . . .*

The message to those on the streets of New York City (and the national television audience) was an age-old one not usually embraced in the public square: God is on his throne, ruling with truth and grace. He engineers the movements of history and the choices of men—and in all these things the nations are proving two undeniable realities: the glories of his righteousness and the wonders of his love.

Sometimes his righteous glory bursts and blazes like a million sequins on as many glitzy gowns; sometimes his wondrous love glows like the light in one child's eyes. The glories are big. They are hard to miss. But the wonders are small—and we walk right by hundreds of them every day!

Why not resolve to tune your heart to God's presence and notice as many of them as you can today? They're there. You'll see them: *wonders of his love, and wonders of his love, and wonders, wonders of his love.*

Who is like You among the gods, O Lord? Who is like You, majestic in holiness, awesome in praises, working wonders?
EXODUS 15:11, NASB

Blooming in the Dark

I most often purchase my Christmas poinsettias from Brookwood, a residential/vocational ministry for adults with disabilities, some thirty-five miles west of my city. I was once fortunate enough to spend the better part of a day there, meeting many of the residents and talking to them about their work. Every person I met happily described the job they were doing, introduced me to other residents, and even invited me to join them in their task.

I learned that planning for the community's annual crop of nearly forty-seven thousand poinsettia plants had begun in early summer. The day I visited, residents at work in the horticulture greenhouses were preparing potting soil in containers, separating and placing seedling plants into flats, and moving the plants into their temporary growing spaces. In just a few weeks, a master gardener explained, these growing plants would be placed in complete darkness to encourage their blooms.

In complete darkness for up to fourteen hours a day for at least forty days. Without that long period of darkness, there can be no brilliant red, pink, or soft-white blooms. Just the smallest exposure to light during this time can adversely affect the eventual crop. But when the darkness is respected and endured, the end result is row upon row of vibrant beauty.

Just like the poinsettias, Brookwood itself was born out of a dark and uncertain time: its founder is the mother of a child with special needs. She envisioned and sought something more for her daughter than a lifetime in an institution. But before Brookwood bloomed, there was plenty of darkness.

A wise and kind friend of mine once observed that good things seemed to be coming from my own unwanted stretch of darkness. Creative work finding new expression. A stubborn resurgence of joy. Even a few wild splashes the color of hope. And why not? God's greatest gift was born in the deepest dark.

Are the lights seemingly out where you live? Do not despair. God is working, even in the dark—and he alone knows the time required to nurture the manifold blooms that he has in mind.

Even the darkness is not dark to You, and the night is as bright as the day.
PSALM 139:12, NASB

a Misfit's Gifts

I look forward to Christmas with delightful expectancy, and I am always a little sad when the season is done. But even so, I never feel more like a shiny, neon-lit misfit than I do at Christmas.

I feel awkward arriving solo at holiday parties. I even feel a little out of place at church, where I know everyone but belong with no one. I tried explaining this seasonal malaise to an old friend recently, and she responded, "Leigh, you have a good life." I do. Oh, I do! But at Christmas I am most assuredly the odd woman out. My friends will *not* receive from me a beautifully photographed card of my spouse and/or children that says, "Love from the McLeroys." There's just one McLeroy at this address. I will host my family's Christmas dinner, planned and prepared alone, and be thankful for each beloved face around my table. But when they go home in pairs, I will remain alone.

Years ago, my parents would take my sister and me to a department store with a special area for children to shop in. We would be given money that we could then spend on our family as we shopped "secretly" but well supervised. The gifts we purchased for my parents were bought with their own money, so in essence, we gave them what they had already given us.

This Christmas, I'm wondering how I might return to Jesus a few of the treasures that he has given me—and give them with greater love and gratitude. How can I give him both my fierce independence and my ache for company? Can these be packed together? How can I give my sorrow over the children I never had and my keen longing for a husband and family, even now? Perhaps he'll know what to do with these misfit gifts. After all, they are the gifts I have to offer back to the lover of my soul. He is good, and he does all things well.

Merry Christmas, precious Jesus, from just me. Transform the meanness of my offering into something useful, beautiful, and true. Let the life I live be pleasing to you, even through seasons where it seems strange to me.

Everything comes from you, and we have given you only what comes from your hand.

1 CHRONICLES 29:14, NIV

Bending Low

Every once in a while, God reminds me that he gives grace to the humble, not the proud. That he made himself little and lowly to love the little and lowly like me.

I had been asked to speak at a dinner for a church where I'd spent a good bit of my working life—and where I still knew and loved a lot of folks. I had friends in the room. My former boss—the senior pastor—was there with his wife. I wanted to do well for God and for the person who'd graciously invited me. And for myself.

Although I don't typically eat before I speak, to be polite I made a pass along the back of the lovely buffet table prepared for the guests. About the time I arrived at the green beans, I felt something brush my legs. I looked down and saw my half-slip in a puddle around my ankles. Its elastic had given up the ghost at the worst possible moment. Any thoughts I'd had about being graceful or looking self-assured died. For a half second I considered diving under the skirted table after my errant undergarment, then thought better of it and stepped out of the loose circle of nylon around my feet, kicking it further under the table. Then I bent low to try to retrieve it with one hand, but I realized there would be no way to hide it when I stood up again.

I felt a soft tap on my shoulder, looked wildly around, and saw a female server smile at me with her hand outstretched. I silently and gratefully handed her my slip, she disappeared into the kitchen, and I never saw it again.

For the rest of the evening, including my time at the podium talking about how Jesus made himself little and lowly for the good of a lost world, I felt my cheeks flush in embarrassment. Likely no one but the server and me knew how little and lowly I'd become, and I'm certain I learned more that night than anyone else. The message is what matters most, and it is the messenger's job to bend low, be grateful for her rescue, and try to be as inconspicuous as possible.

When the time came, he set aside the privileges of deity and took on the status of a slave, became *human*!
PHILIPPIANS 2:7, MSG

DECEMBER 24
For unto Us . . .

Christmas Eve dawned wet and cold in my hometown: a dozen small errands and last-minute deliveries drove me out into the drizzle when I'd just as soon have stayed home. The streets were surprisingly free of traffic—perhaps that's why I noticed sights I might have otherwise missed.

A few blocks from home, on a freeway overpass, red plastic cups inserted into the chain-link fence spelled out a joyous invitation: "Marry me." I smiled, imagining the surprise that must have greeted the one morning traveler meant to read these two simple words and reply, "Yes."

Not far from this handmade message, a blinking electronic sign read "Lost Elderly, Bedford, Texas," and my heart sank. Somewhere someone was celebrating. And somewhere else, an elderly person's family was frightened for their loved one's safety. I prayed for the person to be safe and found. Then as I exited the freeway and passed a tiny cemetery, I noticed a man in a windbreaker setting up a small Christmas tree. A blue camp chair waited nearby, and I wondered if, when he finished, he planned to sit for a while and share the tree with someone he loved.

In just a handful of miles, the morning told me three distinct stories of strangers whose names I'd never know. *For unto people like us,* I thought, *a child is born* (see Isaiah 9:6). For us, God became a man. He attended wedding celebrations, wept unashamedly at the grave of a friend, and declared he'd come especially to save the lost.

Ours is the world he entered—this messy tableau of beginnings and endings, of joy and grief, of fear and uncertainty, sorrow and celebration. He came to write the climax of redemption's sweeping story and to write himself into our small, everyday dramas in a way that changes them forever.

Driving home in dropping temperatures and misting rain, I mouthed to the rhythm of the windshield wipers, "Unto us, unto us, unto us . . ." and offered up silent thanks for a God brave and good enough to come so far and draw so near, out of his love for us.

For to us a child is born, to us a son is given, and the government will be on his shoulders.
ISAIAH 9:6, NIV

You Shall Call Him

For more than twenty years, I've sent out Christmas cards with no family pictures, no beautiful graphics, no pop-up figures or flowery script. Even though I feel a little silly doing it, each year I write and send to family and friends an original poem. I meant to do this only once, but my mother must have thought I would continue, because the next year, she asked me if I'd forgotten to send "her poem." So I kept writing them, mostly for her. (If you've received one or many of these, don't think you aren't loved and special too. You are. But my mom was not someone you wanted to disappoint.) I'm not sure which one was Mother's favorite, and I can't ask her now. But this is mine. Thirty-three words. One for each year of my Savior's earthly life. Because no number of words about him will ever be enough.

> *You shall call His name*
> *Sea-calmer,*
> *Wine-maker,*
> *Fish-finder,*
> *Friend*
> *Wound-healer,*
> *Truth-teller,*
> *Soul-seeker,*
> *Lamb*
> *Love-walker,*
> *Star-hanger,*
> *Tear-keeper,*
> *Mine*
> *Bread-breaker,*
> *Kiss-taker,*
> *Grave robber,*
> *Thine.*

And there are also many other things which Jesus did, which if they were written in detail, I suppose that even the world itself would not contain the books that should be written.

JOHN 21:25, NASB

Come, Thou Long Expected Jesus

"A savior is born for us," Martin Luther preached on Christmas Day in 1534. "That really climaxes all. . . . That is the chief point and greatest reason why we ought to be joyful. . . . Those people are lost who neither know nor have heard this. . . . For these words melt heaven and earth together, make death into sugar, and turn all ills, of which there are plenty, into delectable wine."*

The incarnation changes everything.

One evening deep into Advent, I found myself in a room so filled with longing I thought the walls might burst. So full, with only eight souls' collected hopes and dreams and fears. There has never been a time that the world has not ached for a Redeemer, and never a time when I myself have not needed one. That God, in love, sent just what was needed is beyond my wildest imagination. And because he has come, has lived, has suffered, died, and risen again, we may keep on bringing to our long-expected Jesus "the hopes and fears of all the years." He expects them. He was made for this.

> *Slipping on humanity like a coat*
> *You left the rarest air that is*
> *and settled here.*
>
> *Never mind the glory once laid by—*
> *You plunged into a world bereft of majesty*
> *and stayed to woo us into life again.*
>
> *Heaven's purest hope contained*
> *in flesh put on to die:*
> *Your dwelling changes nothing more than me.*

The people who walked in darkness have seen a great light; those who dwelt in a land of deep darkness, on them has light shone. You have multiplied the nation; you have increased its joy; they rejoice before you as with joy at the harvest, as they are glad when they divide the spoil. For the yoke of his burden, and the staff for his shoulder, the rod of his oppressor, you have broken as on the day of Midian.

ISAIAH 9:2-4, ESV

---

* Eugene F. A. Klug, ed., *Sermons of Martin Luther: The House Postils* (Grand Rapids, MI: Baker, 1996), 1:116.

All Is Calm and Bright

When I asked my eighty-seven-year-old aunt to name her favorite Christmas carol, she replied without hesitating, "Silent Night." I was surprised. This is the aunt whose home was the nexus of many a family holiday gathering. The music *I* most associate with her at Christmas is something a bit more upbeat by Dean Martin or Andy Williams. But she said, "Silent Night."

Sometimes, when you know something well, you cease to recognize its goodness. I'm afraid I've become numb to "Silent Night." I mouth the words now without connecting them to anything in my heart. But when I try to hear this carol as if it were new to me, one line lights up in contrast to the others around it: "All is calm, all is bright."

Calm and *bright* are not words that seem in sync with each other or with the world in which we live. But together they evoke a longing and a curiosity. Whisper them together now, under your breath. Really. No one's listening. "Calm and bright. Calm and bright." What do you feel?

I feel peace. And hope. *Calm* and *bright* are common, everyday words for immanence and transcendence. The calming peace of Christ lies in his nearness. He has come. He is here. And the bright hope found in his presence is, in baby form, not so much as to overwhelm. His transcendent glory is a flame that could incinerate and stupefy the merest man or woman—but in the Christ child it is a bright gleam of hope I'm not afraid to be near.

Because "all is calm, all is bright," I can sleep in the heavenly peace of Christ.

Peace is . . . the one thing that is permanent. Strife has only a temporary tenure. Trouble is like a cloud that cannot last. It is like a shadow that must pass. But peace is the eternal blue in God's sky which clouds may dim, but not destroy. Peace is . . . God's program for our world, and He Who is to reign forever and ever has said: "Peace I leave with you."*

Peace I leave with you; My peace I give to you.
JOHN 14:27, NASB

---

* James I. Vance, *In the Breaking of the Bread: A Volume of Communion Addresses* (New York: Revell, 1922), 65.

It's on the Card

Since Christmas I have been carrying in my wallet three Starbucks gift cards, gratefully received from friends who clearly appreciate my love of coffee at almost any hour of the day or night. I have no idea how many collective lattes or cups of decaf the cards contain, but knowing they are there, tucked away in advance of my next coffee run, is oddly satisfying.

Last week while I was on a trip, my hotel was steps from a Starbucks. As I passed by it, I remembered my gift cards and stopped in on impulse. I ordered a tall, nonfat latte and handed over one of the cards to the barista.

I experience a tiny jolt of joy each time I order a "free" coffee. I simply enjoy what has been secured in advance for me. And I think, *I can't believe I didn't have to pay for that!*

Day by day, I continue to receive more grace than I could ever afford. There's no way I could hope to cover my own shortcomings, but someone else has. Hurtful words spoken in haste? Paid for. Wanting something that belongs to another? Paid for. Pride? Laziness? Envy? "On the card." The blood of Jesus Christ is always enough. Always.

At Starbucks these days, I'm feeling a little giddy at my good fortune (and my good friends). My cards are gifts that keep on giving, and I am enjoying the satisfaction each cup of coffee brings. Sin, on the other hand, is never so enjoyable beyond its initial buzz. Regret and remorse quickly kick in, and on my best days repentance is not far behind. When I confess and apply the ancient payment, I am grateful all over again for the goodness of the one who knew just what I would need and when. Thanks be to God for his indescribable gift. I can't believe it's paid for.

Christ made a single sacrifice for sins, and that was it! Then he sat down right beside God and waited for his enemies to cave in. It was a perfect sacrifice by a perfect person to perfect some very imperfect people. By that single offering, he did everything that needed to be done. . . . Once sins are taken care of for good, there's no longer any need to offer sacrifices for them.

HEBREWS 10:12-14, 18, MSG

Welcome

When I was a little girl, welcome was always certain at my Aunt Billie's house, where I was met with open arms from the moment my feet touched her driveway. She didn't have to say she was delighted to see me, because everything about her said welcome.

Later, in high school, welcome was just a few steps across our suburban street at a kind neighbor's house. Many afternoons I knocked on her door and was welcomed inside. She made two glasses of iced tea, and we sat and talked about anything that crossed my mind as worthy of conversation. She welcomed me.

Welcome is a powerful thing.

At the end of a year that left me bone tired and empty, I planned for a few days away, alone. I chose places where I believed welcome would await me. For three days, I retreated to a favorite spot in the Texas Hill Country: a cabin on a bluff near the Frio River where I've spent many precious hours in the past.

It was God's welcome I felt as my feet walked the cool stone floor and the canyon's rocky trails; it was his embrace that gathered me as I napped in the window seat with the windows open wide and rocked in the hammock before sunset. In the dark, the light, the silence, and the solitude, I was welcomed. I was not alone.

On the way home, I stopped for a final day of rest in a place I'd never been: a hotel housed in an old riverside brewery. Everyone I encountered was kind. Everywhere I looked I saw beauty. When the restaurant hostess asked if I was alone, I said yes. I told her I'd decided to treat myself to a birthday splurge en route to my Houston home. "New Year's Eve is your birthday?" she asked. I nodded yes.

A few minutes later, my smiling waiter appeared with a small treat I didn't order. "Happy birthday," he said with a wink. When strangers (not relatives or neighbors) are kind—it's easier to see the true origin of that kindness. When you travel alone and are welcomed with love, you understand better whose love surrounds you everywhere you go.

"I will welcome you. And I will be a father to you, and you shall be sons and daughters to Me," says the Lord Almighty.
2 CORINTHIANS 6:17-18, NASB

Dive!

When you're sure the water's deep enough, the best way to enter a freezing-cold river is not to wade or ease in. It's to dive. Waders would surely reconsider the second the chilled water met their toes. (I almost did when I tested it with mine.) But when four other slightly crazy adults decided to commemorate the New Year by plunging into the Frio River on a bright December afternoon, I thought, *Why not?*

It was something I'd never done before. But since it was my birthday, too, I thought it would be a fun way to celebrate. I didn't have a swimsuit (who packs that in the dead of winter, for Pete's sake?), but when the water is freezing, blue jeans and two T-shirts make for more appropriate attire.

So at two thirty in the afternoon with the cameras of saner people poised to record the moment, the five of us went off the dock and into the river. Just before we did, I turned to the friend on my right (also a birthday girl) and asked her, "Jump or dive?" She said, "Dive," and on the count of three, we did.

How does it feel to hit the river in deep December? Electrifying. Breathtaking. Shocking. I'm pretty sure I screamed when I surfaced, and I couldn't turn around and swim back to the dock fast enough. But it was oddly exhilarating, too. Freeing. I felt jolted awake and utterly alive. And although I doubt I was in the water for more than thirty seconds, I believe I left more than a few needless things behind when I climbed out.

Like the grown-up fear of looking foolish. Regret at a precious moment lost. Uncertainty, procrastination, and an adult-sized fondness for appearing artfully poised and in control. Because when real life beckons—when a jarring challenge awaits—when a cold river you're facing crooks its finger and says, "I dare you," the surest way to avoid retreat (and regret!) is to breathe deeply, close your eyes, and dive.

I came that they may have life and have it abundantly.
JOHN 10:10, ESV

Old and New

When the phone rang at 7:15 a.m. on December 31, I knew without looking whose voice I'd hear. My dad's.

"Happy birthday!" he boomed when I answered.

"Now which one is this?" he asked—and for half a second I thought he might not remember. Then I heard "Sixteen?"

He'd set me up. The corners of my mouth turned up, and my day was officially made.

"No, Daddy," I said. "It's *seventeen*."

"I missed a year," he laughed. "How'd that happen?"

I am far from seventeen. I have boots older than seventeen. To someone who *is* seventeen, I am certain I am identified as "old." I wouldn't argue—there are mornings I feel every one of my years. But there are moments I forget them too.

I forget when I'm with a roomful of friends I've known for life—friends whose crayons I borrowed and who I giggled through slumber parties with. I forget when I pull on those beat-up Tony Lamas and sink into their perfect broken-in-ness one more time. You'd think I might remember when I open the pages of my latest crumbling Bible and see the highlights and marginalia of my own hand—but I don't. Instead I think, *Today I'll discover something here I've never seen before, because your mercies are new—utterly new!—every morning of my life.*

I love so many things about this God I've followed since childhood. But perhaps the thing I love most is that he is always old and new. He was the shaping of my youth and the North Star of my early adulthood. He was the tall mast of my thirties and the strong anchor of my forties. And I'm certain he will be my beacon of hope in the years to come.

Where will he meet me today? I can't say for sure, but I am certain that he will. What will I learn by sundown? I don't know now, but give me a few hours, and I'll report back. Where will we go, my good God and I, when I pull on these old boots and step out my front door? He knows. I do not. But he'll tell me when I need to know—and until then, I'll treasure his old, new company every blessed step of the way.

His compassions never fail. They are new every morning.
LAMENTATIONS 3:22-23, NIV

A Closing Prayer

Father God, make me present with you today in my thoughts, my actions, and my words. Sharpen my focus and increase my attention so I can see the places where you are at work, where your great love is breaking through.

Lord Jesus, remind me that you—by the miracle of your incarnation and the power of your resurrection—are present with me here today. Nothing I encounter will surprise you. Nothing I attempt will be done alone. You are here.

Holy Spirit, heighten my senses (as much as I can bear!) to the beauty of the gospel. Give me gratitude for the God who calls, convicts, rescues, makes righteous, and restores—and who has never stopped doing so. Move through me. Speak through me. Show yourself in and to me.

In the name of the ever-present Father, Son, and Holy Spirit, amen.

acknowledgments

The devotions in this book began years ago as a way of recording sightings of God at work in my everyday life. I began writing them as a spiritual exercise and a creative discipline. I wanted a record—in my own voice—of God's movement and his loving presence. And I wanted to share them. So each week, on Wednesday, I sent out an e-mail devotional called "Wednesday Words" to a faithful readership of family, friends, and friends I've never met. I'm still writing them.

So thank you to the readers of "Wednesday Words." You feel like family. Your responses from week to week are a gift to me and a confirmation that this small thing is worth doing and doing well. I know you long for his presence too.

Thank you, also, to my church family at Houston's City of Refuge EPC; the solid, loving, praying women of my small group, near and far flung; my precious CBS sisters (how I miss you!); and to the handful of dear ones whose lives have shaped and are shaping mine, as iron sharpens iron: I do love you.

God places us in families. I am thankful for mine. You all have my heart. You always will.

about the author

LEIGH MCLEROY is an author, a teacher, and a speaker with a passion for God and a keen eye for his presence in everyday life. She is the author of five books, including *Treasured*, *The Beautiful Ache*, and *The Sacred Ordinary*, and a collaborator on more than twenty other books. Her writing has been published in *Discipleship Journal*, *Indeed*, *In Touch*, and *Christian Single* and has appeared online at ExploreGod.com and TheHighCalling.org. For more than fifteen years, she has written a weekly devotional called *Wednesday Words*, which has found its way around the world and back. Leigh holds degrees in journalism and apologetics, and she lives and works in Houston, Texas.

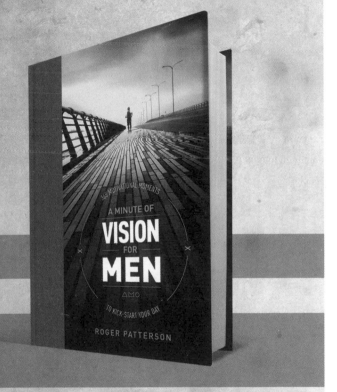